Kabbalah and Catastrophe

Stanford Studies in Jewish Mysticism
Clémence Boulouque & Ariel Evan Mayse, EDITORS

KABBALAH AND CATASTROPHE

*Historical Memory in Premodern
Jewish Mysticism*

———

Hartley Lachter

Stanford University Press
Stanford, California

Stanford University Press
Stanford, California

Printed in the United States of America on acid-free, archival-quality paper

Library of Congress Cataloging-in-Publication Data
Names: Lachter, Hartley, 1974- author.
Title: Kabbalah and catastrophe : historical memory in premodern Jewish mysticism / Hartley Lachter.
Other titles: Stanford studies in Jewish mysticism.
Description: Stanford, California : Stanford University Press, 2024. | Series: Stanford studies in Jewish mysticism | Includes bibliographical references and index.
Identifiers: LCCN 2024012403 (print) | LCCN 2024012404 (ebook) |
    ISBN 9781503640214 (cloth) | ISBN 9781503640900 (epub)
Subjects: LCSH: Cabala—History—To 1500. | Mysticism—Judaism—History—To 1500. | History—Religious aspects—Judaism.
Classification: LCC BM526 .L33 2024 (print) | LCC BM526 (ebook) |
    DDC 296.1/6—dc23/eng/20240509
LC record available at https://lccn.loc.gov/2024012403
LC ebook record available at https://lccn.loc.gov/2024012404

Cover design: George Kirkpatrick
Cover art: Children of Mars, from the *Heidelberg Bilder Katechismus* (~1455–1458).
Typeset by Newgen in EB Garamond Regular 10.5/15

For Zoe and Mollie
With all my love

Contents

Acknowledgments

Many colleagues and friends have helped me during the years in which I wrote this book. The research for this project began as I started a new position at Lehigh University in the Department of Religion Studies in the fall of 2014, where I also directed the Philip and Muriel Berman Center for Jewish Studies. The environment in our department has been uncommonly collegial and supportive, as well as intellectually rich. My deepest gratitude goes to my colleagues: Dena Davis, Chris Driscoll, Jodi Eichler-Levine, Khurram Hussain, Nitzan Lebovic, Annabella Pitkin, Michael Raposa, Rob Rozehnal, Lloyd Steffen, and Ben Wright, and to Bob Flowers, dean of the College of Arts and Sciences, who genuinely values scholarship and has supported our work. I extend my heartfelt thanks to the coordinators of the Department of Religion Studies and the Berman Center, with whom I have had the good fortune to work over the past nine years: Marian Gaumer, Tara Coyle, Jodi Imler, Maria Ioannidou, Alex Farkas, and Mandy Fraley. Without them, this book would not have been possible.

Like all academic works, this one has benefitted in countless ways from conversations with colleagues at conferences and seminars. To those who have shared their time and ideas with me, in many often delightful locations around the world, I offer my gratitude: Daniel Abrams, Michal Bar-Asher Siegal, Jonathan Bennaroch, Na'ama Ben-Shachar, Nathaniel Berman, Clémence Boulouque, Yossi Chajes, Noam Cohen, Jonathan Dauber, Glenn Dynner, Iris Felix, Eitan Fishbane, Pinchas Giller, Roee Goldschmidt, Andrea Gondos, Ellen Haskell, Joel Hecker, Marc Herman, Moshe Idel, Zvi Ish-Shalom, Nitza Kahn,

Avi Kallenbach, Ruth Kara-Ivanov Kaniel, Nitza Kann, Sharon Koren, Noam Lev-El, Shaul Magid, Gene Matanky, Alan Mittleman, David Myers, Gene Matanky, Ronit Meroz, Idan Pinto, Biti Roi, Marla Segol, Jonathan Schnytzer, Kocku von Stuckrad, Josh Teplitsky, and Steven Weitzman.

The Oxford Summer Institute in Modern and Contemporary Judaism has been a joint project that I have co-convened together with my colleagues Jodi Eichler-Levine from Lehigh, Miri Freud-Kandel from Oxford University, and Adam Ferziger from Bar-Ilan. They have all read and commented on aspects of this work, and I am deeply grateful for their feedback and for the opportunity to work with them. My thanks as well to all of the participants who have attended and contributed to these seminars over the past eight years.

Access to primary sources located in rare book and manuscript collections has been crucial in researching this book. Many thanks to Ilana Tahan, lead curator of Hebrew manuscripts at the British Library, and Cesar Merchan-Hamann, curator of the Oxford Bodleian Hebrew manuscript collection. At the National Library of Israel in Jerusalem, I would like to extend thanks to Zvi Leshem, head librarian of the Gershom Scholem Reading Room, and to the staff at the Institute for Microfilmed Hebrew Manuscripts.

To the editors and staff at Stanford University Press I owe a deep debt of gratitude. Sincere thanks to Clemence Boulouque and Ariel Evan Mayse, the founding editors of the new series, Stanford Studies in Jewish Mysticism, for supporting this project and for their helpful feedback. Caroline McKusick, associate editor at Stanford, offered many important and insightful suggestions that have made this a better book. I thank her for her care and diligence in bringing this book to press. Aviva Arad's work in copyediting the manuscript was meticulous and thorough, for which I offer my sincere gratitude.

I have the very good fortune to be married to my favorite intellectual conversation partner and scholar of Jewish studies. To Jessica Cooperman, who has discussed the ideas in this book with me for years, and who has read every word and offered countless helpful suggestions, words cannot convey my gratitude. Over the course of writing this book, my daughters, Zoe and Mollie, grew from young children to young adults. I owe them more than I can say for their patience with all the late nights spent working or time away from home on research trips, and for the good-humored and kind-hearted support.

Kabbalah and Catastrophe

Introduction

In the early fourteenth century in Spain, Joseph Angelet composed a kabbalistic commentary on the Torah titled *Kupat ha-ruchlin*. Only the portion on Genesis has survived, in a unique, 239-folio manuscript held at the Bodleian Library in Oxford. Medieval kabbalists rarely give many autobiographical details. In fact, a significant number of these texts are entirely anonymous.[1] Angelet, however, offers a rare break into the first-person voice at the end of his commentary, stating that he completed it on the twenty-fifth day of the month of Av, in the Hebrew year 5071, which corresponds to the Gregorian year 1311 CE. He also, interestingly, says that this was the fifth year of the *shemittah*, or Sabbatical cycle, the thirty-third year of the Jubilee cycle, 1243 years since the destruction of the Temple, and "the sixth year since the exile of our brothers in France."[2] Angelet's strategy for situating himself within the flow of Jewish history reflects the three modes of measuring time that developed during the rabbinic period. Time can be measured based on the duration since the creation of the world, or according to the cycles of Sabbatical and Jubilee Years, or since the destruction of the Second Temple in Jerusalem.[3] However, the marking of historical time within the broad sweep of world and Jewish history does not end, for Angelet, with the destruction of the Temple. Events affecting Jewish communities of his own day fit into a comprehensive linear historical time frame, as well as a recurring succession of repeated periods. As we will see in what follows, such a schema was of central importance to how many kabbalists between the early fourteenth century through the early sixteenth century understood the world and the place of Jews and Judaism in the course of historical time.

Premodern kabbalists were deeply invested in the meaning of the events of Jewish history. That interest did not end with the closing of the biblical canon or the destruction of the Second Temple in Jerusalem. The experience of the Jewish people in exile, and the realities associated with their status as a politically disempowered minority, such as expulsions and outbreaks of violence, demanded explanation. Kabbalah was one lens that medieval Jews deployed as they peered back through the Jewish historical record, and as they attempted to anticipate the Jewish future. This book considers some of the ways that premodern kabbalistic texts provide insight into how Jews understood the Jewish historical condition. The complex theosophies and world views advanced in kabbalistic texts reveal an abiding interest in the meaning of Jewish history and the destiny of the Jewish people. Kabbalists did not live outside of history, and their interests were not confined to the timeless mysteries of the divine realm. Kabbalistic texts contain a vast trove of valuable primary evidence for learning about how premodern Jews engaged with their own history, and how they sought to shape it.

Christian Constructions of Jewish History

Covenantal theology is fundamentally about the relationship between divine providence and human history. Since antiquity, the conflict between Christianity and rabbinic Judaism has been deeply entangled with conflicting views regarding how to read the meaning of historical events. Was Jesus the promised messianic redeemer, or is the messiah yet to come? Does the mantle of biblical Israel pass to the Jewish people as their biological descendants who continue to perform the commandments revealed at Sinai, or does the life, death, and resurrection of Christ shift that legacy to the community of his faithful adherents? Is the exile of the Jewish people a sign of temporary divine punishment, or permanent divine rejection? Does the future entail the long-awaited arrival of the messiah and ascendancy of the Jewish people, or will it involve the triumphant return of Christ? The Jewish-Christian debate is, at its core, a conflict over the meaning of Jewish history.

For many Christian thinkers, as Robert Chazan notes, the evaluation of the role of Jews in the course of human history became increasingly negative over the course of the Middle Ages.[4] Jewish historical suffering was understood as just punishment for their rejection of the true messiah. Jews were not regarded as historical actors; the postbiblical experience of the Jewish people was regarded as a cautionary tale. The wandering Jews[5] were living reminders of the calamity that awaits all who refuse the message of Christianity and its understanding of the pivotal historical role of Christ as redeemer. The final resolution of the current period of history will entail, according to many medieval Christian exegetes, the disappearance of Jews and Judaism. In the meantime, the Jews persist as a vestigial people, present yet mired in the past, unable to recognize the new phase of history in which they live. The doctrine of supersession stipulates that Jews and their covenant with God had its moment in the past, which then came to an end with the advent of Christ. The Jewish people's ongoing adherence to the laws of Moses and the rabbinic oral law was regarded by many ancient and medieval Christian thinkers as conclusive evidence that the Jews have been unable to play a meaningful role in the course of human affairs. Since the moment of their rejection of Jesus as their messiah, the claim goes, Jews have been frozen in time. In other words, Jews were regarded as the ultimate nonhistorical actors on the stage of human history. Their role is to serve as objects of a Christian gaze, living reminders that those who reject Christ will be banished from history, remain frozen in the past, and ultimately be deprived of the rewards of redemption in the future.

An important and instructive example of this view can be seen in the works of Augustine of Hippo (354–430 CE), whose elaborate discourse regarding the role of Jews in human history had a significant influence on medieval Christian thinkers.[6] As Jeremy Cohen has pointed out, Jews factor prominently in the world-historical schema constructed by Augustine in his *De Genesi contra Manichaeos*. He divides history into six dispensations, or ages, corresponding to the six days of creation mentioned in Genesis. The third age begins with Abraham, and the fourth with the kingdom of David. However, there was a decline at the end of that period, such that with the beginning of the fifth age, which involves the "advent of our lord Jesus Christ," the events that entail the rise of redemption and divine grace for the rest of humanity bring about the decline of Jewish life and history. As Augustine described it:

And so, for the people of the Jews that age was, in fact, one of decline and destruction. . . . Afterwards, those people began to live among the nations, as if in the sea, and, like the birds that fly, to have an uncertain, unstable dwelling. . . . God blessed those creatures, saying "Be fertile and increase . . ." inasmuch as the Jewish people, from the time that it was dispersed among the nations, in fact increased significantly. The evening of this day—that is, of this age—was, so to speak, the multiplication of sins among the people of the Jews, since they were blinded so seriously that they could not even recognize the lord Jesus Christ.[7]

The Jewish experience of exile and political disempowerment is presented here as part of a divine plan for human history. The onset of the fifth age is immediately preceded by a period of Jewish sinfulness so severe that it blinds them to the truth of Jesus's identity as messiah. The rise of the historical epoch of the Christian church involves the decline of Jewish historical fortunes. Their "unstable dwelling" in the realm of human affairs condemns them to live as a ubiquitous, yet subjugated people among foreign nations. Sacred history, for Augustine, includes Jewish collective misfortune as part of the broad sweep of successive ages encoded in Scripture through the seven days of creation. At the same time, he accounts for the persistence of the Jewish presence in Christian territory, and even the growth in their numbers since the death of Christ, through a reading of Genesis 1:22, in which God blessed the fish of the sea and fowl of the air (symbols for Augustine of the itinerant, homeless Jews) by saying "be fertile and increase." Jewish life as a disempowered minority, and Jewish survival and persistence over the course of human history after the time of Jesus, are both understood in Augustine's reading to be a fate foreordained in the first chapter of the Hebrew Bible.

Augustine buttresses his argument for the inevitability of the survival of the Jews with an interpretation of the mark of Cain.[8] As recounted in Genesis 4:8–15, God condemns Cain to a life of toil and homeless wandering for murdering his brother Abel in a jealous rage. When Cain objects that his punishment is "too great to bear," God places a mark upon him to indicate that anyone who kills him will bear a seven-fold punishment. In Augustine's reading of this passage, Cain's sin of fratricide and subsequent punishment represents the Jews' betrayal and murder of Jesus, their own kinsman. Cain's punishment to spend the remainder of his days as a "restless wanderer" (*na'va-nad*) is, in Augustine's view, a prophetic foreshadowing of the Jewish condition throughout history after their betrayal of Christ. Like Cain, they live as vulnerable wanderers throughout the course of sacred history. Yet also like Cain, Jews bear a distinctive and ironically protective signifier in the form of their observance of Jewish law and customs. God's granting of this particular "mark of Cain" prevents them from completely disappearing. Jews, it would seem, have a role to play in God's plan for humanity, and for this reason they require divine protection to ensure that their punishment as the vagabonds of history does not lead to their early disappearance.

The fact of Jewish survival is, for Augustine, yet another facet of the unique role that Jews play in human history because of their culpability for the death of Christ.

> Now behold, who cannot see, who cannot recognize how, throughout the world, wherever that people has been scattered, it wails in sorrow for its lost kingdom and trembles in fear of the innumerable Christian peoples . . . ? The nation of impious, carnal Jews will not die a bodily death. For whoever destroys them will suffer sevenfold punishment—that is, he will assume from them the sevenfold punishment with which they have been burdened for their guilt in the murder of Christ. . . . Every emperor or king who has found them in his domain, having discovered them with that mark [of Cain] has not killed them—that is, he has not made them cease to live as Jews, distinct from the community of other nations by this blatant and appropriate sign of their observance.[9]

Jewish exile and Jewish religious life and cultural distinctiveness are understood here as signs of divine punishment. The scattered Jewish nation who "wails in sorrow for its lost kingdom" and who lives in fear of the power of their Christian rulers, will never die out altogether. They will persist, according to Augustine, and they will never be made to "cease to live as Jews, distinct from the community of other nations," since it is their destiny to bear the mark of their shame as the killers of Jesus. This mark, significantly, is the practice of Jewish law itself. A fervent "Jewish exceptionalism" can be detected in the view that Jews alone play this uncanny historical role, guilty of deicide/fratricide, yet also protected by God and thereby indestructible. So important is the Jewish role in sacred history that, like Cain, those who try to destroy them will be punished sevenfold. The Jewish condition, in this view, is both grievously negative and historically essential. And yet, Jews themselves are not proactive agents on the stage of history; they are the subjects of history, suffering a fate long-since established by the sins of their ancestors and codified in biblical prophecy.

Augustine famously argued that Jews serve as a "witness"[10] throughout history, conveying through their very being the truth of the Hebrew Scriptures, as well as the horrific fate that awaits those who follow their path by rejecting the message of Christianity. The subjugation of the Jewish people by Christian rulers fulfills what Augustine regards as a prophetically anticipated reality. As Augustine puts it, "Throughout the present era (which proceeds to unfold in the manner of seven days), it will be readily apparent *to believing Christians* from the survival of the Jews, how those who killed the Lord when proudly empowered have merited subjection."[11] The abject state of the Jewish people reflects their guilt, while their continued existence serves both as cautionary tale and confirmation of prophecy.

Jews, for Augustine, enable Christians to perceive biblical truths to which Jews themselves are blind. In one evocative image he argues, "For what else is that nation today but the desks (*scriniaria*) of the Christians, bearing the law and the prophets as testimony to the tenets of the church."[12] Like the insensible desks that hold books for their readers, the Jewish historical condition is properly understood, according to Augustine, only by the Christians who observe it. Jews provide valuable prophetic testimony by preserving and transmitting the books of the Hebrew Bible, but they are no more able to understand the meaning of those books than inanimate reading desks can understand the books that are placed upon them. In another remarkable image, Augustine argues that over the course of history, since the death of Christ and the destruction of the Temple, "the Jews inform the traveler, like milestones along the route, while themselves remaining senseless and immobile."[13] Just as the markers or signs that direct a traveler along a roadway do not themselves move through space, Jews, as signifiers in the historical drama of humanity, do not move forward through time. Instead, their subjugated condition merely marks the way for others. The Jews themselves are frozen in time.

In the Christian reading of Jewish history established by Augustine, Jews exist both within and outside of history—they serve a necessary purpose for

Christians without progressing through history themselves. By refusing to abandon their law and accept Jesus as their messiah, Jews collectively have become trapped in a bygone era. As Miriamne Krummel describes it, "According to Augustine's reasoning, Jews ceased to be physically possible and transformed into portable signifiers at the moment when Jewish belief was simultaneously invalidated and retained to service Christian formulations of time and temporality. Augustine's image of the temporally frozen Jew effectively weakens the independent foundation of Jewish temporality and its backstories on which Christianity was built."[14] In Augustine's construction of a Christian theology of Jewish historical fate after the time of Jesus, Jews are simultaneously historically meaningful and blind to the meaning of history. The truth of Christianity creates, in Krummel's felicitous phrasing, "the temporally frozen Jew" who does not move forward through time, who lives as the subject of Christian power, and whose historical fate can only be understood through a Christian gaze. And as Krummel has also argued, the attempts to create a "universal" Christian way of marking time further marginalized Jewish historical memory. Even the Jewish calendar was superseded.[15]

Once Jews have finished serving their historical purpose of helping to spread Christianity to the world through their function as witnesses, what destiny can exist for the Jewish people if not to disappear? As Amnon Raz-Krakotzkin has observed, "In the Christian view . . . history was *historia sacra*, the history of the Church, which only embraced the believers—those who accepted the Gospel and therefore entered the domain of Grace. The Jews, in their stubbornness, had taken themselves out of history when they refused to accept the Gospel. Significantly, Christian authors also claimed that history would reach its fulfillment only when Jews *returned to it*: that is, when they accepted Christianity as the truth of the Gospel."[16] That is to say, Jews can enter history only by leaving Judaism. To remain Jewish is by definition to remain frozen in the past.

Medieval Jews and Jewish History

Christian readings of Jewish history in the Middle Ages were deeply influenced by Augustine's legacy. Jewish historical misfortune was regarded, by both Jews and Christians alike, as theologically significant. While Christians regarded Jewish history as a sustained confirmation of Christianity, Jews developed their own strategies for understanding Jewish historical experience, and for situating it within a long timeline that culminates in redemptive triumph.[17] The so-called "argument from history," or the suggestion that the negative events of Jewish life since the time of Jesus demonstrate that the Jewish covenant with God has ended, featured prominently in medieval Jewish-Christian polemics.[18] Robert Chazan has observed that "medieval Jews argued with deep conviction for the unbroken and unbreakable continuity of their historical experience as the true people of Israel. This perception of the Jewish past, present, and future colored every aspect of medieval Jews' perception and representation of self and other."[19] Jews, like their Christian counterparts, were deeply invested in understanding the meaning of Jewish history. The genres and discursive modes in which they wrote were not often what might be regarded today as historical writing. They tended to speak less with the voice of the chronicler, and more commonly as the exegete. This is due to the fact that, as Chazan notes, "medieval Jews saw themselves and their neighbors in highly archetypical paradigms, in terms drawn from the vast reservoir of biblical and rabbinic imagery. . . . Biblical events are assumed to serve as precedents for subsequent Jewish experience."[20]

How did medieval Jews engage with what we might call medieval Jewish history? Were they interested in the particulars of the events that happened to Jews throughout the world since the end of the Talmudic period? Or were they more focused on the timeless matters of the law and the mysteries of the eternal Godhead?[21] As Yosef Hayim Yerushalmi has famously argued in *Zakhor: Jewish History and Jewish Memory*, medieval Jews engaged very little in historiography, or the chronicling of specific events, aside from a temporary period in the wake of the expulsion from Spain in 1492 when a number of Hebrew books of this sort were composed.[22] For the most part, Jewish historiography has been a largely secular and modern phenomenon, while in the Jewish Middle Ages, "there was much on the meaning of Jewish history; there was little historiography."[23] That is to say, the absence of a particular mode of historical writing—historiography—does not imply a lack of historical memory. Yerushalmi's point is simply that Jewish views regarding the meaning of Jewish history were expressed in other modes, such as biblical commentary or homiletical exposition. As he notes elsewhere, "We possess, in all branches of Jewish literary creativity in the Middle Ages, a wealth of thought on the position of the Jewish people in history, of *ideas* of Jewish history, but comparatively little interest in *recording* the mundane historical experiences of the Jews since they went into exile."[24]

This claim has been the subject of robust scholarly debate in the decades since the publication of Yerushalmi's influential book.[25] Amos Funkenstein has argued that "with or without historiography proper, creative thinking about history—past and present—never ceased. Jewish culture was and remained informed by an acute historical *consciousness*, albeit different at different periods."[26] Halakhic discourse entails its own unique brand of historical consciousness, according to Funkenstein. He notes that these sources reflect "clear distinctions of time and place throughout: distinctions concerning customs and their context, exact knowledge of the time and place of messengers and teacher of the *halacha*, the estimated value of coins mentioned in sources, the significance of institutions of the past."[27] While this might not constitute historiography in the formal sense, Funkenstein maintains that it certainly is a kind of engagement with history. An examination of the many different kinds of texts produced by medieval Jews reveals that they were not only aware of their historical reality—they were fascinated and perplexed by it. That is to say, "their existence was to them a source of perpetual amazement . . . it remained always in need of explanation."[28] The various discourses produced by medieval Jews thus reflect not only an attempt to give meaning to Jewish history, but also to account for the past and ongoing realities of Jewish life and "the perception of the distinctness of Israel."[29]

In evaluating Yerushalmi's distinction between history and memory, Robert Bonfil suggests that conventional historical texts and those that fall into what might be termed "Jewish memory," or the attribution of meaning to events of the collective Jewish past, might not be so different after all. He has observed that when medieval Jews sought "to reflect upon extraordinarily tragic events and the bearing they have upon their own self-perception . . . [they] need not necessarily express their reactions in historical writing. Such reflections could be assigned to the realm of memory, making liturgy, homiletics, halakhah, or theology the appropriate channels of literary expression. And yet, as far as *interest in past events* is concerned, I personally feel unable to grasp that there is a substantial difference between memory and history."[30] The fact that medieval Jews composed a far greater number of scriptural commentaries than historical chronicles did not mean that they were uninterested in Jewish history or current events in the world around them. It merely suggests that they wrote in a different register. The intellectual context in which Jews functioned used the Bible as a primary discursive reservoir of meaning; Jewish law was the unquestioned blueprint governing Jewish life; and rabbinic texts were understood to be authoritative legal guides. In such a cultural setting, engagement with Jewish history was not absent—it was merely expressed in the idiom appropriate to the context. The issue facing medieval Jews, according to Bonfil, was "how to find a proper formula for Jewish history regarding both contents and literary genre."[31]

What exactly did Jews remember? What history called out for meaning? While there were many facets of Jewish history that engaged the attention of medieval Jewish writers, the overarching context of exile, or *galut*, demanded explanation.[32] Amnon Raz-Krakotzkin has observed that for Jews in the Middle Ages, "it is impossible to discuss the topic of 'Jewish memory' without emphasizing the crucial role of the idea of exile in its construction."[33] The importance of this phenomenon is something upon which premodern Jews and contemporary scholars of Jewish history largely agree. The condition of living as a dispersed minority without political autonomy has in fact been a crucial factor in Jewish history and the development of Jewish identity. And as noted above, Christian thinkers since Augustine have regarded the presence of the Jews in exile as a theologically significant confirmation of Christianity. For medieval Jews, as well, Jewish exile entailed a critical theological dilemma. Did the exile of the Jewish people imply that they have been abandoned by God? What was the cause of the exile, and how can it be corrected? Why is the messiah so delayed? Is it simply the result of Jewish transgression, or is there a more complicated dynamic at play? The combination of Christian weaponization of Jewish historical suffering, together with the theological dilemmas that Jews faced when trying to square their own history with notions of covenantal promise, created a strong incentive for Jewish thinkers to respond to the challenge.

And respond they did. Medieval Jews, including kabbalists, were far from silent on these matters. They addressed many questions about the workings of human history in relation to divine providence. The misfortunes of Jewish history were key features of the medieval Jewish-Christian debate. Jews could not avoid the Christian claims regarding the historical fate of the Jewish people; it permeated the culture and architecture of the societies in which they lived. Images of the royal and dignified *Ecclesia* and the blindfolded *Synagoga* who could not perceive her own place in history gazed down upon them from cathedral walls, and reminders of their minority status under the rule of the Christian majority were constant. Any alternative perspectives on the meaning of Jewish history that they might articulate, even if they were drawn from ancient, pre-Christian sources, could not help but be a rejection of Christian theology and *historia sacra*.

Jews and Christians shared some basic assumptions regarding history. Both, for instance, regarded the present as a painful transitional period leading up to a messianic redemption. Where they differed was in the meaning of the present in relation to the biblical past and the covenantal promise. Was the destruction of the Temple and the exile of the Jewish people a sign that God had abandoned them?[34] At stake in the attribution of meaning to the events of the past and present for medieval Jews was the looming specter of Christian claims to be the true inheritors of the legacy of Israel and the divine promise of redemption. This supersessionist orientation of Christianity toward rabbinic Judaism entails the sweeping claim that all Jewish history since the death of Jesus has been nothing but an affirmation of the truth of Christianity and a rejection of the Jewish people by God.

Jewish and Christian readings of history are in many important respects both a form of what Funkenstein refers to as "counterhistory." He observed that "counterhistories form a specific genre of history written since antiquity. . . . Their function is polemical. Their method consists of the systematic exploitation of the adversary's most trusted sources against the grain. . . . Their aim is the distortion of the adversary's self-image, of his identity, through the deconstruction of his memory."[35] Neither Jews nor Christians could escape the fact that claiming the legitimacy of their own place in history necessarily meant rejecting the core claims of the other. And while Jews feature far more prominently in Christian discourse than Christians do in Jewish Scripture or rabbinic literature, Ram Ben-Shalom has demonstrated persuasively that "many medieval Jewish sources reveal an interest not only in Jewish history but in Christian history too. There was an awareness that the Middle Ages was a period in which historical events of significance to Jews took place and important Jewish figures lived."[36] The cultural dynamics were such that Jews could not and did not simply immerse themselves in the world of ancient texts and ignore the theological implications of the postrabbinic historical experience of the Jewish *and* Christian peoples. For example, Ellen Haskell has demonstrated how Zoharic literature is replete with both subtle and overt countertheologies directed toward Christianity.[37] Through the novel idiom of Kabbalah, the thirteenth-century Jews responsible for the creation of Zoharic literature created, in Haskell's words, "a hidden space from which they contested Christendom's dominance." The subversive strategies at play in the Zohar thus "challenged the public Christian transcript of Jewish subordination and upheld their own versions of Jewish identity and self-definition."[38] In what follows, I explore how late medieval kabbalists deployed kabbalistic ideas in the service of reimagining the meaning of Jewish history. Jewish exile and Christian dominance demanded an explanation. As we will see below, Kabbalah was one way that premodern Jews sought to provide it.

Medieval Kabbalah and Historical Memory
Gershom Scholem has exerted tremendous influence over the academic study of Kabbalah and the ways that these texts have been understood by historians and other researchers working in related fields. Scholem tended to regard premodern Kabbalah as a factor that worked within Jewish history, rather than as a repository of Jewish historical memory. At one point he describes his interest in studying kabbalistic sources as motivated by a recognition that kabbalistic texts reveal "forces which vitalized and sustained the Jewish people as a living body throughout the peregrinations of our history."[39] Yet, at the same time, he suggests that kabbalistic texts are of value to scholars seeking to understand how Jews in earlier periods understood their own experience.

> Wherever you touch, it is as if you touch gold, if you but have eyes to see. There is opened up here a world of profound personal and human experience, combined with the historical experience of the nation. Daring ideas

were formulated with great clarity or in allusive language; the very soul of an entire period speaks to us through these obscure and halting symbols, and through its strange customs and ways of life we have come to understand the terrors of life and death of pious Jews.[40]

Scholem was more interested in seeing Kabbalah as an agent of Jewish history than as a resource for understanding Jewish theories for the unfolding of historical events in their own time. In particular, he regarded the kabbalistic texts written before the expulsion from Spain as uninterested in history and more focused on the mysteries of the emergence of the world from God. Kabbalistic images and ideas that were created during this period, were, according to Scholem, "in the last resort ways of escaping from history rather than instruments of historical understanding; that is to say, they do not help to gauge the intrinsic meaning of history."[41] It was only after the expulsion that Kabbalah "triumphed because it provided a valid answer to the great problems of the time. To a generation for which the facts of exile and the precariousness of existence in it have become a most pressing and cruel problem, kabbalism could give an answer unparalleled in breadth and depth of vision. The kabbalistic answer illuminated the significance of exile and redemption and accounted for the unique historical situation of Israel within the wider, in fact cosmic, context of creation itself."[42]

Hannah Arendt, in an essay written in 1948 discussing, among other things, Scholem's *Major Trends in Jewish Mysticism*, critiques Jewish historians of the previous century for ignoring "all those trends of the Jewish past which did not point to their own major theses of Diaspora history, according to which the Jewish people did not have a political history of their own." She observed that in the gaze of those historians, "Jews were not history makers but history-sufferers."[43] Arendt praises Scholem for redeeming Jewish history and revealing the ways that Jews have been historical actors, who, ironically, through the Kabbalah, have contributed to key aspects of modernity. She accepted Scholem's thesis that the messianic movement of Shabbtai Zvi was an essentially kabbalistic phenomenon, and that through its failure it generated Jewish modernity. Arendt cites with interest Scholem's description of how kabbalists transformed Jewish law into theurgic actions, such that "every mitsvah became an event of cosmic importance. . . . The religious Jew became a protagonist in the drama of the World; he manipulated the strings behind the scenes."[44] Arendt understands this as part of the historical appeal of mysticism, both past and present. In her view, "These speculations appeal to all who are actually excluded from action, prevented from altering a fate that appears to them unbearable and, feeling themselves helpless victims of incomprehensible forces, are naturally inclined to find some secret means for gaining power for participating in the 'drama of the World.' "[45]

Scholem's insights were a significant step in bringing Kabbalah into greater contact with the study of Jewish historical memory, and Arendt is certainly correct in observing that Scholem's work with kabbalistic sources provided an important corrective to historians who reinscribed the Christian view of Jews as the passive subjects of history. Yet Scholem still relegated kabbalists before the time of Luria to the murky realm of mystical speculation disengaged from the historical realities of Jewish experience.[46] Such an assumption about what is—and is not—present in kabbalistic texts might account for the fact that kabbalistic sources are absent in most studies of medieval Jews.[47] It would seem that kabbalistic compositions have been regarded as devoid of historical consciousness, specificity of place and time, and engagement with the predicament of Jewish collective experience. Kabbalah has been taken perhaps too literally as an esoteric discipline addressing arcane matters of the transcendent divine realm, accessible only to the most expert of kabbalists (and, by extension, the most skilled of contemporary scholars). This has resulted, ironically, in a scholarly perception of medieval kabbalists that is similar to the medieval Christian perception of Jews; they are regarded as living outside of history.[48] Kabbalah, as a mode of discourse, is perceived as disengaged with the lived historical experiences of Jewish people. In this book, I argue that the project of making sense of the meaning of Jewish history was an important aspect of premodern kabbalistic discourse. Below I consider some of the ways that the texts they produced in the fourteenth to early sixteenth centuries constructed a comprehensive explanatory model for understanding Jewish history.[49] I also show that Kabbalah was more than a compensatory delusion. The very act of producing, consuming, and preserving kabbalistic discourses about the meaning of Jewish history is itself a way of engaging history. By developing elaborate new images and strategies for ascribing meaning to Jewish history, kabbalists developed new modes for imagining viable Jewish identities within the realities of premodern Jewish life.

It should be stated at the outset that I do not argue that the events of history can be used to explain or account for the creation of kabbalistic ideas. The Crusades did not create the Zohar any more than the expulsion from Spain created Lurianic Kabbalah. The intention in what follows is instead to better appreciate how kabbalistic discourses were used by premodern Jews to understand the events of Jewish history. When viewed from that perspective, the texts composed in the centuries that fall between the completion of the main body of the Zohar in the late thirteenth century and the rise of the kabbalistic community of Safed in the mid-sixteenth provide particularly interesting evidence for how ideas from earlier kabbalistic compositions—the Zohar prominent among them—were creatively redeployed in the service of thinking through the meaning of Jewish history during the difficult final two centuries of Jewish life in much of Christian western Europe.[50]

Texts from this period are often regarded as less creative and original than those produced during the mid- and late thirteenth century, and as a result, they have received less scholarly attention. For example, many monographs and articles have been dedicated to the study of the Zoharic corpus, but only one book (a doctoral dissertation from 1980) has been written about the *Sefer ha-peli'ah* and *Kanah*, and no monograph has ever been written about the *Sefer ha-temunah* and related literature, both of which were composed in the fourteenth century. The tendency in the field to dedicate more attention to the study of medieval kabbalistic texts which went on to enjoy popularity in the sixteenth to nineteenth centuries, such as the Zohar, has resulted in a significant lack of scholarly attention to the many less famous texts produced in the fourteenth, fifteenth, and early sixteenth centuries. While Spain was the center of kabbalistic creativity during the second half of the thirteenth century, we find kabbalistic texts from a growing range of geographical locations during the following two centuries, including the Byzantine Empire, Italy, Germany, eastern Europe, North Africa, and the Ottoman Empire. While many of these texts were less well known than some of the earlier compositions from Spain, they are no less interesting when considered from the perspective of what they can tell us about how Jews during that time used Kabbalah to make sense of their own experience of Jewish history.

As noted above, medieval Jews could not avoid Christian claims regarding the meaning of Jewish history, nor could they avoid the need to account for the tragedies that occurred over the course of their exile. Biblical and rabbinic theodicies tended to regard the misfortunes of the people of Israel as divine punishment for transgressing the law. Kabbalists engaged with these questions by adding an additional discursive layer. Medieval Jewish experience, as they saw it, connected with the biblical past and was contiguous with the long history of the Jews through concealed divine forces, known only through the kabbalistic tradition. The correspondence of the hidden attributes of God (known as the ten *sefirot*, or ten divine luminous emanations) with earthly events reflects, in their view, the fact that the true driving force of history and human affairs is to be found in the secret divine realm. Such knowledge, they claimed, was revealed only to Jews, and could be found in the traditions preserved by the kabbalists. Implicit in this is the suggestion that the standard cannon of rabbinic Judaism was not adequate to account for the present conditions of medieval Jewish life. Kabbalah provided medieval Jews with a new explanatory model for understanding Jewish history, Jewish suffering, and the fate of the Jewish people in the future. Medieval kabbalistic ideas were projected back onto biblical and rabbinic Judaism in a fanciful act of transformative memory. As Eitan Fishbane has noted, the fictional attribution of kabbalistic knowledge to the second-century Rabbi Shimon bar Yohai and the other rabbinic characters of his time as represented in Zoharic literature creates a new Jewish history that is "'remembered' through the lens of medieval fiction." The Zoharic narrative that details the secret conversations of famous rabbis from the founding era of rabbinic Judaism is, in fact, a discursive device that, Fishbane suggests, "irreversibly recasts cultural memory, and the imagined world becomes—for all intents and purposes—the enduring truth of the culture, a representation of the real."[51] In remembering a new, kabbalistic Judaism, medieval kabbalists were able to regard themselves as the inheritors of an authentic revelation from antiquity that explains the divine plan for history.

Jonathan Z. Smith has observed that religious myths are not timeless, ahistorical engagements with universal themes. Religious discourses, he argues, provide a mechanism for people to engage with their "situation" in a particular time and place in which people encounter an "'incongruity' between cultural norms and expectations and historical reality."[32] The realities of postrabbinic Jewish history were hard to reconcile with the expectations associated with Jewish self-conceptions of divine election and covenantal legacy. Chazan has noted that the misfortunes of Jewish history were underscored in Christian polemical discourses as a primary reason why Jews should abandon their religion and adopt Christianity.[33] This led medieval Jewish authors, including kabbalists, to search for meaning in the catastrophes of Jewish history, since "the pain of catastrophe is mitigated considerably by understanding; it is profoundly exacerbated by a sense of meaninglessness."[34]

The historical consciousness reflected in medieval kabbalistic texts evinces a greater interest in finding meaning in tragedy than it does in understanding the periods of calm and prosperity. Salo Baron famously argued that medieval Jewish life, and Jewish history in general, should not be regarded as merely a succession of moments of oppression.[35] Despite the expulsions, outbreaks of violence, legal and social restrictions, and church-backed anti-Jewish polemicizing, Jews found ways to flourish in many places throughout the Christian West in the Middle Ages. A "lachrymose" history of premodern Jewish life, he argued, creates an incomplete picture of Jewish history. Nonetheless, many medieval Jewish thinkers—kabbalists among them—could not avoid the significant theological dilemma posed by the conditions of Jewish life. The basic claim of the covenant—that Jewish acceptance of divine law and performance of the commandments will be reciprocated by divine protection and messianic redemption—was difficult to reconcile with the realities of Jewish historical experience in the medieval Christian West. Even those Jews who lived in moments of relative security did so with the constant awareness that their fate was contingent. Moreover, they were acutely aware of the misfortunes of Jews in other regions, past and present. In the passage cited from Joseph Angelet at the start of this introduction, he does not measure time in relation to positive events. For him, the orienting events of Jewish history are the destruction of the Second Temple in Jerusalem and the exile of the Jews from France. While Baron's caution against an overly "lachrymose" history of premodern Jewish life is certainly sound advice for contemporary Jewish historians, we must also be open to the fact that many medieval Jews embraced a narrative of decline in Jewish historical fortune. As Adam Teller has observed, "When pre-modern Jews thought about themselves and their place in the world, they did so not in liberal, but in lachrymose terms."[36]

One strategy deployed by medieval kabbalists is an *inversion* of history. This is slightly different from Funkenstein's idea of "counterhistory," in that it both responds to the historical claims and consciousness of the Christian other, and it seeks to reorient the meaning of historical reality itself. While the main contours of Christian assertions regarding the meaning of Jewish history could not go unaddressed, countering Christian claims alone was insufficient to address the problems raised by Jewish history and medieval Jewish experience. Tragic events, such as expulsions, violence, and the generally declining state of Jewish life in western Europe during the fourteenth and fifteenth centuries, required more than a rejection of the Christian narrative. The historical reality itself was a problem, and Kabbalah provided one attempt at a solution. When refracted through the prism of the kabbalistic imagination, Jewish history appears in the inverse. Exile, oppression, misfortune, and tragedy are placed within a vast historical time frame, and recast as necessary, virtuous suffering that actively moves history forward. The setbacks in Jewish history are reimagined as markers of forward progress that only Jews can see. In the kabbalistic world view, Jews are transformed into the *agents* of history, and the non-Jewish nations of the world the unwitting pawns. Kabbalists claim that by adhering to Judaism and persisting through the traumas of Jewish experience, Jews secretly move history toward its final, triumphant conclusion.

The negative aspects of Jewish life in exile are not, in this view, a sign of divine abandonment, or proof that history is off track. Through a variety of strategies, kabbalists found ways to imagine an inverse of Jewish history; even negative events are depicted as elements of a divine plan nearing its culmination in a grand reversal of fortune. For them, Jewish suffering is neither an unfortunate byproduct of history, nor is it a meaningless accident created by unrestrained human free will. For the kabbalists, Jewish suffering on the stage of history is one of the ways that Jews secretly exert their power and move history toward its culmination. Each collective trauma is reimagined by the kabbalists as a mechanism for Jews to purify their souls and complete the final, necessarily painful steps of the present historical era. Soon, they assure their readers, history will come to an end and Jews will be rewarded. But until then, Jews are not waiting passively. For the kabbalists, Jewish perseverance through painful historical setbacks is the secret central drama of the divinely designed historical process. In the kabbalistic view, Jewish endurance of subjugation and oppression at the hands of their enemies is the way that Jews push history forward. The "history-sufferers" are transformed into the agents of history who ironically exert their agency through suffering.

In the chapters below, I explore some of the ways that premodern kabbalists crafted discourses of Jewish historical experience. The first chapter considers the basic strategy evident in medieval kabbalistic sources for making sense of negative historical events in Jewish history. The establishment of historical time begins with the sin in the garden of Eden, which created the conditions for history. Free will, in the form of the evil inclination and the capacity to freely choose, set the stage for transgression, which in turn threw the divine world out of balance. Since then, the kabbalists claim, the flow of divine energy has been warped. The nations of the world have been empowered, while the Jewish people, as a result of ongoing transgression, have been cut off from the divine realm that was intended to grant them earthly dominance. This chapter considers how kabbalists describe the hidden theosophical undercurrents that account for the tragedies of Jewish historical experience and the reality of national disempowerment. These sources demonstrate how such discourses served to alleviate the "terror" of history, which is the fear that all events are arbitrary and hold no meaning. Despite the many undeniably negative aspects of the Jewish historical legacy, kabbalists claim that there is a divine plan and purpose revealed in the esoteric tradition, and known exclusively by Jews. The goal envisioned for Jews as actors in the world is to serve their role faithfully while enduring history, so that they can bring history to an end.

Chapter 2 focuses specifically on the meaning of Jewish experience in the context of exile among the nations. A surprising number of texts are explicit in naming Christians and Muslims as the people who have been empowered by God to rule over Jews during the present historical moment, and they provide a number of ways to understand the meaning and purpose of this particular fate. Kabbalists from this period created a number of narratives to ascribe meaning to human history during the interim between the expulsion from Eden and the arrival of the messiah.

Chapter 3 expands the discussion of kabbalistic notions of history by exploring the doctrine of *shemittot*, or cosmic Sabbatical cycles. This idea, which was particularly popular among kabbalists in the fourteenth and fifteenth centuries, suggests that the present world has a defined duration of seven thousand years, and that there are seven such worlds of the same duration, comprising forty-nine thousand years in total. This macrohistorical model was deployed by kabbalists to give meaning to their present reality by situating it within a vast sweep of time covering multiple worlds. Imagining other realities in this successive multiverse provided an occasion for understanding the comprehensive divine plan behind all of cosmic time, and the relatively brief moment of pain that constitutes the present eon.

The fourth chapter moves from the history of the cosmic order to that of the individual Jewish soul by exploring the ways that reincarnation is related to the question of historical memory and meaning. Each lifetime is, like the cosmos, only one in a series. Jewish identities of the past and future are bound to one another through the rebirth of souls. According to these sources, the suffering that Jewish individuals experience over the course of multiple lifetimes serves the historically vital purpose of purifying Jewish souls in order to enable messianic redemption and usher in the end of history. Reincarnation is also a tool used by God to guide history on its course, returning specific souls into the world at the right time and in the proper place in order to bring about the intended order of historical events. The persistence and reiteration of the soul across time is, for the kabbalists, yet another indication that God has not abandoned the Jews to the arbitrary winds of history.

Messianic redemption was a question that no medieval Jew could avoid when thinking about the meaning of their history, and kabbalists were keen to point out that their secret tradition offered new ways of understanding the ultimate destiny of the Jewish people at the end of days. Chapter 5 addresses kabbalistic discussions of history's meaning in relation to its anticipated end. The prominence of descriptions of the world after redemption and calculations of dates for the arrival of the messiah indicate just how important these kabbalists felt it was to orient historical time toward its conclusion, and to give some sense of where the present falls on the full historical timeline. Even though the present world will be followed by others, the endpoint that the kabbalists offer as hope for their Jewish readers is not that of the absolute end of being, but more specifically, the end of history and the chain of events driven by human free will. The rebalancing of divine powers that kabbalists maintain will happen at the end of days will bring an end to the channeling of energy to the nations of the world, which in turn will re-empower the people of Israel. But the world of Jewish dominance will not be one in which Jews simply switch places with their oppressors. In the messianic future envisioned in these sources, the dominance of the Jewish nation will happen in a balanced, static world, which is to say—after history ends.

The final chapter brings many of these points together through an examination of the ways that kabbalistic texts, especially those composed during the generation of the Spanish expulsion, describe the role of kabbalistic discourse itself in helping to shape Jewish history. In an intriguing double move, a surprising number of kabbalists depict the writing and sharing of kabbalistic texts as a way for Jews to survive exile and mend the broken course of history. The physical weakness of the Jewish people is compensated, in their view, but the power of their words. The very act of unveiling history's secrets is itself regarded as a form of power that Jews wield in shaping human affairs. The partnership with God that kabbalists claim for Jews through the practice of Jewish law is also manifested in the composition and dissemination of kabbalistic books. This final chapter demonstrates that kabbalists not only produced extensive discourses regarding the meaning of history; they were also explicit regarding the role that they believed their own particular genre of literary production could have in sustaining Jewish identity in exile. Such claims render explicit the argument made throughout this book—that kabbalistic texts have much to tell us about how premodern Jews sustained a meaningful sense of self in the face of history's challenges.

ONE

Terrors of History
Finding Order in a World of Chaos

The challenges of Jewish life in the fourteenth and fifteenth centuries demanded explanation. The length of the exile, and the obvious disparity between Jewish fortunes and those of their Christian and Muslim counterparts, became only more difficult to square with the basic terms of covenantal theology. Kabbalah presented a model that situated Jewish experience within a comprehensive divine plan for historical time. The decline of Jewish historical fortune, and the meaning of the extended final exile, were recast in kabbalistic discourse as purposeful, even foreordained steps in the divine plan for human history. Like many prekabbalistic and rabbinic authors, medieval kabbalists often depicted Jewish suffering as a consequence of Jewish transgressions. They also suggested that the empowerment of gentile nations was merely a way for God to punish his holy people and eventually to restore them to their glory. But Kabbalah adds an important new layer to this interpretation of history. For them, earthly historical events are all part of a supernal drama taking place within the Godhead. The forces that control the course of history and the rise and fall of the nations of the world reside in the realm of the *sefirot*. The fate of Israel over the course of history can only be understood, according to the kabbalists, through the Jewish esoteric tradition. In their view, the veil of history is opaque for every nation but the Jews.

Kabbalistic readings of the meaning of exile and historical misfortune are much more than purely theoretical interpretations of biblical or rabbinic texts. The course of events in postrabbinic Jewish history, which kabbalists often depict as a prolonged and agonizing series of afflictions at the hands of powerful nations, are rendered comprehensible through a claim to privileged knowledge afforded by the kabbalistic tradition. The suffering experienced by Jewish communities in different historical periods and geographic locations was regarded as a reflection of events taking place in the divine realm, with forces out of balance that result in earthly catastrophes. Gershom Scholem has noted that kabbalistic discourses regarding exile and redemption "transformed the exile of the people of Israel into an exile of the whole world, and the redemption of their people into a universal, cosmic redemption."[1] The misfortunes endured by Jews in exile are not, in the kabbalists' eyes, disconnected and without purpose. Jewish historical suffering, they claim, enables the eventual rebalancing of divine attributes, correcting the flaws in the Godhead caused by transgression. Perhaps more significantly, medieval kabbalists asserted that the meaning of the vicissitudes of Jewish history has been secretly revealed to the Jewish people. The kabbalistic tradition contains, they argue, the answer to the meaning of all events in Jewish and world history, from the beginning to the end of time. The true, unseen forces that create historical events are known only to the kabbalists, who in turn were eager to share these secrets with their Jewish readers in order to stave off historical despair.

The diverse circumstances of Jews in various locales and times are all connected in the kabbalistic imagination. Though Jews endure the pain of exile differently depending on time and place, all events in Jewish history are part of the same story taking place in the world above. The tendency of most medieval kabbalists to talk about Jewish history in terms of a general conception of the effect of divine forces on human events as a whole is not the result of a lack of interest in the particular fates of postrabbinic Jewish communities. As I noted in the introduction, there is good reason to believe that they were well aware of the main events of Jewish history as they pertained to communities in various regions throughout the world. But their project was not that of chronicling and documenting history in particular times and places. Their goal was to provide a key for understanding history in a way that could make sense of *all* of Jewish history, and to chart a hopeful future. In their thinking about history, kabbalists constructed models for making sense of the totality of historical time.

Kabbalistic views of history accord well with what Jacob Taubes describes as the apocalyptic/gnostic approach to the particularities of historical events. In his view, such texts provide a way to understand the specifics of history by answering the more general question, "How is history possible in the first place? What is the sufficient condition on which history as possibility rests?"[2] For the apocalyptic and gnostic writers that Taubes describes, as for the kabbalistic authors who are the subject of this book, history cannot be understood merely through its discrete events. The meaning of the present requires an appreciation of the full arc of time. As Taubes puts it, "In apocalypticism history is not recorded in the form of a chronicle; rather, apocalypticism attempts to gain knowledge about the future from the past and the present."[3] By constructing myths of creation, the origin of history, and the anticipation of redemption, apocalyptic discourses render events in the present meaningful. Even tragedies and disasters can be recast in the apocalyptic imagination into hopeful signs of the approaching future transformation. Suffering, in such a view, is not incomprehensible or random when its meaning is understood in terms of the hidden forces at play, with a divine plan stretching from the primordial past to the messianic future.

Mircea Eliade described the religious engagement with history in his landmark book, first published in French in 1949, and then in English in 1954 under the title *The Myth of Eternal Return: Cosmos and History*. In that study he advanced the claim that "archaic" civilizations engage historical time cyclically, imagining a continuous process of decay and renewal that gives meaning to particular historical events by relating them to eternal archetypes. The ancient Hebrews, he suggested, were the first civilization to think of time as primarily linear, with God controlling the events of human history, such as the rise and fall of nations through military conflict. In Eliade's view, the biblical prophets turned catastrophes of history into "negative theophanies."[4] He argues that "for the first time, the prophets placed a value on history . . . and discovered a one-way time."[5] Eliade regards the God of the Hebrew Bible as one "who reveals his will through events (invasions, sieges, battles, and so on). . . . The Hebrews were the first to discover the meaning of history as the epiphany of God, and this conception, as we should expect, was taken up and amplified by Christianity."[6] The biblical narrative presents one-time events as divine measures that are manifest within history, not as repeating nodes of renewal. These are singular episodes that serve a divine purpose in moving human history in the right direction. For instance, Eliade notes that "the moment of revelation made to Moses by God remains a limited moment, definitely situated in time. And, since it also represents a theophany, it thus acquires a new dimension: it becomes precious inasmuch as it is no longer reversible, as it is a historical event."[7] The novelty of the Israelite approach to finding meaning in history, in Eliade's view, is that the events of the biblical narrative are not exemplars of an eternal process of repetition and renewal. Biblical events happen once, by the will of God, in order to push history purposefully forward toward a divine objective.

Eliade's oversimplified conception of Israelite, and by extension, Jewish, history as linear has been rightly criticized.[8] As we will see over the course of this book, and as other scholars have observed, premodern kabbalistic notions of time were complex, and incorporated bother linear and cyclical characteristics. Nonetheless, Eliade's primary observation regarding the way that Jews, as well as other, more "archaic" religious traditions, give meaning to historical time should not be dismissed out of hand. His main objective is not simply to categorize the Israelite approach to history as linear in opposition to all other ways of understanding history up to that point. Eliade was interested in the many ways that religious traditions advance strategies for giving *meaning* to the events of human history. In his view, both the linear and cyclical models for understanding historical events are ways of coping with what he calls the "terror of history."[9]

The fear that history evokes is not simply the possibility of misfortune, suffering, and death. The most salient aspect of this terror, in Eliade's view, is the fear that the suffering might be arbitrary and devoid of any greater significance. Both archaic and Israelite strategies for understanding negative historical events grapple with this question. According to Eliade, the primary question is, "What could suffering and pain signify?" He claims that the response, in various forms, is that history is "not a meaningless experience that man can tolerate insofar as it is inevitable, as, for example, he tolerates the rigors of climate." Eliade refers to historical tragedies as "events," such as war, enslavement, or disempowerment, and he suggests that for the *homo religiosus*, "if it was possible to tolerate such sufferings, it is precisely because they seemed neither gratuitous nor arbitrary."[10] Eliade notes that both linear and cyclical religious conceptions of history always advance a "reason" for historical misfortune, which means that "the suffering becomes intelligible and hence tolerable." Religious discourses of historical disaster create a structure in which one "tolerates it morally because *it is not absurd.*"[11]

Like Taubes in his discussion of apocalyptic conceptions of time, Eliade regards religious approaches to history as engaged with the broader contexts of meaning in which human history takes place. This is not a discourse of the historical detail or the recounting of individual events. The question that animates them is the possibility of meaningful history as such. There is no use in seeking to understand the meaning of every historical event and detail, since either all events are meaningful, or none of them are. Each religious discourse, in its own way, constructs an overarching system of meaning in which transcendent forces are at play in the world, giving purpose to particular events, whatever they might be. This does not mean that they were not interested in particular events. It merely means that the *way* that the episodes of human affairs are understood is through a broader discourse of the divine architecture of history. Eliade argued that this is why (in his view) archaic civilizations are not particularly good at retaining the details of historical events over long periods of time.[12]

Eliade is certainly right to point out that the lack of attention to particular events does not represent an indifference to them. A comprehensive theology of history gives meaning to the totality of events that comprise human history. He observed that "among the Hebrews, every new historical calamity was regarded as a punishment inflicted by Yahweh, angered by the orgy of sin to which the chosen people had abandoned themselves. No military disaster seemed absurd, no suffering was vain, for, beyond the 'event,' it was always possible to perceive the will of Yahweh. Even more: these catastrophes were, we may say, necessary, they were foreseen by God so that the Jewish people should not contravene its true destiny by alienating the religious heritage left by Moses."[13]

One last observation that Eliade makes deserves brief mention. In his discussions of both the cyclical and linear conceptions of time, he suggested that both are, in their own way, antithetical to history and seek to abolish it. For archaic civilizations, there is the continual return to the mythic time of origins—*in illo tempore*—that generates the renewal of history. The Hebrew Bible, on the other hand, used the idea of a messianic savior "in order to 'tolerate history,' that is, to endure their military defeats and political humiliations."[14] Yet Eliade points out that even in this case, "messianism hardly succeeds in accomplishing the eschatological valorization of time: the future will regenerate time; that is, will restore its original purity and integrity. Thus, *in illo tempore* is situated not only at the beginning of time but also at its end."[15] By creating a narrative of the origin of historical time in the garden of Eden, and a vision of the end of time at the point of messianic redemption in which the purity of the origin is restored, Eliade perceives in Judaism another strategy to accomplish the same objective as that of myths of historical cycles. In both cases, the events of the present are rendered meaningful through their relationship to a transhistorical sacred power, with a mythical origin that also serves as the final destination of the historical process. Israelite temporal linearity is thus also, ironically, a closed loop. Such a discourse, in Eliade's view, renders the present legible, since "in the Israel of the messianic prophets, historical events could be tolerated because, on the one hand, they were willed by Yahweh, and, on the other hand, because they were necessary for the final salvation of the chosen people."[16] Yet Eliade also observes that "when the messiah comes, the world will be saved once and for all and history will cease to exist."[17] That is to say, the redemption entails the end of history. In this regard, the biblical and rabbinic tendency to perceive the workings of God within time is not an uncomplicated embrace of history. Like Christianity, Eliade observes, the goal is not to sacralize history, but escape it, since "the will to put a final and definitive end to history is itself still an antihistorical attitude."[18]

Reading History's Heroic Victims

Premodern kabbalists constructed a wide variety of historical discourses in which the aspiration to escape a process of human history that has gone wildly off course is part of a broader strategy to make sense of contemporary historical events. One particularly dramatic example of such a discourse is provided by Isaac of Acre in his 'Otzar hayyim, written in the early fourteenth century.[19] In a curious reworking of the myth of Prometheus, he relates the following story:

I, the young, Isaac of Acre, heard from the mouth of an uncircumcised gentile a very strange thing . . . and even though this is not true in the literal sense, it is true in the manner of the concealed secret. This is what he told me: he said that a pious man from among the pious gentiles, a notable wise man in the wisdom of the powers that go from potentiality to action visible to the sensible eye, a wandering ascetic, was traveling by means of shortening of the way (qefitzat ha-derekh) and deception, among the byways and deserts, until King Solomon was shown to him in a desert very distant from human settlement. He was sitting upon his royal throne, and he was forced to remain there and not to move. While he was sitting there, many ravens would descend upon him from the sky and peck at his flesh and eat from it until all of the flesh was consumed from his bones. Over the course of one day, his flesh would regrow until his entire body was restored as it was, and then the ravens would return and consume his flesh in the same manner. This they would do every day. And the wandering man said to him "Who are you, who is so afflicted with suffering as severe as this?" He responded, saying "I am King Solomon, son of David, king of Israel." And he said to him, "Why are such grievous afflictions cast upon you from the heavens?" He said to him, "Because of the transgressions that I committed against the will of my creator." And he said to him, "For how long must you suffer these severe afflictions?" He said, "Until the messiah comes, who is of my descendants. By his merit, the Holy One, blessed be he, will pardon me and I will be at rest and quieted." The secret that I perceived in this is that this Solomon is the "king to whom peace belongs," and he is Kenesset Yisra'el, the Shekhinah that dwells within the souls of the children of Israel who are immersed in exile under the yoke of the nations of the world. The ravens are, by way of mystery, the nations of the world who oppress the children of Israel with all types of suffering, and subjugate their bodies and possessions. However, by way of the secret, this Solomon alludes to *Tifferet* and *'Atarah*, and the ravens according to the kabbalist wise men of Sepharad (Castile) allude to the external gradations that have ascended and afflict the divine gradations. In the days of the messiah, may he arrive speedily in our days, the external gradations will fall and return to the domain of the earth, the place from which they emanated, which is their annulment. And the overflow from *Pahad* will be removed from *Tifferet* and *'Atarah*, and they will receive the effulgence of *Gedulah* and *Pahad*.[20]

Isaac of Acre makes the unconventional choice to interpret a story related to him by a gentile as though it contained a multilayered kabbalistic secret about the nature of Jewish life in exile. In his first reading, he takes the Solomon/Prometheus character to be a representation of the Jewish people in exile for their sins. And like the rabbinic notion that the Shekhinah accompanies the Jews in their wandering and suffering,[21] he understands Solomon's tortures to represent the suffering of the Jewish people that they share with God.

But this is the point where Isaac of Acre's similarity to the general rabbinic view of history ends. For him, there is an extensive unseen drama in the divine realm that accounts for the travails of Jewish life over the period of exilic history. The Shekhinah, or Divine Presence, refers here to the last of the ten *sefirot*, and it is manifest in the world not as an accompanying presence with the Jewish people, but rather as the substance of their very souls. When Jews suffer at the hands of the gentile nations, God suffers with them, since their souls *are* divine. The nations of the world, represented by the ravens, are merely tools in a divine plan for punishing Israel, and God himself shares in this suffering. The torment, however, is not permanent. The tortured king eagerly awaits the arrival of the messiah, who, as tradition has it, will be from the house of David, and therefore one of his own descendants. In that transformed future, his suffering will end. Jewish life in exile and their subjugation by foreign nations is understood here as an aspect of the wider arc of divine action over time, with a distinct origin in the past and an assured end in the future.

At an even more recondite level of meaning, Isaac of Acre claims that this story also relates a supernal drama within the Godhead, according to which the suffering King Solomon is the conjunction of two sefirot, *Shekhinah*, the tenth and final *sefirah*, and *Tifferet*, the sixth. The ravens represent the external "gradations," referring to the idea of the ten *sefirot* of impurity that parallel the ten divine *sefirot*.[22] These entities empower the non-Jewish nations in the material world, and under normal circumstances, they are subordinated to the *sefirot* of purity. However, as a result of past Jewish transgression, the divine balance has been disrupted and the impure powers have been enabled to afflict the *sefirot* of purity. On the historical plane, this takes the form of the subjugation of the Jewish people to the nations of the world, reflecting the imbalance in the divine realm. But this situation, he assures his readers, will not persist indefinitely. When the final messianic redemption arrives, the external entities that empower the nations will fall to earth, the lower realm from which they originated, and be eliminated. The sefirotic attributes *Tifferet* and *'Atarah* will once again receive the flow of divine energy from *Gedulah*, or *Hesed*, the fourth *sefirah*, as they did in the past, thus restoring the divine powers to their proper, *original* configuration. And on the plane of human history, the people of Israel will be relieved of their suffering, and their prominence will be restored.

In this reading of an admittedly fanciful tale, Isaac of Acre presents a kabbalistic view of history as a marionette performance. The fates of nations on earth can only be properly understood by those who know how to perceive the interactions of the supernal divine forces that guide historical events. World affairs are, properly speaking, the final visible manifestation of a divine drama. Looming over Isaac of Acre's interpretation of the story is the powerful claim that only Jews who are learned in kabbalistic lore are able to know the true meaning of history. Through an emphatic inversion of the Christian claim that Jews are the blind conveyers of the divine word who lack the insight to perceive its truth, Isaac of Acre's tale portrays kabbalists like himself as the only ones who can properly decode the gentile wise man's story. And what he claims his kabbalistic wisdom to reveal is nothing short of the truth behind the agony of Jewish history.

In what follows, we will consider some of the ways that kabbalists described the place of Jews within the sweep of historical time. The perception of history that they construct is one in which the Jewish experience of exile and subjugation is both painfully apparent, and at the same time eminently explicable. The fate of the Jewish people over the course of their long and final exile is not minimized—if anything, the misfortunes are exaggerated—but it is also not regarded as absurd or incomprehensible. That is to say, history is terrible, but it is not, in Eliade's parlance, terrifying. Kabbalistic discourse provides a way for Jews to make sense of their collective fate by accounting for catastrophe and attributing meaning to historical setbacks. At the same time, it also suggests that the future in store for the Jews is a restoration of the conditions of the world to its original purity. The arrival of redemption is both a return to the beginning and the end of the curse of history.

Storm from Paradise: Original Sin and the Origin of History

How do medieval kabbalists talk about the beginning of history? This is a different question from that of the origin of time. The issue I wish to consider is the specific question of kabbalistic discourses of the beginning of *historical* time, with events driven by human action and free will. In considering kabbalistic approaches to the origin of history, my interest is in how medieval kabbalists account for the state of world affairs in their own time, with wars, plagues, oppression, and other often tragic events that serve as the context in which the Jewish experience of exile takes place. In all discussions of this question that I am aware of in medieval kabbalistic texts, history begins with the transgression of Adam and Eve in the garden of Eden, when they ate from the tree of knowledge of good and evil. History does *not* begin with creation. Had things gone in the garden of Eden as God originally intended, there would have been no history as we know it. The world of human affairs, with nations that rise and fall in a process of continuous change, was not, in the view of most kabbalists, the intended ideal state of affairs. The Edenic life would have been a static paradise. A world driven by the whims of human free will, with the competing forces of the good and evil impulses, is a deviation from the original divine intent. History is what happens in the interregnum between the transgression in Eden and the arrival of messianic redemption.

In a famous image regarding the historical process, Walter Benjamin describes Paul Klee's painting *Angelus Novus* as a depiction of the "angel of history." The angel is moving backward into the future while staring into the past. Benjamin notes that "where we perceive a chain of events, he sees one single catastrophe which keeps piling wreckage upon wreckage and hurls it in front of his feet." And while the angel would like to pause and heal the world, "awaken the dead, and make whole what has been smashed," he cannot, because "a storm is blowing from Paradise; it has got caught in his wings with such violence that the angel can no longer close them."[23] Benjamin's depiction of the angel of history as a supernal power rendered powerless specifically by a storm "blowing from Paradise" is an image that bears a striking resemblance to the kabbalistic view of history. The sin in the garden of Eden is what sets the great tempest of history in motion. And like Benjamin, the kabbalists regarded history as an accumulation of wreckage, rather than an incremental progression toward a better future. The world will be healed only when the storm from paradise is quelled and history ends. In an essay dedicated to interpreting the meaning of Benjamin's Angel of History,[24] Scholem described the angel as "a melancholy figure" seeking to overcome history "in a leap leading out of the historical continuum into the 'time of now,' whether the latter is revolutionary or messianic."[25] History as such is irredeemable, and the escape from history is the only hope. Kabbalists shared the conviction that the historical process unfolds like a storm from paradise, and as such, kabbalistic reflections on the course of history therefore begin with Eden.

The concept of original sin—the notion that all humans are born into a "fallen" state and implicated in sin from birth as a result of Adam and Eve's transgression—is commonly regarded as foreign to Jewish thought.[26] To be sure, some Jews took grave exception to the Christian doctrine, and discussions of it were common in medieval polemical literature.[27] Nonetheless, kabbalists in the thirteenth century drew upon earlier rabbinic motifs in order to formulate a number of interpretations of the nature of Adam's sin that bear certain resemblances to the Augustinian notion.[28] Azriel of Gerona, for instance, held that before the sin of eating the fruit from the tree of knowledge, Adam was an incorporeal, spiritual being. The three main aspects of his soul, *Nefesh*, *Ruah*, and *Neshamah*, were united with the upper three *sefirot*.

Adam existed in a primordial state of perfection, lacking free will, since he had no evil inclination, for a period of two thousand years before the creation of the world. Only after the sin in the garden of Eden did humanity take on corporeal form. In the messianic future, Azriel maintained that humanity will regain their incorporeality, and be relieved of the blight of the evil inclination.[29] The corollary to Adam's sin, in Azriel's view, is corporeality and individuation.

Nahmanides, on the other hand, considers the most significant outcomes of Adam's sin to be the creation of free will[30] and the phenomenon of death.[31] In his comment on Genesis 2:9, he argued that "originally, Adam naturally did that which was right. . . . It was the fruit of this tree that gave rise to will and desire, such that those who eat of it would become able to desire one thing or its opposite, for good or evil. . . . After he ate from the tree, he possessed free will according to his desire, to do evil or good, either to himself or others. This is a divine characteristic from one perspective, and yet bad for a person, in that he comes to possess a drive and desire." Had Adam not sinned, life would have been eternal,[32] yet also static. There would have been none of the drama and change over time that constitutes what we have come to call human history. The "Era of Torah," which takes place during what Nahmanides calls the "Era of Desire," is the period between Adam's sin and messianic redemption.[33] The primary characteristic of this period for Nahmanides is the existence of human free will. In the messianic future, as in the prelapsarian past, humanity will revert to their original state of proper behavior by nature.[34] Human history in its present form is a deviation from God's original plan.

Kabbalistic interpreters of Nahmanides expanded considerably on his cryptic remarks regarding the exact nature of Adam's sin and how it gave rise to the historical era. Unlike the Christological notion, in which the emphasis is on the need for redemption from hell in the afterlife, these authors were more concerned with redemption from historical time. Some of these kabbalists, who make up what is loosely referred to as the school of interpreters of Nahmanides, describe Adam's sin as a form of "cutting the shoots."[35] This enigmatic Talmudic phrase[36] is understood by medieval kabbalists to refer to the separation of the Shekhinah from the upper *sefirot*, caused by human acts of transgression. Nahmanides himself never uses this phrase in reference to

Adam's sin, though he may have hinted at it in his comment on Genesis 3:22 that "Adam sinned with the fruit of the tree of knowledge below and above, in action and in thought." Isaac of Acre, for example, says that the tree of life and the tree of knowledge in the earthly garden of Eden had supernal corollaries in the divine realm. The tree of life represents the realm of the "east," associated with mercy and light, while the tree of knowledge of good and evil is associated with the "north," the realm of darkness and satanic power.[37] When Adam sinned by eating from the tree of knowledge, he separated it from the tree of life. This was a problem because "when the tree of life is bound to the tree of knowledge, which is the aspect of the north, the aspect of Satan, the aspect of evil, Satan cannot oppose, because the tree of life, which is the attribute of peace, overpowers him. When it separates from it, its power remains and it opposes . . . this is 'cutting the shoots.' "[38] Isaac of Acre goes on to describe the far-reaching consequences of this act in some detail:

> You already know that man comprises all things, and his soul is bound to the supernal soul. . . . When he follows the evil path of Satan, he cuts and separates the soul from the supernal soul . . . distancing and separating soul from soul is like cutting . . . therefore, when Adam ate the fruit of the tree of knowledge, and separated it from the tree of life, the evil inclination gained control over him . . . this caused impurity and death and distancing of soul from soul. Thus, it is made clear that through his eating [of the fruit], he severed below and above, and divided the powers of the tree of knowledge away from the powers of the tree of life. . . . This is cutting the shoots, since after he separated the fruit of the tree of knowledge from the aspect of evil from the tree of life, the power of the evil inclination was augmented and he satisfied his soul with it. Soul was distanced from soul, and power was given to the emissaries of the tree of knowledge to do evil.[39]

Like Nahmanides, Isaac of Acre regards the introduction of the evil inclination and death into human experience as outcomes of Adam's sin. But he creates a much more complex image of what happened in the divine realm that led to this outcome. Adam separated the divine powers connected to the two trees in the garden when he ate the fruit of the tree of knowledge. This led to a destabilization of the divine powers of good and evil, giving evil satanic influence a foothold in the world. Moreover, Adam himself was fundamentally changed, since his soul was separate from the divine soul, rendering him mortal. Reality itself shifted, impurity was brought into the world, and the original divine plan for a perfect universe was pushed off course. In Isaac of Acre's telling, this leads not only to a world driven by human volition and temptation, but also one in which the "emissaries of the tree of knowledge" are given free reign. This last comment may hint at the notion of the heavenly *sarim* or archons (to be discussed below) that are appointed over the nations of the world, and that are empowered to afflict the people of Israel during the time of exile.

R. Bahya ben Asher in the late thirteenth century was more explicit in his assignment of sefirotic associations for the trees in the garden in Nahmanides's comment: "The tree of life and the tree of knowledge above are *Tifferet* and *'Atarah*, and 'Adam sinned in action and thought,' with the tree of knowledge and its correlate. And his sin was that he cut the shoots, which is to say, he severed the power of the divine name that entered the shoot, which was the reason that the shoot dried up and was killed. It was fitting for the shoot to exact vengeance, and thus he was punished with death, wherein his soul is severed during his death from his body, as he severed the supernal power from the shoot."[40] Bahya's emphasis here in describing the theosophical correlates to Adam's transgression is less on the creation of individual will, and more on the reason for the finitude of the human lifespan. Just as the plucking of the fruit caused the "shoot" to die, Adam, along with all of his descendants, was punished with death. And just as the twists and turns of human history are unimaginable without individual volition, it is similarly impossible to imagine the dramas of history in the absence of death. Untimely demise is the key to tragedy, and the threat of death is central to the leveraging of collective power. In the mythic time, *in illo tempore*, of Eden and redemption, death and free will are abolished. The interregnum of historical time is, in Joshua Ibn Shuib's view, corrupted: "According to the opinion of our rabbis of blessed memory,[41] the entire world and all of creation was cursed as a result of that sin . . . and in the approaching [messianic] future, when the original intent of creation is achieved, all things will return to their primordiality and being."[42] The primordiality of creation is, as of yet, unattained according to Ibn Shuib. Only the future redemption will attain the original objective of creation. Life in between, which is history as we know it, is infused with the evils of death and transgression. In the redeemed future, reality will finally attain its divine objective, which means that history will of necessity come to an end.

Some kabbalists argue that Adam's sin caused the light emanating from the attribute of *Yesod* to become concealed, and this in turn is the cause of death. According to the anonymous *Ma'arekhet ha-'elohut*, "Because [Adam] intended to separate the fruit from the tree, which was the tree of life, he and his descendants were punished with the separation of the soul from the body, measure for measure, for it was previously appropriate for him to live eternally."[43] The current historical period is therefore one in which death reigns, as a result of changes in the divine realm brought about by Adam's sin. The text notes that "in the current historical period (*zeman ha-hefetz ha-zeh*), which is a time when the evil inclination prevails, the light that alludes to *Yesod* from which life derives, cannot be perceived. This concealment is the cause of death, since the snake cast filth into Eve. The sinner who wishes to cleave to life is prevented by the attribute of *Din*, by the flame that is before it."[44] The *sefirah* of *Din* is associated with the power of strict judgment. The empowerment of that divine attribute is understood by this anonymous author as the way that the light that brings eternal life to humanity from *Yesod* was concealed after Adam's sin. It functions like the "flaming sword" mentioned in Genesis 3:24 that prevents humanity from reentering the garden after their expulsion. The new condition of humanity then becomes congenital, passed on through all future descendants: "Since Adam was the root of all [later generations], all who came after him were punished for his sin, and no person since ever made use of that light [that was concealed] as it was appropriate to do before the sin."[45] To be locked out of the garden is, for this text, to be deprived of the divine light of life, and therefore subject to death. The author, in fact, regarded the twin phenomena of death and the human will to do evil as primary signifiers of the "current period," meaning, the duration of human history. As the text notes, "Death exists only in the current period, since the world pursues their evil inclinations on account of the first sin."[46]

For these kabbalists, the sin of Adam and Eve becomes a complex theosophical etiology for explaining far more than the existence of sexual shame, the need for work, pain in childbirth, and the legless snake. It also accounts for something different from the inherently "fallen" and irredeemable nature of humanity (as in some Christological readings). The transgression with the tree of knowledge explains both the origin and end of history. The sin in the garden explains why the light that was intended for the world stemming from *Yesod* is blocked, and why the unity between "knowledge" and "life" has been severed. The result is a world in which *humans* are capable of creating catastrophe. But the prelapsarian/postmessianic reality will be categorically different. As Joseph ben Shalom Ashkenazi notes in his commentary on Bereishit Rabbah, "In the future, the evil inclination will be removed from us, and the commandments will be natural and not by choice and free will. . . . Thus was the intention with humanity. But, when [Adam] sinned, the commandments became a matter of choice and free will."[47] While such an accounting does little to stem the horrors of human-made catastrophes such as war and oppression, it does serve the purpose of making them comprehensible, or at very least, to put it in Eliade's terms, *not absurd*. Moreover, by claiming knowledge of an esoteric, divine tradition that explains such phenomena, the kabbalists assert ownership over powerful and exclusive insight into the travails of history.

The Archons of the Nations and the Inversion of Power

The world as constituted after Adam and Eve's sin is one in which history has been driven off course and the supernal powers are out of balance. Many medieval kabbalists take this as the basis for a theosophical understanding of the origin and nature of the power of non-Jewish nations and their capacity to oppress and subjugate Jews. For these kabbalists, the disarray in the divine realm explains the jarring historical-political reality of the chosen people living as subservient minorities under foreign domination. Joseph Gikatilla, active in Castile in the late thirteenth century, gave the fullest early articulation of the notion of the seventy *sarim*, or supernal archons, that represent the seventy nations of the world.[48] Each archon in the divine realm has an appointed nation and geographical territory over which it holds sway. In an ideal state, all of the supernal archons are subject to the power of the *Shekhinah*, the last of the *sefirot* and the connecting point between the divine realm and the material world. However, since the sin of Adam and Eve, and further exacerbated by ongoing human transgression, the supernal powers are out of balance. The result in the divine realm is a reversal of the proper order, with the archons receiving power from the upper *sefirot* and exerting influence above their station, while the overflow from *Shekhinah* to the people of Israel is vastly diminished. In the human realm, this imbalance is expressed in history, with non-Jewish nations overpowering God's chosen people.

Gikatilla's discussion of the seventy archons builds upon the naming of seventy nations in Genesis 10, and the rabbinic notion of the seventy angelic beings that surround the throne of glory, mentioned in Pirkei de-Rebbi Eliezer,[49] and alluded to in Nahmanides's commentary on the Torah.[50] The archons of the nations are, in Gikatilla's view, part of the complex balance of powers in the realm of the divine "chariot," or the Godhead. As he states the matter, "The archons of the nations are very important for the service of the divine chariot."[51] The problem is not the existence of the nations of the world and their corresponding archons, but their capacity to overpower Israel. In a fuller description, he explains:

> Know that the supernal archons have two portions in the world below; one portion on the earth, in the particular place where that archon rules, and one portion among the nations, the particular people who dwell in that place. Each of the seventy archons has a designated portion upon the land and among the nations. . . . During the generation after the flood, each nation was paired with their archon . . . and at that time, each archon took possession of their portion upon the earth and among the nations, and God, may he be blessed, took his portion; upon the land, Jerusalem, and among the peoples of the world, Israel.[52]

In the proper arrangement of divine and human power in the generation after the flood, the intention was for the nations of the world each to have its own geographic region, together with its own supernal representative. The people of Israel, however, would be a special case. Their land—traditionally understood to be the centermost point on earth—would be the land of Israel, and God himself would be their supernal representative and guardian. Such, according to Gikatilla, was the intention for the postlapsarian world. History would exist, and nations would function in the world, but the people of Israel, living in the land of Israel, would have special divine protection.

Human history after Eden was to be one that, according to this kabbalistic conception, would have placed the people of Israel literally at the center of worldly and divine affairs. As Gikatilla further elaborates:

> Just as all of the supernal archons are arrayed around the name YHWH, may he be blessed, so too, their families below surround the people of Israel, who are the portion of the name YHWH, may he be blessed. Thus, it is said, "All nations surround me; by the name of God I will cut them down" (Ps 118:10). . . . What is the reason why the people of Israel are in the center? It is due to the fact that they are God's portion, and have inherited the land with God's portion below, which is Jerusalem. . . . There are three things placed in the center: The name YHWH above with all of the archons around it. . . . The people of Israel below in the center of the nations . . . and Jerusalem, the inheritance of God, which is the land of Israel, with the lands of the non-Jewish nations surrounding it. . . . Thus, it is made clear to you that the name YHWH, the people of Israel, and Jerusalem are all three in the center, and the rest of the archons and their domains are the periphery.[33]

The proper arrangement of both divine and human powers, according to Gikatilla, is with the people of Israel and their land serving as the central foci of power. This would correspond with the placement of the divine name designated over the people and the land of Israel, the tetragrammaton, YHWH, which occupies a central place in the divine realm, corresponding to the sixth *sefirah*, *Tifferet*. But like the first divine plan in the garden of Eden, this second, more historical arrangement in which Israel would have been ascendant was also undone by human transgression. Israel's sins upended this arrangement and fundamentally altered the flow of power to the archons and their respective peoples, leading to an inversion in Israel's fortunes. Instead of being the most powerful people in the middle point of the world, they became dislocated, embattled, and surrounded by foreign enemies who had been given a free hand to oppress them. As Gikatilla describes it,

> Therefore, the people of Israel are plundered, scorned, shamed, and laid waste by all of the nations. And thus, the channels that were once directed toward Israel with all of the goodness that flowed from the name

YHWH, they were all destroyed and spilled down to the lands of the archons of the nations. Regarding this, Solomon, peace be upon him, said, "Concerning three things does the earth shudder; a slave who becomes king" (Prov 30:21), these are the supernal archons who steal overflow from the channels that are directed toward Israel that were broken and now pour to them. They become kings in place of Israel. "A scoundrel sated with food" (Prov 30:22), these are the idolators among the seventy archons who are sated and fattened from the many forms of goodness that come to them from their archons, deriving from the overflow that once came to Israel. The channels were broken and the archons received that overflow. When the archons of the nations are filled with the goodness that was designated for Israel, then their peoples look forward to when Israel will sin so that their archons can intercede between the name YHWH and Israel, so that they will receive the overflow that was supposed to reach Israel from YHWH.[54]

History in its present form, with the people of Israel exiled from their land and subjugated to the authority of non-Jewish nations, is a reflection, according to Gikatilla, of a change in the intradivine balance of powers brought about by Jewish transgression. The proper subordination of the archons to the Tetragrammaton in the divine realm would have resulted in the subordination of gentile nations to the Jewish people on earth. But Jewish transgression on earth has caused the opposite, in Gikatilla's telling, creating the present reality in which the Jewish people are "plundered, scorned, shamed, and laid waste by all of the nations." His interpretation of the verse from Proverbs further emphasizes the upside-down nature of the present condition of history, and explains how it is that the "slave became the master"—that is, how non-Jews became the overlords of the people of Israel.

Gikatilla's picture is much more complex than the general theodicy that Jewish transgression is the cause of Jewish misfortune. He presents a behind-the-scenes glimpse into the inner workings of the divine realm in order to lay bare the secret structure of divine power that accounts for the rise and fall of nations. By breaking the "channels" that connect the *sefirot*, Jewish transgression has enabled the supernal archons of the nations to subvert the power that otherwise would have been bestowed exclusively to Israel. The dominance of non-Jewish nations is therefore an ironic reflection of Jewish power. Without Jewish transgression, the nations of the world would be significantly weakened. Gikatilla goes so far as to suggest that the archons of foreign nations eagerly anticipate Jewish sin and transgression, since it is on account of this that they can benefit from the divine power that otherwise would flow to the Jews from God.

Gikatilla's assessment of the secret role of supernal archons in the dynamics of national/political power on earth is not confined to the past and present. He also anticipates the role of this mechanism in the future destiny of Jewish history. Gikatilla's implicit claim is that Kabbalah decodes the full arc of time. The course of human affairs and the fate of Israel is rendered legible, and all individual events fit into place, through a kabbalistic accounting of the origin and end of history. The heavenly archons play an important role in Gikatilla's accounting of history.

> Know that all blessing used to come initially from YHWH, may he be blessed, directly to *Kenesset Yisra'el*, and from *Kenesset Yisra'el* to the people of Israel. Through the people of Israel, all of the seventy nations and idolatrous peoples were blessed and sustained below. Thus, it is said, "By you, all of the families of the earth shall be blessed" (Gen 12:3). When Israel sinned, the channels were broken, and the nations of the world gained access to the blessing that previously came to Israel. . . . But, when God returns the exiles of Zion, and unites the divine name of Israel and removes all of the impediments between them, then not a single one of the archons of the nations will receive overflow or blessing or goodness, except by means of *Kenesset Yisra'el*, who dominates them all and rules them all, and she gives them sustenance. All of the archons and idolators will receive sustenance from the end of all of the final gradations, from the remainder of *Kenesset Yisra'el*. . . . Then, all of the archons will be subservient to Israel, and all of them will receive sustenance from Israel. . . . Therefore, since this is the case, it shows that when God, may he be blessed, unites with *Kenesset Yisra'el*, and they unite with one another, then all of the archons will be made into a single fellowship to worship God, may he be blessed, and to

serve *Kenesset Yisra'el*, since their sustenance comes from her. Just as the desire and will and passion of the seventy supernal archons will be to serve *Kenesset Yisra'el*, so too will the desire of the seventy nations be to serve the people of Israel below, to cleave to them, and they will all serve God.[55]

In Gikatilla's portrait of the sweep of history, he describes the disastrous result of Israelite transgression on the divine realm. By rupturing the channels between the *sefirot*, Jewish violation of divine will brought about the circumstances in the divine realm that in turn generated negative consequences in the human realm. In the period after Eden, history was inevitable, but it did not, according to this view, need to entail the exile and subordination of the Jewish people. Had Jews not violated the commandments, Gikatilla claims, their history would not have been a litany of tragedy. But with the archons of the nations receiving the divine blessing that was intended for Israel, history went badly awry. In the most biblical of moves, Gikatilla understands the misfortunes of Jewish history—and here he implies specifically the relations between Jews and Christians, descendants of Jacob and Esau[56]—in terms of a stolen blessing! Through hidden theurgic mechanisms, transgression begets usurpation of divine favor.

The situation, in Gikatilla's assessment, is, however, not without hope. History moves in the direction of redemption, which is also a return to the proper arrangement of divine and human powers. The return of the Jewish exiles to Zion will entail a repair of the damaged channels in the Godhead. The nations of the world will then be united in "a single fellowship to worship God," and more importantly, they will be subservient to Jewish authority. Jews, he suggests, as representatives of the *Shekhinah* on earth, will be objects of adoration instead of scorn. Just as the archons above will once again be subordinated to *Kenesset Yisra'el*, or the tenth *sefirah*, all non-Jewish nations will be subordinated to Jews. The redemptive future is one in which the "desire" of the enemies of Israel will be transformed. Nations will no longer be in conflict with each other. Instead, they will be the willing subjects of Jews.

In this particular vision of redemption, time continues, but history ends. The return to Zion is also a return to a time of balance and harmony in both the human and divine realms. All nations will be united in their worship of God and service to the Jewish people, just as their archons above will once again serve and derive sustenance from the *Shekhinah*. The misfortunes of Jewish life in exile are deviations brought on through the power, as opposed to the powerlessness, of Jewish actions. Jewish suffering in exile is, in Gikatilla's view of history, a consequence of the theurgic capacity of Jewish violations of divine will. Because of Jewish transgression, the world order was turned upside down. But in the future, all will be made right.

And what of the present? In this view of the covenant, the unique relationship of Jews to God, with the tenth *sefirah*, the *Shekhinah*, serving as their personal archon, is retained to protect them over the course of their exile. As Gikatilla puts it, "This is the secret [meaning of the verse] 'For the sake of his great name, God will never abandon his people' (1 Sam 12:23), which is to say, even though the people of Israel may not be so very righteous, he will not abandon them. What is the reason? Because they are the portion of his great name, and just as his great name can never change, so too, the people of Israel will never disappear."[57] Gikatilla deploys the doctrine of supernal archons in order to make sense of his own present. As we saw above, he describes Jewish historical experience in the decidedly lachrymose terms of Israel being "laid waste by all the nations." But the present is only part of the story. When understood in terms of past and future, even Israel's suffering (and survival) is a sign of divine favor. The historical misfortunes of the Jewish people are all the result of a secret drama of interconnecting divine forces in which Jews and Judaism take center stage. What might appear as clear evidence of God's abandonment of the Jews is recast as signs of Israel's centrality in a divine plan for human history. At the end of history, the full story will become visible. In the meantime, the kabbalistic tradition is portrayed as the secret Jewish weapon against the terror of history. While Jews might suffer during the current historical moment, Gikatilla and other kabbalists assert that Jews alone have received the true divine revelation regarding the secret mechanisms that govern and direct history. The story it tells is one in which even Jewish suffering is part of the noble fate of the chosen people.

The discourse of the archons plays a prominent role in the works of many kabbalists in the generations after Gikatilla. In one anonymous text, the author's perception of the present state of Jewish history as one in which Jews suffer under foreign dominion is related to Jews "straying" from their proper place, thereby falling under the sway of the archon of another nation: "Corresponding to the kingdom of the house of David is a different power called the 'Kingdom of the Evil One.' When the people fall into the hands of the archon on account of their straying from the proper path, it rules over them, as our own eyes observe, due to our many sins."[38] The hidden world of the supernal archons helps this kabbalist understand far more than the enigma of *biblical* misfortune. The relationship of the people of Israel to the archons, and their capacity to stray from God's domain into foreign territory, is an explanatory mechanism for understanding the author's own historical predicament as a Jew. The notion that Jews have wandered from their "proper path" and fallen under the authority of an evil kingdom with a similarly evil archon helps this kabbalist to understand the historical reality that they and the presumed reader observe with their "own eyes."

An anonymous text closely associated with Gikatilla's depiction of the seventy archons suggests that "the people of Israel occupy the center of the palace, and if they deviate to the right or the left and break forth from the palaces, they immediately enter into the domain of the external archons, and [they] afflict Israel, since they are in the center. This is the secret of the exiles and the destruction of the Temple, since Israel occupies the palace of the Lord, and the rest of the nations and their archons occupy the byways."[39] Here again, Jewish historical tragedy is attributed to Jewish actions that distance them from direct divine oversight and place them under foreign authority. The rightful place of the Jewish people, in this author's view, as well as that of Gikatilla discussed above, is to be at the center of the divine plan. When Jews venture into the periphery, their fortunes decline.

Another anonymous text sometimes referred to as *Kabbalat Saporta*[60] described the origins of the archons in the following terms: "The seventy archons of the nations are emanated from the domain of the forefathers, which is *Hesed*, *Pahad*, and *Tifferet*. Regarding these archons, Scripture says, 'The host of the heavens in the heavens' (Isa 24:21)." The author then suggests that "the souls of the nations of the world are emanated from the archons," while Jewish souls are emanated directly from the *sefirot*. Because of this, "the nations of the world worship the archons, and the people of Israel worship the central pillar, and none else."[61] The governing power of the archons over non-Jewish nations is attributed by this author to the ontological connection between the supernal archons and the earthly people whom they govern. The Jewish people likewise have a special connection between their souls and God, which makes them uniquely connected to the divine. Through a discourse of archons and nations, the anonymous author asserts a historical, covenantal theosophy. The archons may have conditional power, but Jews alone bear divine souls and live on earth as divine subjects. Other nations are, in fact, idol worshippers who have only at best an indirect relationship to God through their archon. As a result, this same author asserts that Jewish men who sleep with gentile women or commit other sexual transgressions are like "one who commits idol worship and nullifies the central pillar, and is drawn after the archons of the gentile nations and accepts them upon himself as gods."[62]

The connection between non-Jewish nations and their archons provides a template for making sense of historical events. Wars between nations and the rise and fall of world powers are regarded by kabbalists as reflections of unseen interactions between archons on the divine plane. As the author of the early sixteenth-century *Kaf ha-qetoret* quips, "Just as there are enemies in the material world, so too above."[63] Menahem Recanati,[64] a kabbalist active in Italy in the late thirteenth and early fourteenth centuries, argued that such historical events can only be properly understood in this manner: "Know that when God wishes to uproot a people and cast them down, he first casts down their archon above. . . . When the archons above are stricken, in every respect so too are those under their authority. . . . Know and understand that when Pharaoh pursued Israel, the entire battle took place above and below."[65] Historical events, in Recanati's view, cannot be fully understood by observing only their material, earthly manifestation. The real "event" takes place in the divine realm, and only those with visibility into that world—namely, the kabbalists—can understand the events of history. As Recanati puts it in another composition, "Regarding that which occurs below among kings on earth, there is no nation that does not have an archon appointed over it above, other than Israel, since they are the portion of the glorious God, and he did not appoint an archon over them."[66] In order to understand events that occur among earthly kings,

Recanati resorts to the idea of the supernal archons, and the fact that Israel alone are under the direct providence of God.

The particular nature of the archons of the nations of the world is also used as a way of understanding their actions. The anonymous early fourteenth-century *Ma'arekhet ha-'elohut*, written in Catalonia, describes the seventy archons as deriving from the supernal *'ilan*, or tree, an image invoked to refer to the divine realm of the *sefirot*. The text states that "from the seventy branches of the tree derive the seventy archons appointed over the seventy peoples, and the archons are called the 'gods of the gentile nations,' and the glorious God, may he be blessed, [is called] 'God of gods,' and the archon of Israel, and they are his portion and his people."[67] The archons of the nations are imagined as part of a multifaceted divine structure. Non-Jewish nations are distinct from one another, yet together as a group they are categorically unlike the people of Israel, who have God as their supernal representative. The anonymous author also suggests that the particular location in the realm of the *sefirot* from which the archons of the nations of the world derive their power is that of *Pahad* or *Din*, the divine attribute of strict judgment. This attribute is also associated with the angel Gabriel and with the element of fire. As the text states it, "*Pahad* is Gabriel, which is the archon of fire, which is the archon of the nations, and it pursues strict judgment. Therefore, when the people of Israel sin, they fall and are exiled under the power of the gentile nations to serve them."[68] The power of the non-Jewish nations under whom Jews live in exile is explained by this author as a function of the source of origin of the power of the archons of those nations. Since they draw power from the harshest of divine attributes, non-Jewish nations are likewise powerful in all the wrong ways.

Other texts also take an interest in associating the supernal archons with particular powers or entities in order to account for historical events. The *Tiqqunei Zohar*, for example, suggests that the Torah was given with two powers, *Hesed*, the fourth *sefirah* associated with loving-kindness, and *Pahad*, the fifth *sefirah*, associated with harsh judgment, in a deliberate move intended to empower the people of Israel to overcome the seventy nations and their corresponding archons.

What are "other gods?" They are the appointees over the seventy nations, and Samael and Nahash make seventy-two. On account of this, the Holy

One, blessed be he, gave the Torah from the right, which is *Hesed*, and from the left, which is *Gevurah*, possessing seventy faces, in order to redeem [Israel] from the seventy nations. The Torah was given from fire and water, which are two, in order to redeem Israel from Samael and Nahash, which are composed of fire and water. Concerning this it is written, "You shall not have other gods before me" (Exod 20:3). And corresponding to the seventy peoples, seventy souls. One who transgresses the seventy faces of the Torah . . . the seventy appointees and people of the evil inclination dominate the seventy souls.[69]

The right and left aspects with which the Torah was given correspond to the evil angelic entities Samael and Nahash. The seventy direct descendants of Jacob in Egypt (Exod 1:5), or "seventy souls," correspond to the seventy archons. So too with the seventy faces of the Torah mentioned in Bamidbar Rabbah 13:16. These are the tools given to the Israelites to overcome foreign domination by the peoples ruled by the seventy supernal archons. However, the text warns that transgression will cause them to fall under the domination of the archons and peoples of the "evil inclination." A similar comment can be found in the anonymous Hebrew writings of the author of the *Tiqqunei Zohar* and *Ra'aya mehemna* sections of the Zohar: "When Israel's sins overpower, the nations of the world prevail in the realm below, and the angels of destruction, which are the hosts of Samael and the serpent, prevail above."[70] The empowerment of nations on earth is, for these kabbalists, a function of Israelite actions, and the nations ultimately are given their power from God.

According to the anonymous *Masekhet 'atzilut*, likely composed in the fourteenth century, "Samael and his seventy archons are not nourished by the supernal light, but rather from the back side of Metatron."[71] This passage contrasts the direct Jewish connection to God with the indirect pathway whereby divine energy reaches non-Jewish nations. While Jews are sustained by the *sefirot*, all other peoples are sustained by archons who in turn draw their power from the "back side" of the angelic entity Metatron. The idea of supernal archons representing each of the nations of the world and connected, in one form or another, to the flow of divine energy, is used as a way of both describing the proper relationships between peoples, and of accounting for the conflicts between nations.

According to the anonymous *Sefer 'ohel mo'ed*, likely composed in Spain in the fifteenth century,[72] the fifth *sefirah*, associated with the attribute of *Gevurah* or *Din*, is

> the power of Samael, which is the primordial serpent, which is the evil inclination and the angel of death, and it is the Satan which is the archon of Esau, and it is the chief among the supernal accusers, called Laban the Aramean who deceives all, since it is from the side of harsh judgment. When he brings forth accusations against the people of Israel, then Isaac, who is from the left side, silences him and brings forth a defense on behalf of his children.[73]

The archon representing Christianity is associated here with a long list of images traditionally associated with evil. The power of Christianity derives from their supernal archon, which in turn derives from the *sefirah* of *Din*, or judgment, and it seeks to use power from this attribute to prosecute the case against the people of Israel in the divine realm. However, the power of Isaac is also associated with this divine attribute, and it is he who, according to this author, intervenes on behalf of Israel and overpowers the archon of Christianity.

The anonymous author of *Sefer pokeah 'ivrim*,[74] written in Castile in 1439, argued that it is the *Shekhinah*, the tenth *sefirah*, that opposes the forces of Samael in the world on behalf of Israel. The biblical commandment in Exodus 17:18 to wage war against the people of Amalek "from generation to generation" means that the power of Amalek continues to exist in every generation "in the secret of Samael, archon of Esau, who possesses power in the supernal entities, and has power to afflict Israel grievously, thus requiring a great divine power to lessen his power. Therefore, it is necessary in every generation that there be for Israel and their kings a war with Amalek and his accursed offspring, to weaken the power of the evil Samael, until the holy time of the messiah arrives, be it speedily in our days."[75] The ongoing war with the Amalek, the biblical enemies of Israel, is manifest on the plane of human history, according to this author, in the form of the conflict between Jews and Christians. Even though Christians, or Esau, guided by their archon, Samael, appear to be winning, the people of Israel are represented by a much more powerful divine entity that will, one day, succeed in defeating their enemies.

Menahem Ziyyoni, active in the late fourteenth to early fifteenth centuries in Germany, suggested that contemporary world events can be decoded by means of the secret interactions of the supernal archons.

> Our rabbis of blessed memory have said, a nation does not fall until its archon above falls first.[76] When the overflow is reduced, and the overflow [to another nation] increases, the appointed [archons] are annulled, and when an appointed [archon] is annulled, then a war occurs between kings upon earth. When Pharaoh pursued the people of Israel, there was a mighty and strong battle in heaven, for the archon of Egypt, which is Uzah, conjoined with Samael, the archon of Esau.[77]

Ziyyoni's comments are a reworking of a passage in Gikatilla's *Sha'arei 'orah*,[78] in which the archons are used to explain "the subject of wars." In this case, the conflict between Israel and Egypt is understood as a clash between the divine powers and an alliance with Samael, commonly understood as the archon of Esau, or Christianity. The enslavement of the Jews in Egypt as described in Exodus and the life of medieval Jews in Christian territories in medieval Europe are both, Ziyyoni argues, part of the same long conflict in the divine realm. Drawing upon the midrashic tradition that the fates of nations on earth are the product of the divine manipulation of archons in heaven, Ziyyoni suggests that all world events, with the exodus from Egypt serving as merely one example, are contingent upon the fates of the archons above. The travails of medieval Jewish life are portrayed as part of a cosmic conflict spanning the full sweep of Jewish history.[79]

Isaac of Acre is careful to point out that the archons from which non-Jewish nations on earth derive their agency are ultimately under divine providence. He rejects the notion that the archons function independently. Their power stems from God, even if it is, at present, much greater than originally intended. As he puts it,

> Even though they [the archons] are appointed over all of the rest of the peoples, and they have authority over them as gods (*'elohim*), they have no power except from the lord our God, may he be blessed and exalted, for he created them and he sustains them. Regarding the *Shekhinah*, which is our portion and inheritance, Scripture says regarding these archons, "For he is

the God of gods and the Lord of lords" (Deut 10:17). For they can do nothing small or great even in their own lands and to their own nation, except under the providence of the central pillar, which is 'Atarah.[80]

The functioning of all nations, even in their own territory, is under direct divine providence. National power is merely a function of the flow of divine energy to their supernal archons, which God can choose to grant or withhold at will. According to Isaac of Acre, the power of non-Jewish nations derives from God, but in a manner that is distinctly contingent.[81] In this kabbalistic view of history, national power is an illusion. For those who can peer behind the veil of world events—that is, for the kabbalists who claim privileged insight into the secret divine realm—the figment of mighty nations is dispelled. The course of human events is the long shadow cast by the interaction of entities in the world above. What appears to the untrained eye as a world in which Jews are disempowered, dispersed, and possibly forgotten by God, is transformed in the kabbalistic imagination into a cosmic drama in which their suffering is due to their centrality in the concealed scope of history.

Theosophies of Exile: Kabbalistic Etiologies of the Medieval Jewish Condition

Rabbinic texts are replete with references to the notion that God suffers alongside the people of Israel in their exile.[82] In the Babylonian Talmud, for example, a comment attributed to Rabbi Shimon bar Yohai states that, because of God's love for Israel, "to every place where they were exiled, the Shekhinah went with them."[83] While exile is often described in rabbinic literature as punishment for Israel's sins, God shares in the pain of that punishment. Kabbalists elaborate upon this notion by describing in rich detail the theurgic implications of Jewish transgression. The lengthy exile of the Jewish people and their subjugation by foreign nations was always hard to reconcile with their status as God's chosen people. Medieval kabbalists were quite willing to acknowledge this contradiction, and they developed a variety of strategies to make sense of this reality. But in all cases, they explicitly resisted the nihilistic view of history as arbitrary, or the pessimistic perspective that God had simply abandoned the Jews.

One interesting example can be found in the anonymous *Sefer berit ha-menuhah*, composed in Spain in the late thirteenth or early fourteenth century.[84] The author states:

> Consider how great is the esteem of the Holy One, blessed be he, for Israel. In the present you can see how much inconceivably wiser the wisdom of Israel is, and you can see that which is written, "You are sons of the Lord your God" (Deut 14:1). And you can see how great is the loftiness of all of the angels, yet they were only created for the sake of Israel. And even the greatest of the angels were not called "sons," only Israel. . . . And if you were to say within your heart, "If the God of the world is our father, why has he sent us away from his table? Why has he scattered us? Why has he forgotten us for these [many] days?" you have not descended to the ends of the paths of truth. If you had, you would know how many watches were changed by the Holy One, blessed be he, on the day the Temple was destroyed. When Israel was exiled, the supernal beings were exiled. All of this is because he is a true judge. . . . When the guardians were blocked, the channels of the chariot [between the *sefirot*] were blocked . . . and when they were blocked, the ministering angels began to cry out for overflow that was no longer reaching them, causing their power to contract. . . . The legions that were appointed over Israel in their watches were exiled with them. . . . After this, the Holy One, blessed be he, appointed other, lesser angels over the watches, without the same dominion as the first. . . . All of the appointed angels long for the elevation of Israel, to behold the love of the Holy One, blessed be he, with them unto *'ein sof*.[85]

The exile of the Jewish people is described here as part of a much broader process that happened in the divine realm. Despite the fact that they have, in this author's view, superior wisdom, and although they are the "sons" of God, Jews suffer on the historical plane. This is explained as a result of the blockage of the "channels" between the *sefirot*, which has deprived the ministering angels of their power. They, along with the people of Israel, cry out for overflow from God. The text also claims that the supernal beings were exiled alongside Israel, watches were changed, and the new forces appointed in their place are not as strong. The exile of the people of Israel on earth is portrayed here as parallel to a process of diminishment in the divine realm. The result is that these angelic beings "long for the elevation of Israel." According to this text, the Jews are far from alone in their exile. While on earth the Jewish people may appear like a people who have been "scattered" and cast away from the divine table, a vast gathering of divine beings is secretly cheering for the Jewish people's loving and infinite restoration to God, "unto *'ein sof.*"

The anonymous authorship of the *Sefer ha-temunah* and its accompanying commentary, composed in the middle third of the fourteenth century, likely in Byzantium,[86] took particular interest in the meaning of the Jewish experience of exile. For these texts, the displacement and oppression of Jews at the hands of other nations changed everything. The decline in the political fortunes of the Jewish people was part of a much broader change in the Godhead and all levels of reality. Even the shape of the letters of the Hebrew alphabet (the *Sefer ha-temunah* is organized as a commentary on each of the letters) is altered as part of the historical exile of the Jews. The present form of the Hebrew letters, for this text, contains secrets regarding the historical fate of Israel. As the author of the commentary to *Sefer ha-temunah* puts it in one passage:

> The secret is that the letter *kaf* (כ) that is part of the form of the letter *tet* (ט) alludes to the *Shekhinah*, and because of the sins of the people of Israel, she is bent over, and because the people of Israel are in exile, she is with them. This makes it known that there is none to have mercy upon or comfort them in exile except for the Holy One, blessed be he, alone. The gods of the foreign nations have no power to heal or rectify them. Concerning this it is said, "For your ruin is as vast as the sea; who can heal you?" (Lam 2:13). Which is to say that she has no remedy other than that which comes from the Holy One, blessed be he, for he is the God, the healer, the great, the mighty, the wondrous, while the gods of the foreign nations have no healing power. This "bent over" state [of the letter] is similar to and alludes to the exile of the people of Israel. For it would have been appropriate for the letter *tet* to be thus (i.e., upright), however, due to the transgressions of the people of Israel, it is bent over thus. . . . In this way it indicates and says to

the people of Israel, "See if the gods of the foreign nations possess power like me to come and rectify the warped, and to bring the people of Israel out of exile."[87]

The bent shape of the letter *kaf* (כ) which is incorporated into the letter *tet* (ט), expresses, according to this author, the historical fate of the Jews during exile. The letter, like the *Shekhinah* herself, is stooped, weighed down by the burdens of exile. Though such a suggestion does little to ameliorate the Jewish historical condition, it does reduce its terror. Jews, this author suggests, are not suffering in indifferent silence. God is not only aware of their pain, but suffering it with them. The Jewish burden of history is even encoded into the letters of the divine language. The holy tongue cannot speak without giving voice to the Jewish pain of exile. Such far-reaching implications of the exile of the Jews demonstrate, according to this author, that only God can remedy the situation. The historical misfortune caused by the "sins of the people of Israel" is not a typical case of national decline. Jewish exile weighs upon God and changes reality. Therefore, the author asserts, no solution can be sought through direct appeal to the foreign nations to whom Jews have been subjugated. They and their "gods," or archons, have no capacity to fix the Jewish historical predicament. Escape from exile can only be achieved through direct appeal to God and by observing Jewish law.

The above-cited passage seems to suggest that the Jewish condition cannot be addressed through this-worldly means. The author is adamant that the Jewish redemption from history requires a deus ex machina. They cannot count on other nations "to have mercy upon or comfort them in exile." In other words, the solution to exile does not happen *within* the forces of history. The author of the *Ma'arekhet ha-'elohut* similarly argues against Jews seeking to take history into their own hands through direct confrontation with gentiles. In this author's view,

> During the time of exile, when the Temple has been destroyed, it is our duty to engage in many prayers, acknowledgments, and supplications [to God] continuously, so that the nations of the world will not oppress us with harsh decrees, and it is best for Israel to remain servile to them. . . .

However, in the days of the messiah, the evil inclination will cease . . . and the memory of Amalek will be wiped out from the under the heavens, for peace shall be bound to the world completely, and Esau will no longer receive power . . . and then sinners shall cease from the land, "the evil ones shall be no more" (Ps 104:35), since the fall of Israel results in the elevation of the gentiles, the elevation of Israel will result in the fall of the gentiles.[88]

Oppression at the hands of the nations of the world is depicted here as the inevitable fate of the Jewish exilic condition. It is therefore better to remain "servile" rather than die in hopeless rebellion. But it would be a mistake to regard this as an entirely passive attitude to Jewish historical fate. The anonymous author states that it is a Jewish obligation to engage in prayer to God in order to reduce the severity of anti-Jewish decrees. Moreover, the clear aspiration is that such worship will eventuate in the "days of the messiah" when humans will no longer be driven by their evil inclinations, which is to say, when history as we know it comes to an end. The power relations between Jews and non-Jews will then reverse, with Esau, or Christian peoples, losing their strength. Sinners will cease to exist, and peace will reign. For this author, as for other kabbalists, history will resolve only through an extrahistorical divine intervention. In the meantime, the Jewish historical condition is not engaged directly. Joshua ibn Shuib makes a similar argument in his commentary on the Torah: "What we can understand from this Torah portion is that even though Jacob perceived and understood his place and station in the supernal realm, he did not become arrogant . . . he was always fearful and anxious, sending tributes . . . all of this alludes to our exile."[89]

For many of these authors, the dominance of non-Jews is not an accident. Kabbalists create elaborate accounts of the events in the divine realm that lead to the historical power of foreign nations over the Jewish people. Menahem Recanati, writing in Italy in the late thirteenth and early fourteenth century, suggested that the different points of origin for the emanation of Jewish and non-Jewish souls account for the dominance of the nations of the world over the Jewish people. Recanati accepts the kabbalistic claim that Jewish souls derive directly from God: "The emanation of the souls of Israel is from him, may he be exalted, as it is said, 'your fruit is provided by me' (Hos 14:9), which is not the case with the nations of the world."[90] However, Jewish transgression causes the exile of the *Shekhinah*, which in turn connects God with the "concubine," or supernal mother of the foreign powers. She is brought "within" the divine realm, occupying the place that rightfully belongs to the *Shekhinah*. As a result of this, "when the concubine is within, the channels of impurity are filled with the souls of gentiles, and sometimes the concubine requests from the king that her children be able to rule over the children of the beloved, and the king swears it to her on account of the sin of Israel. Therefore, the peoples of the world rule over Israel, in the secret of, 'and Isaac loved Esau' (Gen 25:28)."[91] Jewish transgression brings about a change in the divine household. Gentile souls are bestowed upon the world via the concubine, and they are given the power to dominate the Jewish people on the historical plane. As one anonymous kabbalist notes in a commentary on the Torah regarding the relationship between Esau and Jacob, "because they were twins, deriving from a single emanation and source, therefore, there is only one blessing [between them] and not more."[92] Jews and Christians, according to this author, cannot both enjoy good fortune at the same time. The success of one requires the downfall of the other. In this sense, periods of Christian empowerment necessitate Jewish misfortune, since the twin brothers of Judaism and Christianity derive from the same point of origin, and cannot draw from it simultaneously. The conflict between them is encoded into the divine economy from whence they came.

Patiently bearing the pangs of history is, for many kabbalists, not only a fate that God shares with the Jewish people, but also one that Jews endure for the benefit of the world. Joseph Angelet, in his commentary on Joseph Gikatilla's *Sha'arei 'orah*, draws upon the metaphor of the suffering servant in Isaiah 53 to describe the Jewish role in history.[93] In a move clearly designed to counter the Christian use of this image as a prophecy regarding Jesus,[94] Angelet interprets Isaiah as a meditation on the fate of righteous Jews during exile.

> The righteous bear the sin of the generation. This is the secret of the verse, "He was wounded because of our sins" (Isa 53:5). They are struck first by the attribute of *Din*, be it through death or afflictions, which are worse than death. . . . They are the essence of the world. The wicked are

compared to thorns, thorns cut down, as it is said, "thorns cut down, set
ablaze" (Isa 33:12). [The righteous] are also caught in these afflictions, and
the generation is redeemed, as it is said, "by his bruises we were healed"
(Isa 53:5). This is known in the *Midrash ha-ne'elam* in the portion of
Pinhas[95] through the parable of the physician. When people say they are
suffering, they let blood from the right arm, and by means of if all of the
limbs are healed. Thus, it is said, "By his wounds we were healed." The
letting of his blood is the cause of healing for us all. This is the reason
for the exile of the people of Israel, who are close to God. Their downfall is greater than any other people, and the righteous among them, a
downfall greater than anyone. For when the head rises first, with the
turning of the wheel, the head is below and the leg is above. Such is the
nature of the miracle performed for these righteous ones through an alteration of nature.[96]

When the fifth *sefirah* of *Din*, or strict judgment, afflicts the world because
of the sins of the generation, the righteous, according to Angelet, are the first
to suffer. But were it not for the presence of the righteous, the wicked would
be lost, like the thorns consumed by fire mentioned in Isaiah 33:12. When the
righteous suffer the punishments directed toward the wicked, the "generation
is redeemed." Angelet draws upon the comparison made in the Zohar between
the medical remedy of bloodletting and the suffering of the Jews. Just as ail-
ments of the body can be cured by letting blood from the right arm—the most
prized of limbs—the shortcomings of a sinful generation are repaired through
the affliction of the righteous. And this, according to Angelet, explains the
Jewish experience of exile. The downfall of the Jews is so great because they,
like the right arm, are close to God and dear to him. The righteous among the
Jews are even more precious, and hence their downfall is even more severe. In
the somewhat cryptic concluding remark, Angelet suggests that the turning
of the wheel of time that brought the Jews so low from their previous high
status will once again return them to God in the future. However, this will *not*
happen naturally, which is to say, it will not happen within the normal flow of
history. This completion of the Jewish task in history to bear the sins of the
generation will only happen through an "alteration of nature." The suffering

of the righteous in the interregnum before the miraculous extrication of God's people from history is, in Angelet's view, neither pointless nor a sign of divine abandonment. Jewish suffering is for the sake of humanity. In a reversal of the Christian notion of Christ as the servant who suffers for the benefit of the world, Angelet argues that by enduring exile, it is the Jewish people who will save a sinful world that would otherwise be consumed in divine wrath. Such a discourse ennobles the Jewish experience of history, and suggests that Jewish life carries the secret for moving history in the direction of its miraculous conclusion.

For some kabbalists, the notion that Jewish suffering has secret meaning is explicitly related to specific historical events of their own day. Isaac of Acre, for example, regarded the oppressive measures taken by Christian kingdoms against the Jews of his day in the early fourteenth century as a divine strategy to provide the Jewish people with an opportunity to publicly manifest their sanctity before the nations of the world. As he states the matter in his *'Otzar hayyim*: "'When I manifest my holiness [before the nations of the world] by means of you' (Ezek 36:23). By means of suffering with which they will be afflicted in the lands of the gentiles: the righteous of Ashkenaz with death by sword; the righteous of France with death by the sword; the oppression of the nobles of Spain with very great taxes; the wretched of the land of Ishmael with lives of suffering and great disgrace."[97] Isaac of Acre is very clear in his comment that actual historical catastrophes affecting Jewish communities of his day can be understood as manifestations of divine holiness. Jewish suffering, it would seem, is how God communicates with the rest of humanity.

In some cases, deprivation is described as spiritually healthy for the Jewish people. The physical security and pleasure enjoyed by non-Jews are seen as a vice and a sign of low moral character. Isaac of Acre, for example, quips that "the delights of the body are the inverse of the delights of the soul. . . . Our rabbis have praised the diminished state of Israel and their poverty and exile and dispersion, for that is what builds up and elevates the intellective soul, causing it to cleave to the supernal truth."[98] Drawing upon philosophical language, Isaac of Acre argues that the conditions of exile enable Jews to attain mystical communion with God. Joshua ibn Shuib also regards suffering in exile as beneficial for the Jewish faith in God. In a discussion of the sending forth of the dove from Noah's ark as a typological allusion to the successive future exiles and redemptions of the Jewish people, he says, "When Israel are in exile and they suffer trials and afflictions, they strengthen in their faith and intentionality more so than they do during times of security. It is known to masters of natural wisdom that when the dove is satiated, it draws apart from its mate, and when it is hungry, it cleaves to them. This is [as it is written], 'Behold, I have refined you, but not as silver. I test you in the furnace of depravation' (Isa 48:10). The Holy One, blessed be he, regards no state as beneficial for the people of Israel as poverty, as they have said, poverty is good for Israel."[99]

Kabbalists such as these accepted the fact that Jews could not solve the problem of exile through conventional means. At the same time, they could not simply ignore the glaring theological questions raised by Jewish historical experience. Jewish suffering had to mean *something*. Kabbalists deployed a variety of discursive strategies based on the claim to an esoteric tradition in order to offer readings of Jewish history against the grain. Displacement, oppression, expulsion, impoverishment, and episodes of violence at the hands of foreign powers were recast as part of a concealed divine plan in which Jews were the valiant, suffering heroes of history. But they can attain victory over their enemies only by means of the theurgic power of the commandments, and not through the worldly power of the sword. Joseph ben Shalom Ashkenazi, for example, suggests in his commentary on *Sefer yetzirah* that "all of Israel's victories occur only by means of the commandments, through the overflow of the power of *Binah* upon them. In this manner, they prevail without sword or spear or weapons of war, 'for the Lord can grant victory without sword or spear' (1 Sam 17:47). When they neglect the commandments, *Binah* immediately abandons them, and they descend to the ultimate depths."[100]

In the passages considered in this chapter, history is something to be endured. Jews are not commanded to shape history by creating an ideal society within the present conditions of historical reality. Their mandate is to pray for history to end. Jews exert power over the course of history by suffering and observing Jewish law. Perhaps these authors were conscious of the problem raised by Jacob Taubes that "every attempt to bring about redemption on the level of history without a transfiguration of the messianic idea leads straight into the abyss."[101] And for sure, recreating anything like the ancient Israelite kingdom in medieval Palestine would have been absurdly out of reach for medieval Jews. But this is not to say that by accepting the Jewish burden of history, these kabbalists regarded themselves as living their lives, in Scholem's terms, "in deferment."[102] Jews, even kabbalists, were no more "outside of history" than any other medieval people. Within the parameters available to them, they created discourses that engaged the Jewish historical condition and attempted to render it meaningful. Medieval Jews were not in control of powerful armies or vast territories. But in the kabbalistic imagination, they were armed with theurgic weapons that could not only shape history, but also hasten its conclusion. The production of discourses of this sort reflects a desire on the part of the kabbalists to perform important social work. By offering Jews a way to understand their own problematic history, and to imagine a world *beyond* history, the kabbalists sought to create a viable Jewish identity *within* historical reality.

TWO

Meaning in Exile

Kabbalistic Readings of History Gone Awry

In what ways are the histories told by premodern kabbalists different from the mode of historical writing as it has come to be known in the modern West? As noted above, kabbalists did not write chronicles or document evidence for the occurrence of events. In terms of style, these are very different genres. But in terms of the enterprise itself of making sense of human history, there are more similarities than one might suspect. Like modern historians—along with premoderns from the time of Herodotus—medieval kabbalists sought to understand the horrors wrought by other humans. Teofilo Ruiz has pointed out that "suspecting or knowing that there is probably no meaning or order in the universe," historians work to construct "explanatory schemes that seek to justify and elucidate what is essentially inexplicable. These half-hearted attempts to explain the inexplicable and to make sense of human cruelty are what we call 'history.' It is the writing of history itself."[1]

Like all histories, religious discourses provide a particular kind of explanatory model for historical events. Their aim is not fundamentally different from other types of historical writing. The explanations they offer to help understand the forces driving human affairs are, of course, based on different premises. Religious texts also have different assumptions regarding the sources of authoritative knowledge that can illuminate the darkness of history. But like their modern secular counterparts, premodern religious authors formulated explanatory discourses that were intended to make sense of past and present events. As Ruiz observes, "Religion posits the terrors besetting one's own personal life and the weight of collective history as part of a divine plan and as the sum total of inscrutable but always wise actions of an all-powerful, all-knowing deity (or deities). . . . There is always the reassuring belief that the deity knows why such things need to happen. . . . In the end, all events, awful and good, form part of an overarching sacred project in which we all play a part."[2] When it comes to making sense of the terrors of history, premodern religious discourses are not so very different from those of modern historians.

From the fourteenth through the early sixteenth centuries, kabbalists continued to recombine elements from earlier kabbalistic texts in order to render meaning out of Jewish collective experience. They often did this through discussions of biblical events, such as the exodus from Egypt, but it should be emphasized that this was not merely an exegetical exercise. The ways that kabbalists constructed grand narratives about the arc of history and the role of Jewish suffering within the present era reflects a clear attempt to understand the events, peoples, religions, and world powers of their own day. This was particularly pressing in light of the challenge to covenantal theology posed by the ongoing Jewish exile. In the kabbalistic sources discussed below, the painful path of Jewish history is depicted as a grand concealment cloaking a secret divine plan. Jewish life in exile, for these authors, was much more than mere waiting. Through their suffering, and by means of the theurgic power of their practice of Judaism, they envisioned the Jewish people as the key drivers of human history. For these authors, Jewish life in exile is not passive. In their view, Jews are deeply engaged with the ongoing events of history, even if it is not apparent to the uninitiated observer.

The authorship of the anonymous pseudepigraphic compositions *Sefer ha-kanah* and *Sefer ha-peli'ah*, likely composed in Byzantium in the late fourteenth to early fifteenth centuries,[3] provides extensive discussion of the meaning of Jewish historical exile. Ideas developed in earlier sources are deployed in order to construct a synthetic kabbalistic discourse of Jewish historical experience. The text, written in the voice of figures from the rabbinic period, assumes an omniscient perspective, peeling back the layers of concealment in order to uncover the supernal divine forces behind historical events. Biblical misfortunes, such as the exile in Egypt, are rendered alongside postbiblical and contemporary events as part of a comprehensive accounting of Jewish history as a whole. The text claims that the traumas of Jewish history all have knowable causes—knowable, that is to say, to those who have access to the kabbalistic secret. Jewish transgression is, for this text, centered as a reason for the misadventures of Jewish history. But like other authors discussed above, this is all due to the vast theurgic power of Jewish actions. Jewish behavior reverberates above, and as a result, Jewish history is painful. Nonetheless, the text assures its readers that the Jews will not be entirely abandoned during the cosmic course correction that is the duration between Eden and redemption, since "the Holy One, blessed be he, scattered them among the nations to punish them and not to disown them. The proof is, 'And you I shall scatter you among the nations' (Lev 26:33)."[4] Jewish exile and disempowerment fulfill prophecy and ironically signal divine favor.

The *Sefer ha-kanah* goes to great lengths to explain and justify the ongoing meaning and relevance of Jewish life in exile. For this author, like many kabbalists before him, the phenomenon of Jewish exile begins in the Godhead. As a result of human transgression,

> *Yesod 'Olam* is gathered above, and the *Shekhinah* remains alone below, lacking her consort. . . . Know that this attribute called *Malkhut* judges the people of Israel . . . and we, the people of Israel, alone, are called her nation. And when the children sin, their sin causes their mother to depart from her consort, and to be separated from her rank and her glory, 'the glory of the princess is hidden' (Ps 45:14), and then the mother also chastises the children and casts them into the hands of one or all of the seventy heavenly archons. And the archons enslave them 'with mortar and with bricks, and all manner of tasks in the field' (Exod 1:14), as well as beheading, burning, and forced conversion, and there is none to offer comfort. And *Binah*, the mother of the mother, sees Israel deserving of redemption, and she redeems them. And if they are not deserving, she does it for the sake of *Kenesset Yisra'el*, called the name of God.[5]

The origins of the Jewish historical condition are to be found in the realm of the *sefirot*. Transgression causes separation between the ninth *sefirah*, *Yesod*, and the tenth, *Shekhinah*, or *Malkhut*. In her capacity as *Malkhut*, she becomes the chastising mother who metes out punishment. In this case, the punishment entails handing the Jewish people over to the seventy archons of the nations to be enslaved by them. The condition of Jewish subjugation to foreign power is associated with the biblical enslavement in Egypt mentioned in Exodus 1:14, but also with postbiblical suffering at the hands of non-Jewish powers in the form of execution and forced conversion. Like the Israelites in Egypt, the Jews in their ongoing exile are envisioned as the captives of supernal gentile powers. For the anonymous author of the *Sefer ha-kanah*, the suffering of medieval Jews under the tyrannical governments of their day is part of the very same phenomenon as the exile of Jacob's descendants in Egypt. Both were divinely ordained. And both, the author assures the reader, come to a happy conclusion. When the third *sefirah*, *Binah*, the supernal "mother of the mother," perceives Israel to be worthy of redemption, exile will end. And even if the Jewish people never attain that merit, exile will eventually be brought about through the mercy that the upper mother will have upon *Shekhinah*, the lower mother. One way or the other, the present historical condition of the Jews, for whatever duration it may continue, will not last indefinitely. The secret longing of one mother for another within the realm of the *sefirot* is offered as proof of the eventual redemption of the Jews from exile.

The passage continues with further reflection on the intradivine dynamics of primordial sin, the exile in Egypt, and the eventual exodus. As the paradigmatic example of God's use of foreign powers and historical events in order to punish and correct his chosen people, the author is particularly keen to uncover the underlying theosophical events at play in the upper world during this key moment in the history of the Israelite people.

> Come and see and understand the exile in Egypt, how it was and how they were redeemed. Adam sinned and separated *Malkhut* from her consort. What did *Malkhut* do? She selected the chosen son of Adam, the son who was called "Adam," as their father's namesake, which is Israel, who is called "Adam," and gave him over to one of the seventy supernal archons, the greatest of them, called "Egypt," since Egypt's archon is "Ishmael," bound to *Hesed*, the attribute of his father. But the supernal archon of Egypt did not have mercy upon the people of Israel . . . everything that Abraham had

he gave to Isaac, and to the children of his concubines, he gave gifts[6]—external entities that function with impurity. Because of this jealousy, they did not treat Israel justly, for it would have been sufficient for them to leave them alone in their land [of Egypt], and enough for them to undergo exile, for there is no suffering like exile. However, they added great afflictions and suffering upon them, and proclaimed decrees that were not divinely mandated, and thus the children of Israel cried out, for the greater the suffering, the greater the cry. Immediately their sighing and wailing ascended to *Kenesset Yisra'el*, mother of the children, and the mother had mercy upon her children. And the cry of that mother [ascended] to her mother, which is *Binah*, the mother of the mother, and immediately, "And God heard their cry" (Exod 2:24).[7]

As we have seen above, Adam's sin resulted in a rupture within the Godhead. *Malkhut*, the final *sefirah*, was divided from her male "consort," *Yesod*. However, that mere fact alone was not regarded by this author as sufficient for explaining the ongoing conditions of Jewish history. How, for example, did Egypt come to be empowered to enslave Israel? According to this passage, *Malkhut* selected the people of Israel to be the chosen son of Adam specially designated to suffer punishment on account of their primordial father's sin. The retribution designated for them was to be handed over to "Ishmael," the supernal archon of Egypt. The intention was that since this particular archon is bound to the *sefirah* of *Hesed*, or mercy, associated with the patriarch Abraham, the Egyptians as earthly people under that archon's control would treat the people of Israel kindly. However, the archon Ishmael was jealous of Jacob, since Abraham favored Jacob over Ishmael on account of his mother's status as wife rather than concubine. As a result, the archon of Ishmael then led his earthly people, the Egyptians, to torment the Israelites with slavery and other forms of suffering, despite the fact that they had no divine mandate to do so. God had only wanted them to undergo the suffering of exile in Egypt rather than slavery.

This treatment at the hands of the Egyptians led the Israelites to cry out in anguish, which inspired the mercy of the "mother," which refers to *Kenesset Yisra'el* or *Malkhut*, the final *sefirah*, which in turn aroused the sympathies of the "mother of the mother," or *Binah*, the third *sefirah*. Such was the hidden dynamic of the Godhead, this text suggests, hinted at in Exodus 2:24, "And God heard their cry." It is significant that the author does not shy away from describing the course of human history, even as presented in the Torah, as taking a path that God did not intend. Just as Adam's transgression was not what God had wanted, the exile of the Israelites in Egypt was only meant to be a moderate punishment in order to punish the favored son at the hands of the lesser child. The perspective this text offers its medieval Jewish readers is that free will, and in this case, sibling rivalry, both among humans and their supernal archons, are the driving forces behind the events of history. The kabbalistic tradition is presented as a window into the hidden divine plan for history, as well as the ways that that plan has been pushed off course.

As the discussion in *Sefer ha-kanah* continues, the relationship between divine forces and human history is described in more overtly theurgic terms.

And now my son, I will remove the veil of blindness from your eyes and make known to you what has been revealed to me from the emissaries of God. . . . Judgment is passed in the court of *YHWH*, and the judgment is passed on to *Yesod*, and from there to *Malkhut*, and for this reason destruction and exile and evil seasons exist. And this is [the meaning of] "on account of evil, the righteous are taken away" (Isa 57:1), which is the attribute of *Yesod*, and the attribute of *Malkhut* remains devoid of all supernal goodness, and filled with judgment and retribution and all manner of grievous suffering. But, when the name *'Ehiyeh* manifests upon the name *YHWH*, then all of the *sefirot* are filled with all forms of goodness, and all of the interconnecting channels straighten and bestow overflow and blessing to the name *Adonai*. When *Malkhut* receives from the names *'Ehiyeh* and *YHWH*, then it is a "time of favor" (Ps 69:14), and all creatures below and above experience happiness and rejoicing. One who knows how to set these three arrayments in order, knows how to ward off evil and harsh decrees, like the prophets and the masters of the Mishnah, who fended off all misfortune through their prayers, who brought about a "time of favor" through their prayers, and the *sefirot* were all filled with mercy and great light unto *'ein sof*, as it is written, "the Lord is God, he has given us light" (Ps 118:27).[8]

Claiming supernal revelation as his source, the anonymous author, speaking in the voice of Kanah to his son Nehunya, offers to remove the "veil of blindness" from his eyes regarding the secret forces of history. He claims that the rendering of judgment above for transgressions entails the separation of *Yesod* from *Malkhut*, which fills the latter with the forces of judgment, which brings about "destruction and exile and evil seasons." The manifestation of the most supernal divine name, Ehiyeh, upon the Tetragrammaton, associated with *Tifferet*, brings about the opposite effect. Moreover, possessing this knowledge enables one to "ward off evil and harsh decrees." Such was the power, the text claims, of the biblical prophets and rabbis from the time of the Mishnah. Their prayers, the author claims, could ameliorate the worst events of Jewish history, because they knew the inner workings of the *sefirot* and their relation to historical misfortune.

The text then returns to the specific event of the exodus from Egypt. The great battle that God waged against the Egyptians on behalf of the Israelites is presented as a *supernal* battle in the divine realm that paralleled the events on earth.

> At the time when it came to be aroused to bring about redemption, so that the children would go forth from slavery to freedom, the supernal archon of Egypt took external blessings and added them to his chariot and came forth to do battle with *Tifferet*, who grants power to the archon of Israel, which is *Kenesset Yisra'el*. . . . And "the Lord waged battle for them against Egypt" (Exod 14:25), and they could not flee, and they fell to the ground, and all of his people were drowned in the sea, above and below. . . . Thus, they came forth from Egypt and were beloved to the point that he sustained them with manna for forty years, and gave them the Torah, 248 positive commandments, and 365 negative commandments, some made contingent upon the land [of Israel] . . . and some general for outside of the land [of Israel] for which there is no mention of the land or soil. And he said, "If you listen to me, I will perform for you many forms of goodness, and I will establish

you in the land [of Israel]. And if you do not listen to me, I will punish you with harsh forms of suffering. I will give you over into the hands the seventy archons, 'and you I will scatter among the nations'" (Lev 26:33).[9]

Once again overstepping its mandate, the archon of Egypt drew power from the "external blessings," or evil powers that draw from the forces outside of the *sefirot*, in order to wage battle against God. By attacking the central *sefirah* of *Tifferet*, associated with the Tetragrammaton, the archon of the Egyptians intended to deprive *Kenesset Yisra'el*, the tenth *sefirah* and divine archon of Israel, of its source of power. But this plan of attack, the text claims, backfired terribly. The divine response to this assault in the supernal realm is what explains, according to this text, the defeat of the Egyptians and their drowning in the Sea of Reeds as related in the book of Exodus. The Egyptian forces "above and below" were destroyed, while the final *sefirah* was redeemed along with the earthly people of Israel. Moreover, the Israelites were then "beloved," and given the gifts of manna and the 613 commandments. But the passage ends with the admonition that failure to observe these commandments will result in historical catastrophe. The supernal archons will be empowered to overcome the *Shekhinah*, and the earthly people of Israel will be exiled from their land and rendered subject to foreign nations. The author of this passage suggests that the collective Jewish experience of many "harsh forms of suffering" over the course of their troubled history emerges from the double-edged sword of Jewish theurgic power.

The author does not end the discussion on an entirely pessimistic note. They are quick to point out that being cast out into exile and subject to the pangs of history is not irreversible. Even in exile, God accompanies the Jews and longs for their return to the proper path, since only Jewish fulfillment of the law will return history to its proper course.

> In truth, God is with us in exile, and since *Adonai* is with us, filled from the supernal source, which is the supernal *Keter*, by means of *'El Hai*, which is *Yesod 'Olam*, he sustains the needs of all creatures, and the world exists in a state of fullness, with all forms of pleasure, for when the king is rich, all of his servants are rich. But if the attribute of *Adonai* is not filled from the supernal source, and the attribute of *'El Hai* departs, then the

attribute of *Adonai* is left barren and empty, lacking all goodness, and he exacts from them measure for measure, since all of Israel have neglected the Torah and the commandments and spurned them, and therefore the "righteous one" has departed. Thus, how much more so must we who are in the exile, outside of the land, bind and draw *Adonai* near to *YHWH* through the performance of the commandments, since their performance draws all of the overflow from above to below. If we continue to neglect the commandments and be lenient with them, then *YHWH* departs from *Adonai*, and *Adonai* loves *YHWH* in the manner of, "but Rebecca loved Jacob" (Gen 25:28). It thus creates division in the tent, so she too conducts herself measure for measure and sends forth plagues, war, famine, and calamity.[10]

Returning to the theme of the barren final *sefirah*, referred to here by the divine name *Adonai*, the text notes that when it is bound to *'El Hai*, a cognomen for *Yesod*, the ninth *sefirah*, the world is blessed. But when there is "division in the house" caused by Jewish transgression, the empty final *sefirah* punishes the Jewish people justly, "measure for measure." All Jews, the author claims, have been lenient with the law, and therefore they must all suffer collectively over the course of history until the damage they have caused has been reversed through proper observance. Until then, they will experience "plagues, war, famine, and catastrophe." But again, the text is careful to point out that the presence of such historical evils should not be taken as reason to give up hope. Jews living in exile "outside the land," they suggest, have a very particular role to play in reuniting the divine powers through their diligent engagement with Jewish law and ritual.

This long reflection on Jewish history in the *Sefer ha-kanah* ends with an admonition not to despair. The author assures the reader that through adherence to the law—and *only* through the law Jews will be saved from history and brought beyond time into eternal life: "All of the world is his, and he separated you from all of the nations, but you sinned, and he scattered you among the peoples to punish you. . . . Therefore, one who is lenient and neglects even a hair's breadth of the commandments of God ruins themselves and the entire world . . . for if we do not observe the commandments and do not engage in the study of Torah, then by what virtue would we merit eternal life, and by means of what would we be saved from the harsh decrees that come upon us from the seventy nations?"[11] The only path beyond history is through it. And the only way to engage history and return it to its proper course, as well as bring it to its ultimate conclusion, is by means of Jewish law and the study of Torah.

The circulation of such a discourse suggests an acute awareness of the need to account for Jewish suffering. It also tells us something about the ways that some Jews drew upon kabbalistic theosophy and theurgy in order to persuade their coreligionists (and themselves) that the covenant between God and the Jews remained in effect, despite the painful anxiety that Jews had been abandoned to the cruel and senseless forces of history. The result is a view of history as something very much like Eliade's "negative theophany," in which God's action, and even God's favor, is revealed through historical misfortune. History's pain for the Jewish people is imagined here as evidence of history's meaning. The focus on Jewish ritual practice and adherence to *halakhah* is not, in the eyes of this anonymous author, a retreat from history. By practicing the law, Jews repair history and return it to its proper course, which culminates in the end of history itself.

Consequences of History

The anonymous author of the *Sefer ha-peli'ah* and *Sefer ha-kanah* describes the fate of the Jewish people of his own time in terms of reward and punishment for the actions of both their ancestors and themselves. At one point, for example, the exile of Jews into Christian and Muslim territories is described as a punishment meted out to earlier generations: "You should know that God judges his world measure for measure, and our forefathers, through their forgetfulness of God, sinned. Due to this, they were given over into the hands of two emissaries in order to correct us—they are the archons of Edom and Ishmael: Jesus the Nazarite, and Muhammad the Ishmaelite."[12] By identifying Jesus and Muhammad as archons who serve a divine purpose to correct the Israelites, Jewish life as a religious minority in Christian and Muslim territories is regarded in this text as an ongoing consequence of the transgressions of the ancestors, who were then handed over to these secondary powers "measure for measure." The power of the majority cultures under whose authority Jews lived is theosophized in a very specific way. The divine decision to punish the

Jewish people by means of the supernal representatives of these two religions is a strategy to account for the radically disproportionate power relations of Jews to Christians and Muslims. The "argument from history" in the medieval polemical literature that suggests that Jewish disempowerment is a sign that their covenant is no longer valid is addressed by this way of reading the Jewish condition. In the eyes of this text, the balance of power between Jews and their Christian and Muslim neighbors is exactly as God intended. It is all part of a longer story in which Jews are being corrected in preparation for their eventual redemption. Kabbalah provides the extra insight into the inner workings of the divine realm that create historical realities in the physical world by identifying Jesus and Muhammad with supernal archons, and by giving them a divinely designated role in correcting Jewish transgression over the long arc of history.

Why then does the exile persist? After all, any Jewish reader in the fourteenth or fifteenth centuries would likely have asked why, after such a long duration, Jews are still suffering as an exiled minority among these two much larger and more powerful religions. The answer, according to this text, is the ongoing Jewish neglect of the law.[13] In at times quite sharp language, the author describes the behavior of their community in an unflattering light. At one point the author describes the "wicked" among the Jewish people: "The wicked, they are the ignorant, those who disregard the Torah, who commit transgressions, who eat bread impurely, who spurn the commandments. Woe to them, and woe to their neighbors, woe to those who dwell among them, woe to those who consort with them. They lengthen the exile, bringing suffering to the upright who live in their generation."[14] The implication here is that the exile persists by virtue of the actions of a subset of the people. The rest of the Jewish people suffer as a result of the transgressions committed by these individuals. And they suffer through the further delay of redemption and the continuation of the conditions of life in exile. Elsewhere the author states, "I have observed, my son, the poor conduct of the children of the exile. It is not enough for them that they eat like a lion and grow fat like a bear. How are they not ashamed? For they bring instability upon us through their evil behavior and cause the Holy One, blessed be he, to punish them. For the mother punishes the children, and they themselves are the ones who have caused anger, and not others."[15] By forcing God to take on the role of punishing parent, the wicked create bad outcomes for the entire people. As the author puts it elsewhere, "You who engage in vanity and emptiness, who accrue wealth to leave to others, for it is not yours; don garments only to cast them off on the day of death with shame; eat and drink so that it will turn to stench in your bowels—God will judge you for extending the exile."[16] The punishment that the Jews receive as a result of focusing on material gain and earthly pleasures is specifically identified here with "extending the exile." The duration—and not just severity—of life in exile is explained, according to this text, by Jews turning their minds from the law and focusing on worldly pursuits.

The choice of prior generations to conceal Kabbalah is regarded as a prescient decision to prevent such sacred knowledge from falling into the hands of unworthy future generations. According to the author, "Due to our sins, only a very small measure of this knowledge remains in our hands today of the many traditions that our ancestors received. Know, my son, that the great men of our people concealed them due to the inadequacy of the generations to come after them, who would concentrate their minds and attention only on the vanities of this world."[17] More than divine retribution is at stake in the ongoing decline in Jewish moral life, according to this author. The loss of the Jewish esoteric tradition was a move by the "great men" of the Jewish people who prophetically anticipated the inadequacy of the future generation in which the author lived. But the loss of Kabbalah, of course, also causes history to become opaque. In this respect, both the decline of Jewish fortunes, and the inability of Jews to understand their own historical condition, can be accounted for by Jewish moral laxity. But for those readers of the *Sefer ha-kanah* who gained insight into the workings of history based on kabbalistic principles and who took its message to heart, the situation, in their minds, was different. They were offered a privileged view of Jewish history and a glimpse into the hidden divine realm that holds the true forces behind world-historical events. Unlike the wicked among the Jewish people who suffer without knowing why, the righteous understand their fate, and know that they are not the ones responsible for the persistence of exile. In fact, their actions have the opposite effect, as the author notes, "when tefillin are upon our heads and arms . . . by means of this we are sustained among the foreign nations."[18] Practicing Jewish law and ritual is, for this author, the most direct possible form of Jewish engagement with history.

If such is the way of understanding God's reasons for punishing Jews with exile, what is to be made of the apparent divine favor shown to Christians and Muslims? In his commentary on the Torah, Menahem Recanati suggested that the blessings that accrue to non-Jews were a consequence of their connection to Jews: "When the supernal tree is blessed, all of them are blessed along with the blessing of the tree, even though they are of no benefit. Such is the secret of, 'Catch us the foxes [the little foxes that ruin the vineyards]' (Song 2:15), even though they 'ruin the vineyards,' they are to be blessed along with us, since they are intertwined (ne'ehazim) with us. The nations of the world are intertwined with Israel in this manner."[19] For Recanati, the good fortune of non-Jewish nations is an unintended consequence of the blessing of the Jewish people. Jews are simultaneously distinct from non-Jews, and yet also deeply interconnected with them.

The author of the Peli'ah and Kanah texts puzzled over this question. At one point in the dialogue, the question comes up without an entirely conclusive answer. "A blessed year is also blessed for the nations [of the world]. This was difficult for me. I said to him, what relation do the nations [of the world] have with Israel? He said to me, what concern is it of yours to understand the relation between Israel and the nations at the time when Israel is blessed? 'You have no business with concealed matters,'[20] for 'concealed things are for the Lord our God' (Deut 29:28)."[21] This response is designed to emphasize the highly esoteric, and therefore valuable, nature of the secret of the relationship between the fates of the nations of the world and the fate of the people of Israel.

Not one to be so easily put off, the questioner persists: "I said to him, tell me, what is the nature of Israel and the nations, and how are they blessed one from the other? He said to me, It is written, 'You shall fashion a world of Hesed' (Ps 89:3), and it is the beginning of the circuit (hathalat ha-hekef), and the circuit is the seven sefirot, Hesed, Pahad, Tifferet, Netzah, Hod, Yesod, Malkhut. They are called 'circuit,' since each of the sefirot leads six thousand years, and one thousand is a Sabbath. They are the seven *shemittot*."²² The notion of a succession of universes that exists in a series of *shemittot* or Sabbaticals is an idea that gained currency in earlier kabbalistic sources and was embraced by quite a few kabbalists from the early fourteenth through the mid-sixteenth centuries. This idea will be addressed below in detail in chapter 3. For the moment, it is only important to note that the author of *Sefer ha-peli'ah* resorts to this idea, as well as the idea of the seventy supernal archons of the nations of the world, in order to make sense of non-Jewish power in the current historical moment. The author continues:

> Behold and understand that the seventy supernal archons are the representatives of the nations arrayed outside the curtain. . . . I will also make known to you that beyond the seventy supernal archons arrayed to the right and left, there are other beings further beyond them, and they are entirely outside, called shells of *'orlah*, and they are called impure powers. And know that one *shemittah* of seven thousand years has passed. It was the *shemittah* of *Hesed*. But this *shemittah* is the *shemittah* of *Pahad*, a harsh *shemittah*. Thus, there is war, plague, and famine throughout the world. . . . The left side, which is *Gevurah*, is the current *shemittah*.²³

The arrayment of archons of the nations of the world outside of the "curtain" separating the sacred and profane supernal realms, as well as the even more remote domain of the impure *'orlah*, is not in and of itself regarded as inherently problematic for the Jewish people. In the previous world, or *shemittah*, which was governed by the *sefirah* of *Hesed*, or loving-kindness associated with the patriarch Abraham, no evil afflictions reached the Jewish people. The current world, however, is entirely different. The present reality is governed by the *sefirah* of *Din*, or harsh judgment, associated with the patriarch Isaac. As a result, according to the author, historical calamities such as "war, plague, and famine" occur in the world.

The author then goes into even more detail in order to explain how this idea can account for the particular experiences of the Jewish people of his day living in Christian and Muslim territories.

> From the left side of our father Isaac a chariot was fashioned for the left attribute called *Pahad Yitzhak*. Isaac was not completely refined, since he

had dross within himself from which Esau was derived. The dross served an important purpose within Isaac, in order to serve as a node of connection for the supernal archons arrayed outside the curtain. Behold and understand that Isaac had two aspects—pure and profane. Those facing outside are profane, and by means of them, Esau is connected, and to Esau are connected the supernal archons bound on the left side. Behold and understand that the archons are connected on the side of Ishmael, which is the side of Abraham, are called "nobles" (*nedivim*), and the ones on the left connected to the side of Esau are called cruel, harsh, "wicked who borrows and does not repay" (Ps 37:21). I said to him, if so, why are the ones on the right [also] harsh and evil toward the people of Israel? He said to me, despite the fact that they are nobles, they are nonetheless external, hating their opposite. Be that as it may, the harshest and most evil toward the people of Israel are the supernal archons of the left; those of the right are not as harsh.[24]

As we have seen above, the nations of the world, along with the archons above in the divine realm, were not accidents of history. They were part of a divine plan which, according to the kabbalists, would have placed them under the authority of the Jewish people, who have God as their supernal representative. The archons "outside the curtain" were intended to be of inferior status and power. However, the sin in the garden of Eden, along with ongoing Jewish neglect of divine law, has led to an inversion of power and the subordination of Jews to the archons of the nations of the world. What is interesting in this passage is the notion of the division of the seventy supernal archons into two camps:[25] "All of the seventy nations are arrayed on the left, outside the curtain, to cast off sustenance for them; thirty-five on the right connected to Abraham by way of Ishmael, and thirty-five on the left connected to Isaac by way of Esau."[26] This arrangement of archons is mapped onto the two general domains of medieval Jewish life: Muslim and Christian. The Muslim people are connected to the divine realm on the right side, associated with Abraham and loving-kindness, while Christian people are conjoined to the sefirotic realm on the left side, the side of Isaac and harsh judgment. This is the reason, the author suggests, for the less harsh nature of Muslim rule when compared to the conditions of Jewish life in Christian territories. This is not to say that Muslim authorities are never oppressive toward their Jewish subjects, as the author notes. The claim is merely that the position of their supernal representatives in the divine realm accounts for the historical reality that Jewish life under Muslim rule was generally better than the fate of Jews in Christian kingdoms.[27] As the anonymous author puts it, "Esau is the tallest of all of the archons of the nations of the left."[28]

In another discussion of this division of the seventy archons, the author of *Sefer ha-peli'ah* is even more explicit about the correlations between the major religious powers of his day and the two camps of supernal archons.

> Know and understand that that in the [realm of the supernal] chariot there are thirty-five supernal archons on the right, connected to the chariot by means of our forefather Abraham, may he be blessed, and all of them follow the religion of Ishmael [i.e., Islam]. So, too, on the left of the [realm of] the chariot, there are thirty-five supernal archons connected to the chariot by means of our forefather Isaac, and all of them follow the religion of Esau, the father of Edom . . . which is the religion of Jesus the Nazarite. Similar to the nations of the world, with the seventy supernal archons, the people of Israel, issue of the thigh of Jacob, were seventy souls. When [their] transgressions became too numerous, the inner entities were driven outside, and the external entered [within] and assumed rule over the chariot, and prophecy departed and the *Shekhinah* [ascended] to the upper heavens. "A slave who becomes king" (Prov 30:22), "a maidservant who supplants her mistress" (Prov 3:23). For Samael, the archon of Esau, presently reigns, [and it is he] who is the slave of *Tifferet Yisra'el*, the archon of Israel, the archon of Jacob. As it is said, "The elder shall serve the younger" (Gen 25:23). And, "a slave-girl who supplants her mistress," refers to Hagar, the maidservant of Sarah, her mistress. Hagar is an external Egyptian, and Sarah is within.[29]

The seventy nations of the world are grouped together under the two leading archons—one corresponding to Ishmael, and one to Esau. The world, or at least the world that mattered for this kabbalist in seeking to understand the broader political landscape in which the Jews of his day primarily resided, was either Muslim or Christian. And yet although Muslim and Christian peoples have much greater numbers and superior political power, he claimed that all seventy of the supernal archons of the world population are balanced against the original seventy Israelite souls who descended to Egypt in Exodus 1:5, and from whom the Jewish people descended. The archons of Muslim and Christian nations were relegated to the external, left-sided realm, while the Jewish people were "within," enjoying direct divine oversight.

However, Jewish transgressions led to a catastrophic inversion, driving the "inner entities" outside and allowing the "external entities" to enter within. This led to the reversal of the intended historical fortunes of the Jewish people, with the nations of the world, led by Esau/Jesus/Samael/Christianity on the left, and Ishmael/Islam on the right, becoming dominant and powerful. Disorder on the plane of human history is the consequence of this imbalance in the divine realm. When the archons of non-Jewish nations took control of the "supernal chariot," they caused the *Shekhinah* to depart from the world, and prophecy to cease. Such is the meaning, the author asserts, of Genesis 25:23, "The elder shall serve the younger," a phrase much debated in medieval Jewish-Christian polemical literature. For this author, Esau/Christianity is the younger brother who, like the "maidservant who supplants her mistress," has usurped the dominant role. But this does not, in the author's eyes, change the fact that Samael is, by all rights, the slave of *Tifferet Yisra'el*, the supernal representative of the Jewish people in the realm of the *sefirot*. Their present historical reality is an effect of the reversal of the intended arrangement of power in the Godhead. And for the author of the *Sefer ha-peli'ah*, Jews alone have been granted knowledge of this secret, which means that only Jews have been given insight into the meaning of Jewish historical fate.

Returning to the question of how blessing enters the world, and why the non-Jewish nations appear to receive more of it than Jews, the author asserts the centrality of the Jewish people, despite all appearances to the contrary. "When the circuit is blessed, the external supernal archons also receive. The circuit is only blessed by means of Israel. Were the nations of the world only to know the damage they cause by afflicting the people of Israel, they would make peace with Israel and seek to emulate their ways, like the greater and lesser Sanhedrin. I said to him, 'What purpose is there in *'orlah*, and the shells of *'orlah*?' and he said to me, 'I will reveal it to you another time. May God grant me merit to hear these secrets from his mouth.' He then left me and departed."[30] The author suggests that the blessing that enters this cycle, or "circuit" of the universe comes only by means of the people of Israel. The blessing that accrues to non-Jewish nations by means of their archons is incidental, and entirely attributable to the people of Israel. This is the secret that the nations of the world fail to understand—and that the readers of the *Sefer ha-peli'ah* are offered as a glimpse into the workings of human history. In fact, it is the withholding of this secret from non-Jewish people that leads to their misguided affliction of the Jewish people, which is even counter to their own self-interest.

The arrangement of the supernal representatives of the nations of the world in the divine realm is also of interest for this author in considering the question of the viability of Jewish diasporic life. The question is not only why the exile has been so long, but also how Jews have been able to survive in exile. As the author of the *Sefer ha-peli'ah* puts it, "We [dwell] in this exile among Edom and Ishmael, and we survive among them by means of a wondrous miracle from the Lord, may he be blessed."[31] The miracle of survival results from the theurgic power that Jews exert when they obey the law and perform Jewish rituals properly. Prayer, for example, is often associated with advancing the onset of redemption. The Talmud asserts that one must connect *ge'ulah*, or "redemption," to *tefillah*, or "prayer," by mentioning redemption immediately before the recitation of the eighteen benedictions.[32] Does the delay of redemption imply that Jewish prayer is ineffective? Does prayer even serve a purpose, or does the persistence of exile imply that all previous Jewish worship has been in vain? Puzzling over this question leads the authorship of the *Sefer ha-peli'ah* to craft the following dialogue:

> Why were they not redeemed from the first day that a wise man connected *ge'ulah* to *tefillah*? He said to me, one person cannot attach them beyond the measure of a single individual. However, if all of Israel were to connect [them] fully and sufficiently, uniting *ge'ulah* with *tefillah*, then they

would be redeemed. . . . There is a measure of benefit when the individual performs this, since by means of this the people of Israel are saved from the decrees of the nations. Were it not for this, what are we and our lives before them?[33]

Were the entire Jewish people to pray in a fully coordinated manner, the author suggests that they would be rewarded with immediate redemption. Laxity on the part of some results in delayed redemption for all. However, the diligence of the portion of the Jewish community that does recite their daily prayers has benefits for the entire Jewish population, since they save the Jewish people from the harshest of the "decrees of the nations." Were this not the case, the author implies that Jews would be unable to survive in exile. The prayers that a small number of pious Jews perform might not result in the immediate onset of the messianic age, but for this author, such prayer is most emphatically effective and powerful, in that it enables Jews to move forward through history, painful though it may be.

Despite all of the detail present in this accounting for the historical reality of Jewish life in the author's particular moment, mysteries remain. What, for example, is the reason for the creation of a domain of evil within the realm of the *sefirot* referred to as the impure shells of *'orlah*? Why would God construct the universe in this way, creating evil, and creating an entire eon of harsh judgment filled with misfortune? Such questions are, in this passage, fully acknowledged, but marked as a secret still withheld, to be revealed at another time. As the author states elsewhere regarding the inscrutability of the historical suffering of the Jewish people, "The Holy One, blessed be he, emanated *Pahad*, and *Pahad* emanated overseers and taskmasters . . . and their like was emanated into the lower world below, the seventy supernal archons, and they were placed in the world to exact judgment from sinners. Souls were sent forth to be tested and to thereby accrue merit by means of undergoing challenge. Therefore, no created being can comprehend the reason for [such] challenge and its purpose."[34] Nonetheless, the richness of detail with regard to the concealed *mechanisms* of history provided the medieval Jewish reader with a way of imagining and making sense of the divine plan behind historical events. The dynamics of the divine realm, spelled out in their many particulars, account for the pain of Jewish life under foreign rule. The conditions that render history in its current form possible in the first place are what interests this author. By explicating the secret divine forces behind history, and by advancing a claim to revealed esoteric knowledge, the author presents a message that is ironically reassuring. The darkness of history has its reasons, and Kabbalah enables Jews to see at least some of history's secrets. As the *Sefer ha-peli'ah* puts it, "The *sefirot* are the eyes of Israel, and Israel, when they perform the commandments, are the eyes of the *sefirot*."[35]

Pangs of History

History has a shape in the kabbalistic imagination. While this doesn't provide a complete theodicy, it does give the medieval authors and readers of these texts a way of making sense of historical events and their place in the flow of historical time, even if the ultimate causes of suffering remain in some measure concealed. Giving too much shape to history's course runs the risk of impinging upon human free will and the influence that the choices made by individuals plays in human affairs. But giving too little shape to history can make the flow of time seem chaotic, unjust, and devoid of meaning. The kabbalists tried to find a place in the middle, in which humans could be free-acting agents, and yet God had a hand in preplanning and controlling the full course of history.

Writing in the middle of the fourteenth century in Spain, Judah ben Solomon Canpanton[36] offered an interesting example of a general structure to the flow of history. In a composition entitled *Leqah tov*, he listed the astrological entities that govern each millennium, with the assumption that the full cycle of historical time takes place over a total of seven thousand years. He counted down from the seventh millennium and ended with the first, but for the purposes of this discussion I reversed the order in order to get a sense of how he envisions the forward flow of time. The moon governs the first millennium. This was the period during which "the Holy One, blessed be he, created the world from nothingness, and placed the *'adam*, which he fashioned in the image of the form of his shape, in the garden of Eden."[37] Mercury governs the second millennium, during which the flood was brought upon the earth. Venus was appointed over the third millennium, when the people of Israel were liberated from slavery in Egypt, the Torah was given at Sinai and "all of them attained the level of prophecy."[38] He states further that "the Sun was designated for the fourth millennium, in which the Temple was destroyed and in which the people of Israel were judged." However, the Temple, he notes, was also rebuilt during that millennium, and the "the people of Israel possessed the fullness of Torah." Mars rules the fifth millennium, when "the house of Israel was destroyed by acts of annihilation and decrees pronounced over Israel, since Mars represents the spilling of blood, because the people of Israel were killed for the sanctification of his name, may he be blessed, and they were exiled from their dwelling places."

Moving from past events to the present and future, Canpanton notes that the sixth millennium is governed by "Jupiter (*Tzedek*), because of the justice (*tzedakah*) that the Holy One, blessed be he, will perform in the sixth millennium with the people of Israel in their exile in the land of their enemies. They are the pangs of the messiah. In the midrash [it says that] everything that happened to the forefathers will happen to the children."[39] Finally, Saturn (*Shabtai*) corresponds to the seventh millennium, "in which the souls [of Israel] will enjoy a respite that the mouth cannot speak, as it is said, 'A psalm, a song for the Sabbath day' (Ps 92:1), because it is entirely a Sabbath for eternal life[40] in which the righteous will sit and be nourished by the luster of the *Shekhinah*."[41] The present period of history, in Canpanton's view, is one in which the "pangs of the messiah" are to be expected. Historical tragedy is a sign of the approach of inevitable redemption. But the overall character of the age is reflected in the name of the planet appointed to rule the millennium, *Tzedek* (Jupiter), which is justice. The events of Jewish history—even disastrous ones, are foreshadowed in the lives of the patriarchs as revealed in the Torah. For those with the right insight, Canpanton suggests that history is legible. The proper reading of history reveals that the world has a predetermined duration of seven thousand years, with high and low points. And he claims that he and his readers are in the final, tumultuous period before the ultimate justification of the Jewish people, which culminates in messianic redemption and eternal reward.

Historical templates such as this, along with the notion of imbalance in the divine realm caused by human sin, which leads to the reversal of the intended power relations between nations and peoples, served to help make sense of painful chapters in Jewish life. This is not to say that particular historical events give rise to new kabbalistic ideas. But there is no doubt that the choice to make recourse to kabbalistic explanations of historical suffering in the aftermath of traumatic events was part of a broader project to address the perception of a downward slope in the fate of the Jewish people, and an assertion that such misfortunes were not a sign of divine abandonment.

Shem Tov ibn Shem Tov, for example, lived and wrote in Castile in the aftermath of the catastrophic violence that claimed approximately one hundred thousand Jewish lives during the summer of 1391.[42] He described the supernal dynamics behind such moments of disaster for the Jewish collective as a result of the imbalance of the impure "arrayments" (ma'arkhot), similar to the archons appointed as governors over the nations of the world, in relation to the people of Israel. "Sometimes human transgressions overpower to the point that the verse is fulfilled, I have concealed my face,[43] and these arrayments come forth through the concealment of the [divine] face. . . . In this manner, the seed of Israel have been given into the hands of the accursed arrayments, and despite his [divine] providence over them, he hides his face from them. . . . It is all just, the arrayments acting in keeping with the permission granted to them through the concealment [of the divine face]."[44] Like the authorship of the Peli'ah and Kanah texts, as well as many other kabbalists from this period, Ibn Shem Tov attributes the power of non-Jewish nations to oppress the Jewish people to the improper alignment of supernal forces brought about by transgressive human behavior. When the supernal archons of non-Jewish nations are empowered through the theurgic effects of Jewish sin, historical disaster ensues. But interestingly, Ibn Shem Tov deploys this idea together with the notion of the concealment of the divine face mentioned in Deuteronomy. This underscores the notion that Jewish transgression both causes the empowerment of non-Jewish nations and leads God to turn away from protecting the Jewish people from the forces of history. While it may have been painful for medieval Jewish readers to think of God acting in such a manner, it also likely rang true. The alternative to divine self-concealment is divine abandonment. The claim that God responds to Jewish transgression by concealing his face and enhancing the power of gentiles preserves the divine role in human history, while placing a degree of separation between divine action and the suffering of the Jewish people at the hands of other nations.

Another instructive kabbalistic analysis of the meaning of history can be found in the anonymous *Sefer pokeaḥ ʿivrim*, composed in the northern Spanish town of Medina de Pomar in the year 1439. Only one complete copy exists, preserved in MS Parma 2572. This substantial text comprising 193 folios is divided into five sections, each constructed as an extended commentary on a biblical verse. The first section deals with the status of the Torah as an eternal, unchanging document of divine revelation, comprising many secrets known only to the people of Israel. The second deals with the reasons for the commandments, both exoteric and esoteric, praising in particular the virtue of the Jewish people as those who "submit" themselves to them. The third section deals with the unique and superior status of the Jewish people among the nations of the world, with a focus on the divine nature of Jewish souls and the theurgic capacity of Jewish actions, and the eternality of the people of Israel and ultimate destruction of non-Jewish peoples at the time of messianic redemption. The fourth chapter deals with the origins and nature of Kabbalah, though kabbalistic texts, authors, and ideas are cited generously throughout the book. The fifth and final section deals with the conditions of the Jewish people in the kingdom of Castile, and their many virtues as they endure their particularly difficult historical circumstances. The text has a certain eclectic sensibility, citing at times at length from the Talmud, Midrash, *Sefer ha-bahir*, and *Sefer ha-Zohar*, *Tiqqunei Zohar*, *Sefer ha-peliʾah*, *Sefer ha-kanah*, as well as many medieval authors by name, including Maimonides, Rashi, Abraham ibn Ezra, David Kimhi, Rabaad, Nahmanides, Judah ha-Levi, Bahya ibn Pakuda, Jacob ben Sheshet, Shemayahu ben Isaac ha-Levi, Moses de Leon, Joseph Gikatilla, Joshua ibn Shuib, Joseph Angelet, Joseph ibn Shoshan, Vidal Ben-veniste, and a number of anonymous kabbalistic texts. Boaz Huss dedicated two studies to *Sefer pokeaḥ ʿivrim* in the early 1990s,[45] but beyond that this text has received relatively little attention in the scholarship on medieval Kabbalah, despite the important light it sheds on the circulation of kabbalistic ideas and texts in Spain during the mid-fifteenth century.

Though *Sefer pokeaḥ ʿivrim* was composed five decades after the mass violence of 1391, the author was deeply invested in accounting for the tragic loss of life, which according to some estimates was as high as one hundred thousand. The author also addressed the ongoing challenges facing Castilian Jews during the intervening years. This text demonstrates how kabbalistic ideas regarding the unique nature of the Jewish self and the theurgic power of the performance of Jewish ritual were deployed to help Jews understand difficult historical experience. *Sefer pokeah 'ivrim* is focused on the meaning of suffering in exile, and the author was acutely aware of the challenge such suffering poses to the sustainability of Jewish covenantal theology. The phenomenon of Jewish conversion to Christianity is never directly addressed in the book, but it may inform the author's motivation to craft a compelling message regarding the meaning of Jewish tragedy. Throughout the book, the author acknowledges the sufferings of the Jews of Castile and offers a vision of hope for their redemption. Kabbalah plays a central role in this discourse of despair and hope, serving as a strategy for imaging not only a future messianic redemption in which all Jewish suffering will be resolved, but also a present reality in which Castilian Jews can help to overcome the forces of evil through the theurgic practice of *mitzvot* and the embrace of their fellow Jews in love and collective *devekut*, or cleaving to God. Such cleaving is part of what the author depicts as the reason why the Jewish people will never be completely annihilated by foreign nations: "Of necessity, they [the people of Israel] will never be [completely] destroyed, because they cleave, truly, to he who is eternal and permanent, according to the secret of 'For I am the Lord, I have not changed, and you, the children of Jacob, will not cease to be' (Mal 3:6). Even during a time when the nations are capable [of this], the children of Israel will continue to exist."[46]

The author of *Sefer pokeah 'ivrim* speaks explicitly and directly to the issue of the suffering of Jews in Castile. Though the question of Jewish exile in general receives significant attention throughout the text, the specific travails of Castilian Jewry take center stage. The author begins the fifth and final section by citing the Babylonian Talmud Sanhedrin 20a and its interpretation of Proverbs 31:30; "'Grace is deceitful,' this is the generation of Moses, 'and beauty is vain,' this is the generation of Joshua, 'a woman who fears the lord shall be praised,' this is the generation of Hezekiah." The author argues that the Jews of Castile have borne their burdens admirably, in particular through the three "sacrifices" of submission to the will of God, prayer, and Torah study.

> And now, after all of these matters about which I have written concerning the secret of the Torah and the commandments, the secret of the superior status of the people of Israel, and the secret that one must "bask in the light of life,"[47] and the secret of the loftiness of the wisdom of the holy Kabbalah, I will now write concerning a wondrous matter that is a consolation for all of Israel, who dwell in this long and evil exile, to prove that although they may be few in number, by means of the sacrifice of [their] great submission [to the will of God], the sacrifice of prayer, and the sacrifice of heeding the words of Torah, they have attained a level superior to the level of those who stood at Mount Sinai, and the generation of Joshua.[48]

Jewish suffering in exile is treated here as not only the final subject to be addressed by the text, but in many respects as the overarching purpose of the entire book. The "consolation" that the author offers to his fellow Jews is that, though small in number and therefore politically and militarily weak, the Jewish people of his generation have attained a level of spiritual perfection higher than that of the biblical Israelites who were witness to the revelation on Mt. Sinai or who entered the land of Canaan. The Jews of Castile, in this author's view, are the historical heirs to the biblical covenantal promise par excellence.

The author does not castigate the community for their shortcomings in order to account for Jewish suffering, as we find, for example, in the case of Solomon Alami,[49] who lived and wrote at around the same time. Instead, the author of *Sefer pokeah 'ivrim* praises the Jews of Castile for their devotion to Jewish life and tradition.

> Every time the people of Israel perform these three types of sacrifice perfectly, they ascend to a level higher than . . . the generation of Moses or the generation of Joshua, through the secret of the sanctity of their souls and the performance of the commandments in their entirety, and the three above-mentioned types of sacrifice. What also arises from this is a powerful consolation for those who dwell in this kingdom [that is, Castile],

for they have ascended to [the level of] the generation of Hezekiah, for in this exile they have performed, for many years, these three types of sacrifice—submission, prayer, and Torah—to the utmost of perfection. Submission, since for these past fifty years there have befallen them many evil afflictions . . . and they have been oppressed, lowly, and despised these past years, and yet they have always trusted in the Lord, may he be blessed. So too, with regard to sacred prayer, throughout this kingdom, each day they perform it with utmost perfection. . . . So too, with regard to Torah, for throughout the kingdom . . . in every city there is an able teacher with an ample income, and there are many students. If so, we may say regarding the people of this kingdom, "a woman who fears God is praiseworthy."[30]

The author makes no attempt to minimize the suffering of the Jews of Castile during the "past fifty years"—an explicit allusion to the events of 1391, since the text was completed in 1439. The ill fortune of the Jewish people is treated as an unqualified tragedy, and the author's description of it is filled with pathos. The ongoing suffering of the Jews of Castile is no illusion or mere privation of the good, according to the author of *Sefer pokeah 'ivrim*. The "consolation" offered is that, by enduring that suffering without losing faith, and by offering the three "sacrifices" and sustaining functional Jewish communities, the Jews of Castile are not merely waiting passively for messianic redemption. In fact, the advent of the messiah receives scant attention in the book. The author, it would seem, wanted to address Jewish suffering in the present, and a deferred reward was not enough. Instead, he argues that, by virtue of the divine souls that Jews, and Jews alone, possess (the author gives significant attention to this kabbalistic subject in section three of the text), and through their collective suffering at the hands of their neighbors, Castilian Jewry have attained a spiritual level equal to that of the generation of Hezekiah—a strong image of national success and fulfillment of covenantal promise. That is, the Jews of Castile need not merely wait passively for their reward. In many respects, they already enjoy the fruits of redemption, not despite their suffering, but because of it.

Sefer pokeah 'ivrim ends with an uncharacteristically explicit and candid description by the author of the overall message they intended to convey to their readers by writing their book.

There is likewise great consolation in this for all of the seed of Israel in this kingdom who have trod the paths of sheep to seek after God continuously and to trust in his great name, may he be exalted and sanctified, despite the fact that they have endured many plagues, afflictions, and various forms of death, multiplied and continuous sorrows, concerning which they have said, "for Your sake we are killed all day long, we are reckoned as sheep for the slaughter."[51] "All of this has befallen us and we have not forgotten you, nor have we nullified your covenant."[52] Therefore, sacred seed [of Israel], strengthen your hearts! We shall place our hope in God, for though [we suffer] many plagues and unending injuries, the Lord, may he be blessed, is full of mercy, "before the wound, the bud of healing blooms."[53]

For this author, the goal of providing this compendium of rabbinic and kabbalistic material was to provide "consolation" for the Jews of Castile, and to convey to them that, despite the many forms of suffering that they have endured, God is nonetheless full of mercy. Castilian Jews are once again depicted as particularly meritorious for their unwavering trust in God and dedication to his law—a comment that no doubt sought to counter the impression that the conversion of a significant number of Jews to Christianity during this time implied that they had failed to live up to expectations. In fact, collective historical suffering and trauma, past and ongoing, is presented here as a unique opportunity to display Jewish commitment. And for this author, Kabbalah is part of how the meaning of Jewish persistence through history is understood.

History's Necessary Afflictions

For kabbalists who claimed that history has a purpose and meaning, misfortune must also, somehow, be part of a broader divine calculus. In some cases, the historical condition of suffering and oppression in exile is understood not merely as an intended outcome, but also as one that is ultimately for Israel's benefit. Far from being a sign of God's abandonment of the Jews, such authors describe the pain of exile and disempowerment as signs of divine favor. One example can be found in an anonymous text titled

Kaf ha-qetoret, written either shortly before or shortly after the Spanish expulsion.[54] The meaning of exile and suffering in Jewish history is a matter
that the author addressed throughout his work. He asserted that "the afflictions of Israel do not happen randomly (*derekh mikri*), but rather, as divine
chastisement with which God chastises each generation, and therefore [it
is written], 'say to my soul, I am your deliverance' (Ps 35:3), for by means
of afflictions, the soul is redeemed, if the body is able to withstand them."[55]
The author speaks directly to the anxiety discussed by Eliade and Ruiz,
namely, that history is all the more frightening if it is arbitrary. In rejecting
this possibility, he suggested that the painful events in Jewish history are
God's way of punishing his chosen people. And more than that, history's
misfortunes are instrumental in redeeming Jewish souls through afflictions
of the body. Were it not for the difficulties of Israel's past, its future would
not be so bright. As he observes in another passage, "Had the Israelites not
been slaves to Pharaoh . . . they would not have merited redemption with so
many miracles and wonders. So too, had the people of Israel not been exiled
for many bitter days, they would not merit the world that is entirely good."[56]
For this author, the suffering that Jews experience over the course of their
unfortunate history is how they are refined and prepared for redemption.
As he puts it elsewhere, "This world, which is temporary, has been given
to gentiles and evildoers, and Israel is refined like silver . . . the nations of
the world will be consumed by fire . . . and the people of Israel will remain,
refined seven-fold."[57]

One of the ways that exile prepares Jews for redemption, according to *Kaf
ha-qetoret*, is by offering them the opportunity to appropriate the merit of the
nations who oppress them. Building on the time-tested image of the competing biblical brothers, Jacob and Esau, as a way of talking about the Jews and
Christians of his day, the text describes the grand inversion that will happen at
the end of exile for those who suffer it patiently.

> Happy is he who bears exile and displacement at the hands of foreign peo-
> ples, for in the future he will receive a great reward on account of this. And
> not only that, but also regarding the gentile who harms him, in general or
> in particular, if they had previously done good and had merited a portion

in the world to come, the Jew is granted his portion, and that of the gentiles who had done him evil. Due to the fact that Esau is Jacob's brother, he lost his place in paradise, and in the world to come he will be covered with shame on account of his brother Jacob.[58]

Suffering under foreign domination in diaspora is depicted here as an ironic turn of good fortune. The author posits, as noted above, that the one who endures exile merits redemption. But in addition to that, he suggests that Jews who suffer at the hands of the people of Esau are secretly acquiring whatever future reward might have been granted to Christians for the good deeds they had performed in this world. Viewed from this perspective, when Jews experience oppression and violence at the hands of Christians, the Jews accrue additional heavenly reward to themselves from the very Christians who have done them harm. In the world to come, the Christian peoples, or "Esau," will be made to bear their shame, which they acquired in this world by afflicting Jews during their period of exile.

The author of *Kaf ha-qetoret* situates his perspective on Jewish exile and historical suffering within a broader framework for conceptualizing the totality of Jewish and human history. In a discussion of Psalm 22, he focuses on the image of the "hind of the dawn," *'ayelet ha-shahar*, as a metaphor for the condition of the Jewish people in exile.

"For the leader, on the hind of the dawn (*'ayelet ha-shahar*), a psalm of David" (Ps 22:1). The *'ayelet ha-shahar* is a star that goes forth and ascends before the breaking of the dawn. . . . The movement of the stars indicates the movement of the people of Israel on Earth. And the *'ayelet ha-shahar* alludes to the two exiles, which are the two exiles mentioned by Ovadia the prophet, "And the exiled host of Israel . . . and the exiles of Jerusalem in Sefarad" (Obad 1:20). . . . Just as the *'ayelet ha-shahar* presages the dawn and the morning, so too the exiles presage the redemption. And just as this star hurries forth and ascends and proceeds to its proper place, so too the children of the exiles go forth and return to their place in the land of Israel. . . . Every place in which it is said, "for the leader, a psalm" (*la-menatzeah mizmor*), and every place that states *la-menatzeah*, corresponds to the attribute *Netzah*. This is the leader that arouses his loving-kindness for Israel. . . . Israel must cleave perpetually to the attribute of *Netzah*, which is the mystery of the right on the verge of shifting to the left, and is called *Netzah*, which would bring victory (*menatzeah*) to Israel and their wars. . . . At the time when this hind of the dawn (*'ayelet ha-shahar*) appears with the attribute of *Netzah*, great wars will be aroused in the world.[59]

The fate of Israel in its exiles is represented, according to this text, by the movements of the stars, in particular the *'ayelet ha-shahar* that rises immediately before the dawn. Just as the "hind of the dawn" anticipates the coming of the morning light, the exiles of Israel are to be regarded as indicators of the coming redemption and return to the land of Israel. In both cases, be it of the predawn darkness of the night, or the premessianic suffering of exile, the coming change is not always apparent in the present moment. Therefore, according to *Kaf ha-qetoret*, the psalm carries the comforting message that redemption is often anticipated by conditions that would appear to be its opposite. The beginning of Psalm 22 with the familiar refrain *la-menatzeah*, "for the leader," is interpreted in this passage to refer to the seventh *sefirah*, *Netzah*, an attribute associated with the right-hand side of the divine realm of mercy, and whose name literally means "victory," or "eternity." The author argues that this suggests that during the darkness of the predawn, or the period right before messianic redemption, the Jewish people should cling to this divine attribute, and expect that there will be many wars and conflicts in the world. A world of suffering and disorder is interpreted to mean that the redemption of Israel is at hand.

This passage continues with the assertion that it was "for such times that David, our king, servant of the God of Israel, wrote this psalm." The present, he acknowledges, is painful, and it is reasonable that Israel calls out to God. Citing the famous words of Isaiah, the author continues:

> "My God, my God, why have you abandoned me?" (Isa 22:2) . . . for so long to the constellations of the heavens. "So far from my deliverance, and the utterance of my roaring" (ibid.). . . . The psalmist is saying that the redemption will be at the far reaches of times and seasons, and before

the redemption arrives, there will be numerous "roars," meaning, cries of anguish that will be cried out by the children of the exile. . . . Days that are dark as night are days of affliction and exile and wandering and adverse deaths for the entire house of Israel. "And you are the Holy One, enthroned, the praise of Israel" (Ps 22:4). The psalmist sang his song as a preemptive argument against complaint, suggesting that the Primordial Will foresaw all of the afflictions and evil events to come, and this is why he created the evil shells that cause so many misfortunes and destructions for the Israelite people. For because you are holy, it would have been right for you to sit upon your throne with the "praise of Israel," and not the throne of *Gevurah*, which is the attribute of harsh judgment, which empowers the impure shells and the "whore," the handmaiden below. Upon Israel, [it bestows] evil and not good, and upon the nations of the world, good and evil: good is the secret of apparent successes, and bad is their loss from the eternal world. The accusers below, which were created to perform God's command and his will, are only nourished by the evil Samael, and they are only guided by his power and hand. . . . The primordial serpent was created to oppose Israel with the attribute of harsh judgment . . . and the reason is that the primordial will perceived that during the current period of six thousand years, creation cannot . . .⁶⁰ survive in this world except by means of the attribute of harsh judgment, since the evil inclination has been brought into this world, and the supernal Wisdom [saw fit] to create it in order to exact vengeance by means of it. . . . This demonstrates that the shells and foreign nations were created from the outset for the benefit of the Israelite people, since any good accumulated by the nations of the world by means of the shells will be left for Israel.⁶¹

With anguished cries, Israel is depicted in Isaiah as calling out to God from their exiles, asking why they have been abandoned to the "constellations of the heavens," or forces of nature. But another passage from the Psalms, the text argues, was written in direct response to precisely this concern. The "darkness" of the present moment is undeniable, but also, according to this text, foreordained as part of a broader plan. To explain the present, the author of *Kaf ha-qetoret* returns to the very beginning of history. The problem derives from the introduction of the evil inclination with the sin in the garden of Eden. During the current dispensation of time, before the onset of the messianic days in the seventh millennium, God had to occupy the throne of the attribute of *Gevurah*, the fifth *sefirah*, associated with harsh divine judgment, to sustain the postlapsarian world. This, in turn, led to the empowerment of the primordial serpent, gentile peoples, the external "shells," and the evil archon Samael. The people of Israel suffer under the dominion of these forces. But such suffering was not simply an unintended consequence, or a side effect of history. The second *sefirah*, *Hokhmah*, divine wisdom, perceived from the very beginning that God would take revenge upon the oppressors of Israel by means of the very same attribute of harsh judgment that has temporarily augmented the powers of the foreign nations. As such, all of the misfortunes that have occurred in the world since the beginning of history have been, according to this author, for the benefit of the people of Israel, who will one day claim for themselves the good that the gentile peoples have accrued. The passage concludes the discussion with a reminder that "the psalmist declares with this psalm that all of the calamitous events that will befall Israel, from the day in which the signs of the hind of the dawn (*'ayelet ha-shahar*) appears in the world— they are a sign of the [approaching] redemption."[62] Here again, misfortune is recast as a sign of hope.

The image of hope for a historical reversal of fortunes between the Jewish people and their enemies is emphasized in *Kaf ha-qetoret*'s commentary on Psalm 70.

> "Oh God, hasten to my aid" (Ps 70:2), grant me strength and support from your sacred dwelling, that I might do to my enemies as they have done to me. . . . "Let those who proclaim 'Ha! Ha!' turn back in frustration" (Ps 70:4), which is to say, may the destiny of those peoples who threaten the lives of Israel be to perish in their faith. Those who say to me "Ha! Ha!," these are two words of mockery, as when one engages in mockery and says "Ha! Ha!," [and] when they say, "Your messiah will never come. When will he come?" With this, they embarrass the Jews for the great length of the exile, and the Jews have no answer for this except hope. They express mockery and say, "That for which you hope will come upon us."[63]

Evident in this passage is the author's awareness that the prolonged exile is a significant weak point in the polemical discourse between Jews and non-Jews. In his depiction here, the length of the exile, and the mystery of when the messiah will finally come, are both elements in the outright mockery of the Jewish people. And indeed, the exile is a serious problem that "embarrasses" the Jews in this imagined interaction. In response, they hold on to hope. They even have words of mockery of their own in the form of an assertion that the glorious destiny that Christians anticipate for themselves will, in the end, go to the Jewish people. In the meantime, their reward, like their future destiny, remains hidden. As *Kaf ha-qetoret* puts it elsewhere, "Just as the punishment of the righteous is revealed, the reward for the commandments, which is the goodness of the Holy One, blessed be he, is concealed and hidden."[64]

Meir ibn Gabbai,[65] a Spanish exile living in Ottoman Turkey in the early sixteenth century, offered another kabbalistic reading of Jewish history in the wake of the expulsion from Spain. Like many kabbalists before him, he regarded the present state of human history, with the Jewish people subject to foreign rule, as a reversal of the intended divine plan for creation. The problem of subjugation of Jews to non-Jewish powers results from Jewish transgressions stemming all the way back to the garden of Eden, causing them to cleave to the aspect of harsh judgment or the *sefirah* of *Gevurah* or *Din*, as well as the evil aspect of the tree of knowledge. Before the sin in the garden, he argues, Adam was so close to God that "it was as though there was no distinction between him and his creator, but the transgression separated between them."[66] Since that time, humans have been subject to free will, sin, and death. The transgressions that Jews have made against their law are the cause of their ongoing historical condition of exile. Past transgressions mean that Jews "will be sold into the hands of the foreign nations who derive from the power of that aspect [of harsh judgment], and everything is in keeping with that which they arouse."[67] Or, as he states the matter elsewhere, "When they do not perform the will of God, they become slaves of slaves, since the foreign nations, who are subjected to the rule of the archons, become their masters."[68]

One of the reasons he gives for the Jews' experience of exile and their subjugation to foreign nations is the need for Jewish souls to be refined by means of such hardships in order to remove the impurities they retain from the sin of Adam. These experiences over the course of history enable them to carry out their theurgic task of redeeming the world. In several places in his works, Ibn Gabbai connects the exile of the Israelites in Egypt with just such a process.[69] As he notes in *Tola'at Ya'akov*:

> We have already written in the opening of this composition[70] that the sin of Adam caused the opening of the "muddied spring" (Prov 25:26), the source of filth, which then flowed forth upon him and his descendants. Those forms then required refinement and cleansing, and this is the reason for the exile into Egypt, for it is the "iron forge" (Deut 4:20). Israel was exiled there to be purified of that dross, and to deposit their contamination and filth that was intermixed into their forms from the power of the shrewd snake.[71]

Adam's sin introduced impurity not only into Adam, but also into all subsequent generations. The correction of that sin could only come about, according to Ibn Gabbai, through the collective suffering of the Jewish people. Events that might otherwise read as evidence of divine indifference to the fate of Israel, like exile and enslavement, are read kabbalistically as necessary steps in a historical process whereby Jewish souls are purified in order to be able to bring about the full rectification of the unity of God and the rebalancing of the forces of good and evil. Like the author of *Kaf ha-qetoret*, Ibn Gabbai described the pain of history as having a necessary, purifying effect on the Jewish people.

Ibn Gabbai accepted the tradition that the revelation of the Torah on Sinai had the potential to finally correct Adam's sin.[72] Through their suffering in Egypt, the souls of the Israelites were sufficiently purified to be able to receive the Torah, which would have pushed history back on track. However, like the process of creation, the revelation at Sinai did not go as planned. The commission of idol worship with the incident of the golden calf described in Exodus 32 had disastrous consequences, according to Ibn Gabbai, following the rabbinic tradition, for the removal of the impurity acquired from Adam's sin.[73] At the very moment when the project of creating the world was about to be brought back in line with God's original intent through the revelation of the Torah to the Jews, they sinned once again, plunging themselves and the world back into another exile. All subsequent Jewish experiences of subjugation to foreign rule are a consequence of that transgression. As Ibn Gabbai described it:

The Torah is a writ of liberation from death, for the Torah is life devoid of death. It also grants freedom from foreign nations. Sin arouses its corollary above, which is the aspect of impurity, the angel of death, which is the power of the other nations. For this reason, it is necessary that sinners fall under their dominion in the world below. By means of the observance of the Torah, that side [of impurity] has no power at all to be aroused, and for this reason, it cannot dominate those who observe it. Foreign nations will not be able to rule over them in this world below, but rather they [Israel] will rule over their enemies. . . . Because Israel committed idol worship [with the golden calf at Sinai], the *Shekhinah* departed from them, and she is their souls. This was therefore their downfall and the reason they were sent into exile among the foreign nations that derive from that power [of impurity] to which they cleave. This is similar to Adam, for when he sinned, the soul of life departed from him, and the spirit of impurity dwelt upon him, rendering him subject to death.[74]

The susceptibility of the people of Israel to foreign rule since the transgression at Sinai is similar, in Ibn Gabbai's formulation here, to the susceptibility of humanity to death since the sin of Adam in the garden of Eden. Both involved a negative form of *devekut* or "cleaving"[75] to the divine forces of impurity that puts them out of balance and creates outcomes in the world that were not part of the original plan for creation. Were it not for the sin of the golden calf, Ibn Gabbai argues, the proper alignment of the *sefirot* would have been restored. The people of Israel, living in the land of Israel, would then have been connected to the supernal forces of purity such that they would have held sway over the forces of impurity. Since the foreign nations draw their power from the realm of impurity, they would have been unable to dominate the people of Israel in the world below. Instead, Israel would have been able to "rule over their enemies."[76]

Ibn Gabbai does more, however, than merely lament the Jewish predicament. He offers the possibility of a remedy through corrective theurgic action. The recovery of God's original plan for creation and restoration of the proper alignment of the *sefirot* will entail, according to Ibn Gabbai, a reversal of the power dynamics between Jews and non-Jews: "When the people of Israel perform the will of their father in heaven, they reign on earth, and that power [of harsh judgment, deriving from the *sefirah* of *Din*] is subject to them like a servant, and then all of the gentile nations are subordinate to them. Such was the original intention of creation—that they should reign above and below."[77] Redemption will mean the reversion of the world to its proper balance, which for Ibn Gabbai, means the subjugation of non-Jews to Jewish power. Just as the exile of Israel among the nations of the world signifies the fallen state of the present reality, the rectification of the world will be embodied in the reversal of the power dynamics between Jews and gentiles. But in order to reach that state, Jews must endure the pain of history. Exile and disempowerment, according to this view, is not merely a consequence of past transgression. The tragedies and misfortunes of life as a subject nation are instrumental in correcting history's course. Jews, on such a reading, are *agents* of history even when they are the subjects of other nations. By suffering, they bring history closer to its dramatic conclusion.

THREE

The Shape of Time

History and Cosmic Cycles

How does historical time move forward?[1] Is it a straight line? A circle? A spiral? Does the cosmos have a secret temporal rhythm that helps to explain the events that people experience on the plane of human history? The previous chapters have described some of the discourses employed by kabbalists for imagining the meaning of Jewish historical experience. The present chapter considers another aspect of how medieval kabbalists describe the grand arc of history. For many of the kabbalists under consideration here, historical time has a shape. They claimed to have access to a secret doctrine that interpreted the biblical *shemittot*, or "Sabbaticals," as cosmic cycles of seven.[2] This notion is based on an interpretation of the biblical laws regarding the Sabbatical year, or *shemittah*, requiring Israelites to allow their fields to lie fallow and to forgive debts every seven years,[3] as well as the commandment to count seven of these cycles, culminating in the *yovel*, or Jubilee, every fiftieth year.[4] The kabbalistic interpretation understood the biblical doctrine of the *shemittot* to allude to the secret idea that the entire cosmos undergoes a series of cycles: seven cycles of seven thousand years, with each cycle constituting its own "world," governed by one of the seven lower *sefirot*. The 50,000th year entails the great Jubilee, a final redemption in the form of the return of the cosmos into *Binah* and the re-assimilation/annihilation of the souls of the Jewish people, along with the world, into the Godhead. In some versions, the cycle of seven cycles then begins again.

While the present historical period is linear, in that it moves from the transgression in the garden of Eden through the twists and turns of human history until messianic redemption, the present reality is not the only iteration of the world. There are past and future worlds described by the kabbalists. Each of these worlds, according to these texts, has its own unique character. The historical time of the present age is merely a single embodiment of the multiple ways that cosmic time can manifest itself.

This reiterating of temporal eons challenges the notion advanced by Eliade that Jewish sources depict time as linear.[5] In the texts considered below, the direction or flow of time is complex. As Sylvie Anne Goldberg has observed, Jewish temporalities combine "circular aspects of traditional societies with linear aspects of theological societies."[6] This discourse about the shape of historical time reflects the kabbalistic notion of temporality itself. Elliot Wolfson has written extensively on the question of temporality in a wide range of Jewish, non-Jewish, and philosophical sources.[7] Rejecting the simple dichotomy between linearity and circularity, he suggests that kabbalistic temporality can best be understood as a "linear circularity." Wolfson argues that

> in kabbalistic teaching, time in its primordiality is not extrinsic to God, but is the radiance of divine becoming recounted in the narratological telling of enumerated duplication. The twofold depiction of *sefirot* as line and circle suggests that the interminable telling of the timeless time proceeds linearly, but in a succession that is subject to disruption by the eruption of the cycle of the eternal return of the moment that has perpetually never been.[8]

In such a conception of time, novelty and repetition converge as they diverge. In paradoxical discourse typical of kabbalistic sources, the line and circle are images for depicting kabbalistic time only when used in conjunction. As Wolfson states the matter elsewhere, Kabbalah reflects a "dual deportment of time as an extending line that rotates like a sphere or as a rotating sphere that extends like a line. Rendered in an even more appropriate geometric figure, we can speak of time as a swerve in which line and circle meet in the sameness of their difference."[9] The doctrine of the *shemittot* reflects at the cosmic level this basic feature of kabbalistic temporality. Repetition of the past is an instantiation of the future in the present. Cosmic time is not a simple, linear movement from creation to the end of being. Instead, the kabbalistic cosmos repeats itself with variations of sameness and difference.

Why imagine such a succession of worlds? What work does such a discourse do? A part of the answer can be found in the fact that in virtually all of the examples of Jewish discussions of the doctrine of the *shemittot* that I am aware of, the present world is regarded as uniquely problematic, containing evils not to be found in prior or future worlds. The claim that the Jewish tradition contains a secret doctrine that accounts for the suffering that Jews have experienced over the course of history by revealing a deeper, hidden structure of the grand divine scheme for the cosmos, played out over multiple iterations, is a powerful assertion of Jewish knowledge of the workings behind history and the structure of time. Contained in that secret doctrine is the notion that the future world of redemption beyond history, identified with *Binah*, the third *sefirah*, is already present as the future. Despite the pain of the present, the redemption of the future is attainable as, in Wolfson's turn of phrase, the "not yet now." In a discussion of Rosenzweig's comment that "eternity is the future which, without ceasing to be future, is nevertheless present," Wolfson observed that "messianic hope hinges on preparing for the onset of what takes place as the *purely present future*, that is, the future that is already present as the present that is always future, the *tomorrow that is now because it is now tomorrow*."[10] To speak of the end of history, or the time beyond history and time, is not to despair. By describing the messianic future, and the future worlds beyond that, the kabbalists drew attention to the future remedy of Jewish historical suffering that is present in its futurity. Imagining the future world is an act in the present that releases the trap of purely linear time, with redemption placed in the unattainable beyond. In the revolving spiral of time constructed in kabbalistic texts, redemption becomes attainable since it is, as Wolfson describes it, "the present that is always future."

To possess the secret that the current era of the world is particularly problematic is to hold the key to understanding the reason behind historical misfortune. Eliade took note of the social utility of claims to esoteric knowledge of this sort. He pointed out that the Hindu notion that the present age is that of Kali Yuga, or an "age of darkness" that entails an unusual amount of human suffering compared to other ages, is nonetheless consoling in its way. It helps one to understand the reason for such suffering, since one is "conscious of the dramatic and catastrophic structure of the epoch."[11]

The Hindu and Jewish examples are not unique in this respect. Notwithstanding Eliade's conflation of biblical and "Jewish" conceptions of time, and his tendency to oversimplify the supposed linearity of Jewish historical thinking,[12] his insightful analysis of cyclical temporal discourses is useful for thinking about medieval kabbalistic texts on this question. Eliade observes, for example, that

> a common characteristic relates all the cyclical systems scattered through the Hellenistic-Oriental world: in the view of each of them, the contemporary historical moment (whatever its chronological position) represents a decadence in relation to preceding historical moments. Not only is the contemporary eon inferior to the other ages . . . but, even within the frame of the reigning age (that is, of the reigning cycle) the "instant" in which man lives grows worse as time passes. This tendency toward devaluation of the contemporary moment should not be regarded as a sign of pessimism. On the contrary, it reveals an excess of optimism, for, in the deterioration of the contemporary situation, at least a portion of mankind saw signs foretelling the regeneration that must necessarily follow. Since the days of Isaiah, a series of military defeats and political collapses had been anxiously awaited as an ineluctable syndrome of the messianic *illud tempus* that was to regenerate the world.[13]

For discourses that endorse the idea of cosmic cycles with defined natures, the evils of the historical present are in many ways built into the broader structure of cosmic time. Framing the realities of historical experience in this way limits free will and human agency as a primary driver of historical events. But on the other hand, it provides a clear rationale—a *divinely ordained* reason—for the existence of the travails of history. Though the course of human affairs may be somewhat circumscribed by this larger framing, it is also rendered more comprehensible, since the tragedies of the moment can be understood as a reflection of the nature of the current cosmic eon, and the divine plan for the full arc of cosmic unfolding.

The discourse of successive eons can serve as a strategy for making sense of a troubling present. Hence Eliade's observation that under such regimes, "history could be tolerated not only because it had a meaning, but also because it was, in the last analysis, necessary. For those who believed in the repetition of an entire cosmic cycle, as for those who believed in a single cycle nearing its end, the drama of contemporary history was necessary and inevitable."[14] Being stuck in a difficult cosmic cycle might seem like a morose view of history. But it can also help address the even larger problem of the terror of history itself, and the anxiety that historical traumas have no meaning. As Eliade notes, cosmic cycles provided premodern people with a unique language for suggesting that "none of the catastrophes manifested in history were arbitrary. Empires rose and fell; wars caused innumerable sufferings; immorality, dissoluteness, social injustice, steadily increased—because all this was necessary, that is, it was willed by the cosmic rhythm, by the demiurge, by the constellations, or by the will of God."[15] Such grand narratives of the divine structure of time give "historical events a metahistorical meaning, a meaning that was not only consoling but was above all coherent, that is, capable of fitting into a well-consolidated system in which the cosmos and man's existence had each its *raison d'être*."[16] The kabbalistic doctrine of cosmic cycles, or *shemittot*, accomplishes a similar task. These elaborate and detailed descriptions of the hidden divine historical map of the universe, both past and future, serve as occasions for thought regarding the meaning of events in the present. As Elisheva Carlebach has noted in a study of sixteenth-century Jewish chronographs, depictions of the full sweep of history conveyed the sense that "historical time was shaped by a divine plan and that both good times and bad were preordained."[17]

The kabbalistic doctrine of cosmic cycles presents an extended meditation on the nature of historical time, and the place Jews have in the interaction of forces that result in world events. As Scholem has noted, kabbalists who embraced the doctrine of the *shemittot* "wrestled no less than Yehudah Halevi in his *Kuzari* with the problem of the history of Israel."[18] For such authors, "the history of the world unfolds according to an inner law that is the hidden law of the divine nature itself."[19] This discourse involves the claim that both Jewish and world history holds a secret, and that Kabbalah provides Jews with exclusive access to that concealed truth. The experiences of the Jewish people in history, and their struggle with exile and subjugation to foreign powers, are recast not as setbacks or divine abandonment, but rather the opposite—such experiences are necessary steps in a carefully designed divine process that cannot be avoided, a process that reflects the structure of the inner life of God. The travails of the present moment of history, according to these texts, should not be regarded as challenging the validity of covenantal theology, but instead as confirming what the secrets of the kabbalistic tradition have anticipated all along. Wars among nations of the world and suffering inflicted upon the disempowered people of Israel, according to these texts, are unavoidable parts of a hidden divine historical process. Such experiences for Jewish souls on the stage of world history are a consequence of the nature of the present stage of cosmic time. Negative events in Jewish history reflect the *presence* of the divine attribute of *Din*, or "harsh judgment," in the current *shemittah*, and not the *absence* of divine providence or the abrogation of the covenant. The authors of these texts also offered the reassurance that, after a final cataclysm that will soon come to an end, an inversion will take place, and the imbalances in the world that have persisted since the sin of Adam and Eve in the garden of Eden will be corrected. The bodies and souls of the Jewish people will finally be cleansed of their dross and returned to their proper, sanctified state. The hoped-for future is one in which the enemies of Israel will be defeated, and history as we know it will come to an end.

Shemittot: Mapping Cosmic Time, Making Historical Meaning

The idea that the biblical commandments regarding the Sabbatical and the Jubilee contain a concealed kabbalistic secret regarding the progression of cosmic time in units of seven thousand years began in the thirteenth century,[20] but was endorsed more broadly in the fourteenth and fifteenth centuries. However, the embrace of this idea was not universal. Important Castilian kabbalists from the late thirteenth and early fourteenth centuries, including the authorship of the Zohar, Moses de Leon, and Joseph Gikatilla, either ignored or rejected the idea of cosmic cycles. Starting in the latter half of the sixteenth century, Moses Cordovero and Isaac Luria polemicized vehemently against the most common formulations of this doctrine.[21] Some important kabbalists who embraced this idea included Nahmanides[22] and the subsequent school of his interpreters,[23] as well as the texts associated with the *Sefer ha-temunah*, the *Sefer ha-peli'ah*, and the *Sefer ha-kanah*,[24] and many other kabbalists from the fourteenth through the early sixteenth centuries.[25]

In a relatively early formulation of this idea, David ben Judah he-Hasid describes the progression of worlds/*shemittot* as follows:

> You must understand that the secret of the *shemittah* is a wondrous and concealed matter. . . . The secret of the *shemittah* is, "A generation goes and a generation comes, and the earth lasts forever" (Eccl 1:4). . . . Thus, each *shemittah* departs and another arrives, and each *sefirah* [of the seven lower seven *sefirot*] rules over one *shemittah*. In keeping with the character of the *sefirah*, so too the nature of the *shemittah*. If the *sefirah* inclines toward judgment, the *shemittah* is judgment. If the *sefirah* is compassion, the *shemittah* is compassion. If it is justice, so too is the *shemittah*. The true Kabbalah that we have received, one from the mouth of another, back to Moses our teacher, peace be upon him, is that the previous *shemittah* was of *Hesed* (loving-kindness), while the *shemittah* we are in now belongs to *Gevurah* (harsh judgment). That is why so many harsh decrees have been aroused in this *shemittah*, as well as severe judgments, numerous persecutions, due to our many sins, and the harshness of exile. On account of this, the present overpowering exile is an indication of *Gevurah*, [the *sefirah*] that is now ruling. When six thousand years pass, which is [the duration] of the world, then twilight will immediately commence, when the righteous will sit with their crowns upon their heads, basking in the splendor of the *Shekhinah*. They will adorn themselves to enter the Great Sabbath, mother of the children. When the Sabbath begins, all worlds, gradations, and chariots will be drawn up to *Binah*, as it is written, "dust you are, and to dust you shall return" (Gen 3:19). Nothing will remain but He and his name, as before the world was created.[26]

Each *shemittah* cycle of seven thousand years, according to this view, is governed by one of the seven lower *sefirot*, taking on the character of that particular divine attribute. According to David ben Judah he-Hasid, the progressions of worlds or *shemittot* begins with the fourth *sefirah* counting from above to below, which means that the previous world was governed by *Hesed*, the attribute of divine loving-kindness. However, the next world is ruled by the second of the seven lower *sefirot* counted from above to below, which is the attribute of *Din*, or strict judgment. He associates this directly with the reason for the "present overpowering exile" experienced by the Jewish people. The progression of sevens occurs not just between the seven *shemittot*, but also throughout the seven millennia that occur within a given *shemittah*. Hence, the argument goes, in the present cycle, redemption begins to dawn at some point in the sixth millennium, which in the Hebrew calendar begins in the Gregorian year 1240, and culminates in the assimilation of all being in the "Great Sabbath," or the *sefirah* of *Binah*, in the seventh millennium.[27] The fine-grained particulars of history might not be completely preordained, but according to this view, history follows a basic outline, and there are certain broad patterns that are to be expected. Knowing this secret, which David ben Judah he-Hasid claims was revealed esoterically to Moses, enables Jews to place themselves within the flow of time in the present cosmic eon, as well as imagine the other, better worlds that have existed before and will come after.

This is not the only model that circulated in the Middle Ages when it came to thinking about the doctrine of cosmic cycles. A few early fourteenth-century kabbalists, such as the anonymous author of the *Ma'arekhet ha-'elohut*, stated that they did not know in which *shemittah* human life currently takes place,[28] while Joseph Angelet adopted the unique position that the present cycle is the final one, governed by the *sefirah* of *Malkhut*.[29] Moses of Kiev, writing in the late fifteenth and early sixteenth centuries, suggested that each "world" or *shemittah* is 49,000 years rather than seven thousand, since each is comprised of seven *hekefim*, or "orbits," "alluding to the fact that each *shemittah* is multiplied by seven thousand [years], which equals forty-nine thousand, and then they return to their mother (i.e., *Binah*)."[30] Abraham Adrutiel, a Spanish exile living in Fez in the early sixteenth century, suggests in his *'Avnei zikkaron* that this topic was a matter of controversy. His discussion of the topic opens with the statement: "Thus says the young one: I have seen fit to write here a matter regarding the secret of the *shemittot*, despite the fact that this subject is prohibited due to the great danger it poses for one who is not accustomed to these ideas. But due to the fact that there is forgetfulness of the divine command in the world, I have seen fit to write about it here."[31] It seems that Adrutiel

regarded this topic as dangerous, and yet also a remedy for the neglect of Judaism. One might speculate that when it comes to this topic, he felt torn between
the downside of predeterminism, and the benefits of a strategy for making
sense of historical events. With regard to the question of which *sefirah* governs
the current reality, he says, "Know it truth that we do not know which cycle we
are currently in, be it the first, the middle, or the last. According to the words
of the wise ones, all of them agree that we are not in the first . . . and since I
observe the lions roaring concerning this matter regarding which *shemittah* we
are in, some [enumerating] from below to above, some from above to below,
I therefore chose not to write it here, for I feared my teachers, the wise men of
the generation, lest they overtake me."[32] Adrutiel says this right before citing
the words quoted above from David ben Judah he-Hasid on this topic.

Despite this diversity of opinion among the kabbalists who embraced this
conception of time, they all agreed that the cosmos undergoes a cycle of seven
iterations.[33] Each *shemittah* reflects one of the *sefirot*, and as a result, it constitutes its own world, since, as Shem Tov ibn Gaon puts it, "all of the *sefirot* are
called worlds,"[34] and with regard to the *shemittot* he points out that "each one
is a single world and a single holiness of its own."[35] Or as Joseph Angelet described it, "Know that every *shemittah* is called world; all of the *shemittot* until
the great Jubilee. And one can reason that the Jubilee is also called world. 'And
he shall remain his slave forever (*le-'olam*)' (Exod 21:6), the world (*le-'olamo*) of
Jubilee."[36]

This structure of seven worlds in cosmic and historical time is a reflection of the divine structure of the seven lower *sefirot* beneath *Binah*. Many
kabbalists claim that the understanding of time in the kabbalistic doctrine
of the *shemittot* is alluded to by Rav Katina in the Babylonian Talmud, Rosh
ha-Shanah 31a, in his cryptic statement that "the world subsists for six thousand years, and is desolate for one [thousand]." The anonymous authorship
of *Ma'arekhet ha 'elohut* described the many manifestations of the supernal
heptad in the following terms:

> The divine structure consists of seven [*sefirot*] which are the supernal
> world, and from it emanates the lower world. Corresponding to these
> seven pillars of the world are seven firmaments . . . the dwelling place of

the intellects. From them derive the seven planets . . . and corresponding to them are the seven land regions upon the sphere of the earth . . . and they are divided into seven climatic zones. And the establishment of the world is through seven [people]; Adam and Eve were created, and from them were born Abel and his two twins, and Cain and his twin. . . .[37] There also remained seven people after the generation of the flood, which was like a new creation; Noah and his three sons and their three wives. . . . The seven worlds are each seven thousand years, as will be explained below, and the entire world consists of seven, which alludes to the divine structure. So, too, the days of the week and the Sabbatical years and the seven Sabbaticals of the Jubilee, as well as the days of Passover and the days of the counting of the *omer* for seven Sabbaths [leading up to the Feast of Weeks]. Regarding seven, the Holy One, blessed be he, has said that in the future he will fashion seven wedding canopies for the head of each and every righteous person,[38] which alludes to the fact that the light of the righteous will be seven times greater. And the seven are called "days," which are the days of creation mentioned in the portion of Genesis, and six of them are called the "six days of creation," which are the days of action, since during them the world was created, and the seventh, Shabbat.[39]

The supernal structure of seven lower *sefirot* echoes throughout the eons and cycles of worlds. Just as there are seven successive worlds, so, too, are there many types of sevens that exist in the current cosmic cycle. Within the present eon of historical time, the seven days of the creation, seven days of the week, seven days of Passover, and the seven weeks of counting the *omer*, all reflect the divine construct of seven, just as the seven planets, continents, and climates also serve as manifestations of the divine seven. The many repetitions of seven create a pattern across time, and across worlds, whereby the vast flow of time becomes legible. This passage suggests that the rhythm of specifically Jewish time during the week and calendar year is how the secret of this supernal pattern is encountered. The author also contends that the events of human history after the expulsion from the garden of Eden have been encoded with the divine mystery of seven. History began with the seven original progenitors of humanity, and its ending will be marked by the seven canopies that will adorn the heads of the righteous in the future redemption at the end of history.

The time of "desolation" at the end of history evoked speculation among kabbalists. For many, this desolation was the necessary prelude to regeneration and renewal. The idea of successive worlds involved the notion that the cosmos and time undergo destruction, followed by recreation. Interpreting Rav Katina's comment, the *Ma'arekhet ha-'elohut* describes this aspect of the flow of cosmic time and worlds in the following terms:

> Concerning Rav Katina's statement, "the world subsists for six thousand years, and is desolate for one [thousand]" (b. Rosh ha-Shanah 31a), what you must understand in Rav Katina's utterance is the matter alluded to by two words, which are "and desolate for one [thousand]" (*ve-had haruv*). This is a great principle. It is desolate for one [thousand] since time will remain, but [the world] will be desolate of humans and animals. During that period of one thousand years, the *'Atarah* longs continuously for when she will be acknowledged and renewed, "and desolate one [thousand]" indicates the renewal after one thousand [years]. . . . This is the matter of the Sabbatical and the Jubilee. The six years refer to the six thousand, and the year of the Sabbatical refers to the world to come, which is the seventh millennium, in which the inhabitable world will be desolate and the earth will be at rest, and everything will be nullified.[40]

Cosmic regeneration, according to this view, requires periodic annihilation. The rhythmic, predictable macropattern of the universe entails a "week" of millennia, during six of which the world is active, and one, like the earthly Sabbath on the seventh day, in which the world is "desolate." The author of this text contends that Rav Katina's statement implied the subsequent renewal of the world after a thousand years of desolation, since it would be impossible for there to be a measurable duration of time for that period if it signified the end of time itself. The millennium of desolation, which the *Ma'arekhet ha-'elohut* also identified with the world to come, is a return of the world to its primordiality, *in illo tempore*, that results in subsequent recreation.

In another discussion of the cycling of the cosmos through the duration of forty-nine thousand years, the author employs the image of a *hekef*, "orbit," or "circuit," to describe the movement from one world to the next.

> Each of the days of creation refers to a world which is called a single orbit (*hekef*). Know that the world orbits seven times, and these are the seven worlds that orbit, corresponding to the seven supernal [*sefirot*], since each of those *sefirot* is called a "world." They are the forty-nine years, which are forty-nine thousand, until the beginning of the fifty thousandth. It corresponds to the great Jubilee, as will be explained further. They are seven times seven, corresponding to the seven supernal [*sefirot*], since each one is composed of seven, and the seventh millennium of these orbits will be holy, corresponding to the Sabbath comprised of *zakhor* and *shamor*. Therefore, it is said regarding the Sabbatical, "Sabbath to the Lord," just as with the Sabbath it says, "Sabbath to the lord," since in that millennium *'Ateret Tifferet* is renewed, and then after that a new heaven and a new earth are created, and the *'Atarah* is made the cornerstone. The days of the portion of Genesis refer to these orbits, each day a single orbit, and six orbits to the six days of creation in which the forces are active, and the seventh orbit is entirely sacred and a Sabbath to the Lord, and it is the day that is entirely Sabbath and a world that is entirely one and a rest of eternal life. That rest flows to the great Jubilee that we will mention in the discussion of eights.[41]

Just as six of the millennia within a given world are active, and one is a kind of Sabbath, the same applies to the seven worlds: six are active and one is a "rest of eternal life." And while the *'Atarah*, or *Shekhinah*, longs for renewal at the transition from one world to the next, during the final world, she is bound to *Tifferet*, and "made the cornerstone." In other words, the seventh world is one in which all traumas and evils of history are overcome. The exile of the *Shekhinah* ends in the seventh and final world. The cycle of cosmic eons ends with a period of time utterly devoid of history.

Bahya ben Asher suggested that the cycle of destruction and renewal is what allows the world to regain its pristine purity.[42] He understood Rav Katina's notion that the world will be "desolate for one thousand" to mean

that "after the destruction of the seventh millennium, and after the elimination of the [evil] powers and their removal, dominion returns and is renewed in the world as it was."[43] The period of desolation entails, among
other things, the purging of evil forces from the world. When the world
is renewed, dominion is regained by the forces of good, which establishes
a new order in the world, one more in keeping with divine intent. Bahya
even applies this principle of renewal to the entire cycle of forty-nine thousand years, arguing that after the annulment of the cosmos within 'ein sof,
the entire process begins again: "When the great Jubilee arrives, all ten [of
the sefirot] return to their root in 'ein sof." In Bahya's view, this accounts
for why "all being is annulled and void. After the Jubilee, being is renewed
in its entirety, to be revealed from 'ein sof, and divine flow returns above
and below as in the days of old, and thus it is from Jubilee to Jubilee for
eighteen-thousand iterations."[44]

Designating the transition from one shemittah to the next as a divine act of
destruction followed by renewal underscores the notion that the regeneration of
time is always connected to the generation of every temporal eon and world. The
authorship of the Sefer ha-peli'ah makes this point in a comment on Ecclesiastes,
"'A time to cast down and a time to build' (Eccl 3:3) . . . this refers to casting
down and building another shemittah. 'A time to slay and a time to heal' . . . slay-
ing is the destruction of the vessel of life, which is the shemittah that passes, and
healing is the rectification of the vessel that receives life, with is the shemittah to
come after the shemittah that passes."[45] The same author articulates this idea elsewhere by employing the terminology of the flame bound to the coal, taken from
Sefer yetzirah 1:7, where this image refers to the interconnections between the
sefirot. For the anonymous author of Sefer ha-peli'ah, the binding of beginnings
to endings is a sign of divine forethought in structuring cosmic time.

At the end of all of the shemittot, they will all return to the coal, as they
were previously in potentia. Come and see how they are emanated from
one another, grasped by one another, sustained by one another, like a
chain with no boundary between them. The end is bound in its beginning. Beware, and be on heightened guard for your soul, for there is one
who rules over them—he is the one who ordains—there are none who can

comprehend his ordinances. Only by this is he indicated; that its ending is bound in its beginning; first in thought is last in deed.[46]

The divine reign over the entire succession of cosmic iterations is indicated, for this author, by the return that happens at the end of the seventh world, when all worlds ascend to their origin in the Godhead. In the largest sense, this is the end that is "bound to its beginning." The plan for time, and for the emanation and return of worlds from the divine, was, this text claims, part of a divine plan from the start. The same applies to the point of transition between worlds, where the ending of one is the point of origin of the next. In each case, the convergence of ending with beginning indicates the presence of a divine intention for the unfolding of each world before its creation. The regeneration of time and the cosmos in each *shemittah* is the design of the "one who rules over them." And while there may be "none who can comprehend his ordinances," meaning, though the events of history may be inscrutable, they are, for this author, most definitely planned by God. The divine reasoning for creating the particular history evident in the world remains hidden, but the fact that there is a divine calculus behind the design of historical time is the point this author seeks to emphasize here. The many tribulations of history were all part of an extensive and unknowable divine plan, present first in divine thought at the origin of cosmic time, and bound to the events that take place in the world. Such a discourse depicts a reality that may be troubling, but it is not arbitrary.

Such seems to be the implication of Meir Aldabi's comment in his popular text *Shevilei 'emunah* from the second half of the fourteenth century. This book was written for a more general readership, and it is not by any means an exclusively kabbalistic book, though it makes mention of kabbalistic topics and texts. In a comment on the Sabbatical cycles, he observes:

> Know that there is a further secret in this matter [of the Sabbatical cycles], received by a few of the wise men of our Torah. They contain an allusion from the masters of the Torah, since truly this matter did not come to be through random chance, but rather only through God's intentional will, may he be blessed. Therefore, the sevens were designated in the Torah; the

sevens of days, years, and weeks of years. So too for the days of the world, which are six thousand as the duration of work, the conduct of the world proceeding according to the days of creation, and the seventh millennium corresponding to the Sabbath day. This is the Kabbalah in the possession of a few of the wise men of Israel from the mouths of the prophets, and they contain a deep secret that is not appropriate to write down in a book. And one must not ask what comes after this, for blessed is the one who knows.[47]

It seems likely that Aldabi knew more about this subject than he was willing to write in this passage. But his interest in stating here that the Sabbatical and Jubilee laws contain a kabbalistic secret is that he does not want his readers to believe that they came to be through "random chance." He then suggests that the Torah structures all time around units of seven, including the duration of the world for seven millennia. This idea is part of a larger "secret that is not appropriate to write down in a book," though Aldabi clearly felt some need to allude to the general notion, and to embed it within the larger body of Jewish esoteric knowledge that exists beyond the scope of his own treatise. But what is the problem that such a comment seeks to solve? It would seem that Aldabi wanted his readers to know that just as the flow of time at the level of weeks, Sabbaticals, and Jubilees has a divinely ordained pattern, the full arc of history is also the result of God's direct choice and deliberation.

The *shemittot* doctrine enables a comprehensive discourse for mapping out the entirety of time. Worlds come and go, and periods of decompensation are followed, after a duration of desolation, by renewal and regeneration. This apocalyptic view of time is, as the term suggests, an act of unveiling—in this case, it is the screen that conceals the divine workings behind time and history that is pulled back. The disclosure of this secret reveals the shape of time. The cosmos repeats itself, with variations that follow the pattern of the inner divine world of the *sefirot*. And the iterations of the universe are not random, but structured in a series of sevens. Some kabbalists are reluctant to say what happens after the end of the seventh millennium of the seventh world, when everything returns to *Binah* or *'ein sof* at the end of the 49,000th year. The author of *Sefer ha-kanah*, for example, states that "after the completion of the seven circuits, which are the seven *shemittot*, everything returns to *Binah*. Beyond that one may not enquire even in thought."[48] Bahya ben Asher, as we saw above, is among those who boldly stated that the entire process begins again after the Jubilee, and repeats itself eighteen thousand more times.[49] The present eon of seven thousand years, like the series of seven worlds, is structured time, and not an amorphous flow. But whether the cycle of seven *shemittot* occurs only one time or many, such a framing of time is essentially rigid, leaving no room at the macrolevel for a spontaneous, drastic change of course. The strategy at work in these discourses is not one designed to unfetter time and history from a predetermined course. The goal is to give time and history meaning, and to show that they are the result of careful divine planning, and even a reflection of the inner divine self. When placed within such a schema, the dramas of history are not random or devoid of purpose, since God himself is cast as the grand architect of the pattern of time.

The many different kabbalistic discussions of the doctrine of the *shemittot* are all, in various ways, meditations on the nature of divine control over historical events. The fate and destiny of the Jewish people are situated within a broader divine plan for the ultimate fate of the cosmos. Bahya ben Asher notes that Mishnah Avot 5:9 states that the violations of the Sabbatical are among the reasons for the exile of the Jewish people from their land because "one who rejects the commandment of *shemittah* denies the creation of the world and the world to come, and this is clear."[50] The implication for Bahya is that the full timeline of history from creation to redemption is encompassed within the commandment of *shemittah*. The fitting punishment for the sin of transgressing this commandment, which is tantamount to rejecting the divine control over the course of historical time, is to be displaced from the promised land. To accept the view that history has no master is, in Bahya's view, to spurn the divine gift of historical destiny, purpose, and protection promised to the Jewish people. Imagining a cosmos that moves through the seven cycles of the *shemittot* allows for a discourse of time that has a secret, all-encompassing divine purpose. In certain moments, history may be traumatic and terrifying, but the claim to know the full plan for the entirety of time allows for the placement of historical events into a much broader macrocontext. In such a world, the pain of the present moment comes to be understood as one, very brief passing stage in the development of the world in the image of God.

Shemittah and Exile

The majority of medieval kabbalists who embraced the doctrine of cyclical worlds accepted the view that the current world takes place in the *shemittah* governed by the *sefirah* of *Din*, or harsh judgment.[51] As noted above, it seems that there was some degree of debate regarding this question. The author of *Ma'arekhet ha-'elohut* states the following: "Know that we do not know which orbit we are currently in, be it the first or the last or the middle. According to the words of our rabbis of blessed memory, and according to the simple meaning, it would appear that we are not in the first, for they said the verse 'and there was light,' teaches that 'he would construct worlds and destroy them' (Kohelet Rabbah 13:4)."[52] This Spanish author, likely writing in Catalonia in the early fourteenth century, regarded the question of the *sefirah* governing the current *shemittah* as one in which there was no unambiguous kabbalistic tradition. He seemed to surmise, based on the midrashic tradition, that because God created and destroyed worlds prior to this one, the current world must not be the first one, but he is unwilling to venture anything more certain beyond that. The author of *'Avnei zikkaron* observes much later in the early sixteenth century that there are those who interpret the order of the *shemittot* as they correspond to the days of creation as "the first day to *Tifferet*, the second to *'Atarah*. And there is another opinion that the first day corresponds to *Hesed*, the second to *Gevurah*, the third day to *Tifferet*, the fourth day to *Netzah*, fifth to *Hod*, sixth to *Yesod*, seventh to *Malkhut*."[53] This indicates that there was some degree of diversity regarding the current *shemittah*, indicating that it was not a foregone conclusion that the majority of kabbalists would come to accept the view that the present cosmic cycle is governed by the divine attribute of *Din*.

Why, then, did the notion that the present world is an embodiment of the harshest divine forces come to be so widely accepted? If this was not clarified in the earliest sources, the fact that so many kabbalists came to regard it as an unquestioned doctrine suggests that this idea was useful. As noted earlier, Eliade argued that the notion that the present iteration of the cosmos is the most difficult and filled with the greatest degree of misfortune is, in a way, a comforting notion for those who experience historical distress. If, when time is mapped out in its entirety, the present is a uniquely problematic world, the troubles of the present seem less mysterious. The wheel of history, such an idea suggests, will eventually, inevitably, turn again, ushering in a new, better reality. And in the meantime, the historical events of the present are part of a divine plan, inscrutable though it may be. In such a discourse, the difficult events of the present can be attributed to the current *shemittah*, just as harsh weather can be attributed to the season. Such is the suggestion of an anonymous comment from the year 1390 on Joseph ben Shalom Ashkenazi's commentary on *Sefer yetzirah*: "Each *sefirah* serves for six thousand years, and then it serves for one thousand years, and then the service passes to the *sefirah* that comes after it. The six-thousand-year period that we are currently in, which is to say that we are now in the year 5150 since creation (1390 CE), the *sefirah* of *Gevurah* serves, and thus the plagues, wars, and exiles."[34] The dread of history is understood by this author to be an unavoidable reality associated with the present state of the world.

The authorship of the texts associated with the *Sefer ha-temunah* literature dedicated considerable energy to this topic as an important esoteric doctrine. As one text put it, "[Knowledge of] the *shemittah* is a form of wisdom of the Kabbalah."[35] This anonymous literature, composed mostly in the mid-fourteenth century, emphatically embraced the notion that the present world takes place within the *shemittah* cycle of strict divine judgment. According to *Sefer ha-temunah*, all of the other cosmic cycles are spiritual paradises in comparison to the present world. In a very real sense, the author regarded the present *shemittah* as the worst of all possible worlds.[36] The negative character of the current cycle is described in stark terms in *Sefer ha-temunah*:

> In the current *shemittah* one finds every intense and overpowering thing, such as demons and impure powers and evil spirits, the evil inclination and many bastards and rebels, and peoples of diverse languages, forms of idol worship, and powers confined to the territory of their lands and peoples, harsh decrees, sins, transgressions, sexual immorality, lengthy exiles, defiled powers, defiled forms of intercourse, impure animals and beasts, fiery serpents, plagues, and all kinds of impurity.[37]

Exile is included in the list of evils manifest in the present world as a result of the power of the attribute of harsh judgment that controls the current reality. The category of exile is used in a double sense, referring both to the exile of the body, in the form of the collective displacement of the Jewish people from their ancestral land, as well as the exile of the soul through the experience of reincarnation.[38] As the anonymous author of the commentary on the

Sefer ha-temunah puts it in a discussion of the above-cited passage: "Due to the excessive harshness of the attribute [of Judgment], he would 'build worlds and destroy them' (Bereishit Rabbah 3:7), such that God had to stipulate for all of the work of creation that it would be [performed through the attribute of] Judgment, and upon this condition everything was created. It was due to this stipulation that all souls must undergo reincarnation, and all bodies must experience exile."[59] The wandering of the soul through reincarnation, and the wandering of the body in diaspora, are cast here as the inevitable consequences of the state of the cosmos in its current temporal incarnation.[60]

Collective historical misfortune is accounted for as a result of the divine attribute governing the span of time in which Jewish life currently takes place.[61] As the anonymous commentary to *Sefer ha-temunah* put it, "During the present time . . . the attribute of *Din* is powerful and harsh in order to carry out harsh judgment upon the wicked. Concerning this the prophet said, 'And the Lord of Hosts is exalted in Judgment' (Isa 5:16)."[62] Roee Goldschmidt has observed that this approach to cosmic cycles unsettled later kabbalists like Isaac Luria because of the limitations it creates for free will and the agency of the Jewish people to play a proactive role in bringing about redemption.[63] For the authorship of the *Sefer ha-temunah* literature, the more pressing question seems to have been how to make sense of Jewish collective suffering in the present, rather than to safeguard the principle of unencumbered free will. The strategy in these texts for addressing this problem is to claim that Kabbalah reveals the divine forces at play behind the events of human history, and by arguing that Jewish suffering is an unavoidable feature of the current historical cycle that will nonetheless culminate in redemption for the Jewish people. It should be emphasized that this doctrine is not typically associated with a comprehensive theodicy that reveals the underlying justice behind every historical tragedy. On the contrary, the impossibility of making sense of the specifics of particular events of historical misfortune is often emphasized.[64] As the author of this text states the matter, "We are unable to grasp a single one of the thousands of myriads of wonders of the Holy One, blessed be he, that are alluded to in the harshness of this *shemittah*, and [how] all of the difficulties that the people of Israel have experienced have occurred because of the power of this *shemittah*, even concerning Pharaoh, Sennacherib, and Sisera."[65]

According to the authorship of the *Sefer ha-temunah* and its commentary, the current *shemittah*, especially since the sin of Adam and Eve, grants the supernal archons of the nations of the world temporary capacity to overpower the divine forces sustaining the people of Israel. This, they claim, results in catastrophic world wars, with tragic consequences for the people of Israel.[66] The anonymous commentary predicts the onset of the process of redemption to begin in either 1409 or 1531. In the meantime, they anticipate that

> all kingdoms, Greece and Edom, will battle one another, these against those, and thus the words of the prophet shall come to pass, "[On that day] the Lord will punish the hosts of heaven in heaven, and the kings of the earth upon earth" (Isa 24:21). From this God will begin to arouse the advent of the messiah to redeem Israel. One need not be dismayed and say, "What sign is this, for haven't there always been numerous wars between kingdoms and cities?" . . . The answer is that thus is the truth: at the time of redemption, all of them will be cast into disarray . . . and it shall be a time of suffering for the people of Israel as has never been seen before, and only a few shall remain from among the many . . . and God in his great mercy, through his providence, shall be gracious and have mercy upon them.[67]

These dark predictions of the calamitous suffering brought about by the final pangs of the influence of the attribute of *Din* in the current *shemittah* are instrumental in bringing about the arrival of the days of the messiah over the course of the sixth millennium. Wars and violence between nations, the author suggests, are to be expected in the present cosmic cycle, especially as it nears its end. By that measure, historical disarray is a hopeful sign of the approaching end of history itself. The author urges his readers to observe the historical events around them, and to interpret them using the doctrine of the *shemittot* as a guide. The arrival of redemption will signal the realignment of divine powers in their intended configuration. The result on the human plane will be the redemption of the Jewish people and their elevation over their erstwhile oppressors. A world gone awry, with nations at war, is to be expected by those who possess knowledge of this particular kabbalistic secret. The current *shemittah* empowers and emboldens the archons, ultimately putting them at war with one another in a final cataclysmic upheaval at the end of history. The anonymous commentary acknowledges the apparent disorder on the stage of history, noting, "We perceive that the arrangement of this emanation [of the world] is in disarray, and this is due to the fact that the force of the *shemittah* causes everything."[68] This comment does not imply that the author regarded history as lacking divine purpose. The point is rather that the nature of the present cycle creates the present historical reality, but "God, may he be blessed, acts in each *shemittah* according to its needs."[69]

As noted above, many kabbalists attribute the power of non-Jewish people to the harsh nature of the current *shemittah*. Their power, as well as their desire to oppress the Jews, is understood to be a manifestation of the unbalanced powers of the divine attribute of *Din* that rules the present cosmic cycle. The *Sefer ha-peli'ah* describes *Din* as the attribute from which the primordial snake drew its power, which enabled it to set in motion the entire train of events that constitute human history since the transgression in the garden. The author notes that "this attribute is called 'evil' (*ra'ah*) . . . and it is the *shemittah* that we currently inhabit. Thus, all of the evil thoughts that the nations of the world harbor regarding the people of Israel derive from that attribute."[70] The behavior of gentile nations, and by extension, the historical misfortunes that the Jewish people have suffered at their hands, is, in fact, according to this view, a reflection of the *divine* attribute that governs the present eon.

Despite the inherent problems Jews face in the present *shemittah*, with its characteristic of empowering other nations over Israel, kabbalists suggested that God nonetheless works behind the scenes to guide history in the right direction. And Jews themselves possess a degree of agency through their theurgic capacity to blunt or enhance the power given to the nations of the world to oppress them. In a discussion in *Sefer ha-peli'ah* regarding the power relations between the descendants of Jacob and Esau in the current *shemittah*, the author resorts to the doctrine of cosmic cycles to account for the power imbalance between Jews and Christians during the present exile.

Know that Jacob is small before Esau. . . . The truth is that Jacob being smaller than Esau is caused by the *shemittah*, for he is an offspring of this *shemittah*. Despite this, Jacob is greater in terms of first-born status, truly. For this reason, he is called "my son, my firstborn, Israel" (Exod 4:22). In truth, harsh decrees and bloodshed were all given to Esau. And therefore Esau, since slaughter derives from harsh judgment, comes from that attribute. Isaac intended to bless him in order to reinforce him with harsh matters, so that all harsh things would affect Esau and his external, left-sided descendants that derive from the aspect of the [current] *shemittah*. And the Lord, may he be blessed, to whom no malice can be attributed, knew the secret inner pathways better than Isaac concerning the future, and overruled him. He intended to strengthen the harshness of this attribute among the nations of the world in order that they would keep their distance from Israel. The Lord, may he be blessed, wishes this only when Israel performs the will of the Holy One, blessed be he; the harshness of the attribute then acts against the gentile nations. If not, heaven forbid, then it functions [on behalf of] the enemies of Israel.[71]

The present *shemittah* of *Din* is, according to this author, the attribute most closely associated with Esau. As a result, he is greater and more powerful than Jacob in the present world in terms of capacity for violence and bloodshed. The author suggests that Isaac's intention in selecting Esau to receive his blessing was not to augment Esau over Jacob, but rather to attract all "harsh things" to him and his descendants, thereby protecting Jacob. But God knew better than Isaac how best to engineer the future. Such, the text claims, was the real reason why God commanded Rebecca to help Jacob obtain his father's blessing. Knowing the nature of the present *shemittah* and the role that the nation of Esau (i.e., Christians) would play in the future, God intervened. The intent, according to this passage, was that by consolidating the harsh aspects of *Din* among the descendants of Esau, they would "keep their distance" from the Jewish people. However, such was only God's intent when the Jews fulfill God's will by observing the law. When they transgress the law, as has indeed been the case, the power of the current *shemittah* found among the Christian peoples enables them to do violence to Israel. Such, the author argues, is the secret divine plan behind the reality of the medieval present, with Jews subjugated to Christians, and Christians substantially more powerful than Jews. It was all part, this text claims, of a divine plan for Esau's descendants to be ready to deploy their particular access to the powers of this cosmic cycle in the event that Jews transgress God's law. This discourse accounts for the events of Jewish history in exile in the Christian West, connecting them to a divine plan that originates in the biblical past, and is situated within the vast timeline of the seven *shemittot*.

The moral lesson that emerges from such a perception of history is that Jews should not expect to attain political or military mastery over their enemies before the arrival of the messianic age at the end of the current eon. The power dynamics of the present world are stacked against the Jewish people. The best course is to accept the nature of the current reality, observe the law, and remain dedicated to God. The powers and pleasures of this world are not the true domain of the Jews. The authorship of *Sefer ha-kanah* made a recommendation of this sort to their readers in a description of the functioning of the Hebrew letter *heh*, a symbol for the attribute of judgment in the present world: "In this harsh *shemittah*, the power of the letter *heh* dominates, conducting all of its actions with harsh judgment. Thus, it was decreed from above that its circuit should be with harshness and judgment."[72] After this fairly typical description of the nature of the present world, the author makes a direct appeal to their readers:

> And thus, oh you children of the exile, beware of the letter *heh* and correct your ways and conduct, as it says, "and you shall choose life" (Deut 30:19), for this I will swear to you: there is no benefit or gain for you in this world—only the observance of the commandments and the avoidance of transgression. Woe to you who pursue matters of the body as though they were matters of the soul. Do not let the principle of the divine unity escape your mind day or night. For you see the harsh attribute from which the evil inclination has been sent forth to do battle with you. You, oh son of man, remember Adam who sinned and was driven from the garden of Eden. How much more so for yourself!

In a stark warning to the reader, the anonymous author of this text points out that earthly matters are a dangerous distraction. Jews must, he asserts, keep the "principle of divine unity," meaning the kabbalistic doctrine of the *sefirot*, constantly in mind. This, he argues, will enable them to be mindful of the "harsh attribute" that rules the present *shemittah*, and that has sent forth the evil inclination which leads to transgression. With Adam as the cautionary tale, the author suggests that observing the law and avoiding sin is the true task for all Jews in the present world, and they must not be led astray to treat earthly, corporeal pleasures as though "they were matters of the soul." The correction for the flaw in the course of history since the days of Adam and Eve can only come through observing the Torah and battling the evil inclination. The suggestion here is not that Jews should avoid history. The point this author is trying to make is that Jews can engage and correct the flaws of history most directly through observance of the Torah. By doing so, they are not ignoring history. Rather, they are pushing history back on track so that it can finally end.

Discourses like this both account for Jewish historical reality, and manage expectations. In a world governed by *Din*, calamity is to be expected. There is no point in struggling directly against such inevitabilities. Nor should they be regarded as human injustices, to be addressed on the purely human level. Painful as they may be, such historical events are part of a much larger divine plan for the flow of time. There will soon be a different, better time, but in the present world, the task for Jews is to observe their law and resist temptation. As the author puts it in another direct appeal to readers in *Sefer ha-peli'ah*: "Therefore, oh ye of woman born, beware and on guard, for the *shemittah* is harsh, and the evil inclination wages war. . . . One should be careful not to cause any harm by means of his sins and transgressions written in the Torah, or through neglect of the commandments, for all of them ascend above and prevent the overflow and blessing from descending."[73] Jews may suffer in the present, but they are nonetheless described here as agents rather than objects of historical events. It is ultimately the theurgic power of Jewish transgression of the law, rather than the actions of non-Jews, that causes the present reality to be even worse than it needs to be. Were it not for Jewish neglect of their law, the world would be harsh, but not calamitous. The stakes, this author suggests, of Jewish observance are very high in the present state of the cosmos, and Jews are called to rise to this particular historical challenge that only they can meet.

"Concealed Worlds without End"

Why imagine multiple worlds? Why is a single universe sometimes not enough? What social work does a multiverse discourse accomplish? As Mary-Jane Rubenstein observes in a wide-ranging study of the multi-universe idea in the history of the West, the many ways that multiple worlds have been theorized reflect different modes of inquiry and points of departure. And multiverse discourses tend to scramble the distinctions between disciplines, in that "multiple-world cosmologies consistently rearrange the boundaries between and among philosophy, theology, astronomy, and physics."[74] Speculation about other worlds is a place where human conceptions of reality, through whichever domain of knowledge, are disrupted. The notion of multiple or endless universes, either successive or concurrent, has generated its own multiverse of theories. This reflects, Rubenstein notes, not simply a diversity of views on a single question. Instead, she suggests that "the shape, number, and character of the cosmos might well depend on the question we ask it."[75] The universe, or universes, that people imagine, can tell us much about the problems they are trying to address, or the questions they are trying to answer, when they put forth the possibility of multiple worlds.

What question or questions were medieval kabbalists asking of their universe? What problems were they grappling with when they constructed discourses regarding a multiplicity of worlds? In the different ways that medieval kabbalists approach this question, the issue of the meaning of Jewish history is never far from the surface. The notion of other worlds that are different, and quite often better, than the present universe serves as an instructive point of contrast for thinking through problematic aspects of the medieval Jewish reality. Imagining past and future worlds that are much better than the present can reassure the reader that their own moment is only a brief snapshot in the long and undulating course of the many lives of the cosmos. In the reality these kabbalists put forth, the present moment is an infinitesimally tiny duration in comparison to the extension of time and space covered by the many worlds God has created. From such a perspective, large problems become small. The present becomes but one negligible instant in a grand divine scheme. This is not to suggest, however, that they claim that Jews are insignificant. On the contrary, throughout the many permutations and iterations of the universe, the kabbalists describe an epic, even heroic, journey of the Jewish soul, in which suffering on the plane of history in the present is a temporary, but vitally necessary, step in the divine plan for cosmic time.

The notion of the existence of multiple worlds is hinted at in rabbinic literature, as, for example, in the comment in the Babylonian Talmud that at night,

God rides a cherub through eighteen thousand worlds.[76] The anonymous late thirteenth- or early fourteenth-century text known as *Kabbalat Saporta* mentions this in a discussion of the doctrine of the *shemittot* as alluded to in Nahmanides's commentary on the Torah. In an attempt to reconcile Nahmanides's doctrine with the Talmudic idea, the author suggests that the lower nine *sefirot* create eighteen separate worlds, since "each *sefirah* is two worlds, one for this world, and one for the world to come."[77] Unlike the standard doctrine of the *shemittot* in which there are seven worlds that exist in succession, this text seems to suggest that there are other ways in which there is a plurality of worlds. The late thirteenth-century kabbalist Joseph ben Shalom Ashkenazi described an even more elaborate conception of multiple worlds. In this case, they are the demonic realms that parallel the ten *sefirot*.

> For the demons that were created at the onset of the eve of the first Sabbath . . . they are also created in the order of the ten *sefirot*, except that they are external, permutations of permutations. Just as there are ten camps of angels, so too are there ten camps of demons, and they possess world, year, and soul, heaven and earth and air and stars and planets and moon and sun and day and night and year and months, face of human, face of lion, face of bull, and face of eagle,[78] and inanimate objects and vegetation and animals and speaking creatures, land and sea, and fish and creeping creatures, crawling creatures, mountains, and valleys.[79]

In his typically cryptic mode of expression, Ashkenazi suggests that the "external" demonic realms with their ten camps of demons are their own worlds. Like this universe, they possess time and seasons, heavenly bodies, plants, animals, and terrestrial features. These demonic cosmoi even include the four faces of Ezekiel's chariot vision. And his conception of multiple worlds extends beyond the parallel of ten pure worlds of the *sefirot*, and ten impure worlds external to them. He suggests that, beyond the eighteen thousand worlds mentioned in the Talmud, there are "twenty thousand worlds, two thousand for each world; a thousand for the day and a thousand for the night."[80] Similar to *Kabbalat Saporta*, Ashkenazi described a cosmic doubling or mirroring, but in this case, it is that of day and night.

These comments from authors writing likely in the late thirteenth or early fourteenth centuries offer early examples of how the idea of multiple worlds came to function in kabbalistic texts. There is no coherent, single doctrine expressed in these passages. But there clearly was a willingness on the part of some to claim that the universe is not one, and that the nature of the cosmic multitude is a valuable kabbalistic secret. In both of these cases, the expansion of the number of worlds is connected to the multiplying of the number of *sefirot*. Thirteenth- and early fourteenth-century kabbalists did this in a number of ways, coming to a variety of totals. Isaac of Acre, for example, embraced the notion of *sefirot* nested within each other, such that "the ten ineffable *sefirot* are each encompassed within all ten, which is one hundred. And each one of those one hundred is encompassed within the hundred, which is one thousand. And each one is encompassed within each of the thousand, which is ten thousand."[81] The lack of uniformity on this matter in the surviving textual witnesses suggests that this idea was both malleable and useful. The discourse of a world that is many offered possibilities, and each author exercised a degree of freedom in experimenting with where that could lead.

In texts that focus on the sequenced multiverse of the *shemittot*, some authors produced elaborate descriptions of the superior nature of the other worlds that come before and after the present universe. A highly negative characterization of the current *shemittah* of *Din* is contrasted with the previous cycle, governed by the *sefirah* of *Hesed*, or divine loving-kindness.[82] The commentary on the *Sefer ha-temunah* describes that *shemittah* as follows: "[The beings] were endowed with pure, brilliant souls that did not experience exile or impurities or reincarnations.... All creatures in the *shemittah* that has just passed were sacred and pure, without any evil inclination or transgression or idolatry or jealousy or hatred. Their eating and drinking were like the delectation of the angels of this *shemittah*. ... The beasts of that *shemittah* were like the supernal angels now in this *shemittah*."[83] The previous world, according to this passage, bore some similarities to the present one, in that there were creatures, but they had no evil inclination, meaning, if they had free will, it was fundamentally unlike the power of choice in this world. The previous *shemittah* was a world without negative events or suffering, including exile and reincarnation. Moreover, there was an elevated ontological status of all beings in the world of *Hesed*, in that their lowest forms of sentient life were like the transcendent divine beings of this world. As this author puts it elsewhere, "The essential nature of animals during that *shemittah* was so ennobled and pure that they were like supernal angels in this current *shemittah*."[84] The previous world is like a negative foil to the present one, in that "just as the attribute (*sefirah*) of *Din* administers the world according to the attribute of divine justice, so too, *Hesed* administers the world according to the attribute of divine mercy. This alludes to the *shemittah* that has just passed, which was conducted according to the attribute of divine mercy . . . just as *Gevurah* administers this world according to its attribute."[85]

Just as the previous world was superior to the current *shemittah*, subsequent worlds are also, each in its own way, far better. In a discussion in the main body of *Sefer ha-temunah* regarding the letter *zayin*, representing *Netzah*, the seventh *sefirah* counting from above to below, and the *sefirah* that governs the fourth *shemittah*, the author describes a world with no impurity, exile, or misfortune. "There is no evil inclination, no powers of impurity, or externality, and no death until the end of the *shemittah*; all die by a kiss. Their Torah is simple and strong like a burnt offering. Manna is their food, and not the grass of the field; as the sustenance of their angels is their nourishment. There are six sacred seasons to sing and praise, powerful days and lengthy Sabbaths, prodigious diverse creatures, healthy and strong, with pure, luminous faces."[86] In this other world, there is duration and time in the form of religious seasons and Sabbaths for the offering of praise to God, and there are beings, far superior to the humans of this world, who live without toil or bodily limitation. Time in that world is finite, and the end of life in that *shemittah* is like death by divine kiss—devoid of suffering or tragedy. A key characteristic of this otherworldly paradise is the absence of what we think of as history and historical events. Time is marked only by sacred events and occasions for praising God. There are no struggles between nations as signifiers of history.

The author of the commentary on this passage goes into even greater detail regarding the paradisical character of the fourth *shemittah*:

That world is in a beautiful arrayment, like the garden of Eden in which there was no contamination and no evil inclination . . . souls enter shining, and people walk like angels, as in, "And I shall walk amongst you" (Lev 26:12).

Reproduction occurs in a pure way, since love and hate do not exist. [There are] diverse creatures with beautiful faces shining with rays of light, and there is no veil. That world is beautiful and replete with large, beautiful trees shining "like aloes planted by God, like cedars [beside the water]" (Num 24:6). Everything is like the garden of Eden, with supernal powers constantly singing without cessation, all of them pure, luminous, translucent, most of them of the innermost; firmaments and spheres arrayed in a single order, stars and planets and configurations. . . . [There are] ten appointed holidays, and one hundred Sabbaths, without months . . . a long year with six seasons in place of months, with summer and winter operating as one. Long life, great days, day and night shining as one. The earth brings forth its bounty without cultivation, and fruit is not lacking from the trees all year. All of the world is as one family, with one Torah with the letter *alef* that is currently missing; its law and teaching in keeping with its *shemittot*, all of them truth and faith as one, and it will have only a minuscule measure [of judgment] for the needs of the world, for in each *shemittah* there remains a small measure of worldly need. Everything will be in keeping with law and righteousness, "for the earth shall be filled with knowledge of the Lord" (Isa 11:9).[87]

For this author, the world of *Netzah* is one in which there is reproduction, but no passion or lust. There is also no hate or conflict. The plants, trees, and creatures are all pure and ethereal, and the stars and planets are ordered differently. The duration and marking of time are categorically different as well. The holidays equal ten—perhaps in parallel to the ten *sefirot*—and there are no months at all, only one hundred Sabbaths. The year is "long," presumably in comparison to the length of a year in this world, and the six seasons are in harmony. Paradoxically, summer and winter, along with day and night, function as a unity. All of the beings of that world comprise a single family, obeying a single, radically different Torah that manifests a letter that is not revealed in the present world. In that world, in which the earth, in Eden-like fashion, brings forth food without work, all energy goes toward the single purpose of acknowledging and praising God. In the world of *Netzah*, which is on the right side of the Godhead and under the sway of the forces of *Hesed*, harmony and purity manifest in all registers of reality.

The following world is governed by the *sefirah* of *Hod*, which is on the left side of the divine being. This world is less purely harmonious than that of *Netzah*. Time is marked by "events" of sorts, but the sting of tragedy is absent from them. In a manuscript version of the *Sefer ha-temunah* referred to in the printed text as the "other *girsa*," or "recension," the realm of *Hod* is described as follows:

> From the power of that *shemittah* there are two "great lights," small and great, for the light of the moon will shine like *Hesed*, with many similar powers of the left. There are also lesser exiles, composites, and external- ities [in that world], and angels and powers of the left under the aegis of diminished *Din*, and worldly creatures as at present, through diminished *Din*, without harshness, and all sacrifices are acceptable. There are two exiles, one long and one short, and there is not so much idolatry among the people of Israel. Among the nations of the world, many acknowledge the divine unity, and all of them offer sacrifices upon the altar of the Lord, and the *Shekhinah* is with them publicly, for there are no rebels against God among them, for the attribute does not function harshly. There are holidays and Sabbaths as at present, and many kings of Israel, and the succession of prophets does not cease among them, and all of them embrace faith and Torah. They are not punished in their exiles, for the *Shekhinah* is with them publicly before all. They are all ennobled, beloved, embracing commandments and Torah. There is no excess of im- purity or sin among them, and their punishments of body and soul are light, since the *shemittah* is gentle, multiplying creation, the world full of creatures without violators, wicked ones, or transgressors as at pres- ent. There is abundant divine overflow, delight, reproduction, sagacious prophets, peace, companionship, wealth, glory, all fearing God, for all of this is wrought by God.[88]

In this world, there are events, such as exiles, and there are "external" beings that function under the power of *Din*. But in the world of *Hod*, all manifes- tations of this attribute of divine judgment are "diminished." As a result, the divine and worldly creatures that draw from the power of *Din* do so "without harshness," despite their similarity to the beings of this world. Time likewise more closely parallels this world, with the same holidays and Sabbaths. And unlike the world of *Hod*, there is a kind of history that plays out, marked by what we could call historical events. Kings and prophets come and go. There are Jewish people and gentile nations, and Jews undergo two exiles, one long and one short. However, they are not "punished" in their exiles, and the nations of the world do not dominate and oppress the people of Israel. Because there is no rebellion against God by his chosen people in the world of *Hod*, the *Shekhinah* never departs from them. Instead, she stays with them "publicly," and the *shemittah* operates "gently." The world of *Hod* is presented here as a kind of daydream for what this world could have been more like if only Adam had never sinned, and the Jewish people had never faltered in their dedication to observing the Torah. The world of *Hesed* is entirely other from the reality of this world, but *Hod* is more like a version of getting this world right. The discourse of such a world offers medieval Jews the opportunity to imagine a version of what the history of this world could have been. The conclusion of this text hints that the radical cruelty and suffering manifest in the current world is not the result of a heartless divine plan, but rather the failings of generations of Jews who were heedless of God's broader cosmic temporal plans.

The worlds before and after this one were not the only alternate universes the *Sefer ha-temunah* authorship was willing to entertain. A simultaneous multiverse discourse also attracted their attention, doing a particular kind of work for thinking about their present reality. In a striking section of the text, the commentary notes that "there are many other worlds besides this one, and they are one next to the other."[89] The author is framing for the reader the following passage from the main body of the text:

> There are numerous wondrous worlds and spheres and *shemittot* and Jubilees in each *sefirah*, and within that, other worlds, this within that and this within that, some to the east, some to the west, some to the north, some to the south. Some long, some round, some small, some large, some composite, some simple, some translucent, some luminous; all of them supernal, awesome, hidden, enclosed in concealed laws and statutes, in the thousands and without number. . . . Within them there are numerous other worlds, called supernal in their spheres, paths, powers, rules, laws,

and teachings, in which there are created powers and diverse creatures—concealed worlds without end.⁹⁰

Here the author is not just talking about the specific worlds before and after the present *shemittah*. Instead, the focus is on the notion of many alternate realities or "other worlds" within the present cosmos. These concentric universes nest within one another, each having a unique character. In addition to diverse shapes and appearances, they also have their own "laws," "statutes," and "teachings" that pertain on their plane of existence. God, it seems, is the master of many worlds hidden from this one. Within the present reality, there are "concealed worlds without end."

A number of strategies are used to ground the claim of multiplicity in kabbalistic methods of counting. The author of the commentary says that these other worlds are "concealed, some large and some small, with diverse laws and statutes unique to each . . . concealed worlds emanate from each of the seven attributes, which are divided into forty-nine Sabbaths, which are like gates."⁹¹ The seven "attributes," or lower *sefirot*, are the base multiplier of "Sabbaths," which each comprise seven. The *Sefer ha-temunah* draws upon the idea of *sefirot* within *sefirot* to claim that each of the lower seven *sefirot* contains its own succession of forty-nine *shemittot*: "From each *sefirah* emerges numerous other *sefirot*, until, from the power of the *sefirah*, there arise forty-nine *shemittot*, divided into forty-nine sections from the fiftieth gate. Thus, each *sefirah* has forty-nine *shemittot*. . . . Each of the six *sefirot* contains many worlds."⁹² Not only does the present reality encompass "many worlds," the succession of worlds is far greater and more complex than the mere seven worlds that serve as the basic enumeration of the *shemittot*. One total that is offered is the astronomical, symbolically large number of "fifty thousand generations of Jubilees and *shemittot*."⁹³ Time and reality subdivide into a dazzling array of iterations.

The authorial voice of these passages presents as the master of hidden knowledge par excellence. To claim that this world contains endless other worlds is to assert that reality extends far beyond that which meets the eye. The one who reveals such mysteries lays claim to a highly privileged glimpse beyond the concealing veil of the current universe. They assert unique access to the many worlds that God has created within this one. For the reader who accepts such a discourse, they, too, claim insight into the true nature of the divine creative project. What they learn is that the single world of human experience is refracted into an endless kaleidoscope of other worlds that exist in parallel to this one. In such a view, the reality of everyday human experience is a disguise. Hidden beyond it are other realities that have their own particular nature. The assertion of such a multiverse implies that the current reality is merely one of many, perhaps even infinite, options of how the world not only *could be*, but actually *is*, right now, hidden from view. Or at least, hidden from those who are ignorant of Kabbalah.

Those outside of the chain of transmission of this kabbalistic secret are like the characters in Plato's cave, gazing at shadows, unaware of the wider world that they inhabit. But those who have been granted this insight into the kabbalistic secret of the many worlds that extend within and across time know the truth: present reality obscures the vast, infinite array of worlds that God has created. For the medieval Jews who produced and consumed such a discourse, the traumas of exile were tempered by the recognition that the course of human history in this world is a game played by blinded actors. Jews alone can see beyond this small slice of reality into the infinite alternatives God has created. As such, the Jewish people, so the kabbalists claim, are the only ones who serve as divine partners in a plan that other nations know nothing about. By suffering in this world, Jews help to play out a single, but necessary, aspect of merely one of the many worlds that God has created. The painful reality that Jews were experiencing in the medieval world was presented as a passing moment in the vast, complex unfolding of the cosmic order. But the special knowledge granted to the Jewish people as they endured that suffering on the stage of history, the kabbalists claimed, revealed to them the true meaning of their pain, and offered them special status as the only people with whom God has shared the full scope and purpose of his master plan for historical time.

Connecting Worlds

The different worlds that make up the *shemittot* are not entirely separate from one another. Certain aspects or features of these worlds reach across time and manifest within one another. Like the *sefirot* themselves, the *shemittot* are interwoven. According to the commentary on the *Sefer ha-temunah*, "Every *shemittah* is intermixed with the others. Each contains a small measure of all of them with regard to generations, commandments, practices, and attributes."[94] The descriptions of other worlds serve not only as opportunities to contemplate a better version of what reality could be. Claims regarding the points of connections between worlds are ways of accounting for aspects of the present condition of this world. Both good and bad characteristics of the current *shemittah* can be understood as manifestations of other worlds in this one. As this same author says elsewhere, "Whenever there are evil and harsh events and powerful wars in the *shemittah* of *Gevurah*, and even in other *shemittot*, they all come to be stored in the *shemittah* in which we exist."[95] In such passages, we can observe some of the ways that kabbalists actively sought to make meaning in the present as they described past and future worlds.

In the *Sefer ha-temunah* literature, the *shemittah* governed by the *sefirah* of *Yesod* is a world that spans worlds. Due to its associations with the Sabbath, it was seen as a manifestation of the period of "desolation" that occurs during the seventh millennium, as described in the Talmudic statement attributed to Rav Katina. Like the earthly Sabbath, the *shemittah* of *Yesod* is a period of inactivity, and a foretaste of the delight of the world to come. The peculiar character of that particular *shemittah* is, according to this text, made manifest in the seventh millennium of each of the *shemittot*. In some passages found in this grouping of texts, the *shemittah* of *Yesod* is unique, since "its attribute and *shemittah* is not active in the lower world, except through inaction. . . . One who observes Shabbat is absolved of all sins and merits the supernal Shabbat . . . if one is worthy, they are forgiven, and if not, the attribute of supernal *Yesod* annihilates them from this world and the supernal Shabbat."[96] This Sabbath world, like an island in time, serves a dual purpose. For those who are made worthy by observing the Sabbath, the manifestations of that world are expiatory, and provide access to the "supernal Shabbat" or eternal reward. For those who lack such merits, the power of the world governed by *Yesod* destroys them. This divine world both rewards Jews (observant ones, that is) and obliterates others. The period of the seventh millennium within each *shemittah*, including the present world, is an extended Sabbath in which Jews will reap their temporal reward in this world, and gain access to their eternal reward in the divine realm.

In the *Sefer ha-kanah* and *Peli'ah* texts, we find expressions of the notion that the interconnection of worlds, which is to say, points of contact across time and between the cosmoi of the successive multiverse, are central to how the present universe functions. At the most basic level, the worlds are connected like a chain, and thus, "there is no *shemittah* that is not connected to the one that came before it."[97] The current eon governed by divine judgment, or *Din*, is situated between the two much more merciful worlds of *Hesed*, divine loving-kindness, which came before, and divine beauty, *Tifferet*, the far more balanced and favorable world that comes next. But the present world is in part supported by the prior one. In the words of the *Sefer ha-kanah*, "This *shemittah* cannot be sustained if it is composed entirely of judgment, without something from the past *shemittah*, which was mercy. . . . Noah came from Adam, who combined judgment and mercy, since Noah was from the previous *shemittah*, and the world was established through them. You have no generation in which there is no one from the previous *shemittah* to sustain the world. Therefore, Abraham came from there."[98] According to this passage, three biblical characters—Adam, Noah, and Abraham—come from the prior *shemittah*.[99] Their placement in this world was intended by God to balance the harsher edges of the present reality. For this reason, every generation includes the remanifestation of souls from the *shemittah* of *Hesed* in order to temper the present *shemittah* of *Din*.

This model for describing the divine strategy for balancing the forces of judgment and mercy in the present world suggests that the souls of righteous Jews in the present are holdovers from the previous world that serve to sustain the current *shemittah*. Their role spans time and space, bridging the gaps be-tween worlds, and ameliorating the otherwise unsustainable forces of harsh judgment in the present. These unique individuals move through the multiple worlds that God creates, bearing much-needed elements of the previous world into this one, as they move on through time toward a destiny in the next world. As the *Sefer ha-kanah* describes it, "The righteous will all ascend above and dwell in the *shemittah* of *Tifferet* in body and soul, like Enoch, Jacob, Moses, Pinchas, Elijah, and the rest of the righteous. For every *shemittah* is grasped by all of the others, so that in each there is a small measure of all of them, of their Torahs, commandments, manners, and attributes. Do you not see that in this *shemittah*, which is the *shemittah* of *Pahad*, there is Abraham, Enoch, Moses, and the ram of Isaac?"[100] Adding more biblical characters to the list, including the ram that was sacrificed in place of Isaac, these special righteous souls are emblematic of the epic, world-spanning journey of the righteous Jewish soul through this world. Suffering in the present is a task that the righteous must endure in order to carry out their special divine mission of bridging worlds. The current period is the most difficult, but it is, for this author, only one brief period as they move onward to the much better world of *Tifferet*. In this theodicy, the suffering Jewish soul in the present is secretly part of an invisible divine plan for the grand unfolding of time across multiple worlds. And by serving their heroic role—unappreciated except by those who know the kabbalistic secret—they advance the divine plan for structuring cosmic time. The souls of the righteous are in this way an expression of meaning across time.

For the souls that derive from the prior world, life in the present reality is painful. The journey of those souls from the prior *shemittah* to the current world is described as a descent from paradise. This image of the souls of the righteous traversing worlds fueled the musings of the anonymous author of the *Sefer ha-kanah*. As they described it, the previous world afforded its inhabitants,

> long life without exiles or reincarnations . . . there was no snake or [evil] inclination or eating or sin. . . . In the *shemittah* of *Hesed* the form of all of the creatures was that of cattle, since this is the form of one of the creatures of the divine chariot. Strolling with the supernal luster of the garden of Eden was the pleasure of their sustenance. . . . Abraham knew that he was from there, and that the Holy One, blessed be he, brought him from that *shemittah*. He remembered how it was there, along with Noah, and the two of them brought a small measure of the unity and light of the past *shemittah*, and planted a tree of the root of his unity, which the gentile nations cut down. During the time of the fourth *shemittah*, which is the *shemittah* of *Hesed*, there were no twins, which is to say, judgment—only mercy. Abraham, Noah, Moses, and Enoch, all of them were there, in confraternity in the light of *Hesed*. They remembered the days that were before them, and begged of God that they not be sullied, and they were punctilious in their conduct.[101]

The previous *shemittah*, as we have also seen it depicted in the *Temunah* texts, was radically different from the present reality. The emphasis in this passage is that there were neither "exiles" nor "reincarnation," a topic that will be addressed in more detail in the next chapter. There was also no "snake," the villain of the garden of Eden, nor was there any evil inclination, transgression, eating, or labor. Sustenance came directly from God, and there was never any expulsion from the garden. In short, it was a world without history. As time moved, the events of that world were static, devoid of drama, unpredictability, or choice. And compared to this world, the author suggests, such a life was paradise. Abraham, Noah, Moses, and Enoch lived together in that world, and have been scattered across the generations of the current *shemittah*. Two of them also planted a tree of divine unity from the previous world in order to bring some of its light into the present. But, the author claims, gentile nations destroyed it. These otherworldly souls are described here as openly pleading with God not to be tainted by the impurity of this world. They were meticulous in their conduct, the text explains, in order to accomplish that. And yet the tone of this passage is that these righteous souls from the past world suffer here in the present, even as they serve as instruments of God's will for the benefit of the current *shemittah*. This powerful "suffering servant" image evokes a broader message regarding the meaning of Jewish experience through historical time; suffering in the present is doing God's will, and reward, both past and future, awaits. Moreover, that suffering is essential for this world; without the pains endured by the righteous from the previous world in this one, history would collapse. The only way for God to maintain the present course of history in this eon of harsh judgment is through the suffering of souls from the previous *shemittah*.

Enoch was a particularly interesting character for this author when it comes to describing the previous *shemittah* with the present. As the only character in the biblical corpus described as having been "taken" by God because he "walked" with him (Gen 5:24), the author of the *Sefer ha-peli'ah* regards him as falling into a slightly different category from other souls that derived from the world of *Hesed*.

> Know that in the previous *shemittah* the physical Enoch was at a very elevated level. He never encountered a wicked person or judgment in all of

his time. The Holy One, blessed be he, brought him into this *shemittah* to sustain the world, and to serve as a supernal pattern, Judgment and Mercy, to challenge those created [here], and they did not withstand the challenges, since they chose death over life. Enoch stood and said before God, "All of this generation is wicked, offspring of killers; they lack faith. And truly I know that in the future you will annihilate them. Why have you brought me to be among them? And I was the greatest of my generation, and now I wish no association with their evil ways. Therefore, master of all the worlds, I am worthy of being like one of the ministering angels, since in the generation of the *shemittah* of *Hesed* that has passed from which I came, everyone was superior to the ministering angels, and I was great even among them." . . . Thus, his flesh was transformed into flames, like Elijah, and he was placed among the ministering angels.[102]

Enoch's transformation is depicted as a reward for his high standing not just in the present world, but also in the prior world from which he derived. Like Elijah, he is spared the pain of death. But unlike Elijah, God consents to remove him from the human cycle of birth and death and place him among the ministering angels. This passage underscores the corrupt state of the present world by showing it from the perspective of an inhabitant of the previous world. Equipped with prophetic foreknowledge, Enoch points out that humanity will become so violent and debased that God will annihilate almost all of them in the flood. Why, he asks, must he endure such indignity to live as a human being in the world governed by the *sefirah* of harsh judgment? Unlike with other characters who came from the world of *Hesed*, God agrees to elevate him to angelic status. But the point of the passage remains clear; the present world compares poorly to the previous *shemittah*, and for those who remember their experience there, life in the current reality is unbearable. Those who remain in order to sustain the current world by balancing the divine attributes of judgment and mercy are the suffering servants of humanity par excellence.

Living in a dynamic historical environment creates a burden for righteous souls. Part of how those souls make the present world sustainable is through balancing divine forces by their conduct. One way, the author claims, that they accomplish this is through sexual coupling. As they note, "Seth, Moses, Noah,

[and] Abraham came from the previous *shemittah*, and they had no females. The present *shemittah* is female, and if the male and female are not bound together, the world cannot be sustained. . . . Those who derive from this *shemittah* must create a full world, which is male and female."[103] The binding of male and female is described as a characteristic particular to this world. In the previous, masculine world—devoid of human drama as it was—there was no need for it. But in the present, feminine reality, creating a "full world" requires a union of the powers of male and female. And this is not only a Jewish duty, according to this author. Non-Jews are also required to accomplish the same purpose for sustaining the "external" realm that they represent. As the author states, "Know, my son, that gentiles are also commanded regarding reproduction. . . . Just as there is an inner world, so too is there an external world, and it is in keeping with the needs of the *shemittah*."[104]

Biblical characters are not the only beings that derive from the prior *shemittah*. According to the *Sefer ha-kanah* authorship, "The fish of the sea are from the previous *shemittah*, while land animals are from the present *shemittah*."[105] Because of this, "they are not subject to the judgment of the present *shemittah*, which is slaughtering. Do you not see that if they are brought onto dry land, they die? This is because they are not intermixed with judgment. . . . In the *shemittah* from whence they came, they did not eat or drink. They lived and were sustained by the supernal radiance, like the angels in the present *shemittah*."[106] Building upon the fact that in Jewish law, kosher slaughtering only pertains to land animals and not to fish, the author suggests that this is because the entire species is a holdover from the previous world of divine *Hesed*. Like the other beings in that world, they did not eat and drink, and in the present world, they are unable to survive on land, because they do not combine judgment and mercy.

In passages like these, connecting worlds sustains the present, but accomplishing that task entails suffering. The righteous souls from the previous world suffer in the present eon, as they are subjected to an entirely different reality. Unlike in the world of *Hesed*, the world of *Din* involves the evil inclination, hard labor for survival, and the sting of death. Humans are free to use their drives, for better or for worse. Passions overwhelm human life, even as they can be channeled into the sacred forms of gendered coupling that help to sustain the cosmos. In short, the present world subjects its inhabitants to the terrors of history. The authorship of *Sefer ha-peli'ah* depicts a pathos-laden plea from Moses asking God why he has been brought from the prior world to this one: "Master of the world, why have you brought me into this evil *shemittah*? Why have you allowed me to become liable for death? He said to him, in the past *shemittah* you did not undergo trial, so the Holy One, blessed be he, brought you to wage war with the master of war, and you did not prevail, and thus are liable for death."[107] Even righteous souls, it seems, can benefit from the challenges they face in this world. And even the likes of Moses are prone to failure. On the plane of history in the current reality, the author suggests, the souls from the world of *Hesed* can stumble. And yet, like Moses, they contribute immeasurably to the present cosmic cycle by enduring its challenges.

In these exemplary descriptions of sacred suffering, these texts provide a discourse that helps to account for Jewish historical suffering. The suggestion is that, like the intercosmic souls of their biblical forebears, Jewish experience in the present world is filled with pain. But for those who faithfully serve their role, that suffering is noble and productive. It is not arbitrary or without purpose. Bearing the agonies of a world filled with sin and death is part of the task of righteous Jews in this world. And when they perform their duties well, they keep history on track and hasten its end. The messianic future of this world, and the paradises that await in future *shemittot*, will, like the world before this one, be a paradise. Reaching that point is the sacred function that Jews fulfill by bearing the burdens of their history.

History's Arcs

A basic question that many medieval kabbalists faced when considering their historical circumstance was simply this: Is history getting better, or worse? Despite the fact that the doctrine of the *shemittot* suggests that the previous world was far superior to this one, and despite the reality that earlier periods in the present world, such as the days of the First and Second Temples, seem to have been much better, there were still those who articulated a progressive view of history.[108] In their view, history generally improves over time. Even across the progression of worlds, there were those who regarded the general trend as one of gradual improvement.[109] Menahem

Recanati put the matter succinctly in his commentary on the Torah, "In each of the *shemittot* there will be a greater measure of goodness than of the one before it."[110] Or as Joshua bar Samuel Nahmias stated in his *Migdol yeshu'ot*, written in the early fourteenth century, "All six of the *shemittot* are each better than the previous one, just as in the six days of creation, the last is better than the first."[111]

Contemplating the multiverse provided medieval kabbalists with an opportunity to articulate optimism. Seen from the perspective of the long arc of cosmic time and multiple worlds, the future beyond their bleak medieval present looked bright. As the *Sefer ha-peli'ah* authorship noted, "There is no doubt that the next *shemittah* will be superior to this one in terms of divine mercy (*rahamim*), because 'He will destroy death forever' (Isa 25:8)."[112] This improvement over time is about more than the generally better nature of the future *shemittot*. Progress over the grand arc of history can be observed, according to these kabbalists, in the fates of nations. Recanati suggested that "the peoples of the world and their powers decrease with each successive *shemittah* . . . and their archons decrease with each *shemittah*."[113] Shem Tov ibn Gaon similarly argued that "the gentile nations and their powers diminish in each of the *shemittot*."[114] The author of *Ma'arekhet ha-'elohut* argued that the improvement over the progression of the *shemittot* entails both the degradation of foreign nations and the elevation of the condition of the Jewish people:

> Each of the worlds in their renewal will entail an addition of goodness over the one that came before it. This goodness consists of the reduction of power of the archons of the nations of the world, from one world to the next, and the elevation and strengthening of the power of the people of Israel upwards and upwards. And on the seventh day, which corresponds to the great Sabbath, all of their powers will cease. Just as there is increasing goodness from one orbit to the next, so too there is increasing goodness within one orbit from millennium to millennium.[115]

The movement through worlds entails the attenuation of gentiles. The final point of cosmic redemption will be signaled by the complete disappearance of the powers of non-Jewish peoples. For these writers, the optimistic view of history involved imagining the gradual disappearance of Israel's foes. The final destination of cosmic history is the end of all forces that impinge upon Jewish experience.

When medieval kabbalists contemplated the terrors of their present state, they did not shy away from the reality of the historical problems they faced. They described their own present as undeniably painful. Their strategy for endowing their own historical moment with sacred meaning involved reframing history itself. Their degraded position was understood to be part of the difficulty of their particular cosmic phase. But they were not, in their minds, cast adrift. For these kabbalists, human history, like cosmic time, had a direction. The pain of the present was rendered meaningful, intentional, and even useful, through a discourse of its place in the inevitable approach of a better future. In the vast span of time across multiple worlds described in these sources, the difficult state of the Jewish present was seen as only a small blip on an expansive temporal map. For most past and future time, reality is much better. By the same token, the dominance of non-Jewish nations in the present is brief and insignificant when considered within the full divine plan for cosmic history.

By imagining the present state of human history as a brief moment in a cosmic process that entails worlds beyond all recognizable historical experience, the kabbalists tell us much about the kind of life they dreamed of when they wanted to conjure a better world. Their aspiration was not merely for the opposite of their present. They did not want to simply change places with their Christian neighbors. Their goal was to reach a time beyond history, and live in a world devoid of events. For these kabbalists, the present was bearable not only because it was temporary, but also because it was a stage on the way to future worlds in which the toils and traumas of the current world disappear. The kabbalistic secret of historical meaning is an anticipation of worlds beyond the dramas of human life. In this daydream of the cosmic past and future, the medieval Jewish condition was reimagined as a secret journey through the ever-improving worlds that embody the repetitions of hidden divine forces.

FOUR

Living across Time

Reincarnation and the Course of History

Is one lifetime enough?[1] For some religious traditions, the span of a single life simply doesn't provide sufficient space for the soul's task in the world. For many medieval kabbalists, *gilgul*, or reincarnation, was part of how they described the journey of the Jewish soul through the divine plan for human history.[2] The notion of successive worlds explored in the previous chapter was not the only kind of repetition over time that medieval kabbalists embraced. This chapter will consider how the concept of reincarnation served as another discursive strategy in the medieval kabbalistic toolkit to make sense of the Jewish experience of history. Past and future generations of Jews fuse with the present when the same soul returns in multiple persons.[3] And because God is regarded as the power in charge of choosing which souls return to the world and when, turning the wheel of *gilgul* becomes a way of describing how divine intention guides the course of human events. The discourse of wandering Jewish souls through time over the course of multiple lives was a strategy for expressing the historical condition of the Jewish people. As Scholem has observed, "The horrors of Exile were mirrored in the Kabbalistic doctrine of metempsychosis."[4]

In its earliest formulations, the kabbalistic notion of reincarnation was treated as a highly esoteric subject.[5] In the early fourteenth century, Joshua ibn Shuib struggled to explicate Nahmanides's cryptic remarks regarding the meaning of levirate marriage, which he assumed to refer to the secret of reincarnation. He observed that "the rabbi, of blessed memory, was very circumspect regarding this, as is his way, and he did not allude to it except a very small measure. It contains several matters that require explication, but we have not received it sufficiently. . . . It has been lost over the length of the exile, and there remains of it only that which remains."⁶ Ibn Shuib's claim is that the "rabbi," or Nahmanides, knew much more than he wrote about this subject, which, due to the many difficulties of life in exile, has now been mostly lost from the Jewish esoteric tradition. Ironically, the kabbalistic secret of reincarnation, which served as a discursive node in kabbalistic mediations on the Jewish experience of exile, is regarded here as a secret doctrine that has been partially lost due to the very same historical condition of the Jewish people that it helps to explain.

By the early fourteenth century, *gilgul* was accepted by many kabbalists as a mysterious topic with authoritative status. The fifteenth-century anonymous *Sefer ha-meshiv*,⁷ an important and understudied kabbalistic text, much of which speaks in the first-person voice of God, asserts: "Know that the secret of *gilgul* is a great secret, and this lofty matter should not be degraded in your eyes. It is the secret of my divinity (*'elohuti*), truly!"⁸ But in the absence of a clear, broadly embraced authoritative tradition regarding the details of the secret of reincarnation, a wide variety of views took hold during the fourteenth and fifteenth centuries. Earlier texts were interpreted and mined for hints, and biblical phrases were parsed in order to tease out answers to many questions, such as: How many times does a soul reincarnate? Do all souls reincarnate? What is the purpose of reincarnation? Menahem Ziyyoni, writing in the latter part of the fourteenth century, summed up the range of views on this topic that he had observed:

> Know and understand, oh one who inquires, that there are numerous disagreements among the wise men of the Talmud and the masters of the Kabbalah regarding this secret. There are those who say that reincarnation only occurs three times . . . and others who say four, based on "he visits the iniquity of the fathers upon the sons, until the third and fourth generations" (Exod 20:5). And there are those who say up to one thousand, as is the opinion of the *Bahir*. . . . There is another disagreement with many opinions regarding the reason why a person is reincarnated. Rabbi Solomon ibn Adret and the rest of the kabbalists hold that it is one of two

reasons; either one has not completed their appointed time . . . or one who is righteous, but committed a sin that was not completely rectified, and he has the dust of sin; his soul cannot rise up to God as a result of the excessive weight, like straw mixed with mud, until it is refined from vessel to vessel and it becomes purified and light and it binds to the supernal spirits, from spirit to spirit until its primary dwelling and the quarry from which it was hewn. . . . There is no reincarnation without sin. There are those who say this is only for those who are *beinoniyim* (evenly balanced between merit and demerit). . . . And there is another group of kabbalists who say that even the wicked reincarnate.[9]

Many of the open questions regarding reincarnation discussed by earlier kabbalists are mentioned in this passage. The verse from Exodus cited here is frequently brought forth in discussion of how many times reincarnation can occur to a single soul. While many accepted as authoritative the tradition that this verse alludes to reincarnation, the ambiguity in its language led to divergent views regarding three as opposed to four reincarnations as the maximum number.[10] The meaning of the passage from *Sefer ha-bahir* §198 that reincarnation continues until the "thousandth generation," citing Psalm 105:8, was extensively debated throughout the fourteenth and fifteenth centuries.

The question of who reincarnates and why goes to the heart of the purpose of *gilgul*. Some regard it as a strategy to purify and elevate righteous souls. Judah Hayyat,[11] an exile from Spain who wrote an important commentary on *Ma'arekhet ha-'elohut* in the early sixteenth century, argued that the wicked reincarnate three times to correct the transgressions of negative commandments, while the righteous reincarnate one thousand times in order to perfect the performance of the positive commandments.[12] Others contended that since "there is no reincarnation without sin," only those who are evenly balanced between righteousness and wickedness have a need for reincarnation. The righteous, in such a case, need not reincarnate at all. And still others claim that even the wicked reincarnate in order to remove the "dross" that their soul has acquired.[13]

An important idea that Ziyyoni mentions here and that will be explored in more detail below is the notion that reincarnation serves to purify the soul through a process of refinement. Suffering in multiple lifetimes is part of how the soul attains a state in which it is fit to return to its source in the divine. The traumas of multiple Jewish lives, played out on the stage of Jewish history, have, according to such a view, a redemptive purpose.

One of the reasons that kabbalists give for the necessity of reincarnation is the imperishability of the soul. The author of *Ma'arekhet ha-'elohut* mentions this point in a discussion of some of the unresolved issues regarding *gilgul*.

> [The soul is a] simple incomposite intellect that is never destroyed, and therefore it is refined and reincarnated until God finds it a fitting helpmate to sustain both of them. . . . This is only two and three [times],[14] "for four I will not revoke it" (Amos 2:6). We will accept that from that point on, the soul attains merit in all respects to be purified, or perhaps it does not acquire merit, and it is punished eternally. Or perhaps a place is prepared for it according to its station until the time of the resurrection; blessed is the one who knows. But as we have said regarding the subsistence of the soul, that those that are worthy of eternity are the souls of Israel, since they are emanated from the place of life. . . . If there are those among the souls of Israel that are punished eternally . . . in no way is it ever destroyed.[15]

Citing verses from Job and Amos, the anonymous author ends up with the possibility entertained by other kabbalists that the soul reincarnates either three or four times. But what happens if the soul does not attain sufficient merit? Is it lost, or punished eternally? Is it stored somewhere until the time of resurrection? All of these are entertained as possibilities, since the question of what happens to a soul in the event of a series of reincarnations in which they do not succeed in purifying themselves is acknowledged as unknowable, as indicated by the phrase, "blessed is the one who knows."

One matter, however, is clearly stated in the above-cited passage: Jewish souls are divine and eternal.[16] Many other kabbalists make a similar claim. For example, Isaac of Acre asserted that the soul is "emanated from [God] himself, without any intermediary, as it is said, 'and he breathed into his nostrils' (Gen 2:7), and one who breathes into something from the soul of his spirit gives it of himself. For this reason, [the soul] never ceases to be, forever and ever."[17] Joshua ibn Shuib similarly asserted that "the soul itself can never perish since it is not composite such that it could be dissolved. It is fitting to be eternal, in keeping with the quarry from whence it was hewn."[18] Or as the *Sefer hameshiv* unequivocally states, "The essence (*'atzmut*) of the soul is the essence of divinity, truly!"[19] How does an eternal soul experience time and history? Is there a single life, and then an eternal afterlife? Or does the soul return, and if so, is it a reward, or a punishment? What does it mean to live multiple lives as an exiled Jew?

The idea of reincarnation solves some of these problems, but raises others, since the possibility of many sinful lives in a row is far from remote. Multiple lives of suffering are also very possible. But resolving all such questions does not seem to have been a prerequisite for medieval kabbalists when it came to embracing the doctrine of *gilgul*. Reincarnation and the eternality of the soul functioned as related discursive structures for thinking about the movement of the Jewish self through time. The claim that the soul is never lost enabled a way of imagining how the self, over multiple lifetimes, will inevitably still be present in the anticipated future in which the terrors of history will finally be resolved. Such is the position adopted by the anonymous author of *Sefer 'ohel mo'ed* in the fifteenth century, arguing that reincarnation is "derived from God's mercy, may he be blessed, in order that no soul be lost from among the people of Israel. For if it has not perfected itself, it reincarnates a second and third time . . . and by means of this they perfect themselves and are not lost . . . they completed their reincarnations and perfect themselves and become worthy to experience the arrival of the redeemer and the resurrection of the dead and the world to come."[20] For this author, reincarnation guarantees that all Jewish souls will experience the delight of messianic redemption. The passage continues to note that experiencing the "afflictions" of Jewish history over multiple lifetimes is an act of divine mercy, since such suffering is preferable to fate of the soul in *gehennom*.[21]

One issue that looms over all of the discussions of reincarnation is that of theodicy and divine justice. Making sense of suffering that appears to be at the hands of God, and not directly as a result of any obvious transgression—a question as old as the book of Job—is of course part of what makes reincarnation attractive for monotheistic, covenantal theologies. Tractate Berakhot of the Babylonian Talmud interprets Moses's request of God, "Show me your ways that I may know you" (Exod 33:13), to mean, "Why is it that there are righteous who prosper, righteous who suffer, wicked who prosper, and wicked who suffer?"[22] The incongruity between the expectations of divine justice and the observable realities of human life is an unavoidable problem with a long legacy in premodern Jewish thought. Reincarnation was one strategy embraced by kabbalists for addressing some of the problems associated with this issue. For kabbalists who deployed the discourse of *gilgul*, suffering in the present was understood to be the consequence of transgressions in a past life or lives. The anonymous commentary on the *Sefer ha-temunah* stated clearly that punctilious performance of the commandments can provide an escape from the cycle of death and rebirth, since "those who merit to act in this manner, their soul does not undergo reincarnation from body to body."[23] They even offer the practical advice that during prayer, "one should direct their intention toward *Binah*, the place of repentance, the gate of the letter *nun*, [to] redeem one's soul from reincarnation."[24] The anonymous author of *Sefer 'ezrat ha-Shem* from the fourteenth century claimed that "the soul returns because of its own sin, or that that of the generation. That soul returns until its ways are improved and it attains a positive disposition."[25] Future incarnations are, according to this author, the product of either individual or communal inadequacy. And though additional lives can be a torment, they are also an opportunity for improvement.

Every new life, for these authors, is a chance to exert positive theurgic power through the proper performance of commandments, thereby repairing past transgressions and preparing the self for future reintegration with the divine. Drawing upon the kabbalistic notion that the performance of *mitzvot* causes the divine presence to "dwell" upon the bodily limb that performs the mandated action properly,[26] the *Tiqqunei Zohar* argues that individuals reincarnate until they have caused God to dwell upon every bodily limb: "Meritorious is he who causes him to dwell upon each of his limbs, to make for him a place to dwell; to cause him to reign over each limb, with no limb devoid of him. For if the Holy One, blessed be he, did not dwell upon a single limb, he would have to return in reincarnation because of that limb, until his limbs were complete, all of them perfected in the icon of the Holy One, blessed be he. For if one is missing, he is not in the image of the Holy One, blessed be he."[27]

Attaining the full image of God requires the performance of the law, potentially over the course of multiple lifetimes. Reincarnation is a second chance to fulfill the divine will. Once the indwelling of the divine upon the body has been completed, the cycle of reincarnation for that soul comes to an end. The span of time accorded to a Jewish soul to perform God's will extends across a significant duration of time and multiple human identities.

For the authorship of *Tiqqunei Zohar*, ignorance of the secret of *gilgul* leads to an inability to understand misfortune. Past lives, they claim, account for suffering in the present, and for those who have not received the esoteric knowledge regarding this subject, the suffering is exacerbated by virtue of its incomprehensibility.

> "The pit was empty; there was no water in it" (Gen 37:24). There was no water, but there were snakes and scorpions.[28] So, too, there are ignorant individuals whose houses are filled with angels of destruction, which are the "snakes and scorpions," which strike them with numerous strikes and afflictions, which they caused before they came into the world in reincarnation into these particular bodies and homes. When these snakes and scorpions strike them with afflictions, they cry out, "Woe! Woe!" They have conflict with everyone in the home, and they contend with the masters of *gehennom* who judge them. There are others who pass all of their days in peace and tranquility, without any misfortune of that of the seven lands, and then they are judged in the seven domains of *gehennom*. There are people such as those, and there are people such as these, and only to the wise men of these mysteries has the knowledge of it been transmitted.[29]

Two models for divine justice are suggested in this passage. For some, the transgressions of past lives cause retributive divine forces to torment reincarnated individuals in their present lives. These agents of divine punishment from the realm of the afterlife known as *gehennom* bring misfortune upon their unsuspecting subjects. The suffering that ensues creates disharmony in the individual's relationships as they lash out in a futile attempt to find a cause for the negative events of their lives. Yet for others who are guilty of transgressions in past lives, their present life is completely free of misfortune. Punishment for such individuals takes place in the afterlife and not a reincarnated identity. No specific reason is given for why God sometimes chooses one course of punishment over another. The point the passage makes is simply that the individuals in question cannot understand the meaning of the experiences they encounter over the course of an individual lifetime. Divine justice spans a longer time frame. But, for those who are privileged to have access to the secret doctrine of reincarnation, the author observes that the full implications of the events of human life are better understood. This passage suggests that the kabbalistic idea of reincarnation enables Jews to grasp the hidden divine strategy for punishment and reward as it plays out over multiple lives. Armed with such knowledge, life's misfortunes become more legible and appear less absurd.

To be sure, reincarnation does not resolve all problems associated with questions of theodicy.[30] The world in which souls pass through multiple lives is still one in which the righteous suffer on the stage of history. The fact that such misfortune is the result of the transgressions of a past self only begs the question as to why God does not directly and immediately reward the righteous and punish the wicked. The authorship of *Sefer ha-kanah* acknowledged these problems in a discussion of reincarnation in relation to reward and punishment.

"Righteous who suffer" [refers to] one who came to the world previously, and his acts of righteousness were many, so the Holy One, blessed be he, brings him into the world another time to receive punishments. He is born during the waning of the moon, and all of his circumstances entail suffering and lack. For thus would reason and justice have it, that the righteous should bear diminishment, since he was born diminished, in order that he can atone and rejoice in the world to come. "The wicked who prosper" [refers to] one who came into the world previously and committed many transgressions. God, may he be blessed, brings him another time to receive his meager rewards, and he is born during the fullness of the moon, and he is filled with all goodness, and then he is cast out and sent to *gehennom*. . . . Moses our teacher, peace be upon him, asked why the Holy One, blessed be he, brings such an individual twice in order to receive his punishment or reward [and does not accomplish this] the first time, and he received no answer regarding this.[31]

In an ironic reversal of the apparent fate of the righteous individual who suffers, the author suggests here that this is God's way of providing the opportunity to atone for any minor transgressions from past lives. By enduring a final incarnation in which the righteous soul is born during the waning of the moon, leading to a life of painful misfortune, they are prepared for eternal reward in the world to come. Conversely, the wicked are born during the waxing of the moon so that they will enjoy the temporary delights of this world as reward for the minor good deeds that they performed in their previous lives. But, the author claims, after this final incarnation, they go on to suffer in *gehennom* in the world to come.

Like the author of the *Tiqqunei Zohar*, the *Sefer ha-kanah* regards knowledge of the secret of reincarnation to be the key to understanding the meaning of the fortune, or lack thereof, that individuals encounter over the course of their lifetimes. The suggestion is that things are often the opposite of how they appear. Any individual life is only one step in a multistage process as the soul moves through time. Knowing this secret—which is to say, being informed of the kabbalistic tradition regarding the doctrine of *gilgul*—provides a way to reconcile the suffering of the righteous with divine justice. But as can be seen in the conclusion of the above-cited passage, not all problems are resolved. The anonymous author says that Moses himself asked God directly why the righteous and wicked are not rewarded or punished immediately, in their own lifetimes, for their deeds. Tellingly, the text asserts that no answer was given.

A few later authors take up the question of why the righteous must reincarnate three times, despite their virtuous behavior, and offer creative solutions. Moses of Kiev suggests that the reason why people must reincarnate three times, despite the level of their righteousness, is that because the soul is comprised of three aspects—*Nefesh*, *Ruah*, and *Neshamah*—it must reincarnate three times so that these aspects can return to the tenth, ninth, and third *sefirot*, respectively.[32] Judah Hayyat expressed the same view in his early sixteenth-century *Minhat Yehudah*.[33] The author of *Sefer ha-meshiv* argued that the three reincarnations are part of the progressive development of the soul over three lifetimes, with the first including only the *Nefesh*, the lowest level of the soul, and then *Ruah* in the second, and *Neshamah*, the highest and most divine aspect of the soul, manifesting only in the third. This, the author argues, "is the secret of the *gilgul* of Moses," suggesting that otherwise it would be hard to imagine why a man as righteous as he would need to reincarnate at all. But the author, speaking in the voice of God himself, does not leave the discussion there. The divine voice in the text then describes the state of reincarnation in the present and relates an additional secret. "Know that today only the *Nefesh* and *Ruah* enter the world, and the [souls with a] *Ruah* are few in number. Those who possess a *Ruah* are endowed with a certain spark (*nitzotz mah*) from the power of *Binah*, and not a true *Neshamah* hewn from there. This is the secret of *gilgul* today."[34] The deficiencies of the human world, and the course of human affairs, are, for this author, a consequence of the broader deficiency of human souls, even those of Jews, that manifest in the world. The present state of history thus reflects the imperfections in the conditions of the souls that are reincarnated into the world.

None of this, of course, answers the question as to why God would create such a tortuous, multilived path for the soul in its journey toward completion. Why, then, do these texts continue to use the idea of reincarnation if it cannot resolve the basic problems of theodicy? It would seem that the discourse of multiple lives still does other important work. By expanding the duration for human experience, and by manifesting the soul in multiple persons over time, new possibilities emerge for imagining the meaning of the events of a particular lifetime, or the state of the world in a particular historical moment. The secrets of past and future lives hold enticing possibilities. And by claiming that Kabbalah provides some of the answers—or at least provides a sense of the true dimensions of the question—the Jewish esoteric tradition is portrayed as a way to gain visibility into God's plan for the unfolding of events over time. Perhaps this is why the author of *Sefer ha-peli'ah* states that those who neglect Kabbalah and only study Talmud and halakhic texts are forced to undergo *gilgul* as a consequence![35] Knowing this secret may not provide insight into why the righteous are forced to endure lives encumbered with the inevitable tragedies of the human condition. But it does offer access to a much more complex picture of the forces that influence the journey of the soul through history over multiple lives.

Guiding History

The duration of time during which human history as we know it takes place extends from the expulsion from Eden to the time of messianic redemption. During that tumultuous period, souls reincarnate. According to the *'Or ha-ganuz* commentary on *Sefer ha-bahir*, "The soul reincarnates, according to its deeds, until the great Jubilee, called 'one thousand generations.' "[36] The present reign of history is one of recycled souls. For some kabbalists like Joshua bar Samuel Nahmias in the fourteenth century, death and rebirth are essential to the flow of generations and the movement of history. As he puts it, "Were it not for the departure of one generation, another could not be created in its place. Souls return and reincarnate until the end of the seventh [millennium], for in the seventh, the attributes are completed, and fine vessels are fashioned."[37] This comment offers a zero-sum calculus wherein the deaths in one generation are necessary to make space for the rebirth of those souls in the next. Only in the final eschaton will the soul be "completed," at which point the cycle of reincarnation—and the process of human history—will finally come to an end.

According to some kabbalists, *gilgul* is one of the tools God uses to guide history. The choice of when and in whom to reincarnate a soul is a way to secretly influence the flow of human affairs.[38] The repetition of souls among biblical characters from different generations is one way that, the kabbalists claim, God shapes the history of Israel. Jacques Le Goff notes that in Jacobus de Voragine's late thirteenth-century *Golden Legend*, the soul of any given departed saint can "continue to sacralize time after death" since "at any moment God can send the saint back to earth on a particular mission or to perform a miracle."[39] For the kabbalists as well, death does not prevent the souls of the righteous from serving as instruments of God's will as he shapes the events of human history. Reincarnation was a mechanism for divine action that allowed for a subtle form of intervention into the events of human history. It also suggested that the main contours of future historical events were planned by God well in advance as part of a long-term plan. By bringing certain souls back into the world at specific times and places, God crafts historical outcomes.

To take one prominent example, the authorship of the *Tiqqunei Zohar* embraced the association of Abel, Seth, and Moses as incarnations of the same soul.[40] The Hebrew letters of Moses's name are interpreted as an allusion to this secret. The author claims that the three letters, *mem, shin, heh*, are an acronym in reverse order, "meaning that he is Abel (*Hevel*) and he is Seth (*Shet*) and he is Moses (*Mosheh*). And Moses extends to each and every generation, and each and every righteous person."[41] The recurrence of the same soul in these three important biblical characters suggests that God, according to this author, carefully selected this particular soul for serving the singularly important prophetic role of transmitting the Torah. Judah Hayyat commented on this passage and suggested that Abel's sin was similar to his father Adam's, and that the transmigrations of his soul into Moses through three reincarnations was "in order to correct that which had been made defective, and thus you should understand that Moses is Abel, and know why the Torah was transmitted through him."[42] To advance such a claim is to argue that the foundational event of the revelation at Sinai was most emphatically not an afterthought of history. The spiritual seed for the redemption of Israel from Egypt and the revelation of God's law to his chosen people was planted in the body of the second child born to Adam and Eve. That seed came to fruition through the mechanism of reincarnation over time in order to carry out the divine plan for human history.

Many other kabbalists accepted the idea that the letters of Moses's name indicate the three biblical persons in which he was reincarnated.[43] Another tradition related in the *Sefer ha-meshiv* literature suggests that Abel's soul reincarnated into Noah and Isaac.[44] The exact pathway of the souls of the first people related in the Bible seems to be less important than the claim that it was through these souls that God secretly guided the history and fate of the people of Israel. Other souls from biblical characters are also charted across time through multiple lives in order to show the divine hand behind human history. Isaac of Acre, for example, associated the secret of the reincarnation of Abel with the broader purpose of reincarnation in general. He regarded it as a divine stratagem to create particular historical outcomes.

> Know that the secret of Abel is the secret of reincarnation, alluded to in Ecclesiastes, "one generation goes and another comes" (Eccl 1:4). And it is said in *Sefer ha-bahir*, "the generation that already came."[45] And know that

the Holy One, blessed be he, created this matter out of his great mercy and kindness for the sake of the soul, that it not be lost. He, may he be blessed, created souls in the worlds, and he, may he be blessed, knew why. This is the means for reviving "dead corpses,"[46] which are bodies. For if, heaven forbid, one sins when at first a soul arrives in his body, that man is cut off, and the soul reincarnates and does not return to its place until it has atoned and been cleansed of sin and offense. Therefore, by his power, may he be blessed, the soul returns a second time, in a different body, in order to cleanse the soul when it endures suffering in the second body. In this manner up to four times, including the first time which is not reincarnated. This is as it is written, "The fourth generation shall return here" (Gen 15:16). . . . For this reason, we have been commanded with regard to levirate marriage, for the man who is cut off and dies, certainly his sins are the cause. In order that his soul not be lost, it is incumbent upon his older brother to be the closest relative as a levirate . . . and then his soul will return to the other body and become cleansed, and then "return to God who bestowed it" (Eccl 12:7). The question of Job also depends upon this matter, for he protested continuously and would say "I am innocent and without sin, I am distraught."[47] He did not know the reason [for his suffering] until Elihu came and made known to him the ways of the Holy One, blessed be he, regarding the matter of the soul. Also, regarding the subject of the ten martyrs, they were the ten sons of Jacob concerning the matter of their brother Joseph, and they were punished with death. That was for the sake of the souls' returning to their place. So too with regard to Tamar's actions. She understood this matter and this great secret. . . . And so too Naomi, who knew this. . . . And Scripture says, "who instantly repays those who reject him with destruction" (Deut 7:10), which is to say, despite the fact that a man be wicked, in order to destroy him the Lord provides for him in this world in order to reward him for whatever good actions he did in this world, in order to deprive him of the next world, and then his soul does not benefit from reincarnating three times.[48]

Isaac of Acre adopts the position that the reincarnation of the soul is an act of divine mercy, designed to enable the soul to rectify past transgressions.

Like other kabbalists, he connects this to the biblical commandment of levirate marriage, arguing that when a man procreates children with the widow of his brother who died childless, it enables the departed brother's soul to be reborn in order to atone for the sin that led to his early death. Job's suffering is explained as a result of his actions in a previous life; the ten martyrs are described as reincarnations of the souls of the ten sons of Jacob who must suffer for the act of selling their brother Joseph into slavery in Egypt; and Tamar and Naomi are described as pursuing their particular, idiosyncratic versions of levirate marriage because they were familiar with this secret doctrine and were intent on bringing forth the historically essential souls that would result from those unions. At both the individual and collective levels, reincarnation serves a redemptive purpose.

In the continuation of this passage, Isaac of Acre returns to the particular case of Abel and his multiple lives:

> Now I will return to the subject of Cain and Abel. . . . Seth was incarnated (*hit'aber*) in place of Abel, as it is written, 'God has provided me (*shat li*) another offspring in place of Abel, for Cain has killed him' (Gen 4:25). Seth was also incarnated into Moses, as it is said, "the lord was wrathful with me (*ve-yit'aber*) on your account" (Deut 3:26). Therefore, Moses merited to be worthy and fitting to receive the Torah. This is alluded to in the letters of Seth and Abel; the *shin* of Seth, *heh* of Abel, letters of Moses, *tav* of Seth is Torah, *bet lamed* of Abel are the thirty-two paths of wisdom.[49]

Building upon the notion espoused by earlier kabbalists that the biblical idea of '*ibbur*,[50] or the "impregnation" of the moon, in fact refers to the secret of reincarnation, Isaac of Acre suggests that Abel, Seth, and Moses all possessed the same soul. He then interprets the letters not only of Moses's name, as we have seen above, but also the other letters of Abel's and Seth's names in order to derive the secret meaning of their successive lives. While the three letters of Moses's name represent the three biblical persons of his soul, the other letters in Seth's and Abel's names are interpreted as allusions to the Torah and the thirty-two paths of wisdom by means of which, according to the opening passage from *Sefer yetzirah*, God created the universe. This special soul, and the three important lives it led, is a tool for setting the stage of history. The initial step of manifesting the Torah in the world was taken, according to Isaac of Acre, when Abel came into the world as the first of the three persons his soul would inhabit. Reincarnation for such authors served as a discursive device for describing God's forethought and vision for shaping historical events.

The Hebrew letters of the names of other characters from the biblical narrative are interpreted in a similar fashion to that of Moses. The *Sefer ha-peli'ah*, for example, discusses the kabbalistic tradition that the three letters of Adam's name, *alef*, *dalet*, *mem*, refer to three persons: Adam, David, messiah.[51] The suggestion is that from the ensoulment of the very first human being, even before the expulsion of humanity from Eden, God intentionally set in motion a chain of events that would eventuate in the redemption of humanity and the end of history by means of the messianic king from the house of David. The *Sefer ha-peli'ah* depicts David, rather than Adam, as the actor in this tale who knows the full consequences of his unique, historically important soul. According to the anonymous author of the text, "King David, peace be upon him, was a very wise man who was knowledgeable concerning *temurot*, and when he saw Uriah, he recognized that he was the snake that tempted Eve. And when he saw Bat Sheba, he recognized that she was Eve, and he knew that he himself was Adam. He wished to take Bat Sheba from Uriah, since she was David's soulmate."[52] David's wisdom regarding *temurot* or "exchanges" of one thing for another—a term sometimes used to refer to the doctrine of reincarnation—is depicted in this passage as the reason why David was able to know that he was justified in sleeping with Bat Sheva, the wife of Uriah and his own military officer. David, it is claimed, had the special ability to recognize the origin of his soul, which revealed to him that he was the reincarnation of Adam, Bat Sheva was the reincarnation of Eve, and Uriah was the serpent from the garden of Eden. Armed with this knowledge, the text asserts that David knew how to take action in order to reunite his soul with his primordial soulmate, and to free Eve's soul from the clutches of the evil snake. This action accomplished far more than the perfection of David's and Eve's souls—the very souls responsible for the blunder right after creation that set the present version of human history in motion. This text suggests that by reuniting Adam's and Eve's souls in the persons of David and Bat Sheva, David advanced God's plan for history by procreating the line destined to bring forth the messiah.

Through reincarnation, the end of history is bound with its beginning. Such a discourse offers a stark image of the historical process as one where God secretly orchestrates banal and even morally problematic human events in order to ensure that history moves forward according to plan.

The path of Adam's soul through King David and then into the messiah son of David is understood by some kabbalists as a secret designed explicitly to offer hope to Jews as they contemplate the painful state of living in exile. The author of *Kaf ha-qetoret* argues that knowledge of the secret of the three incarnations of the soul of the first man provides Jews with the motivation to continue moving through history, and a reason not to give in to the despair that history's terror could create. As the text describes it,

> The Holy One, blessed be he, acts like one who is traveling on a path, and his inward parts are wracked with thirst. He asks his companion, "Is there any water to drink along these paths?" He says, "There is, but a bit further. We must continue," until he has led him the entire way by means of hope. Such is how the Holy One, blessed be he, acts. By means of hope, he leads the people of Israel through all pathways, from reincarnation to reincarnation, and until the end of these three reincarnations of Adam, it would seem that Israel moans many moans, until the three reincarnations of Israel have passed, which are Adam, David, messiah.[53]

Living under the conditions of exile is compared here to wandering along a path in need of water. When the traveler asks his companion if there is any water to be found, the author's meaning is clear; the question Jews all must face in exile is whether history has any meaning or purpose. Does God have a plan for Israel, and will they be rewarded for adhering to Judaism? The response is that knowledge of the kabbalistic secret of the reincarnations of Adam's soul is like the companion's encouragement along the thirsty journey. If the Jewish people continue on, there is guaranteed reward in the end. The pathway that Jews must travel is history itself, with its many agonies that leave them "moaning" as they move forward through time. But, the author argues, God has given them hope by sharing the secret that, from the very beginning with the soul of the first human being, God has been planning the redemption of the Jewish people. The full arc of history from Eden to redemption has been planned with the creation of Adam. Armed with this hopeful knowledge, the author encourages his fellow Jews to forge ahead. History is not arbitrary. The end was already planned in the beginning.

Just as Israelite characters like King David move history through the reincarnation of their souls, the author of *Kaf ha-qetoret* also suggests a divinely predetermined path for the souls of prominent non-Jews. He notes that David felt great distress with regard to the power that Esau has usurped in the realm of the supernal chariot. However, this will resolve, according to this author, through the reincarnation and eventual elimination of the soul of Esau. As he puts it, "It is necessary for Esau, who is Edom, to reincarnate three times. This is as the prophet has stated, 'For three transgressions of Israel, for four I will not revoke' (Amos 2:6), which is to say, he will not merit a fourth reincarnation, since he will be cut off at the third. One is the reincarnation of Jesus the Nazarite, and one is Armilus the *satan*, which is Gog and Magog, and that is his end."[54] Christian nations, according to this author, have only temporary power in the present, since their downfall has been divinely predetermined. The soul of their founding progenitor—Esau, or Edom—reincarnated into Jesus, which enables Christians to make use of their stolen power from the divine realm. However, with the final incarnation—the third, that will not be followed by a fourth according to *Kaf ha-qetoret*'s reading of the verse from Amos—the soul of Esau will be eliminated. The end of Christian power will happen when the soul of Esau/Jesus remanifests in the person of Armilus, the last champion of Rome, or Edom, in the great final messianic battle with the messiah son of Joseph.[55] When, as the *Sefer Zerubavel* relates, Armilus is killed by the messiah son of David, then, according to *Kaf ha-qetoret*, David's soul will finally eliminate the soul of Esau from the world, as well as from the realm of the divine chariot. The resulting effect will be the defeat of Christian power and the coronation of the Jewish messianic king. Knowledge of the secret future of the souls of David and Esau offers a glimpse into the divine plan for redeeming the Jewish people from the forces of history.

One interesting question that some kabbalists address is the pain that certain biblical personages may have felt when contemplating their future descendants. If they were given prophetic insight into the ways of reincarnation and the nature of some of their progeny, might they not have reservations about reproduction? Would it be unreasonable for them to feel that history would be better served if they refrained from having children in order to avoid the negative consequences for the Jewish people that their descendants will create? For Joseph ben Shalom Ashkenazi, an important kabbalist from the late thirteenth to early fourteenth century who dealt extensively with this topic,[56] history cannot be engineered by people in this way. He argued that "despite the fact that one is aware that his future descendants will be idolators, like Manasseh and Ravshakeh, [or] the sons of Hezekiah, king of Judah . . . he must not refrain from procreation, and if he does so, he has no share in the world to come."[57] He then observed that the soul derives from the *sefirah* of *Tifferet*, where they are like birds that fly forth from the supernal tree of souls to be born, together with their gendered counterparts, into the world. To refrain from reproduction, Ashkenazi argues, is to deny a divine mandate.

In order to explain why procreation is a commandment despite the fact that history does not move in a linear manner toward steady improvement over time—which means that future generations with wicked individuals are inevitable—Ashkenazi presents a very nonlinear vision for historical progress. He describes a world in which bad things happen, but for the purpose of elevating the soul through historical suffering. History's tragedies are, according to this view, part of a divine plan that entails a complex process of creation and destruction in order for history to attain its purpose.

It is known that all things in the world are subject to being and dissolution, ascending and descending according to *din benei halof,* from ascension to ascension, and from ascension to degradation, and from degradation to degradation, and from degradation to ascension. Therefore, dissolution is not the loss of something for no aim, for the dissolution of one thing is the coming to be of something else, and therefore, despite the fact that one knows that in the future there will be reincarnated individuals from the permutation those who betray the Lord, he must engage [in procreation], and by means of this he will ascend. Despite the fact that it will be obvious to all that this is far off, it is close from another perspective; in order that a process of refinement upon refinement and judgment upon judgment should come upon him, so that he will become like pure silver. Therefore, "one who refrains from procreation diminishes the divine image"[58] for he returns the cast-out and wayward souls.[59]

Using the more general category of *din benei halof*,[60] a kind of principle of destruction and regeneration, Ashkenazi argued that procreation and reincarnation are inevitable parts of this process.[61] Creating future generations who will "betray the Lord" may create historical events and outcomes that seem like the opposite of progress. But when considered from the perspective of the elevation of the soul, historical misfortunes such as these are how souls move forward in the quest for perfection. The "dissolution" of one thing, or the occurrence of an event that is, on its face, negative and destructive, is also, according to Ashkenazi, the coming to be of something new. This is why he claims that the Talmud commands procreation. Not to do so thwarts God's plans and prevents the necessary, albeit painful, steps that history must take in order to resolve the flaws that Jewish souls have acquired.

The assertion that the movement of souls across generations through reincarnation is how God influences the events of history is a claim regarding divine providence over the shape of historical time. The reiteration of certain souls at certain times creates specific historical outcomes, like the revelation of the Torah through Moses with the soul originally given to Abel. It also creates negative events, depending on the nature of the soul that returns to the world, and the pain that it must undergo—or create—in order for the process of spiritual refinement and elevation to take place. The broader point that emerges from these passages is that God uses reincarnation to control history. Any given individual in any particular time or place on the historical timeline is, according to this view, there for a reason. If they live in a period in which history appears to be moving in a bad direction (and when do people not feel this way?), these authors reassure their readers that a secret Jewish doctrine reveals the surprising truth that such moments are hopeful signs of progress. Everything, and everyone, that happens in the world has, they claim, been specifically crafted for a purpose. From this perspective, one should not expect a world in which everything improves over time through human ingenuity and cooperation. The world, for them, is a painful place, and through that pain, history secretly attains a divine objective.

The Crucible of History

Reincarnation and the doctrine of the *shemittot* both entail an analogous form of recycling that extends the temporal frame of both the individual and the cosmos. Bahya ben Asher noted this symmetry at one point in his commentary on the Torah, written in the early fourteenth century: "Just as the *shemittot* of the world return and recycle (*mitgalgalot*), so too the soul, after it has received its recompense in the garden of Eden or its punishment in *gehennom*, returns after a time to the body to receive that which is its due, measure of measure."[62] The cycling of worlds and souls moves through stages, each with its own particular character and nature. Just as each person into which a soul incarnates is unique, so too are the cosmic cycles, as we have seen in the previous chapter. Particularly important for many of these authors is the fact that the present cosmic cycle is that of *Gevurah* or *Din*, harsh divine judgment. The present world is filled with misfortune, and many kabbalists suggested that this is in order to purify souls and eliminate the "dross" that they have acquired in past lives.

But that is not to say that reincarnation is purely a punishment. As the *Sefer ha-temunah* describes it, "[God] establishes a covenant with the righteous as well as the wicked, for he does not desire the death of the wicked,[63] but rather that he should return by means of reincarnation (*gilgul*) . . . this attribute refines silver sevenfold (based on Ps 12:7)."[64] The anonymous commentary on this passage notes: "They shall return, and their souls will be reincarnated from generation to generation, for the Holy One, blessed be he, 'reaches out his hand to transgressors,'[65] so that their souls will be reincarnated and thus cleansed of their sins, 'and they shall return to God' (Ps 22:8)."[66] An anonymous text fragment from the late fifteenth or early sixteenth century also comments on this issue. This unique text, cataloged as *'Inyan ha-gilgul* (On the matter of reincarnation), was copied by Shalom bar Saʿadia ben Zeitun, a scribe known from other sources who may have been among the Jews of Sicily who were expelled in 1492 and settled in the Galilee region.[67] In describing the text that he is about to copy, he states: "I found a long composition when I was in the city of Syracuse that spoke of the secret of *gilgul*, and this is an abbreviated version of what I took from it."[68] The text itself cites a few classic Spanish authorities, such as Nahmanides, Bahya ben Asher, and the Zohar. It briefly discusses some of the main questions concerning reincarnation, such as how many times a soul returns, which biblical characters were connected through reincarnation, and what happens at the time of resurrection if a soul occupied multiple bodies over the course of several lifetimes.[69] As we saw above, there was some uncertainty in the fourteenth-century sources regarding the question of who reincarnates and why. Is it only for the righteous, the wicked, or those who fall somewhere in between? For the author of this text, the answer is unambiguous: both the righteous and the wicked reincarnate in order to attain perfection for their souls. As the text puts it, "The secret of *gilgul* applies to the righteous, in order that they become perfected body and soul. And for the wicked as well it is clear that they will reincarnate so that they can repent and return their souls 'to the Lord who gave it' (Eccl 12:7)."[70] The perfection of the soul over multiple lifetimes is thus a part of the human condition. Each lifetime presents every soul with possibility.

Nonetheless, the present era of the current *shemittah* entails particular challenges. In this world, harsh judgment reigns, and the transgressions of past generations have created a version of history that can only be resolved through multiple lives of suffering Jewish souls. Every Jewish individual must endure the challenges of this world in order to refine their souls. Kabbalists commonly use the image of refining pure metals from ore to describe the purpose of the Jewish soul suffering the torments of exile in the current *shemittah*.[71] This process, in which the "dross" that the soul has accrued in earlier lives is removed, entails a painful course of suffering through the travails of exile. According to this view, both collective and individual Jewish misfortune help to move history forward toward redemption by removing contaminants that Jewish souls have acquired in past lives. Just as the fires of the forge separate gold or silver from impurities, so too, they claim, the agony of exile removes the dross of sin. The collective movement of Jews through history from exile to redemption is, for such authors, attained through the individual process of purging the soul. This way of understanding the hidden divine purpose behind historical events creates a perspective from which historical difficulties can be understood not as setbacks, but as the world proceeding as God intended. Misfortune is the soul's opportunity for improvement. The very act of suffering becomes, for such kabbalists, a way for Jews to move history toward its triumphant conclusion. In their view, when Jews live difficult lives as a subjected minority in exile, they are not the passive subjects of history. Through their many trials over multiple lives, Jewish souls, in the kabbalistic imaginary, are the primary agents of historical progress, moving along the path charted specifically for them by God.

The process of refining souls is often associated with the cryptic comment in the Babylonian Talmud that "the son of David will not arrive until all of the souls of the *guf* have been consumed."[72] The *guf*, or "body," referred to in this passage is interpreted by Rashi to be a kind of supernal storehouse of souls that must be depleted before the messiah can arrive.[73] However, according to *Sefer ha-bahir* § 184, this comment is taken to mean that the messiah will not arrive until "all of the souls in the human body [have been consumed], and then the new ones will merit to go forth, and then, 'the son of David will arrive,' will merit to be born, for his soul will come forth new with the others."[74] In his commentary on the Torah, Nahmanides briefly noted in his exegesis of Deuteronomy 30:2 that this passage from the Talmud entails a "great secret,"[75] which is interpreted by some of his expositors as a reference to reincarnation. For instance, the text known as the *Kabbalat Saporta*[76] explains Nahmanides's allusion as referring to those souls "that will reincarnate in the future, [until] they are purified and no further souls any longer reincarnate in a body, as it is said, 'and you shall return to the Lord your God' (Deut 30:2), which is to say, when they will be purified and will return to God, then, 'the Lord God will restore your former state and have mercy upon you' (Deut 30:3)."[77] Reincarnation, in this view, purifies souls, and when that process of refinement is complete, redemption arrives. As Joseph Angelet puts it,

> If you comprehend the secret of the soul that "returns to the Lord who gave it" (Eccl 12:7), you will understand that this is because it requires purging, and it benefits from this purging. It returns through the secret of impregnation . . . and they do not ascend above until they are rectified as is appropriate, removing all dross from them. "The son of David does not arrive until all of the souls of the *guf* (body) have been consumed,"[78] and the power of the bodily ore is removed from it, which prevents it from returning to its place, according to the secret of "And you shall return to the Lord your God" (Deut 32:2).[79]

When the existing souls have been sufficiently refined, they cease to reincarnate into a human body or *guf,* enabling them to return to their source in the divine and to usher in the messianic era. Exhausting the souls of the *guf* does not mean, as it may indicate in the rabbinic passage, the completion of souls from a supernal storehouse. Instead, Angelet asserts that messianic redemption requires that Jews first refine their souls through a series of incarnations so that they no longer need to return to an embodied state. Reincarnation is thus connected to the progression of the individual soul toward perfection over the course of multiple lifetimes, and the progression of the Jewish collective toward national redemption.[80] Isaac of Acre makes a comment to that effect on the meaning of this obscure Talmudic passage, noting that "the messiah son of Joseph arrives close to the end of the period of reincarnation, so that all those souls that remain from sinners and who are still subject to reincarnation will, through their deaths, obtain absolution and be redeemed from reincarnation. Then, truly, the messiah son of David will arrive."[81]

The need for human souls to reincarnate is attributed by some kabbalists to the same act that set the process of human history in motion—the sin in the garden of Eden. Had they not eaten from the tree of knowledge of good and evil, Adam and Eve, they claimed, would have enjoyed eternal life, and there would have been neither human history as we know it, nor a process of expiatory reincarnation. The anonymous authorship of the *Sefer ha-peli'ah* and *Sefer ha-kanah* texts describe the sin of Adam and Eve as the key event that pushed history off course during the current *shemittah* and created the need for reincarnation. According to the *Sefer ha-kanah,* "There is not a single soul in existence until the end of this *shemittah* that does not undergo judgment deriving from Adam."[82] In an intriguing passage from the *Sefer ha-peli'ah*, Adam and Eve's eating from the tree in Eden caused

> three deaths; one above,[83] second, the corporeal present death—two deaths—and then also the death of the reincarnation that will be reincarnated. When Adam came and was led astray by the woman and took hold of the attribute that he was warned against, divine mercy immediately departed, and it was decreed that everything should be conducted according to this principle until the end of the *shemittah*; sometimes life, sometimes

death, above as below. The Holy One, blessed be he, knew all of this [in advance]. Adam did not heed the command because the *shemittah* required this, so that everything would undergo trial, for if it were not so, then Adam would live forever and never die, since the soul that God breathed into him would grant eternal life, and God did not intend this, except in the *shemittah* of *Tifferet*, since the righteous at that time live forever and ever. Do not say, "If this is so, why did he command him?" For trial is only for those who have been commanded.[84]

In response to the question as to why God would arrange things in the garden of Eden such that death, misfortune, and reincarnation—in short, history itself—would be possible through the transgression of eating from the tree of knowledge, the anonymous author offers a bold reading of Genesis. God knew, the author claims, that Adam would not obey the admonition not to eat from the tree, and this was part of a broader plan to ensure that the current *shemittah* would involve human death rather than eternal life, and the attendant woes of history. By introducing death into the human and divine realms, as well as in future lives through reincarnation, the author suggested that Adam was in fact creating the outcome God intended. An eternal life of bliss is appropriate for the next *shemittah*, governed by the *sefirah* of *Tifferet*. For the present world of *Din*, however, it seems that our author regards death and suffering over the course of multiple lives as a necessary feature: so much so that God felt compelled to contrive a situation in which that would be the inevitable result. The text reflects a degree of anxiety regarding the possible implications of this idea, since this passage concludes with the exhortation to the reader that "this secret must not depart from your mouth, and even though it is written in a book, hide it away and conceal it."

The multiple lives of Adam's soul provide some kabbalists an opportunity to describe history's missed opportunities. *Kaf ha-qetoret*, for example, describes the three incarnations of Adam as each, in their way, a missed opportunity to resolve the problem of history and return to the original, Edenic divine plan. With each incarnation of Adam's soul there was a failure to reach the sanctity of the divine realm.

Adam merited the supernal wine, and Abram, who was Adam through the secret of reincarnation, merited the supernal fire. Adam was not worthy, but instead erred with the "foaming wine, fully mixed" (Ps 75:9), which is the secret of the impure Samael. He did not believe, and he acquired the "foaming wine," which is the secret of darkness, as has been hinted. Noah also desired to acquire enlargement of joy of the lower wine, until he erred in the darkness of Samael. . . . And because he was not worthy, then, due to the iniquity of the generation, he was reincarnated into Moses, and Moses attained the supernal wine and the supernal fire, and for this reason, God appeared to him from the flames of fire at the outset of his prophecy. He wished to attain the supernal sun, but he could not because of the contentiousness among the Israelites.[85]

Adam began with a soul worthy of the sacred fire of the divine realm. The transgression caused him to miss this opportunity, which led to his soul reincarnating into Abram, before his name was changed to Abraham. The author of *Kaf ha-qetoret* understood the nature of Adam's transgression as taking hold of the impure wine of Samael, the "darkness" of the lower world, as opposed to the fire of the divine realm. Noah likewise was led astray by Samael's inferior, impure wine of the world of darkness. But Noah and Moses are said to be forced into reincarnation not only by their own inadequacy, but also by the faults of the generation in which they lived. Healing history through reincarnation, it seems, is a group effort. And Adam was not the only character for whom this was the case. *Kaf ha-qetoret* also notes, "That which happened to Adam happened to David. For had he not sinned, he would have lived eternally in the garden of Eden, and so too, had David not sinned, and had he taken that woman [Bat Sheva] legally, the messiah would have been born at that time, and the people of Israel would have been spared numerous reincarnations."[86]

In the interregnum between the expulsion from Eden and messianic redemption, the cleansing effect of reincarnation takes place, as we have seen, in the realm of human history. Some kabbalists claim that the pain of the current exile of the Jewish people is particularly severe for a reason, in that it enables the final stage of the necessary spiritual refinement. The tribulations of Jewish history, according to this view, are not to be viewed as setbacks in the progression of sacred time, nor as a problem for covenantal theology; they are part of a necessary cosmic unfolding that Jewish souls must endure over the course of multiple lives in order to be refined of their impurities. According to the *Sefer ha-temunah*, of the four main historical Jewish exiles—Babylonia, Persia, Greece, and Edom—the current exile of Edom, associated with Christianity, is the longest and most severe. However, such suffering serves a purpose, according to the anonymous author. Exile, both physical and spiritual, refines the soul and prepares the world for redemption. The present exile is exceptionally harsh and lengthy in order to accomplish this purpose.

> Great is the final exile, longest of them all. By means of its extended duration, sins and evildoers are neutralized, as well as everything that is harsh and difficult, "and they shall return to the Lord" (Ps 22:8). Our exiles and redemption are delayed to purify and distill all souls in order to appear before our God, rectifying form and soul. . . . Thus, souls are reincarnated for purity and cleansing, so that all will return to their point of origin as in the beginning, cleansed of the filth that derives from the [current] attribute with its harsh nature.[87]

The delayed arrival of the messiah during the current extended exile, according to our anonymous author, enables Jewish souls to undergo the necessary reincarnations in order to eliminate dross.[88] This process requires multiple lives that occur in the context of national exile. The severity and duration of the current exile are designed to enable the necessary spiritual refinement to take place in order to bring about the spiritual and physical "return to the Lord." How long this will take is unknown, though there is an "appointed season" for the end of the current exile. The anonymous commentary on this passage notes, "Even though each of the exiles has appointed durations, they have not been revealed to us." However, the commentator also notes that at the end of the process of suffering that plays out over the course of Jewish history, "both the body and the soul will be purified, for punishment and reincarnation are expiatory for them." According to the author of the anonymous *Sod 'ilan ha-'atzilut*, souls that have intermixed with impure spirits or other entities over the course of their permutations in the current *shemittah* "must undergo an exceedingly lengthy and grievous exile in the fourth generation, at the end of which 'he will perform mercies for thousands' (Exod 20:6). Therefore, the soul needs to be purified of all contaminants."[89]

Collective national suffering, together with the individual trials and tribulations associated with reincarnation, are all part of a necessary process that will eventuate in redemption and an escape from the cycle of history. In the meantime, however, the text asserts that historical tragedies, in the form of wars and violence, are to be expected. The commentary on the *Sefer ha-temunah* notes, "It is necessary that the exile of the body and exile of the soul be very long, in order that every harsh and evil thing, sins and transgressions, shall be brought to an end, and they will all then return to God, for they shall all be righteous. Therefore, he sealed this, our exile, and lengthened it in order that the souls shall be purified and they shall return pure before God. . . . For both the body and the soul shall be purified, since punishment and reincarnation are a purification for them."[90] While the anonymous authorship of *Sefer ha-temunah* accepts that the current *shemittah* is filled with misfortune, they also reassure the reader that they are living in the waning years of the dominance of the power of this eon. Soon, they claim, the process of messianic redemption will begin. Before that, however, the negative forces of the attribute of *Din* will become only more manifest in the world in the form of wars and tragedies. As the commentary on the text understands it, "We are already at the end of the harsh attribute, and the exiles are already ending, and the harshness of the attribute is departing, and since it is departing, it functions with greater force."[91] On this reading of world affairs, increasing conflict among world powers is a hopeful sign that the end of history is near.

Writing at the end of the fourteenth century in Castile in the wake of the wave of violence that spread throughout that region, killing as many as 100,000 Jews, Shem Tov ibn Shem Tov[92] suggested a particularly pointed explanation of Jewish history through the idea that Jewish souls require refinement.

All of our exiles, and all who have been slain, and who groan and are oppressed, it is in keeping with perfect justice. This is as they have said, "The son of David will not arrive until all of the souls of the *guf* have been consumed" (b. Yevamot 62a), to reincarnate. And verily the verse says, "For I will not be angry forever, and I will not be wroth eternally; for spirit is

enshrouded before me," in the body, "and souls I have created" (Isa 57:16).
When reincarnation ends, the divine light will arrive by means of the new,
pure forms, and there is no doubt that since the day of the destruction of
the first Temple, there have been no new souls, rather all of them reincarnated. . . . And the generations became increasingly degraded. The more
they progressed, the more the shells gained power, and the ten *sefirot* of
impurity were active. . . . All of the children of the exiles were designated
to reincarnate in exile and to fall under the exile of the archons of the nations . . . for the longer the exile persists, the divine light is more concealed,
and the handmaid reigns and dominates increasingly . . . and the rebels
and heretics of the prior generations reincarnate . . . and the sages have said,
"The Son of David will not arrive until all of the kingdom has turned to
heresy" (b. Sanhedrin 97a). . . . The generations closest to redemption are
the "bad figs" (Jer 24:8; b. Eruvin 21b), and they themselves are the ones
prepared to bear their sins and to enter into the refiner's crucible. . . . The
one who bears the afflictions "and makes of himself a guilt-offering" (Isa
53:10), that is to say, a sacrifice, he shall live eternally in the world that is
entirely good. . . . When all of the souls have ceased and have been refined
and tested in the crucible of deprivation at the hands of the archons of the
gentile nations (*sarei ha-'umot*) . . . then, the supernal God will arouse the
supernal glory to wage his wars, and the time of the great judgment will
arrive, and the rebels and the sinners will be judged for all generations.[93]

Ibn Shem Tov draws upon a combination of some of the ideas that we have
discussed above in order to sketch a comprehensive view of Jewish history and
Jewish suffering at the hands of foreign entities, in a way that demonstrates the
"perfect justice" of the divine plan. Like other kabbalists before him, he asserts
that reincarnation refines Jewish souls and prepares the way for messianic redemption. The refining process entails suffering at the hands of the archons,
gentile nations that draw their negative powers from the external regions of
the divine realm. As history progresses, according to Ibn Shem Tov, conditions deteriorate, and the evil forces gain in strength in order to perform the
increasingly difficult task of purifying the remaining Jewish souls. This is due
to the fact that over time, the souls that remain that require reincarnation are

particularly problematic. Therefore, historical suffering must increase in order to be strong enough to accomplish the task.

The obligation of Jews as history moves toward its final culmination, in Ibn Shem Tov's view, is to accept their fate and "bear their sins" in the "refiner's crucible" of history. Their suffering renders them equivalent to a guilt-offering sacrifice, which will then purify their souls and hasten messianic redemption. An increasing intensity of Jewish suffering is a sign of the impending redemption. Reincarnated Jewish souls must accept and endure their suffering in the "crucible of depravation" inflicted upon them by gentiles as a vital contribution that they make in the final pangs at the culmination of history. The end result, he argues, will be an inversion of the conditions of the present moment—the enemies of Israel will be defeated, sinners will be judged, and the righteous will be vindicated.

In 1542 in Safed, Judah Haleiwah cited this passage from Ibn Shem Tov without attribution in his *Tzafnat fa'aneah*.[94] However, he adds a comment praising those who sacrifice themselves for the sake of Judaism, "as did some of our wise men during the forced conversion in Portugal." He contrasts this with the conduct of Shem Tov ibn Shem Tov's great-grandson, "Levi ben Shem Tov the poet, who sinned and led the masses into error and turned to apostasy and abandoned his religion," who then, in Ibn Haleiwah's view, received eternal punishment.[95] Just as Ibn Shem Tov argued that enduring historical suffering is the sacred task of the Jewish people in order to purify their souls and attain messianic redemption, Ibn Haleiwah suggested (with no small degree of irony, given that he is speaking of a fate that befell one of Ibn Shem Tov's own descendants) that abandoning that task through conversion condemns the soul forever.

Jewish Souls in Foreign Territory

Starting in the late thirteenth century, some kabbalists began to embrace the idea that Jewish souls can reincarnate into the bodies of non-Jews and animals.[96] As Leore Sachs-Shmueli has demonstrated, "Joseph of Hamadan was the first kabbalist to develop this doctrine in an explicit and systematic manner," and his work, via other kabbalists such as Menahem Recanati, came to have an important influence on later authors, including the *Temunah* texts, as well as the *Sefer ha-peli'ah* and *Sefer ha-kanah*.[97] The idea was not without its detractors, and even those who recognized it as an established tradition expressed reservations. Judah Hayyat, for example, refers to the idea of Jewish souls reincarnating into animal bodies as "a matter that is hard to believe."[98] Some take this idea seriously enough that it has implications for how animals are treated. Menahem Recanati, for example, cites the view that the prohibition against eating a limb torn from a living animal can be explained on the basis of the reincarnation of human souls into animal bodies. "If we believe in the secret of reincarnation into animals, one who eats the limb of a living animal is like one who consumes one of the limbs of one of his friends—understand this. Some of the later kabbalists have said that one who egregiously transgresses this commandment and does not repent is reincarnated into an animal that is mauled by animals and eaten while it is still alive. . . . These are their words, and if it is Kabbalah, then we shall receive [*ve-'im kabbalah nekabel*]."[99] While he may have had some reservations regarding this tradition, Recanati embraces it enough to relate it as a matter taught among the "later kabbalists,"[100] possibly referring to Hamadan. In the sixteenth century, David ibn Zimra embraced this doctrine without question.[101]

The wandering of Jewish souls beyond the confines of human, Jewish bodies constituted an extra layer of exile. For some kabbalists, this predicament of the Jewish soul will persist until the world returns to its source in *Binah* at the end of the current *shemittah*. As the main text of the *Sefer ha-temunah* describes it, the final redemption of the Jubilee will entail the return of

> the wandering and exiled [souls] from all of those worlds, due to their many wrongdoings; some in the bodies of human beings in keeping with the cause of the *shemittah*, some in beasts, some in animals, either pure or impure, or in creeping things—all in keeping with a supernal or lower cause. Some are in lifeless vessels, such as the wood of trees or other such things, or in fire or water—everything in keeping with the cause of the supernal or lower gradations of the soul summoned forth since the day of its emergence from its source until its return to the gate of its point of origin; some at times that are near, and some at times that are distant, some confined to bodies, and some in the supernal entities, and some suspended

among the spirits, some to receive punishment, and some at rest. All of these paths are sealed and are known, according to the Scriptures, only by the ones who comprehend—the kabbalists. All of this occurs to bring about the purification of the soul by means of the path upon which it proceeds.[102]

Souls, according to the anonymous author, can end up via *gilgul* manifesting in the bodies of animals, insects, and even inanimate substances and elements.[103] They can also find themselves suspended in the spiritual realm. The duration of such wanderings and the degree of suffering it entails vary from soul to soul. However, all souls undergo these experiences in order "to bring about the purification of the soul." The anonymous author of the *Sefer ha-kanah* argues that the reincarnation of a human soul into an animal is generally the final step in the soul's process of purification. "Even though [the souls of] people can be found in some animals and birds, know that they are completely righteous when they depart from there. They required a small measure of purification, and then they are as the supernal angels."[104] For this author, individuals who require only a limited degree of additional refinement, rather than those who are particularly blameworthy, are among those who reincarnate in animal form.

Some kabbalists understood the fact that righteous human souls can be reincarnated into animal bodies to be the reason why kosher slaughtering practices are designed to involve a minimum of pain. According to the anonymous commentator on the *Sefer ha-temunah*, it is very important that

> there not be any suffering inflicted upon animals, since souls are reincarnated into them. . . . Therefore it has been established that an animal should be slaughtered only with a carefully inspected knife, without flaw or imperfection, and without suffering. . . . Slaughter should be meticulously arranged and examined, as it is written, "and you shall love your neighbor as yourself" (Lev 19:18) . . . for occasionally one will think that they have slaughtered an animal, and in fact they have slaughtered some righteous person whose soul has been reincarnated into that animal, and it is necessary not to cause it to suffer.[105]

In a world in which displaced souls can intermix outside the bounds of the human, encounters with animals always carry the possibility that they involve a wandering righteous soul. For this reason, the author claims, kosher slaughtering must be performed only in keeping with Jewish law. The author of the *Sefer ha-peli'ah* even suggested that unlearned Jews should not eat meat at all, since they lack knowledge of this mystery and are therefore unable to release the trapped Jewish soul by consuming the animal.[106] Some kabbalists also suggest that *gilgul* is the reason for the ritual of animal sacrifice in the Temple. By offering an animal on the altar, a Jewish soul that has been reincarnated into that animal could be released. As the anonymous *Sod 'ilan ha-'atzilut* from the circle of the *Sefer ha-temunah* literature puts it, "If a soul departs from the proper path and intermixes with these [impure] spirits, and through that intermixture with them takes on some of their impurity . . . and it forgets the commandment of God that it received, it transmigrates from body to body to one of the animals or impure creatures. Therefore, the soul needs to return by way of animal sacrifice."[107]

Jewish souls also reincarnate, according to some kabbalists, into the bodies of non-Jews.[108] According to Isaac of Acre, the phenomenon of conversion, both to and from Judaism, can be explained on the basis of reincarnation. He relates the following teaching regarding this question: "I have received a tradition that all of those from among the nations of the world who convert [to Judaism], their souls were among the souls of the children of Israel, and therefore God drew them near beneath his wings 'so that no one be kept banished' (2 Sam 14:14). From this I am inclined to say that, so too, the souls of those who convert away from Judaism were the souls of the wicked from among the nations of the world, and God removes thorns from his vineyard and pushes them away with both hands and returns them to their source, which is the aspect of Samael."[109] The recycling of souls in the conditions of exile creates a kind of ethnic confusion. Jewish souls end up in gentile bodies, and non-Jewish souls, which also reincarnate in his view,[110] are sometimes born into Jewish bodies. Through conversion, this problematic intermixing, as this kabbalist sees it, is resolved. This enables Isaac of Acre and other kabbalists to stabilize the Jewish/non-Jewish binary even as they problematize it. Though the present world is one in which Jews and non-Jews intermix, the underlying nature of their souls remains unchanged, if hidden. He argues elsewhere that famous converts from biblical and rabbinic sources, such as Ovadia, Rabbi Akiva, Rabbi Meir, Shemaya, Avtalion, and Onkolos, were, in fact, lost Jewish souls returning to their true nature, since "truly, the spirit of the *Shekhinah* dwelt upon them, despite the fact that they were not from the seed of Jacob, since they were converts. The correct answer to this is that although their bodies were not from the seed of Jacob, their souls were from the seed of Jacob, and truly, they stood at Mt. Sinai."[111]

The reincarnation of Jewish souls into gentile bodies is presented in some cases as a form of divine intervention in order to move history forward during the course of the present *shemittah*, and to provide covert protection for the Jewish people as they suffer at the hands of gentile nations. According to the commentary on the *Sefer ha-temunah*, for example, "Ruth's soul was originally from among the holy souls of the people of Israel, and because of the fact that she transgressed earlier and was obligated to undergo reincarnation and exile, and she was reincarnated among gentile nations. But then Boaz returned to the world, and Ruth's soul was his soulmate, and she had already received all of her punishment and her time had arrived to be reincarnated into this world together with Boaz, her soulmate."[112] This claim suggests more than the prehistory of the biblical character of Ruth. The implication is that long before the events related in the Bible, God had Ruth's soul undergo reincarnation into a gentile body so that she would be ready at the proper moment to "return" to the Jewish people and serve her unique and essential historical role as the great-grandmother of King David.[113] Ruth's experience of *gilgul* into a gentile body was, the anonymous author suggests, a divine tactic to keep Jewish history on track.

The same text also suggests that the reincarnation of Jewish souls into gentile bodies is a method whereby God blunts the force of gentile oppression of Jews in exile. "Sometimes the souls of righteous individuals are reincarnated into gentiles, and this is for the benefit of Israel, so that they will have mercy upon Israel. . . . It is for this reason that they have mercy and protect those of the people of Israel who speak and act contrary to the gentile nations—not from their own nature that derives from being a gentile and [deriving from] the power of Esau, but rather from the power of those souls that were reincarnated

into their physical matter from the seed of Israel."[114] Instances of Jewish flour-
ishing under gentile authority, or moments of comity with non-Jewish powers,
this text suggests, are, in fact, the result of *Jewish* souls reincarnated among
gentile peoples in order to grant protection to their fellow Jews. Intercommu-
nal dynamics in which Jews encounter sympathetic non-Jewish partners are
not, the author asserts, a reflection of a quality that those who draw from the
"power of Esau," an amplified force of the attribute of harsh judgment that
governs the current *shemittah*. Such moments of calm in the Jewish journey
through the course of history are secretly engineered by divine providence by
means of the strategic reincarnation of Jewish souls.

Shem Tov ibn Shem Tov understood the reincarnation of Jewish souls into
gentiles to be a particularly elevated kabbalistic secret. In his *Sefer ha-'emunot*
he observed:

> Sometimes reincarnation does not occur only among close relatives,
> and sometimes the inner [souls] are brought outside, according to one's
> deeds. . . . Regarding these matters I have discovered wonderous insights
> recorded by the wise ones, and "they are the concealed matters of the
> world" (b. Hagigah 13a), and I have not presumed to record it, however,
> I will convey one matter to you; that Ovadia, who was an Edomite prose-
> lyte, was a prophet who prophesied regarding the fall of Edom, and he was
> reincarnated according to a supernal plan for his body to be in the state
> of a gentile until the arrival of the proper time for him to convert, and
> therefore it would be more fitting for him to prophesy regarding the fall
> of his people. The truth is that his inner form was holy, from "the council
> of holy beings" (Ps 89:8). Thus, the wise ones have said that the souls of
> converts were also present at the giving of the Torah (b. Shevu'ot 39a), to
> indicate that their origin is the house of God, and there they return.[115]

The kabbalistic idea related here, which Ibn Shem Tov claims to have received
from an unnamed source, plays upon the tradition related in the name of
Rabbi Meir in b. Sanhedrin 39b that "the prophet Ovadia was an Edomite
convert, in keeping with the expression, 'from the forest derives the axe [that
cuts it down].'" In the Talmudic context, the claim is merely that Ovadia's
birth among the people of Edom lent a degree of ironic divine justice to his

service after conversion as the prophet who proclaimed Edom's impending destruction at the hand of God. In the kabbalistic rendering of Ovadia's origin among the Edomites, there is far more than irony at play.[116] The implication is that Ovadia's soul was in fact of Israelite extraction, and it was placed into an Edomite body via reincarnation as part of a "supernal plan" that would enable him, over the course of multiple lives, to have the proper impact upon the course of human events in this world. The divine choice of the timing of the multiple lives of this particular prophet, according to this tradition, is another example of a claim that God uses the multigenerational process of reincarnation in order to intervene in Jewish history. For kabbalists like Ibn Shem Tov, the divine use of reincarnation in this fashion provides a discursive strategy for suggesting that God has not abandoned the people of Israel to the arbitrary forces of history. The preplanning implied in a process of reincarnation that began generations before the intended outcome coveys the notion that God has an arrangement in place for ensuring that Jewish historical experience moves forward according to a predetermined course, even if that is not how things appear to observers at the moment. An important tool, according to the above-cited passage, for accomplishing this divine oversight of the historical process is the selective placement of Jewish souls into gentile bodies.

Meir ibn Gabbai provided intriguing evidence for what may be a lost tradition from the literary circle of the *Sefer ha-temunah* regarding the intermixing of Jews and non-Jews through reincarnation. Building upon the classical kabbalistic notion that Jewish souls are emanated from the inner realm of the divine *sefirot*, while non-Jewish souls derive from the "external," he discusses how the present cosmic era has confounded the proper boundaries between Jewish and foreign peoples.

> The souls of the gentiles are from the side of impurity, and they are impure. I have seen in the Book of Unity, by the author of the *Temunah*, a wonderous matter, written thus: "The physical forms of the people of Israel were worthy of being different and distinguished from the species of man, in keeping with their powers and souls. However, the harsh decrees of the *shemittah* dictate that the powers are intermixed and transmigrated in many diverse bodies. All of them will return to their appropriate place

by means of the animal sacrifices acceptably brought upon the altar." The interpretation [of this passage is], it would have been fitting for the bodily forms of the people of Israel to be different from all other creatures, just as their souls and powers are different and distinct from them, so too it was appropriate that their bodies should be [different]. However, the nature of the present *shemittah* and its harshness will not permit this, since . . . the souls of Israel are intermixed with the bodies of gentiles. Those that are intermixed into the bodies of animals are redeemed by means of the animal sacrifice that is brought acceptably upon the altar. However, with the bodies of gentiles, it is not possible to redeem the soul from it unless he converts to Judaism."[17]

The passage that Ibn Gabbai cites from the *Sefer ha-temunah* literature is not found in any of the extant sources from that corpus that I am aware of. But the tenor of the comment is certainly in keeping with the world view of the surviving sources. The suggestion that, given the vast difference between Jewish and gentile souls, it would have been appropriate for them to have different bodies reflects an ethnocentrism that is clearly embraced in these and other medieval kabbalistic sources. The fact that Jews and non-Jews are physically similar is regarded by this author as a negative consequence of the current *shemittah*. The intermixing of Jews and non-Jews through reincarnation is a challenge that, in Ibn Gabbai's reading of this passage, Jews must address. For Jewish souls reincarnated into animals, sacrifice provides a solution. But for those that are trapped in gentile bodies, only conversion resolves their condition. Regardless of the authenticity of the passage from the *Temunah* literature, Ibn Gabbai endorses the view that an important problem caused by the present state of the cosmos is the displacement of Jewish souls into non-Jewish bodies.

The notion that the intermixing of Jews and gentiles is typical of the present age means, according to Ibn Gabbai, that this situation will be resolved at the end of days. However, he argues that Jews should not divulge the secret of reincarnation to non-Jews. If, he claims, gentiles understood the full implications of the kabbalistic secret of reincarnation, they would all immediately convert to Judaism. However, "God does not desire this until the sanctification of his name is brought about among the nations through great and wondrous acts that will be performed during the ingathering of the exiles and the wars of Gog and Magog. . . . Therefore, he made the people of Israel promise not to reveal the secret of reincarnation to the nations of the world."[118] While the knowledge of the kabbalistic secret of reincarnation helps Jews understand their own history and their relation to non-Jews, Ibn Gabbai suggests that *concealing* that secret is historically necessary. In order for gentiles to be present—and to be chastened—by the grand denouement of history, the secret of reincarnation must be preserved exclusively among the Jewish people. Armed with that knowledge, they alone know the true meaning of the present and the real balance of powers between nations. The future also becomes transparent to Jews who understand the winding path of the multiple lives of the soul.

Imagining the Present through Past and Future Lives

When describing the previous and future lives of the Jewish soul, medieval kabbalists were not trying to create a philosophically coherent theology. Claiming multiple lives for the soul solves some theological problems even as it creates others. The question of free will and predestination, for example, is an issue that could be problematic. But for the most part, these kabbalists were not particularly concerned with such questions. The greater emphasis of their efforts was focused on constructing a discourse for giving meaning to Jewish life and practice in the context of a problematic history. They were less anxious to resolve every theoretical problem this doctrine creates than with offering a way to imagine that God is in charge of Jewish history and that Jews who suffer in a particular historical moment are doing so for a reason. *Gilgul* creates a way of talking about the justice of the present by creating a keyhole through which to peer into the past and future.

When the present is considered from this perspective, the meaning of events that seem unjust on their face is recast as part of a divine long game for justice. Take, for example, the following comment by Isaac of Acre:

> Consider those who succeed in all things and encounter blessing in all of their acquisitions, attaining all of their desires. . . . Know without a doubt that their soul is in the first [incarnation], and if they were to follow the paths of God with his entire will, they would not be among those who

reincarnate. But this is impossible, for "there is no righteous one on Earth who does good and never sins" (Eccl 7:20). Therefore, none can escape reincarnation. . . . Know that Abel killed Cain in the days of Moses and Korah . . . measure for measure . . . the one who was slain slew his slayer, "the one who sheds a man's blood, by man shall his blood be shed" (Gen 9:6), but that very man. Therefore, when you see a murderer who dies at peace in his bed, know that it is one of two situations: either he has avenged for himself and is therefore pardoned for the sin of his murder, or it will be avenged in another body.[119]

The divergent fates of individuals, according to Isaac of Acre, can be explained by reincarnation. If they are in their first life, and if they are generally compliant with *halakhah*, they will enjoy many good outcomes. However, he also notes that it is impossible to live a fully blameless life, which means that reincarnation is inevitable for all, and that in future lives, they will suffer as punishment. He then gives the interesting example of how Abel's soul was able to take revenge on Cain's soul for having killed him during his first incarnation. Abel, as noted above, was reincarnated via Seth into Moses, and Cain was reincarnated into Korah. When Moses defeated Korah in the conflict described in Numbers 16, it was a form of measure-for-measure justice that enabled Abel's soul to settle the score with Cain. Isaac of Acre then extrapolates from this to claim that any time a murderer escapes justice, it can be accounted for through reincarnation; either the murder was justified because of an incident in a past life, or the murderer will be brought to justice at the hands of his victim in a future life. Returning in a future life to resolve the transgressions of the past is a way for the soul to heal. But that process of rectification or refinement can involve significant pain. Such discourses of reincarnation allow for a different way of viewing tragic events, including those that are created by other human beings. The message is that all events are part of a divinely ordained scheme of justice that extends far beyond the present lifetime of any given individual.

The authorship of the *Sefer ha-temunah* commentary proposed that Jewish sinners in the current cosmic cycle derive their souls from Datan and Aviram, the biblical characters who were descendants of Reuben and associated with the rebellion of Korah (Num 16:1), and associated in rabbinic texts with a number of transgressions against their own people.[120] In that author's view, "All sinners among the people of Israel in this *shemittah*, generation after generation, they all derive from Datan and Aviram, who were evil, sinners and rebels . . . for there is no generation that does not have individuals who derive from them by way of reincarnation."[121] The predations of gentile powers were not the only instances of injustice that kabbalists sought to explain. Intracommunal conflict and the presence of Jews who oppress or transgress against their fellow Jews also presented a challenge, and reincarnation offered a way to account for their actions. Such individuals, the author suggests, are present in every generation, and derive from these two bêtes noires of the Jewish lineage. Still others, such as the author of *Sefer ha-meshiv*, suggested that humanity developed from an early division between Adam's children and their descendants. Seth reincarnated as Abraham, Abel as Isaac, and the rest of the nations of the world are derived from the soul of Cain that had reincarnated into Ham. Such, according to the author, "is the secret of the nations of the world, which is the secret of the external shells."[122] Through a discourse of reincarnation, the author divides humanity into a stark binary between Jews and non-Jews in order to account for the condition of Jewish history.

Eventually, throughout the ups and downs of Jewish history and life in exile, the process that individual souls undergo over the course of multiple lives will result in a transformation of the collective Jewish experience, and even the state of the cosmos. The current stage of the present *shemittah* will eventually come to an end, and then the world, along with the souls of the Jewish people, will be renewed. Abraham Adrutiel, in the early sixteenth century, offered the following description of the role of Jewish souls in the future transformation of the world:

> When the Holy One, blessed be he, renews the world of the *shemittah*, then, the Holy One, blessed be he, reigns by means of the souls of the righteous. This is the secret meaning of [the statement in the Mishnah that] in the future, every righteous man will create three hundred and ten worlds,[123] equaling the numerical value [of the word] *yesh* (which is 310), as it is written, "To endow those who love me with substance (*yesh*)."[124] The secret meaning of this is that their souls are in themselves the sacred

entities that will be refined and reincarnated in their reincarnations and permutations, for they are the souls that enter the world, and by means of those souls the Holy One, blessed be he, creates all of the worlds, chariots, and hosts.[125]

The souls of the righteous, according to Adrutiel, will be the tool God uses to renew the world at the end of the present *shemittah*. In order for their souls to be prepared for this task, they must be refined through reincarnation. To be on the path toward this goal of serving in close partnership with God to generate the secret, better version of this world—a world without history or suffering—the soul must first traverse history by enduring multiple lifetimes. Life as an exiled Jew is the refiner's fire that prepares the soul for its unique role in the future, when they will create three hundred and ten worlds, the numerical value of "being" (*yesh*). By suffering as a refracted self through the terrors of history, the soul attains the state wherein it can partner with God to bring history to an end.

FIVE

History's Ends

Apocalyptic Secrets in the Present Tense

Raptureready.com is a website devoted to Christian end-times prophecy.[1] One particularly interesting feature on the website is its Rapture Ready Index—a number that is regularly updated based on the degree of "prophetic activity" in forty-five discrete categories of current events. The website gives a 0–5 rating to things like "debt and trade," "inflation," "financial unrest," "moral standards," "globalism," "oil supply/price," "crime rate," "liberalism," "satanism," "food supply," and "global turmoil." The greater the level of activity in each, the higher the rating. Numbers are assigned based on what the managers of the website regard as the degree of correlation in each category to the conditions anticipated in biblical prophecies. The website's designer, Todd Strandberg, claims that he can measure how closely world events reflect the biblical depictions of the period immediately preceding the rapture and seven years of tribulation. The sum of the 0–5 scoring of all forty-five categories produces a raw number that the website refers to as the "Dow Jones Industrial Average of end time activity." The website does not predict exactly when the rapture will happen. Instead, its creators refer to it as a "prophetic speedometer" that measures "how quickly the world is moving toward the occurrence of pre-tribulation rapture." An aggregate rating of 100 and below is described as "slow prophetic activity"; 100–130 is "moderate prophetic activity"; 130–60 is "heavy prophetic activity"; and above 160 is "fasten your seatbelts." The all-time low for the Rapture Ready Index was 58, recorded on December 12, 1993. The all-time high was 189, on October 10, 2016, in the lead-up to the election of Donald Trump as president. At present, November 7, 2022, the index stands at 187.

Observers of world events can find orientation and meaning both by gazing back into the origin of history, as well as by peering forward toward the future end of historical time. Each, in its own way, enables a discourse of meaning around particular events in the present, explaining how the conditions for their occurrence came to be, and how they fit into a comprehensive divine telos. The categories of historical activity in the Rapture Ready Index, for example, could be read as unrelated phenomena subject to the unpredictable, highly dynamic forces of collective human activity, devoid of any greater meaning or purpose. In other words, one could read history as having no direction or meaning. But accepting such a perspective would be to embrace the terror of history that stands deeply at odds with covenantal theology. If historical events are to have meaning, it helps if the conditions of history have a clearly articulated beginning and end. As we have seen above, Adam and Eve's sin serves as the origin of history for many kabbalists, and ongoing Jewish transgression of divine law perpetuates it. But for history to have a direction, it needs an anticipated endpoint. Messianic redemption, the idea of the world to come,[2] and the worlds or *shemittot* that follow the present world, serve this discursive role in premodern kabbalistic sources. As Gerson Cohen has remarked, "A people that would retain its inner autonomy in defiance of defeat must have an ideology of rebirth."[3] For most medieval kabbalists, the Jewish condition is restored beyond history rather than within it.

As we have seen throughout this book, many kabbalists regarded human history as a problem. Were it not for Adam and Eve's sin, the thing that we call history—the chain of often-tragic events that humans create through the exercise of free will—would not have happened. Without the fruit of the tree of knowledge of good and evil, humanity would have remained blameless, and also, according to many kabbalists, devoid of free will, or at least the will to sin. In such a world, historians would be out of work. But once Adam and Eve's eyes were opened, everything changed. Desire, choice, and inevitably, conflict and violence, became part of human life. Edenic time gave way to historical time.

When kabbalists describe the full sweep of history, like many other Western religious formations since late antiquity, they talk about a beginning and an end. The discursive strategies that kabbalists deploy to describe the end of history, at least during the current cosmic cycle, were in part a language for ascribing meaning to the present and the historical condition of the Jewish people. As Scholem has observed, "When we study the Messianic ideal we simultaneously study the nature of the Diaspora, the Galut."[4] The events of history, and in particular, the misfortunes of Jewish history, are accounted for and ameliorated, or at least, compensated, when framed in this way. And as a purported revealed secret Jewish doctrine, all such kabbalistic discourses carry the implication that by knowing how history will end—if not exactly when— Jews have been granted special insight into the hidden workings of God's plan. Kabbalistic apocalypticism thus addresses the present by sharing secrets regarding the divine plan for the end times when the imbalance of history will be corrected and the current world order inverted. As Elliot Wolfson has observed, "Apocalypticism can be classified as theopolitics, since it is predicated on the invocation of the divine being as the counterforce that will topple the imperial oppressors at a given historical juncture and thereby empower the disempowered."[5]

One important feature that many kabbalists ascribe to the messianic era that marks the end of history is the annulment of free will.[6] In one version of his formulation of the messianic era,[7] Nahmanides described a fundamental transformation of human nature that will take place when the messiah arrives. In his explication of Deuteronomy 30:6, Nahmanides stated: "Then the Lord your God will circumcise your heart and the heart of your descendants, to love the Lord your God with all your heart and all your soul, that you may live." He points out that during the entire "duration of the Torah," or the historical period that extends from Sinai to messianic redemption, "humanity has been granted the freedom to act according to their will, be it righteous or wicked." This was the case, he claimed, "so that they should attain merit by choosing good, and culpability for pursuing after evil." The messianic period, he argued, will be completely different, as he notes, "In the days of the messiah, choosing that which is good will be natural; they will not desire that which is improper and will have no craving for it at all."[8] As support for this interpretation, he cites b. Shabbat 151b, in which Rabbi Shimon ben Elazar interprets Ecclesiastes 12:1, "Years will arrive concerning which you will say 'I have no desire for them,'" in the following manner: "These are the days of the messiah, in which there is neither merit nor liability." The end of history will be like the primordial days before history, in that it will involve a return to a state in which humans lack all desire to transgress God's will. And as in many articulations of the redemptive future, there is a convergence of discourses of beginnings and endings. The perfected time of the future in which the evil inclination will cease reinstates the conditions of the ideal past, before things went awry and humans began to choose freely.[9] According to the author of *Sefer 'ohel mo'ed*, the "concealed light" that has been withheld, according to b. Hagigah 12a, until the "future era," will not be fully revealed until the end of the sixth millennium. During the days of the messiah "it will remain slightly concealed, so that sufficient desire (*ta'avah*) will remain in the world for the continuation of the species. All will act according to nature rather than the evil inclination, as it was originally before the sin of Adam."[10]

The author of *Ma'arekhet ha-'elohut* associated the cessation of the evil inclination after messianic redemption not only with the end of the Jewish desire to transgress divine law, but also with the end of the desire on the part of non-Jewish nations to oppress the people of Israel.

> In the days of the messiah, the evil inclination will be annulled. . . . During the time of exile when the Temple is destroyed, which is a time of fury, we must multiply prayers, praises, and supplications continually in order that [the foreign nations] not enslave us with harsh decrees. Since their hand has already been strengthened, it is best for Israel to be contrite and not provoke [them] during the time of exile among the peoples, since the hour is favorable for them. But in the future, during the time of perfection, the filth of the primordial snake will cease, and a strand of *Hesed* will flow forth continually. Sacrifice applies only during the present historical era (*zeman ha-hefetz ha-zeh*).[11]

The removal of the evil inclination during the days of the messiah will reverse the current state of power relations between Jews and non-Jews. During exile, a "time of fury," the nations of the world hold the advantage. It is a favorable period for them, so much so that the author urges their fellow Jews to be submissive before other nations, lest they oppress them even more harshly. The current historical era, referred to here as *zeman ha-hefetz ha-zeh*,[12] is one in which the "strand of *Hesed*" is withheld, and sacrifices are needed. Non-Jews are empowered and driven by a desire to oppress Jews. As a result, direct historical action is not a solution to the Jewish historical problem. The only option is to wait for the transformation of history that will take place, according to this passage, at the end of days, when the evil inclination will be no more, with the consequence that non-Jewish people will no longer have the power or will to oppress Jews. In this anonymous author's sketch of the nature of present historical time in comparison to the posthistorical messianic future, the difficulties of life in exile are accounted for as part of the nature of the current epoch. Just as Jewish and non-Jewish fates are inversely related, the present time and the future time are also inversions of one another.

The sin of Adam and Eve created more than free will. Many medieval kabbalists also embrace the notion that the "filth" that the snake cast into Eve created the phenomenon of death. After a discussion of reincarnation as God's mechanism for giving individuals an opportunity to correct themselves, Menahem Recanati comments on how this relates to human history as a whole, noting that

> by way of the secret of the inner wisdom, there is a wondrous matter, and it is, as you know, that the secret of the filth of the primordial serpent entered into this world through Eve, and on account of this filth, death was acquired by Adam and his descendants. . . . And when the filth will cease and the spirit of impurity will be removed from the land, God, may he be exalted, will renew his world without any other filth, and will awaken, through his power, those who dwell in the dust. . . . For in every respect, the [divine] intention for creation was not in vain, but only that it should go into effect in the future. . . . An example can be taken from the land of Israel, in that it was at first under the sway of another nature, in the secret of the seven peoples who are the secret of the foreskin and impurity, and after that, they were removed from before him and it was not ruled by anyone other than himself, and he bequeathed it to a singular people, singularly designated to his worship.[13]

Recanati's categorical assertion that God's "intention for creation was not in vain," suggests that precisely such an anxiety informed his discourse here regarding the troubling path that history takes from Eden to redemption. His argument is that God's objective—a world without death and suffering—was not thwarted, but merely shifted to the future, creating an interim period, the era of human history. An analogy can be observed, he suggests, in the ancient peoples who ruled the land of Israel. Before Israelite kings reigned over the land, seven other nations held power in Canaan. This was not, according to Recanati, an accident of history, but rather a process similar to the removing of a foreskin. Impurities, he suggests, are sometimes present initially, but it was always God's intent that they would eventually be eliminated. Just as it was God's will that the kings of Israel would rule after removing the impurity of the non-Jewish peoples from the land of Israel, so too, Recanati argues, God created a world in which a period of death and suffering is followed by a messianic future of eternal reward. The conditions of Recanati's present are described as a period of impurity, soon to be overcome in a transformative reversal that will, at last, finally reflect the original divine intent for creation.

The rectification of Adam's sin was a contested topic among Jews and Christians. As Elliot Wolfson has noted, the Zoharic authorship reverses the Pauline doctrine[14] of Jesus as the "last Adam" who corrects the flaw created by the "first Adam," by arguing that "it is not Jesus but Jacob who restores the world to its original ontic condition."[15] That is to say, the messianic redeemer descended from Jacob/Israel, rather than Jesus, will correct the sin of Adam and Eve. That redeemed future is often described as a time of rest, in that the messiah brings relief from history. In many kabbalistic descriptions of the messianic future, foreign nations will no longer hold power over Israel, and Jewish bodies and souls that suffer the conditions of physical historical exile will finally be at peace. According to the anonymous Hebrew text by the author of the *Ra'aya mehemna* and *Tiqqunei Zohar*:

> From that point onward the world will be without death or grief, as it is said, "he will remove death forever" (Isa 25:8), and the world shall rest, "for in six days God created [the heavens and the earth, the seas and all that is within them], and on the seventh day he rested" (Exod 20:11). And regarding Noah it is said, "this one will give us relief from our labor and from the toil of our hands" (Gen 5:29). At that time the verse will be fulfilled, "never

again shall I doom the earth because of man . . . and never again shall I strike down every living thing as I have done" (Gen 8:21). And the Holy One, blessed be he, will renew the souls of the righteous, and renew their bodies, "as eagles grow new plumes they shall run and not grow weary" (Isa 40:31), and it shall be rest for souls and rest for bodies. But the impure bodies, partners of Samael and the serpent, shall be expunged from the world, and so too shall God remove "tears from every face" (Isa 25:8). At that time, the verse will be fulfilled, "the new heavens and the new earth that I shall make" (Isa 66:22).[16]

For this author, the redeemed future is one without death or suffering. Like a cosmic Sabbath, it will be a time when the toil of history ends. The people of Israel will be free from the oppression of non-Jewish nations, and those who are "partners of Samael and the serpent," an allusion to the peoples of Edom, or Christianity, will be removed from the world. The righteous from among the people of Israel, however, can anticipate, according to this text, an entirely different fate. Like the "new heavens and new earth" prophesied by Isaiah, their souls and bodies will be renewed. The cycle of reincarnation for their souls, and the condition of political exile of their bodies, will cease, and they will enter a new dispensation of time.

The same author comments in the *Tiqqunei Zohar* that, unlike the redeemed future, the present world is one that conceals the impending future reversal of fortune for the Jewish people. During the current reign of history, power has been granted to illegitimate heirs. The divine kingdom has been usurped, and the world itself has been cast into darkness. Such is the unfortunate lot of the people of Israel and the divine presence in exile. But, the text warns, history is not as it would appear. Kabbalah, they claim, enables the true reading of history's traumas.

There is no king without a kingdom. In exile, "a handmaid supplants her mistress" (Prov 30:23). When the messiah arrives, it is said, "and let Your Majesty bestow her royal state upon another who is more worthy than she" (Esth 1:19). . . . At present, when she is far from the king, it is said regarding the king, "robe the skies in darkness" (Isa 50:3), and regarding the *Shekhinah* it is said, "do not gaze upon me, for I am darkened" (Song 1:6). Fools look upon the garment, and others look upon the body. In exile, all are fools. But the wise gaze upon that which is within. When redemption comes, dark garments will be removed and cast upon the nations of the world.[17]

The present state of the people of Israel in relation to that of the nations of the world is characterized in this passage as a temporary illusion. The conditions of exile during the present era create a grand deception in which the people of Israel appear to be abandoned by God. Even the kingdom of God would seem to be absent, since "there is no king without a kingdom." During exile, the handmaid reigns, and the *Shekhinah* is supplanted, meaning, the nations of the world overpower the Jewish people. Such a state causes the darkening of the divine presence, and even the world itself. The garment, or external historical conditions of the Jewish people, would appear darkened. But all of this, according to this author, is a figment of the present historical moment. Only fools, they argue, are deceived by this. And in this author's felicitous turn of phrase, "in exile, all are fools." Not so, however, for the wise, meaning those who understand the secret forces of history as revealed in the kabbalistic tradition. For Jews with this privileged access to history's hidden course and destiny, they understand that the present conditions of the Jewish people are temporary. Soon, the author claims, fortunes will be reversed, and the "dark garments" of history will be transferred to the nations of the world.

In some cases, the present historical condition of the Jewish people is related not only to the preredemptive state of the present era, but also the current cosmic cycle. The commentator on the *Sefer ha-temunah* remarked upon "the difficulty of this *shemittah*, causing the Israelite soul to undergo reincarnation and exile." But, the author suggests, Jews are not without guidance as they navigate the difficulties of the present. For this author, the Divine Presence assists them as they move forward through time and eventually ascend the levels of the Godhead, since

> the *Shekhinah* is also a shepherd for the people of Israel, who are called "scattered sheep" (Jer 50:17), until the point when the difficulty of this *shemittah* passes, and they return and ascend, together with the *Shekhinah*

accompanying them from the exile to the sacred mountain, and they shall be as a sacrificial offering in the manner of cattle and sheep, with the attributes of *Netzah, Hesed,* and *Tifferet,* and the word "peace," which is *Yesod,* and from there they ascend to *Binah,* and from there to the 150 praises of David, which is supernal *Keter.*[18]

Harsh though it may be, the present reality is temporary. Behind all events is a destiny for the Jewish people that is, for this author, encoded in the divine realm of the *sefirot.* Eventually, all of the redeemed souls of Israel will ascend to the most transcendent level of the divine.

Kabbalistic discourse adds complexity to the general biblical and rabbinic notion that, at the end of days, the Jewish people will be vindicated, and they will partake of just reward for persevering in God's law, despite the length and difficulty of the final exile. One problem that late medieval authors faced that their precursors did not was the fact that the exile had persisted for more than a thousand years. How, they wondered, could it be just for God to provide only one millennium of reward at the end of this *shemittah,* if the tortured souls of Israel have been forced to undergo an even longer duration of exile? Menahem Recanati raised this question explicitly in his commentary on the Torah. He noted that he "discovered among a few of the later kabbalists who have delved into the secrets of the Torah" that, for some, "it is difficult for them for the days of the messiah for Israel to be such a short period of time; less than one thousand years. To be just, the days of tranquility should be a thousand times greater than the days of the afflictions of the gentiles that we have endured for the sanctification of the divine name, may he be exalted and blessed."[19] The persistence of history has created an imbalance in the system. Because messianic redemption has been delayed for so long, the idea of the one-thousand-year "days of the messiah" no longer seems sufficient. If the duration of the current cosmic cycle is only seven thousand years, the current exile has an over bearing presence in the broad scope of history. Instead of making the pangs of the present seem small and passing, a *shemittah* of that length makes the pain of Israel's exile, at least in the current eon, seem unjustly large.

One creative solution to this problem advanced by some kabbalists is to suggest that divine time differs from human time. The seventh millennium at the end of this *shemittah* will be far longer than one thousand human years, since divine years and human years are measured differently. Isaac of Acre, for example, argued that the duration of the cosmos across all of the cosmic cycles is much longer than forty-nine thousand human years. At one point he speaks directly to his readers and says, "I have seen fit to write a great divine secret that one should conceal carefully. Know that one day for the Holy One, blessed be he, is a thousand of our years. . . . A year above is three hundred and sixty-five thousand years. . . . From there you can calculate and calculate until forty-nine thousand years, in which each year is three hundred and sixty-five thousand years and a quarter day, and each day above is a thousand of our years." By this reckoning, the total duration of the cosmos over the course of seven *shemittot* amounts to 17,885,012,250 years! Isaac of Acre regards this as "clear evidence that the world endures for many years, such that the heart is astonished in contemplating them."[20]

The authorship of the *Sefer ha-temunah* literature goes further and argues that as the end of the current cosmic cycle approaches, time dilates and becomes progressively slower.[21] As a result, the period of reward after messianic redemption is, when measured in relation to premessianic time, significantly longer.[22] In a cryptic comment on the four levels of redemption that pertain to bodies, souls, singers (*meshorerim*), and spheres, the author of the anonymous commentary suggests that the inclusion of the heavenly spheres in the redemptive process means that they will function differently as the end draws near.

> The redemption of the spheres will mean that they no longer need to rotate quickly, but rather, slowly. All of the stars will rest from their rotation, such that they rotate slowly rather than quickly. Therefore, the duration of times (*ha-zemanim*) will be vast, the days long, and the closer the seventh day approaches, which is the seventh millennium, the spheres will spin and rotate more and more slowly, as well as the stars, until the duration of time increases and the days lengthen so much that a day of that time will be like a week for us now. In this manner it will continue for one hundred years. The next one hundred years after that, one of their days will be like two weeks in our time. The third one hundred years, one of their days will be like three of our weeks. In this manner will the centuries

multiply until the end of the sixth millennium. All of this will come about due to the slowing of the pace of the spheres, as well as the rate of the stars. By means of this, the prophecy of Moses our teacher, peace be upon him, will be fulfilled, that says, "Give us joy for as long as you have afflicted us; for the years we have suffered misfortune" (Ps 90:15). This is the secret by means of which God will perform loving-kindness for the generation that merits to see that time, to fulfill this verse, since the days and years have been repaid double for the years that we were in exile, as it says, "for the years we suffered misfortune," the years we have experience evil, "Let your deeds be seen by your servants" (Ps 90:16), which is to say, the *shemittah* performs its actions, and prophecy is fulfilled.[23]

By imagining a slowing of time that gets progressively longer as the end of the *shemittah* approaches, this author describes a world in which the duration of reward after the end of history vastly exceeds the period of historical suffering before messianic redemption. The secret of this expansion of time after redemption enables, according to this author, a fulfillment of the biblical promise of reward for suffering years of misfortune. Even within the current cosmic cycle of harsh divine judgment, the days of messianic bliss in the seventh millennium will far outweigh the difficult period of exile and reincarnation that Jewish souls must endure as they move history toward its conclusion. The waning of the present world will entail a lengthy duration of Edenic bliss, free of sin, the evil inclination, and subjugation to gentiles. Quite telling in such depictions is the fact that the reward for persisting through exile is the opportunity to enjoy a much longer period of time devoid of history and all its terrors. When kabbalists such as the above-cited anonymous author imagined the compensation for experiencing the multiple, difficult lives of a Jewish soul in exile, they did not long merely for Jewish historical dominance. Instead, they dreamed of an escape from the contingencies of history itself.

The Archons of the Nations at the End of History

As we saw in the description of the kabbalistic notion of the supernal *sarim*, or archons, that represent each of the seventy nations of the world, the power dynamics between human nations on earth are determined by the balance of powers in the divine realm. Transgression, starting with Adam and Eve, disrupted the flow of divine energy, resulting in the diversion of blessing from the people of Israel to the nations of the world by way of their supernal archons. The proper order, in which the archons of the nations received their nourishment from the *Shekhinah*, would have left them subordinated to the people of Israel. But in the current state of the world, that order has been inverted. Messianic redemption will entail a reversion to the original divine intent, such that "the desire and passion of the seventy archons above will be to serve *Kenesset Yisra'el*, and so too will be the desire of their nations below, to serve the people of Israel and to cleave to them, and they will all worship God."[24] The end of history is signaled by the emergence of the people of Israel from their subordination to foreign powers. When the divine world is properly realigned, the human world will be one in which Israel is dominant. But it will not be a world in which history proceeds as it has, only with Israel as the people on top. Instead, the future world will be one entirely without conflict.

A tension can be observed in some kabbalistic texts between depictions of the messianic future in which the nations of the world disappear, and others in which they remain, either as humbled penitents devoted to God and to serving the people of Israel, or even as partners with Israel in an entirely new version of human society. In Robert Lerner's classic study of the role of Jews in Joachim of Fiore's apocalyptic thinking, he argued that the notion of a convergence of Christians and Jews in the postapocalyptic future was part of what made Joachim both intriguing and controversial.[25] His followers continued to discuss versions of this idea in the centuries after his death in 1202. At stake is a question debated by all three Abrahamic traditions regarding where to place the identity of the other in relation to the messianic future. Does the final unveiling of the true divine plan for humanity's destiny involve the effacement of the other, or merely their subordination to the self?[26] Will Jews, Christians, and Muslims come together, while still retaining some sense of distinct identity, or will all but one of them disappear? Medieval kabbalistic texts deploy discourses of both effacement and convergence.[27] In some cases, the triumph of Israel at the culmination of human history is described as coinciding with the annulment of the foreign nations and their heavenly archons. But in other cases, gentiles are still present in the messianic future as subordinate nations to emphasize the vindication of the people of Israel as God's chosen nation. In either case, these texts seek to emphasize the same overall message—Jews, by keeping the law, serve as the primary agents of history, exerting a hidden power that only Kabbalah can reveal. Asserting the meaning and power of Jewish practice and identity in the present involves, in such cases, a discourse of the hidden future destiny of non-Jewish peoples.

The author of *Ma'arekhet ha-'elohut* provided an example of this tension in how gentiles are imagined in the postmessianic future. In a discussion regarding the arrival of the seventh millennium, he argues that in such a spiritual age, non-Jews will be lost since they are bound to matter. But he qualifies this somewhat with regard to righteous gentiles, stating: "The righteous among the nations of the world who observe the seven [Noahide] laws that were commanded to the descendants of Noah will not be deprived of their reward, since they have observed that which was obligatory for them and have occupied the position appropriate for them."[28] In this case, some individuals from among the foreign nations will be present in the future state of the world, while others will be lost. But as a group, non-Jews will experience that time in a categorically different way than Jews will. Joshua bar Samuel Nahmias, for example, argued that, despite the fact that gentiles, as descendants of Esau and Ishmael, are able to attain a place in the world to come, the "concealed light" (*'or ha-ganuz*) is available exclusively to Israel.[29]

The realignment of power between nations will result, as noted above, from the change in the position of the supernal archons that oversee the peoples of the world. Descriptions of this impending shift provide kabbalists with an opportunity to account for the political realities of the present and the power that non-Jewish nations wield over them. The key, in their view, is how divine energy is directed through the divine attributes or *sefirot*. Menahem Recanati, for example, describes the oppression and violence that Jews suffer at the hands of Christian nations in the following way: "At first, the power of Amalek was strong because it drew from the aspect of *Pahad*, which is the seed of Esau the wicked. Therefore, they became overbearing and warlike and desired to overtake the power of Israel. However, in the days of the messiah the seed of Esau and Amalek will be blotted out from before the power of Israel, who prevail above."[30] In a world in which the aspect of *Pahad*, "fear," of the *sefirah* of *Din* is dominant, the archon of the biblical people of Amalek, and by association, Esau, is empowered. This, Recanati suggests, accounts for their warlike behavior and their ability to oppress Israel. That capacity is a function of having stolen Israel's power, which is available to them in the upside-down world of historical time. But at the end of history, after the arrival of the messiah, proper balance will be restored, the power of Israel will "prevail above," and the descendants of Esau and Amalek—that is, Christian nations—will be blotted out. This passage does more than simply describe the reversal of fortune that Israel will experience in the future. It also accounts for the conditions that Jews experience in the present. The power that non-Jewish nations have is, in fact, Recanati and other kabbalists argue, only that which their archons have stolen. The implication is that their apparent dominance is only a temporary aberration. When reality reverts to the state God intended, Israel will regain its power, and nations like Esau and Amalek will disappear.

The notion that God allowed the archons of the nations of the world to have access to Israel's power after their transgressions raises a theological problem for some authors. Would it not have been sufficient for them to lose their kingdom and be exiled? Was all of the additional oppression and violence, over such a long duration, really necessary? How is one to account for such events? The author of the *Tiqqunei Zohar* offers an innovative approach to this question.

> Woe to Samael when the Holy One, blessed be he, comes to redeem the *Shekhinah* and Israel, her children, and demands restitution from him and the seventy nations and their appointed archons [regarding] every affliction with which they afflicted Israel in exile. [This is] because, before Israel were exiled, the Holy One, blessed be he, revealed to him that in the future Israel would be under their authority, and he showed them and the seventy appointed archons under his control the reward they would receive if they honored Israel in the exile. Thus, it is written, "And the Lord blessed the house of the Egyptian on account of Joseph" (Gen 39:5).[31]

Samael, associated with the "external powers" in the supernal realm, and the chief archon of gentile nations associated with Christianity, is depicted here as having made a fateful decision. God, the text claims, revealed the future to them. When they learn of the future exile of the people of Israel, they realize that God's chosen people will be under their authority. What is made clear to them, according to this passage, is that if they used their power the right way and "honored" and protected Israel in exile, they would be richly rewarded. The implication is that God had intended the experience of exile to be much less painful, and had hoped that the nations of the world would use their power for the benefit of the people of Israel. But such was not the case. Therefore, the text declares the pain and woe that Samael and the seventy nations will experience when the time of redemption of the *Shekhinah* arrives. At that moment, when the supernal powers will be properly realigned, all those who have oppressed Israel will be called to account for having created an experience of exilic history for the Jewish people that was far worse than the punishment God had sought. As a reading of the present, this text asserts that when Christian nations commit acts of violence and oppression against the Jews, they are overstepping their mandate, for which they will be punished at the time of redemption.

Isaac of Acre combines the ideas seen here in Recanati and the *Tiqqunei Zohar* into a more complete description of the position of the nations of the world relative to Israel in the redeemed state of the world. In his description, some nations will be lost, while others will remain as subordinates to Israel.

For Amalek relies upon the attribute of harsh judgment, which is the power of Esau and Amalek, and through it they wage war against Israel. . . . In the days of the messiah . . . the luster of the light of pure splendor from the *Shekhinah* [will shine] upon Israel, and they will rule over the entire world, and they will exert absolute reign through the power of *'Emet* and *'Emunah*, and God, who is *Tifferet*, will be perfected and united, and the throne, which is *'Atarah*, [will be] perfected and united. Then Israel will blot out the memory of Esau and Amalek, and erase them from the world, and they will no longer be recalled or brought to mind. However, the rest of the archons of the nations of the world will be subordinated to Israel, bringing tribute and offerings to the Lord of Hosts, as it is said, and I have made "kings to tend your children" (Isa 49:23). Then the verse shall be fulfilled, "And the Lord God shall be king over all the earth. On that day the Lord shall be one and his name one" (Zech 49:9).[32]

Like Recanati, Isaac of Acre begins by describing the reason behind the power of Christian nations. Esau and Amalek, he claims, draw their power from the *sefirah* of harsh judgment, or *Din*. However, in the future, when the *sefirot* are brought back into proper balance, the situation will be very different. Isaac goes into more detail regarding the changes that will occur within the Godhead, noting that *Tifferet*, the sixth *sefirah*, will be perfected and united together with *'Atarah*, the tenth, which is also *Shekhinah*, who will shine forth with brilliant light that will empower the people of Israel. With this restored divine endowment, Israel will "blot out the memory of Esau and Amalek," evoking the commandment given to the Israelites in Deuteronomy 25:19, except here, Esau is included together with the biblical people of Amalek as a nation whom Israel is commanded to eliminate, such that even their memory is no more. When read in light of the medieval usage of these names of biblical nations, Isaac of Acre is clearly suggesting that Christian nations will be completely absent in the messianic age.[33] But interestingly, some other nations will remain to serve Israel and bring offerings to God. In this grand reversal of fortune for the people of Israel at the end of history, the non-Jewish nations that remain are used as a foil to the present state of affairs for the Jewish people in exile. The primary interest in this passage is to contrast the current state of the Jewish people with their destiny in the messianic future. Exile is a relational state that describes the condition of living as a subaltern minority within majority cultures and political domains. Redemption, in passages such as these, is also relational. A key feature of the messianic future is the inversion of Israel's relationship with non-Jews, which means that non-Jewish peoples must be present during the days of the messiah in order for that new relationship to be visible. But unlike the present world, fraught with discord, the future imagined here is one where the gentile peoples present no resistance to Israel's dominance. On the contrary, they pay homage to them and their God.

Moses ben Jacob of Kiev argued in *Shoshan sodot*, written in the early sixteenth century, that none of the nations of the world and their corresponding archons will be annihilated in the messianic future. All of them will remain, but in an altered relationship to Israel.[34] He comments that the prayer for redemption in the daily prayer of eighteen benedictions is a plea for release from the powers of the "master of the *shemittah* and Samael, his assistant."[35] With the arrival of the messianic age,

> all of the gates of mercy will open, and all of the supernal archons will be subdued. The attribute of *Binah* will open her gates and sound the blast of the shofar that receives from *Gedulah* with perfect mercy, until every one of the seventy archons directs their faces eastward to receive bestowal of blessing, and bestow upon their nations. By this, their obstinacy will be removed, and they will be gracious toward the people of Israel. "Kings will be their caregivers, and queens their nursemaids" (Isa 49:23), for their supernal power will fall as a result of the emergence of mercy in the *sefirot*. Do not imagine that the supernal archons will be destroyed, for this is not so. It is impossible for the internal tree (*'ilan ha-penimi*) to exist in the absence of the external tree (*'ilan ha-hitzon*). However, their power will be diminished and unable to perform the work of the master of the *shemittah*, due to the profusion of the mercies of *Binah* that have been concealed for the entire duration of the exile. Know this.[36]

The change in the dynamics of the *sefirot* that happens during the time of redemption, according to Moses ben Jacob, will profoundly alter the flow of divine energy to the archons and their respective nations on earth. The mercy that will emerge from *Binah* will emanate through the *sefirot*, affecting the archons in such a way that their power is diminished and thus unable to do the bidding of the forces of *Din*, the "master of the *shemittah*." This will, in turn, invert the historical relationship of the gentile nations to the people of Israel. Instead of oppressing and tormenting the Jewish people, the nations of the world will become their caregivers. And Moses ben Jacob emphasizes that the nations of the world will *not* disappear, because their archons above are part of a necessary aspect of the divine realm. The reason for Jewish suffering at the hands of non-Jewish nations is the concealment of these mercies of *Binah* over the course of the exile. When redemption arrives, those merciful forces will once again emerge, ending Jewish subordination. The hidden divine dynamic behind history, according to this author, is the occlusion of benevolent divine forces—not their absence. When they reemerge, history will be transformed, and the hatred of the enemies of Israel will be transformed into love.

The *Sefer ha-temunah* offers a discussion of the role of the nations of the world and their corresponding archons in the messianic future that suggests that all peoples will remain to experience shame after the messiah arrives.

> Corresponding to them is the seventy families [of nations], half of whom engage in many diverse forms of idolatry, incorporating God into that idolatry, such as Esau and Ishmael; Esau believes in "that man" (*'oto ha-'ish*), saying that he is God. Ishmael, according to their faith. So too, the rest of the peoples according to their faith. Even among the people of Israel, there are many like them, such as the Karaites, who believe in the written Torah, but not the oral Torah, and others like them. The other half [of the world's peoples] engage in idolatry that does not incorporate God into their idolatrous practice, but instead they have forgotten him completely, such as those who worship the sun, the water, the wind, and many others. . . . When the messiah arrives, God will have mercy upon the archons that rule over them, and on account of their worship of them they will be ashamed and receive their punishment, as the prophet has written, "And the moon will be abashed, and the sun ashamed" (Isa 24:23).[37]

The peoples of the world fall into two broad categories for this author. There are those who engage in idolatry, but "incorporate God" into their worship. The nations that fit this description are Christians, descendants of Esau, who worship "that man," or Jesus, and Muslims, the descendants of Ishmael. The author also seems to include Karaites as a people with a faulty, but not entirely erroneous religion. The other half of the world's population, according to this author, have no conception of God at all and are entirely off track in their religious opinions. Interestingly, this author says that when the messiah arrives, God will have mercy upon the supernal archons who rule these peoples, who will then be ashamed for having worshiped their archons instead of God. They will be punished, and, based on the verse cited from Isaiah, publicly bear their shame during the messianic age. In this depiction of the future vindication of Israel, both the archons and the nations who worship them will be present at the end of history in order to bear witness to the error of their ways. In what could possibly be a deliberately countertheological polemic against Christian depictions of the role of Jews in history, the end of days will be a time when the nations of the world serve, through their public shame, as witnesses to the truth and legitimacy of Jewish claims. Like Moses of Kiev, this passage does not suggest an inverse supersession doctrine in which all non-Jewish nations convert to Judaism in the messianic age. Instead, they remain distinct, and they publicly acknowledge the errors of their ways during the preredemptive age of history.

The World at War

The impending change in the power relations between the heavenly archons of the nations of the world and the *Shekhinah*, the Jewish divine representative, is understood by some kabbalists to directly account for wars and international conflict in the present.[38] The author of *Berit menuhah*, for example, suggests that some Jewish observers of world affairs are troubled when they see Jews suffering as a result of wars between non-Jewish nations. This is difficult since the anticipation is that "with the arrival of redemption, the son of David will come forth from his place and visit the sin of Edom upon him,[39] to repay him according to that which he did to the children of Israel, his brothers."[40] How can the dire conditions of Jewish life in the present be reconciled with this promise of impending redemption for the Jewish people? The author argues that the deterioration in historical conditions, and an increase in world conflict, is actually a hopeful sign that the end is at hand. This is because "when the light approaches, the darkness strengthens mightily, and angels of destruction spread forth in the world. This indicates redemption; when it approaches, the exile strengthens. Many among the wise stumble when they see the confusion of the exile and the many afflictions. . . . Happy is the one who holds strong to his purity, walking in the good path, distancing himself from evil during these days. Perhaps he will be saved from the grievous afflictions called the 'pangs of the messiah.'"[41] For this author, the esoteric Jewish tradition teaches that the approaching "light" of redemption causes a temporary increase in the "darkness" of exile. By sharing this secret, the author sought to offer encouragement to those, even among the wise, who succumb to despair when they consider the realities of Jewish history and its "many afflictions."

By claiming that calamitous events are to be anticipated and are part of the divine plan for guiding—and ending—human history, this text suggests a way of reading world events against the grain.[42] The idea of the archons of the nations is important here, since their anticipation of the arrival of the messiah is what accounts for conflict in the human realm, and the attendant suffering of the Jewish people. As the author argues, with the onset of the light of redemption, "the angels of destruction gather to meet this light, and there is a great battle in the heavenly abode; there is no limit to this war. And corresponding to that war which will be in the supernal realm, [will also be] in the lower realm, these with those, due to the great power that derives from the gathering of the lights into one place, in order that the people of Israel shall come to apprehend [these] matters."[43] When world affairs are read in this way, Jews should regard an increase in global military conflict among the nations of the world as an indicator of the approaching end of exile. Revealed in the kabbalistic tradition, according to this passage, is the connection between the supernal archons guiding the peoples of the world and the forces within the divine realm. As the powers within the Godhead begin to correct and revert to their proper state, the archons will wage war, and Israel will suffer. But, for the righteous who hold fast to God's chosen path, the "pangs of the messiah" will soon be over, along with human history as we know it.

Many other kabbalists advanced a similar notion regarding the inevitable deterioration of historical conditions in the final stage before the apocalyptic transformation and end of history. As Scholem has aptly noted, such a view has deep roots in biblical and rabbinic sources, since "Jewish Messianism is in its origins and by its nature—this cannot be sufficiently emphasized—a theory of catastrophe."[44] The commentator on the *Sefer ha-temunah* argued that an increase in world conflict is a sign of the onset of the messianic age.

> There is no people or nation that does not have a heavenly archon above. They are cast into disarray and contend with one another and make war in the heavens. This is why their nations engage more and more in war with one another on earth below. Such is the cause of wars in the world—it is due to their archons above. When you see a kingdom contend and make war with another kingdom, struggling with one another, this is like a message concerning the arrival of the messiah. Thus said the prophet, "I shall incite Egyptians against Egyptians . . . city against city and kingdom

against kingdom" (Isa 19:2). . . . One prevails and another is defeated, this one slays that one, and this one that, until they all fall and rise no more, for the harshness of the attribute of the letter *samekh* takes hold of them and incites them against one another, in heaven and on earth. If an enquirer asks, "There have been multiple years and times in which we have observed wars between nations of the world, and they ended, but the time of redemption did not arrive!" This is the answer: Everything is in keeping with the wickedness of the conduct of the generation, who multiply transgressions, apostasy, evil conduct, following their own path in order to anger God and nullify his commandments and Torah. . . . They make arrangements and edicts contrary to God and contrary to his Torah. Woe to us, for we have sinned![45]

Like the *Berit menuhah*, this passage suggests that wars among nations of the world result from conflict in the heavenly realm among the archons. As redemption approaches, the archons of the nations are "cast into disarray," leading to war throughout the entire world.[46] Such conflicts are to be expected because of the reign of the harsh attribute associated with the Hebrew letter *samekh*, which correlates in the *Temunah* literature with the *sefirah* of *Din* (harsh judgment). The rise and fall of nations—the very stuff of world history—is described here as a consequence of a hidden divine drama known only to Jews through the kabbalistic tradition. And as observers of this history, only Jews understand its true direction and meaning. The author of this text anticipated the objection that could be raised to this argument and noted that some might say that periods of intense conflict have come and gone in the past, and redemption did not arrive. The reason for this, the author claims, is Jewish transgression. Periods of war are opportunities for Jews to hold fast to God's law and enter the messianic age. When they fail at this and "nullify his commandments and Torah," the exile is extended. It is significant to note that for this author, Jews are more than passive observers of history. They alone can pierce the outer veil of world affairs to perceive the divine plan at work. But Jews are also, according to this passage, the primary agents of historical events. If they observe the law during the most difficult moments of war and conflict, they bring history to a close. If they do not, history will continue in order to punish them. Non-Jewish nations are, according to this author, the unwitting pawns in God's relationship with the Jewish people.

The author of *Sefer ha-meshiv* deployed the model of the reign of the *qelip-pot*, or "external shells" that empower the archons of the nations, as a way of reading messianic meaning into the events and catastrophes of current histori-cal events in the author's lifetime. In a comment on Genesis 12:10, "There was a famine in the land," the divine voice that offers revelations throughout the text states, "the secret of this famine is an allusion to and indicator of the present time in which you dwell, in which there are many famines and disruptions in many kingdoms. These are the pangs of the messiah." The purported voice of God continues by saying:

> Know that I shall give you a sign and proof for the arrival of the messiah and his revelation before the eyes of all. At first, [there will be] a great famine in every region; wars and plagues from one end of the world to the other. And if you are among those who will be protected and saved, I shall look upon you with a merciful eye—take courage and be not afraid. When these signs are proven to you, you shall be vindicated; it shall be a sign and proof of the arrival of the "end of the right" (*qeitz ha-yamin*). This will begin presently and continue, in every land, from one end of the world to the other, and you shall behold and hear this secret at the return of the Lord to Zion.[47]

This bold prediction, attributed to God himself, asserts that the impending chaos that will further grip the entire world is a sign of the arrival of the mes-siah. The survival of Israel through these catastrophic events is the proof that God provides to demonstrate that this was his plan for bringing history to a close. The merit whereby the Jews of the "present day" (mid- to late fifteenth-century Spain, when this text was most likely composed), will survive these historical traumas comes from Abraham when he endured the plague de-scribed in Genesis 12:10. According to *Sefer ha-meshiv*, "Know that because Abraham bore this plague, it was an allusion to his descendants who would endure affliction and great distress outside of the land from the power of the external shells. . . . Abraham, peace be upon him, according to this secret, left the land of Israel against his will. He was removed in order to redeem you now, in this time, by his merit. He passed through this suffering and affliction as an allusion to his descendants. This is the secret of the affliction of his wife, which is the secret of the *Shekhinah* at this time [and an allusion to] the war that she wages against the external shells."[48] The author regards the time when the matriarch Sarah was taken by Abimelekh as speaking directly to their present moment, in which the people of Israel suffer in exile. As they observe elsewhere, "At this time, Sarah is in the possession of the one who is Abimelekh, they are all days of misfortune, and then after this Sarah will return to Abraham, after the removal of the power of the shells."[49]

The secrets of history—and in particular the end of history—described in this passage, are not confined to the biblical past. Biblical events, such as the plague that drove Abraham and Sarah down to Egypt, were part of a divine plan to create the necessary conditions for redeeming the Jewish people and preserving them through the present events occurring in the lifetime of the author of the text. The biblical event described in Genesis merely set the stage. The final outcome that God intended was happening in the author's present. By revealing this kabbalistic secret, the text seeks to render the reader's present history legible. The hopeful meaning that it attributes to that history is that it has nearly reached its culmination, and that, thanks to the travails of Abraham and Sarah, the Jewish people will be protected. A world at war is to be expected. By enduring such a world while holding fast to Judaism, Jews fulfill their vital role as the central actors on the stage of human history.

The End of *Gilgul*

For many medieval kabbalists, the body and the soul each have their own experience of the exilic condition. Jewish bodies are forced to wander among the nations of the world, buffeted by historical forces beyond their control, while Jewish souls must cycle through multiple lives, enduring the hardships of multiple Jewish identities in different times and places. In other words, reincarnation is a manifestation of exile. By that same token, the end of exile and the arrival of messianic redemption signals the end of *gilgul* just as it heralds the end of Israel's dispersion among the nations. As Recanati puts it, "There are those among the later kabbalists who interpret the secret of the Jubilee, [stating] that the reincarnation of souls will cease, and all souls will return to their place of emanation, and that this is the meaning of 'and each man shall return to his possession' (Lev 25:10). . . . The allusion is to the redemption of our souls."[30] Depictions of the end of the process of reincarnation reflect an aspiration for the end of the experience of history. The journey of the soul through multiple lives is not a reward.

Righteous souls will of course be rewarded, as Joseph ben Shalom Ashkenazi puts it, "In the future, souls will merit to receive the face of the *Shekhinah*. The soul will become like a scabbard or receptacle for the spirit of the living God, and then *Binah* will bestow her spirit into them, and they will live forever."[31] Wicked souls who do not use their reincarnations to mend their ways will likewise be punished, as the author of the *Tiqqunei Zohar* says, "the wicked who do not repent over the course of these three reincarnations, of them it is said, 'I shall cause that soul to perish from among his people' (Lev 23:30). If so, Rabbi, to where does it descend? . . . The seven regions of hell (*gehennom*). That soul that does not repent over the course of these three, the Holy One, blessed be he, lowers him to these regions of hell. There it dwells for all generations."[32] As the imperishable aspect of the self, souls are never lost, though this text suggests that they can be eternally punished. But what is clear is that the reincarnation of Jewish souls does not continue past the point of messianic redemption.

Building on these traditions from the late thirteenth and early fourteenth centuries, the commentator on *Sefer ha-temunah*, likely in the fourteenth century, described how the end of exile will involve the ingathering of the wandering souls of the Jewish people. Commenting on Isaiah 27:13, "And on that day a great rams' horn shall be sounded, and the ones who strayed in the land of Assyria, and those expelled in the land of Egypt, shall come and worship at the holy mountain in Jerusalem," the author suggests that redemption will be the point when Jewish souls will have completed their tortuous journey over multiple lifetimes. And unlike the author of the *Tiqqunei Zohar*, none of them will be lost or punished eternally. Instead, all of them will be redeemed

in their bodies as well as souls that were reincarnated and exiled until the "fourth"; all of them will be relieved of their exiles. And that which the prophet has said, "and the ones who strayed in the land of Assyria, and the expelled in the land of Egypt," which is to say, those who, because of their sins, have strayed in the land of Assyria, and the "expelled," who were expelled, due to their sins, in the land of Egypt, and even those who lost their souls and spirits completely, will all be gathered at the time of redemption, and will worship God in Jerusalem.[53]

Isaiah's vision of the messianic return of the exiled Israelites and their collective worship in the rebuilt Jerusalem is interpreted here to refer to the ingathering of reincarnated souls at the end of days. All souls who have been exiled into multiple bodies because of their sins will, according to this author, find absolution when the messiah arrives. The image is one of rest from history's traumas, in which no Jewish soul, from any time period, will be left behind. The author's description of the end of *gilgul* is a claim about the purpose of persevering through history.

As noted in the previous chapter, an image that many kabbalists associated with the phenomenon of reincarnation is drawn from the statement in the Babylonian Talmud that "the son of David will not arrive until all of the souls of the *guf* have been consumed."[54] Many understood this to mean that the messiah cannot arrive until all Jewish souls have completed their cycles of reincarnation. In some descriptions of this idea, the completion of the souls of the *guf* will enable "new" souls that bear no taint from the sin in the garden of Eden to enter the world and be granted to the Jewish people. Menahem Recanati makes an argument to that effect in his commentary on the Torah:

> You already know that the souls blossom forth from the attribute called "Sabbath," and if so, then all of the souls there need to be garbed in a body and to die before the messiah comes. With the arrival of the messiah, all of the souls there are completed, and then it is "desolate" of souls, and this is as they have said, "and desolate for one thousand years." Therefore, that day that is called "Sabbath" must ascend and gather new souls in which there is no filth of the snake, which prevents them from descending into this world. This is as it is said, "I shall place a new spirit within you" (Ezek 11:19), and then will be fulfilled, "for one who dies at one hundred years of age will be regarded a youth" (Isa 64:20), "there shall yet be old men and

women [in the squares of Jerusalem]" (Zech 8:4). This period will continue
in this manner for six thousand years, "without adversary or misfortune"
(1 Kings 5:18). Thus, in the seventh millennium that we mentioned, there
are no progeny, since all of the souls in the *guf* will cease, and new spirits
and souls will be gathered to be given to the people of Israel below. Then,
there will be a new world in which there will be progeny in the world,
devoid of pollution or evil inclination. And so, in this fashion, during the
sixth millennium, the messiah will arrive after the cessation of souls from
the *guf*. The dead will be revived, and in the seventh millennium the overflow of souls below will cease. There will be no evil souls in the world for
the duration of that entire millennium, for the attribute of "Sabbath" will
ascend to receive new, pure souls. As it receives them, it will bestow them
below in purity and sanctity. All of them will live in the manner of the
days of the messiah, and this time will extend until the recompense of the
world to come. May God grant us to be among them, amen.[55]

The end of the process of purifying souls through reincarnation will enable
new souls to enter the world. The *sefirah* of *Yesod* will serve as the divine attribute that retrieves these new souls and brings them into the world. During
the days of the messiah, which for Recanati precede the mysterious "world to
come," all Jews will live as pure beings, endowed with these "new, pure souls."
Recanati uses the idea of the cessation of reincarnation to give depth to the
notion discussed above that humans will lack the evil inclination in the messianic age. The end of the desire to do wrong is a feature of the end of the recycling of Jewish souls. During messianic time, as opposed to historical time,
Jews will revert to the prelapsarian state of humanity.

In a slightly different formulation of this idea, the commentator on the
Sefer ha-temunah suggests that a *guf* of souls is present in each of the seven
worlds. In the present *shemittah*, the *guf* serves a particular purpose:

> She (*Binah*) places a *guf* in each *shemittah*, so that those souls, the souls of
> human beings, will arise in that *shemittah*. Thus, in this *shemittah*, there
> is a *guf* filled with souls, concerning which our rabbis of blessed memory
> have said, "The son of David will not arrive until all of the souls of the

guf have been consumed,"[56] and the souls of this *guf* are the souls of the people of Israel, and they come into the world each day. At the time when the redeemer arrives, may it happen speedily in our days, all of the souls will cease to enter into that *guf*, which will then generate different souls— sacred, pure, and sinless souls without filth, without idolatry, without the evil inclination.[57]

As the storehouse of souls, a *guf*, according to this author, is placed in each world by the *sefirah* of *Binah* in order to bring forth souls. In the present *shem-ittah*, the souls of the *guf* are exclusively Jewish. The onset of the messianic age brings about a change in the function of the *guf*. The souls of departed Jews will no longer enter there to be reborn into the world. Instead, new souls will be created that fit with the special nature of the messianic age; they will lack the capacity for transgression. Like in Recanati's comment cited above, this image of the messianic future of the soul culminates in the soul's transformation. The key thing about new souls is that they are innocent, untainted, and incapable of sin. In other words, humans with souls of this sort will no longer be agents of history. The end of reincarnation, like the end of exile, is the end of history. By revealing the secret divine method for bringing this about, medieval kabbalists offered their Jewish readers an opportunity to contemplate the purpose of living through history. The reward for accepting history's hardships, and for moving historical time forward through dedication to God's law, is the opportunity to enjoy time beyond history.

Resting from History: *Shemittah* and Jubilee

In the cycles of time on both the human and the cosmic scales, many kabbalists claimed that there are designated periods of rest. At the cosmic level, the seventh millennium in each world is a period where time changes, and each world is renewed. The present world of the harsh divine attribute of *Din* will see the greatest change with the onset of the final millennium, in that a world of chaos and pain will be transformed into an entirely new temporal dispensation. For many medieval kabbalists, the arrival of that period will entail a return to the divine origin of the soul in the *sefirah* of *Yesod*, the seventh attribute of the Godhead. As *Ma'arekhet ha-'elohut* states, "The seventh day belongs to

Yesod, and it is the great Sabbath, which is the world to come, which is eternal life, and it is the light sequestered for the righteous, for which all souls await, for from it they ventured forth, and there the weary will experience delight."[58] Teasing out the analogy between the seven days of the week, the seven days of creation, the seven lower *sefirot*, the seven millennia of each *shemittah*, and the seven worlds, the anonymous author of this texts associated Sabbath-like characteristics with each of the seventh temporal periods of each of these levels of sevens. Implied here is the notion that relief from work, and rest from the toils of history, is encoded into the structure of time.

The *Sefer ha-temunah* literature occasionally describes the world associated with the *sefirah* of *Yesod* as being present in each of the other *shemittot* during their seventh millennium. The text known as *Sod 'ilan ha-'atzilut* says that the seventh *sefirah* is "a delight and a rest, covenant and goodness for every light and pure emanated soul, and also for essences and *shemittot* existing in their worlds, 'the righteous as a date tree' (Ps 92:13), for the sake of exiled souls. Since it is pure and absolved of all action in the *shemittot*, there is sacred rest, in sanctity and purity, in each."[59] The quality of *Yesod*, the divine attribute of the Sabbath, is associated with the delight enjoyed by "exiled souls" during the final millennium of each world. This is not an era of "action," but rather of rest and reward. In all worlds, especially the present world, it is during the seventh millennium that the forces of history end, and the souls of the righteous are rewarded, just as on the seventh day, work ceases. This author suggested that the divine structure of time, even in the present world, limits historical time to no more than six thousand years. For Jews who believed that they were living in the sixth millennium,[60] the anticipation of the inevitable end of history, even if their soul may not experience it in their current incarnation, would have been a comfort.

The special function of the *shemittah* associated with *Yesod*, which is present in each cosmic cycle, is described by the author of the commentary on *Sefer ha-temunah* in the following way:

> The messiah alludes to *Binah*, which gathers all who are in exile, and supernal and lower exiles, even the two lights, small and great in which male and female souls dwell—they all gather in a single matter and tabernacle

of peace in *Yesod*. . . . The seventh *shemittah*, which is *Yesod* itself, is divided into seven days that are not active among the lower worlds at all. They are the completion of forty-nine gates, even though their days they are not among the *shemittot*. The days of the six *sefirot* are thirty-six, since each [*sefirah*] lasts for six thousand years, and the seventh millennium is a Sabbath, which alludes to *Yesod*.[61]

Here again, the time of messianic redemption associated both with *Binah* and *Yesod* is described as a category of time that is present in every world. The messiah's arrival is not contingent upon the whims of history. Jewish transgression may delay his arrival, but the conclusion of history is, in this discourse, a hardwired feature of cosmic time. The characteristics of the millennia of each world, like each cosmic cycle, are a reflection of God's own inner life. At the broadest level, the unfolding of time in the cosmos follows a predetermined course that matches the structure of the Godhead. Built into that structure is a time of rest and reward for the wandering souls of the Jewish people.

This framing of historical time provides a powerful, deeply kabbalistic strategy for talking about the anticipated end to the torments of history. While virtually all Western religious traditions discuss the notion of a reward for the righteous, be it in the afterlife or the world of messianic redemption or both, in passages such as these we observe a distinctly kabbalistic discourse for giving meaning to Jewish historical experience. By claiming privileged knowledge of the correlation between God's inner life and the design of historical and cosmic time, kabbalists give their readers a way of situating their present moment as a form of participation in God's own internal dynamics. Even moments of misfortune or apparent chaos take on meaning, not merely as periods to be endured by history's unfortunate souls, but as stages in a temporal process in which every time is, in its own way, a reflection of God.

The messianic future as imagined in this text is the place from which creation originates and to which it returns in the *sefirah* of *Binah*. On the human plane, the weekly Sabbath rest on the seventh day and the messianic era in the seventh millennium both correspond to the *sefirah Yesod*. Such a view reflects what Elliot Wolfson has shown to be the correlation between kabbalistic notions of temporality and their ironic and paradoxical discourses of messianism.

Texts such as these express "the possibility of the future diremptively breaking into the present." In the "timeswerve"[62] of kabbalistic time as Wolfson has described it, "messianic hope hinges on preparing for the onset of what takes place as the *purely present future*, that is, the future that is already present as the present that is always future, the *tomorrow that is now because it is now tomorrow*."[63] For the authorship of *Sefer ha-temunah*, the seventh *shemittah* operates as the respite from history during the seventh millennium in each world, just as the seventh day is the day of rest in each week. Messianic redemption is both a thing to be anticipated in the future, and a feature of time experienced cyclically in the present. The end of history is also a return that repeats.

The Jubilee, which in the Bible occurs every fiftieth year, is associated in kabbalistic discourse with the reincorporation of the cosmos into the Godhead.[64] If the transformation that occurs every seven thousand years correlates with the Sabbath "rest," the fifty thousandth year is associated with a more enduring change connected to the idea of "liberation" or "freedom." For many kabbalists, the place of return is the *sefirah* of *Binah*, as the *'Or ha-ganuz* commentary on the *Sefer ha-bahir* says, "At the great Jubilee [everything] will return to *Binah*, as it is said, 'each shall return to his holding and his family' (Lev 25:10). The storehouse of souls is located there."[65] The return of the world to its point of origin, for this author, also involves the return of the soul to its source within the divine. Just as history has an endpoint built into the present *shemittah*, the cosmos as a whole has an endpoint when it returns to its origin after seven cycles.

Is the Jubilee an absolute endpoint, or does the universe emerge from within the Godhead again in order to start a new cycle of seven *shemittot*? Surprisingly, there is no consensus on this question in the early sources, and more than a few kabbalists neglect to weigh in on this point altogether. Bahya ben Asher addresses this issue in a discussion of the *shemittah* and *yovel*, or Jubilee:

> I will explain to you how the destruction of the world and its renewal in the *shemittot*, and also how the annulment of being and its renewal in the Jubilee. It is known that six *sefirot* acted during the six days of creation, each *sefirah* on its day. As one can say, *Binah* on the first day, *Hesed* on the second day, and *Gevurah* on the third day, and so forth for them all,

until the arrival of the seventh day which is *Yesod*, and it performs its function. And what was its function? Enjoyment and rest. For it was rest for itself, and also for all six, for in its rest they all rested. . . . So too, in the case of the six millennia that repeat continuously, it begins to function in the first millennium with *Binah*, the second with *Hesed*, the third with *Gevurah*, and so forth for all, until the arrival of the seventh millennium, which is *Yesod*, and thus it is Sabbath and rest. The world is of necessity desolate, since each *sefirah* functions for the duration of its millennium, and the divine flow ceases to the lower entities when they all return above to receive from *Binah*. . . . This is the destruction when the land is desolate. But it will not be "chaos and void," because in the future they will return as before and bestow that which they received above, and then the world is renewed. Such it will be from seven to seven until the great Jubilee. When the great Jubilee arrives, all ten [of the *sefirot*] return to their root in *'ein sof*.[66]

The *shemittah* and the Jubilee each involve a form of annihilation, and in this passage, Bahya attempts to describe how this difference is understood in the kabbalistic tradition. He begins with a more general description of the progression of the world cycles as analogs to the days of creation, taking the somewhat unusual position that the first world is governed by *Binah*, and the seventh by *Yesod*. Like other authors we have seen, Bahya treats *Yesod* as a unique world that is distributed as the "seventh" in each of the cosmic cycles. Furthermore, within each world, each of these seven *sefirot* are given influence during their own millennium. The return of the world to *Binah* involves a period of desolation," evoking Rav Katina's comment in the Babylonian Talmud, Rosh ha-Shanah 31a, that the world exists for six thousand years and is "desolate" for one thousand. During that time, the land is desolate, but the world does not return to the primordial state of being "chaos and void," *tohu va-vohu*, as described in Genesis 1:2.[67] The destruction at the end of each *shemittah* is followed by a period of renewal and regeneration, which, in Bahya's view, is different from the Jubilee when all of the *sefirot* will "return to their root in *'ein sof*." The implication of Bahya's comment is that the destruction at the end of each *shemittah* is temporary, while the Jubilee implies a comprehensive annihilation after which nothing—not even the divine *sefirot*—will exist. All that will remain is *'ein sof*, the divine infinity. However, as noted above in chapter 3, in Bahya's view, the annihilation of the Jubilee, while much more comprehensive than that of the *shemittah*, is not final. Though it is the case for him that, during the Jubilee, "all being is annulled and void," the cosmos then emerges again to repeat the cycle of *shemittot*. As he puts it, "After the Jubilee, being is renewed in its entirety, to be revealed from *'ein sof*, and divine flow returns above and below as in the days of old, and thus it is from Jubilee to Jubilee for eighteen thousand iterations."[68] For Bahya, the cosmos extends over a vast number of iterations. The preset reality is merely one of seven, which itself is a set of one of eighteen thousand. In this vision of the cosmos, as with others considered above, the present world is infinitesimal when placed within the vast sweep of time. The cycles of the universe may, eventually, come to an end, but Bahya pushes that much farther into the future. In his vision of the cosmic order, being proceeds as a succession of repetitions that are encoded with a divine imprint that follows the pattern of the *sefirot*.

Menahem Recanati is much more reticent when it comes to the state of the universe after the Jubilee. As he argues in his commentary on the Torah, "From the year of the Jubilee onward it is prohibited to contemplate, in keeping with the saying of our rabbis of blessed memory, 'that which comes before, and that which comes after,' for there is only complete nothingness that is beyond the capacity of the imagination."[69] Playing on the famous passage in the Mishnah, Hagigah 2:1, that one must not contemplate "that which is above, that which is below, what came before, and what comes after," Recanati relegates the period after the Jubilee to the realm of the inscrutable. For him, kabbalistic knowledge of the sequence of cosmic time extends only as far as the Jubilee. His main concern is with understanding the difference between the *shemittah* and the Jubilee, and how that relates to the renewal of the cosmic order. This is an issue he addressed directly in another passage:

> Perhaps one may ask, "What difference is there between the *shemittah* and the Jubilee?" Know that there are two answers to this. There are those who say that that which our rabbis of blessed memory have said, "one [thousand] desolate," does not mean that everything returns to "chaos

and void" as in the year of the Jubilee, but rather it is understood to mean "desolate" of man and beast and forms of life. And things composed of the four elements all return each to their basis. And the word "desolate" means that the overflow onto composites, and the heavens and the earth, remain as they are. In this manner, it happens seven times until the Jubilee, when it returns to "chaos and void." This is a foundational opinion for the masters of the Kabbalah. If we wish to interpret "desolate" literally, there will be a distinction between them, since after the *shemittah*, it returns to its regeneration, which is not the case with the Jubilee.[70]

The return and regeneration of the world after each *shemittah* is, according to Recanati, a "foundational opinion of the masters of the Kabbalah." This underscores the importance, in his view, of the idea that all life in the world undergoes a process of destruction and renewal from one cosmic cycle to the next. The material cosmos persists, but living things, including humans and animals, are annihilated, or reintegrated into the divine, at the end of each *shemittah*. Only the Jubilee, in Recanati's view, entails the complete annihilation of the physical cosmos. His reluctance to say what happens beyond that point may simply reflect the fact that, unlike Bahya, he received no reliable kabbalistic tradition about the state of reality after the Jubilee. But it is also telling that he regards this partial knowledge regarding the *shemittah* and the Jubilee to be complete enough to constitute a "foundational opinion" of the Kabbalah. This would suggest that for Recanati, the important insight associated with this secret is the regeneration and renewal of all life from one world to the next, and the idea that the cosmos follows a predetermined course that frames the events of human history in the present world.

For most kabbalists, the *shemittah* and Jubilee were not matters of interest for purely theoretical discussion of the nature of cosmic time. The discourse of the temporal rhythm of the universe is frequently tied back to the historical condition and political state of the Jewish people. The author of *Ma'arekhet ha-'elohut*, for example, builds upon the association made in Leviticus 26:34 between neglect of the Sabbatical laws and exile of the Israelites from the land of Israel in order to describe the nature of the Jubilee. For this author, the Jubilee is associated with emancipation from oppression.[71] The nature of the freedom that will pertain when the Jubilee arrives at the end of the seven cosmic cycles is described in the following manner:

> At the time of perfection, when Israel is in the land observing all of the commandments and the Torah in its entirety, and they possess a Temple and messiah, and they are filled with wisdom and understanding and strength, and there will be peace in the land, and the righteous [will be] redeemed,[72] [and] then the verse will be fulfilled, "on that day the lord shall be one and his name one" (Zech 14:9), as I will explain below. [The land] will no longer cast them out, for the memory of Amalek will be erased, and the evil inclination shall cease, "the name complete and the throne complete."[73] . . . For Israel is the essence of the world and its subsistence. You must consider why Scripture states, "the lord shall be one and his name one," for it should have said, "the Lord and his name are one." The reason is that during the duration when this world exists, it is always governed by [a combination of] loving-kindness and strict judgment, as is the nature of the world. However, during the era of perfection, the powers and blessings of the world will draw near to one another, as was the intention at the beginning of creation. . . . [This is] due to the great unity that will pertain during that time, it is said regarding it, "the lord shall be one and his name one," because the forces will still be active. But, with the cessation of time and the world in the seventh millennium, since that millennium is "the world that is entirely Sabbath,"[74] and the forces are relieved of their work, then, "the lord and his name will be one," and they shall use a single crown. But at the end of all of the generations, the Jubilee will guide the world.[75]

In this description of the state of the world during the days of the messiah in the seventh millennium, or "time of perfection," the powers that afflict the Jewish people in the present will be ameliorated. The messiah will return the people of Israel from exile, rebuild the Temple, and they will be imbued with "wisdom and understanding." And of course, as we have seen in other examples cited above, the evil inclination will disappear. The text then asks why Zechariah 14:9 is written in the future tense. What will be the nature of the unity of God and his name that the prophet alludes to? The answer, according to this passage, illuminates the difference between exile and redemption on the theosophical level. During the time of exile, which is to say, during the period of historical time, the divine attributes of strict judgment, of the *sefirah* of *Din*, and loving-kindness, the *sefirah* of *Hesed*, both play a role in guiding the world. This is why, during the reign of history, there is always a combination of good and bad in human experience. But the author assures the reader that during the "era of perfection," these divine powers will draw close to each other in a manner that reflects the original intent of creation. Such will be the end of history. Beyond that lies the end of time, when the divine powers become a single unity, and the world will be reincorporated into *Binah*. Such will be the complete resolution of both historical time and temporality itself. It is import-ant to note that this discussion of time centers the historical condition of the Jewish people. As the author asserts, "Israel is the essence of the world."

The ever-enigmatic author of the *Sefer ha-temunah* also frequently centers the issue of exile and redemption in discussions of the end of cosmic time. In one passage regarding the end of the seventh *shemittah*, the author states:

> On the Sabbath, all exiles and circuits cease. . . . The seventh *shemittah* is Sabbath for all, in which the six bodies (*gufin*) ascend from the six pillars, since "the son of David will not arrive until all of the souls in the body (*guf*) have been consumed." Then, the exiles above and below cleave to the first light, two lights and two souls as one composed of both, and both as one form. . . . In the seventh, *shemittah* and Jubilee become one entity in the form of the letter *het*, as everything returns to the first redeemer that redeemed everything in peace; for the one sold into servitude, there shall be redemption.[76] "At the Jubilee they shall be released" (Lev 25:31), for they are the supernal days of the messiah. . . . Then everything ascends to the place of its emanation, for that is its place.[77]

The rest of the Sabbath and the freedom of the Jubilee converge, according to this text, at the end of the seventh cosmic cycle. Exile, in all of its forms, will end, as signified by the ascension of the *gufin*, or storehouses of souls, from the six *shemittot* that precede the seventh. The elevation of every *guf* in which souls are stored signifies the true end of the exile of the soul through reincarnation. All of the "exiles" will then cleave to the first light, an aspect of the divine in which they will converge "both as one form." In the realm of the *sefirot*, everything with return to *Binah*, such that *shemittah* and Jubilee become a single entity. The return of everything to its point of emanation is couched in terms of redemption from "servitude," and the end of exile. The historical condition of the Jewish people and the state of the universe reflect one another. And in the secretly revealed divine plan for cosmic time that the kabbalists claim has been esoterically revealed to the Jews alone, resolving the plight of Israel is central to God's design of cosmic time.

Historical time and cosmic time both serve as discursive devices for kabbalists as they describe their tradition's secret teaching regarding the fate of Jewish souls. The *shemittah* and Jubilee are sites of repose for the divine souls of Israel. The Jubilee, in particular, is treated as a time when the liberation of the soul will entail its return to its source within the Godhead in the attribute of *Binah*. The full end of exile entails the reintegration of the soul into God. Regarding the future fate of the souls of Israel, Abraham Adrutiel remarked in the early sixteenth century, "As it is below, so too will it appear above. Thus, each and every soul has a source which is its allotment in a supernal source. When the fiftieth year arrives, which is the Jubilee, then all of the souls ascend to see the face of God, and all of them return to their inheritance and family, truly—to the place from which they emanated and were hewn. Thus, it is written, 'In the year of the Jubilee, each of you shall return [to your allotment]' (Lev 25:13)."[78] The liberation of the soul in the Jubilee is described here in somewhat literal terms as the heavenly manifestation of the individual in the world above. But like the cosmos itself, the Jewish soul does not remain individuated. Redemption for the soul, like redemption for the world, means annihilation within the divine self. Which is to say, the reward for enduring history is the apotheosis that marks its ending. Such a way of framing the progression of time suggests that God has encoded an automatic course correction into the plan for the universe. At the end of cosmic time, which extends much further beyond the end of historical time, everything is resolved through a return into the divine. The kabbalistic secret of the present condition of the cosmos and the Jewish people is that everything, material and spiritual, moves inexorably through cycles and iterations that end where they began in the divine infinity.

Cycling Time, Reading History

When speaking of messianic redemption and the destiny of the cosmic order, kabbalists often speak of the convergence of the end with the beginning. As noted above,[79] Wolfson has shown that the notion of the circularity of time is prominent in kabbalistic discourses of temporality. By claiming that the "end" of all being was part of the first act of creation, kabbalists assert the divine providence over the entire sweep of time. A world in which the future and end of history is crafted from the beginning limits the agency granted to humans to exercise unfettered control over the course of human affairs. On the other hand, such a discourse enables a perception of world events that are divinely intended and not arbitrary or subject to the whims of human choice. By describing the outcome at the end of time as an aspect of God's activity in the very beginning of creation, kabbalists sought to underscore divine control over the course of history. When seen from this perspective, the current state of affairs is not an accident or an afterthought. For these kabbalists, the unfolding of events was crafted from the beginning.

For many medieval kabbalists, the return to the source at the end was inevitable from the very beginning. Joshua bar Samuel Nahmias, for instance, argued that the eventual reintegration of the world into the divine during each *shemittah* at the end of the seventh millennium was known by God from the very earliest stage of creation. At the end of each cosmic cycle, "after the seventh millennium, the causes return to their source, love to its dwelling place. In this manner, things proceed in all of the cycles of seven, until the great Jubilee. Therefore, [at] the 'beginning' that is the wisdom of God, he saw and knew everything."[80] The creation of the world from the "beginning," *reshit*, associated with the second *sefirah*, *Hokhmah*, or divine wisdom, means, for Nahmias, that the divine mind, or "wisdom of God," could perceive and know everything from the beginning. For this author, when God created the world, he foresaw the entire arc of time of each of the seven worlds, as well as the final dissolution in the Jubilee.

The author of the anonymous *Sod 'ilan ha-'atzilut* offers another version of the encrypting of future events in an initial act. Building on the image in Genesis 21 of the tamarisk tree that Abraham planted in Beer Sheva, the text suggests that the eventual historical triumph of the Jewish people over their oppressors was created by this original act of the founding patriarch of the Israelites. As the author states it, "Everything ascends and is swallowed, everything in everything, since everything is in *'Atarah Tifferet*, and from there it ascends and is swallowed, all in *Keter*, the beginning and end of everything, since it is the beginning of all ten *sefirot*, which are called a tree in which Israel are united, and the nations of the world are cut down. It is the tree that Abraham planted, in the secret of, 'he planted a tamarisk tree in Beer Sheva, and there he called out in the name of the Lord, the everlasting God' (Gen 21:33)."[81] The destiny of the world to return to the highest realm of the Godhead in the first *sefirah* of *Keter* is related to the tree that Abraham planted. The author suggests that this very same tree, an embodiment of the *'ilan* or "tree" of the ten *sefirot*, through which the Jewish people are able to unite with God, is also the mechanism by which the nations of the world will be defeated at the end of days. At the very beginning of the establishment of the lineage that will eventuate in the nation of Israel, this author argues, the instrument for the future defeat of the enemies of the Jewish people was simultaneously created. The many historical traumas that they were to undergo were, by implication, also foreseen at that early stage. But so too was the solution to their historical problem, in that Abraham's tree, with its theosophical associations, was created at that time.

The *Sefer ha-temunah* offers a unique way of describing the approach of the end of the current *shemittah*. According to this author, the weakening of the aspect of *Din* at the end of the current *shemittah* will entail a significant slowing of time.[82] For this anonymous author, the arrival of the end is described as a reversal of time and return to the origin of the beginning of the creation in Genesis. As the seventh millennium draws to a close,

> everything returns to its sheath . . . the generations grow fewer and fewer, until there remain seventy pure and good souls. From there to twelve men, and from there to three pillars, and from there to Noah and Enoch, until Adam alone. . . . And then Adam and the *Shekhinah*, together with a being from the supernal entities, recite "a psalm of praise for the Sabbath day" (Ps 92:1), for it is entirely Sabbath for eternal life. Then, everything transcends, and Adam returns to the place from which he was brought forth.[83]

Unlike the calamitous events that usher in the messianic era, the end of the final millennium of the messianic age will entail a peaceful return of things to their source. Humans will not die violent deaths. Instead, there will be, according to this author, something like a reversal of time. The number of humans will grow fewer, until there are only seventy pure souls—evoking the number that went down to Egypt—and then only Noah and Enoch, and eventually Adam alone. The first human, it seems, will also be the last. After he sings the ninety-second psalm together with the *Shekhinah*, Adam himself will be reintegrated into his source. The end of the current cosmic cycle, according to this description, will be a literal reversal of the sequence of events with which the current world began. By that reading, the end of the world was created at the beginning, because the people at the end of the world are the very same as those with which the world began.

The author of this text also suggested that, in every cosmic cycle, events repeat themselves. In a comment on Ecclesiastes 1:8, the main text of the *Sefer ha-temunah* argues that the return of all things to their source also means that, in each world, all events are repetitions of events that came before. "'All things are wearisome; one cannot express' (Eccl 1:8) or grasp the destiny of all things and their details according to their paths. 'The eye cannot be satisfied with seeing, nor the ear [with hearing]' (ibid.), for everything returns to what it was, 'for there is nothing new under the sun' (Eccl 1:9), which is the first agent of all, and therefore the circuits are beneath him, 'for that which was' eternally 'is that which will be' (ibid.)."[84] As the primordial ground of being, God is, according to this author, the source to which all things return. As such, the "circuits," or repetition of worlds over the course of the seven *shemittot*, repeat from previous worlds, even as they move forward in a sequence. As the commentator on this passage understands it, this text is suggesting that

in the end, everything returns to that which it was. And furthermore, everything that will be in the future already exists, for "there is nothing new under the sun" (Eccl 1:90). . . . For that which has been long since in the *shemittot* that have come before, that too shall occur in the *shemittot* that are still to come, as it is written, "There is a thing of which they say, 'Behold, this is new!'" (Eccl 1:10). Do not be surprised by such a thing, for

it has happened in the worlds that have come before, and these worlds are
the *shemittot* that have passed and already completed their time.[85]

The fact that all things derive from and return to the same divine source
in each of the worlds means that, in some sense, the events of those worlds
are the same. As we saw in the previous chapter, each of the *shemittot* is very
different from another, so it is hard to understand exactly in what sense this
author meant to suggest that, for instance, the exile of the people of Israel in
the present world is a repetition of an event from a former world. Clearly, the
author is not trying to convey an exact correlation. But they are suggesting
that events in the present world are not "new." Everything that happens has
in some way happened before, and will occur yet again in the future. The
point is that time is orderly, and events are purposeful reflections of the divine
nature from which they emerged. What happens in this world has analogs
in past and future iterations of the universe, which means that the script for
the present, past, and future has already been written. In this way of speaking of the unfolding of events over time, significant limitations are placed
on the capacity for humans to shape the course of history. But at the same
time, history takes on meaning as a divine pattern that extends across all
seven cosmic cycles. For the author of the commentary on *Sefer ha-temunah*,
the true meaning of events in the present can be understood in light of the
future redemption and ultimate fate of the cosmos. Things occur in the present world "through the power of the second *shemittah* in which we currently
find ourselves, with all of its powers regarding the matter of exiles [of the
people of Israel] in their proper times, and from now until their redemption,
demonstrating the secret of their task in their exiles and redemptions, until
their proper time arrives."[86] Each of the exiles of the people of Israel, according to this author, happens at the right time. When understood in relation to
the final redemption—a matter known exclusively through the traditions of
the Kabbalah—Jews are able to understand the *secret* of "their task in exile."
The claim is that the esoteric doctrine of the *shemittot* and redemption reveals the purpose that Jews serve when they patiently bear the ordeal of exile.
Such discourses of the future were a way for medieval Jews to understand the
meaning of the present.

Predicting the End

Predicting the exact year of the messiah's arrival has a long and controversial history in Jewish sources.[87] A statement in the Babylonian Talmud attributed to R. Shmuel bar Nahmani in the name of R. Yohanan, states: "May those who calculate the end of days be cursed. For they might say, once the end [time] arrived and he did not come, [that] he would not come at all."[88] Precise statements for the specific date of the messiah's arrival always run the danger of creating serious disappointment. They also subject rabbinic authority and claims to esoteric knowledge to the possibility of objective verification or negation. From a purely strategic perspective, it would be better to avoid calculating the messiah's arrival. Staking a claim on a particular date or year is fraught with risk. Yet throughout the late Middle Ages, a surprising number of Jewish thinkers, including many kabbalists, did precisely that, though their predictions varied considerably. For example, Abulafia offered 1280 and 1290 as dates for the messiah's arrival,[89] Joseph Angelet predicted the arrival of the messiah in 1328,[90] and one passage in the 'Idra Rabba section of the Zohar anticipated the onset of a multistage messianic redemption to begin in 1334,[91] while a different passage in the Zohar suggests that the resurrection of the dead is to take place in the year 1648.[92] The anonymous *Sefer ha-meshiv*[93] offers a number of dates for the messiah's arrival, including 1468,[94] and resurrection in 1640,[95] while the anonymous author of *Kaf ha-qetoret*, likely written near the turn of the sixteenth century, suggested a date range for the messiah's arrival between 1440 and 1540, which they regarded as the third century of the sixth millennium.[96] The same general range of dates can be found in the extensive kabbalistic writings of Abraham ben Eliezer ha-Levi.[97] Isaac Abarbanel, arguably the most famous of the exiles from Spain, predicted the messiah's arrival between 1503 and 1531,[98] after a fifty-year period of historical upheaval starting in 1453 with the fall of Constantinople.[99] Joseph ibn Shraga, another Spanish exile, set 1512 as the date for redemption,[100] and the anonymous sixteenth-century *Ginat beitan* predicted that the messiah would arrive in 1598, and argued that he comes in every *shemittah* world on that same date.[101] What compelling purpose did these writers perceive in offering a date for the messiah's arrival that offset the obvious risks associated with the possibility that such predictions might fail? Exploring this question reveals something important about how those who produced and consumed such discourses understood their place in history. It also shows how the anticipation of the end of history served to orient medieval Jews to the present and help them overcome historical despair. An open-ended future of potential suffering was, it would seem, untenable. Predictions of the messiah's arrival, even when they turned out to be inaccurate, were better than no prediction at all.

The social power of "apocalyptic visionaries," as Amos Funkenstein described them, lies in both the vivid imagery that they produce regarding the end of days, and the strategies that they deploy to demonstrate their exclusive access to this body of secret knowledge. The suggestion that one knows God's secret plan for human history and the fate of the cosmos is a powerful claim, and only unique figures are able to succeed in garnering acceptance for their apocalyptic discourses. Funkenstein enumerated three "modes of proof" for such claims: "First, 'uncovered' prophesies (apocalypses in the strict sense): Second, a new method by which to 'decode' old, well-known prophecies (*pesher*): and third, a technique of 'interpreting' the course of history itself 'typologically.' All of these modes have in common the indication of secret knowledge."[102] Funkenstein argued that biblical and Second Temple sources, such as the book of Enoch, the apocalypse of Ezra, and the apocalypse of Baruch, provided elaborate descriptions of the dispensations of historical time, as well as predictions of the imminent end of history. And like the kabbalists, they drew analogies between the days of creation and the duration of historical time. Funkenstein even argued that "the fascination with historical time and its structure was the most important contribution of the apocalyptic mentality to the Western sense of history."[103] And yet, he regarded the Middle Ages as a period in which very few apocalypses were produced—a fact that he regards as "astonishing."[104] From the few examples cited above of messianic calculations and predictions of the end of time based on detailed claims regarding the broader shape of history, I would argue that apocalypticism can be found among medieval Jewish authors if we take kabbalistic texts into account. Funkenstein's thoughtful and nuanced understanding of apocalyptic thinking is certainly valuable, but his claims regarding the absence of such notions among medieval Jews is the result of the general neglect of kabbalistic sources in the study of premodern Jewish historical memory.

For kabbalists who embraced the doctrine of the *shemittot*, the seventh millennium will be the messianic age. The onset of that time, however, was to occur at some point during the sixth millennium, which according to traditional Jewish dating began in the Gregorian year 1240 CE. Writing not long after that time, when there had been a degree of disappointment in some Jewish millennialist circles, Nahmanides offered a prediction for the date of messianic redemption in his *Sefer ge'ulah* (Book of Redemption).[105] He argued that the prohibition against making such predictions no longer applies, since "we are in the End of Days."[106] He then applies a variety of exegetical techniques to argue that the first stage of redemption with the arrival of "messiah son of Joseph" would occur in 1358, and the "messiah son of David" will usher in comprehensive messianic redemption in 1403.[107] The end of history, for Nahmanides, was to happen relatively soon, but not in his own lifetime. Other kabbalists embraced this dating,[108] and for a time it served a purpose similar to what it must have done in Nahmanides's day.

But like all predictions of the messiah's arrival, even those of an authority of Nahmanides's standing were doomed to failure. Kabbalists in the fourteenth and fifteenth centuries would have been painfully aware of the social consequences of failed predictions of the messiah's arrival. What was their perception of such disappointments? And what role did that play in their own willingness to offer dates for the end of history? In a remarkably self-aware comment regarding this question, the authorship of *Sefer ha-peli'ah* depicted a dialogue specifically on this point. Elkana, the text's main character, encounters a mysterious man who offers allusions to the secret of when the messiah will arrive. Elkana complains that the esoteric hints are too obscure. The man says that he will speak more plainly only if he agrees not to reveal what he learns. Elkana replies as follows:

> I said to him, who can refrain from revealing matters that gladden the heart? He said to me, lest he [the messiah] delay, and they fall into despair, and I am to blame. I said to him, on the contrary, when they hear the tidings of redemption, they will feel shame over their transgressions. For they will be reminded that at the time of redemption they will bask in the splendor of the *Shekhinah*, and they will say; "How shall we bask

in the splendor of the *Shekhinah*, and how shall we appear with our faces and hands covered in blood? Therefore, we will repent, and return to our lord." But, if they are deprived of this knowledge, they will despair of the good [that awaits them], and you would be to blame.[109]

Elkana's statement seems to reflect the view of the authorship of *Sefer ha-peli'ah*, while the mysterious man with whom he is speaking holds a view known from other kabbalistic sources that express reservations regarding the entire enterprise of messianic speculations. The disappointment over failed predictions is, in the view of the author of this passage, outweighed by the social benefits of anticipating the messiah's arrival at a particular, impending date. The argument is that, when people hear "tidings of redemption," they are more likely to regret their transgressions, and reflect on how they will appear before the *Shekhinah* when they are weighed down by sin. The author expresses the hope that publicly sharing a date for the onset of redemption will lead to mass repentance and greater adherence to the commandments. For this kabbalist, anticipation of the imminent end of history serves a positive social benefit, which in turn generates more theurgic energy through increased Jewish practice of *halakhah*.

The author of the commentary on the *Sefer ha-temunah* describes a similar hesitation to reveal calculations of the messiah's arrival. However, unlike the above-cited passage from *Sefer ha-peli'ah*, this author is much more concerned about the negative social impact of failed predictions. In a passage discussing the possible ways of calculating the messiah's date of arrival, the anonymous commentator offers this reproach to his readers:

> Do not teach this or speak of it with the foolish or the wicked, and do not reveal it to the ignorant or those who study foreign wisdom, so that when that time arrives, they will regret their derision and mockery and repent and return from their warped ways, and awake from their sleep, and open their eyes. . . . Perhaps they will observe a wise man who spoke and gave a specific time for redemption, because he observed a wayward generation, in order that they not be discouraged, and they trusted in the Lord, and placed their trust in his providence, but then that time passes

and the redemption is delayed, and they are discouraged and lose faith and abscond. Woe to them, and woe to their souls! Such are not of the seed of Israel, but rather of the external powers, for if they had understanding, they would have known that there has never arisen a prophet like Moses our teacher, peace be upon him, and he did not attain knowledge of the time of the redemption. And Jacob, peace be upon him, wanted to reveal it, and the power of prophecy was taken from him. And Daniel, who knew the matter of the redemption better than any prophet, began to reveal and explain, and gave a time, and concealed and sealed it to such a degree that the prophets are unable to grasp the secret and comprehend it. . . . Despite it all, it is incumbent upon us to reveal what we know.[110]

For this kabbalist, the secret of the time of the messiah's arrival should be concealed from the unworthy. Those who are ignorant—or even worse, study foreign wisdom—are not worthy of this knowledge, according to this text. This author prefers for them to remain in ignorance until the messiah arrives, at which point they will experience deep regret, and repent when they "awake from their sleep" at the end of history. The fear is that if a purported "wise man" announces a prediction for the date of messianic redemption that the "ignorant" find compelling, and then the messiah does not arrive on that date, the resulting disappointment will be so severe that those Jews may be lost entirely. Those who make such predictions are described by this author as evil, foreign individuals whose souls derive from the "external powers" in the sefirotic realm. The fact that even the likes of Moses, Jacob, and Daniel were prohibited from announcing the time of messianic redemption is offered as evidence that it is prohibited to do so. That is not to say that the secret of when the messiah will come has been lost to the Jewish tradition. Rather, the suggestion here is merely that it is too dangerous to reveal it.

One would expect that, for such an author, offering a precise date for when to anticipate the onset of redemption would be out of the question. But yet, as the above passage concludes, they note that "despite it all, it is incumbent upon us to reveal what we know." The author then goes on to use a number of techniques to determine the date the messiah will arrive, and gives two possibilities: the Gregorian year 1409 or 1531.[111] Remarkably, after all of the emphatic argumentation regarding the negative effects of failed predictions, and the evil character of those who make them, this author breaks with what they them-selves describe as biblical precedent and suggests two possible dates. It would seem that the allure of messianic hope is not so easily dampened. To simply state that the date of redemption is unknown, or that it cannot be revealed, was, it seems, unsatisfying. Important social work must have been performed by such predictions. For reluctant prophets like the anonymous commenta-tor, the social good that this anticipation will serve (at least until the year 1532) outweighed the potential for disappointment in the future. The community of the present needed something more specific to frame their understanding of *when* they are in history. Looking forward to a date, even one that will be after one's lifetime, when the messiah will come, enables a different view of historical time.

For some kabbalists, a date that is too far into the future can cause a par-ticular despair of its own. The anonymous author of the *Sefer ha-meshiv* liter-ature suggested that God had in fact revealed to Moses secrets regarding the battles that would be waged by Muslim nations against the forces of Rome (which he predicted would be destroyed in the year 1504)[112] during the messi-anic pangs at the end of days, but that Moses "did not wish to reveal them due to the length of the exile. But now, the time has come to reveal them, and from today forward you will hear of mighty wars from one end of the world to the other."[113] Moses, it would seem, understood the future course of history but was reluctant to share it explicitly for fear that it would cause the Jewish people of earlier generations to lose all hope when they learned that the exile would last for such a long time. However, this author, writing not long before the expulsion from Spain, was firmly convinced that they were living on the eve of the redemption during the pangs that are to be expected on the cusp of the messianic era, which meant that those secrets could finally be revealed openly. Knowledge that would have been damaging to Jewish morale in prior gener-ations, according to this passage, has at last become cause for Jewish encour-agement. The catastrophic wars of the present were to be seen as a sure sign of history nearing its culmination with the redemption of the Jewish people. As the author states a few pages later: "We have revealed here the secret of this deep Kabbalah. . . . Happy are you who have attained knowledge of this great secret, for it had not yet been revealed, since it was not the proper time to reveal it, until now, when the time to reveal it has arrived."[114]

The author of the introduction to *Sefer ha-kanah* provides an interesting discussion of the anticipation of the year when the messiah will arrive. The author suggests correlations between each of the ten *sefirot* and the duration of time during the present *shemittah*.[115] Each *sefirah*, beginning with *Keter* and ending with *Shekhinah*, covers five hundred years, which spans the first five millennia. During the sixth millennium, *Keter* reigns for the first five hundred years, and *Hokhmah* reigns for the second five-hundred-year period. After that, the seventh millennium commences. The messiah will come, they claim, at some point during the sixth millennium, but when? They offer the following calculation:

> The messiah, son of David, will receive magnificence and majesty from God, may he be blessed, and he will place magnificence and kingship of Israel upon him, and he will reveal the secret interpretations of the Torah and the twenty-two letters which are the foundation of all glory and all creation. Then the kingdom of Israel (*malkhut Yisra'el*) will return the kingdom of God to its place, and return the crown to its former glory, as it is written, "and the Lord shall be king over all the earth" (Zech 14:9). When will this be? In the two-hundred-and-fiftieth year of the reign of *Keter*. For "the world will exist for six thousand years, and lay desolate for one" (b. Sanhedrin 97a). Know that each of the *sefirot* function for five hundred years, and *Keter* and *Hokhmah* for [an additional] one thousand years. The years begin with *Keter* for five hundred years, and five hundred for *Hokhmah*—one thousand years. Five hundred for *Binah*, five hundred for *Hesed*—two thousand. Five hundred for *Gevurah*, five hundred for *Tifferet*—three thousand. Five hundred for *Netzah*, five hundred for *Hod*—four thousand. Five hundred for *Yesod*, five hundred for *'Atarah*—five thousand for the ten *sefirot*, and it returns again to *Keter* for five hundred years, and *Hokhmah* for five hundred years; a thousand, which is six thousand years.[116]

If the messiah arrives in the middle of the reign of *Keter* in the sixth millennium, and *Keter* reigns for the first five hundred years, it means that the messiah will come two hundred and fifty years after the start of the sixth millennium, which began in the Gregorian year 1340. Hence, the messiah will arrive, according to this author, in 1490.[117] At that time, the author reassures the reader, he will finally reveal the Torah's secrets, and usher in the divine kingdom.[118]

The text continues with a polemical description of how non-Jewish nations, especially those associated with Christianity, will be destroyed when the messiah arrives.

> During the twilight leading into the seventh millennium, the world will be established. The arrival of the messiah will be when five thousand, two hundred and fifty years have passed, which is the middle of the reign of *Keter* for five hundred years. This [is the meaning of the verse] "when the morning stars sang [*be-ran*][119] together" (Job 38:7). And "that man" (*'oto ha-'ish*) [Jesus] called the enslavement of the gentile nations "destruction of the world." It is actually the destruction of the non-Jewish nations, and he did not tell them the truth, that it is their own destruction, because he was afraid of them, lest they turn back. "That man" was crafty, and they believed him that it referred to the destruction of the world, and they did not realize that he proclaimed to them their own destruction, which is the time of the reign of the [Holy One] blessed be he, which is five thousand, two hundred and fifty (1490 CE) according to the tabulation that we enumerate from the creation of the world. If the people of Israel are meritorious through their actions, the time will be advanced.[120]

In possible reference to Jesus's predictions of destruction in Matthew 13 and 24 and Luke 21, the author argues that Jesus was being intentionally misleading by depicting the destruction of the world, rather than the downfall of the non-Jewish nations. The implication is that this was a secret that was known even in antiquity—and remarkably, even by Jesus himself! But, due to the false prophecies, or at least, false interpretations of those prophecies, by Christians, the author suggests that the true meaning of the impending doom has been misunderstood. When redemption arrives, they claim, it is only non-Jews who will be destroyed. The countertheological argument is that the very man that the Christian world reveres as a revealer of truth was in fact the propagator of a lie regarding the end of history and the destruction of non-Jews. As a result, his followers are being led to their own destruction, and only Jews are aware of this. In a slightly different formulation of this passage in *Sefer ha-peli'ah*, the author says that with the arrival of redemption, "the time that Jesus declared to the world as a time of desolation is a time during which there will be a war above, as I will clarify later, and all of the archons of the nations will fall and be subjugated by *Kenesset Yisra'el*, and the peoples will return below and fall under the enslavement of the hand of Israel. This is what 'that man' called the desolation of the world."[121]

The point in both of these passages is that Christians have been misinformed about the nature of redemption. But for Jews to whom this esoteric matter has been revealed, and who look forward to 1490 as the date when the messiah is sure to arrive, the grand unveiling that will occur at the end of history for the nations of the world has already happened for them. And if, as the author of *Sefer ha-kanah* suggests, the Jewish people are meritorious, the date of the messiah's arrival will be advanced. That possibility aside, the text goes to great lengths to persuade the reader that there *is* an absolute final date by which the messiah must come. An open-ended future was, it seems, too much to bear. The passage, and the entire text known as *Hakdamat ha-kanah*, concludes with the following tale as confirmation of this prediction:

> Listen, my son, to all of the words of your father that have been spoken. Know that I placed myself in great danger, and I made a glass cage and entered into it and closed the door behind me to protect myself, and I cast myself into the sea in order to comprehend the work of the great and awesome God. When I was in the sea, a great light appeared before my eyes, and I saw a fish rushing toward me, heralding and saying, "The arrival of the messiah will be in the two hundred and fiftieth [year] of the reign of *Keter*." I ascended from the sea, and on the path, there was a man greeting me, and he said to me, "Sir, in the two hundred and fiftieth [year] of the reign of *Keter*, Israel will be redeemed." And I asked, "In what manner?" He said to me, "Know that when Israel descended to Egypt, the *Shekhinah* descended with them, and when the time arrived, the supernal archon of Egypt arose to wage war with *Tifferet*, and *Binah* took them by way of the path of the tower that floats in the air, and placed them above the grasp of

Egypt. . . . God took them out and brought them to the land of Israel, and they conquered the thirty-one kings who deny God. They dwelt there and reigned in a kingdom to which all nations offered tribute, since their supernal archons had fallen. But after that, they corrupted their ways once, twice, and three times, and the judgment had come forth from *Adonai*, and the present exile went into effect. . . . The time of the end will occur in the two hundred and fiftieth year of the reign of *Keter*. . . . This is the foretelling of the redemption."[122]

This passage, a dialogue between the eponymous Kanah and his father, Even Gador, provides miraculous confirmation that the messiah will arrive in the year 1490. First, the father claims that he entered the sea in a glass diving bell and was informed by a fish that the middle of the reign of *Keter* is indeed the date of redemption. Then, when back on land, an anonymous man greets him with the same news. In response to the question of how the messiah will arrive, the man offers a reprise of all of Jewish history, from the descent to Egypt and subsequent exodus, to the reign of Israel's kings in the land of Canaan, followed by the succession of exiles as a result of Israel's corrupted ways. When the "time of the end" arrives in 1490, the Jewish people will be redeemed, but the anticipation of their triumphant future is understood in terms of their problematic past. Much as we have seen in many other examples, the Jewish journey through history, including periods of suffering, is depicted as part of a divine plan. God, they claim, was present all along, guiding the people of Israel toward their final reversal of fortune. The path to redemption is fraught with many challenges, but in kabbalistic discourses such as this, the pangs of Jewish historical suffering have been part of a hidden divine process. The inevitable resolution of the Jewish historical condition is, for this author, written into the divine structure of the *sefirot* that serve as the pattern for historical time.

The subsequent prominence of the *Peli'ah* and *Kanah* texts posed a challenge for kabbalists writing after 1490, when the messiah failed to appear, and the Jewish population of Spain was expelled only two years later. In a scribal gloss on a copy of this text preserved in MS Vatican 187, written shortly after the expulsion from Spain, an alternative dating of 1503 is offered, citing the "misfortunes that have afflicted the Jews in all of the kingdoms of Edom from

1490–1495," as well as the invasion of Italy by King Charles VIII of France, as sure signs of the "birth pangs of the messiah."[123] The same year features prominently in a document preserved in the Cairo Geniza and discussed in a study by Isaiah Tishby.[124] Rabbi Moses of Kiev held the *Sefer ha-kanah* and *Peli'ah* in very high regard, using it as the basis for his book *Shoshan sodot*, which was completed in the year 1511. In one passage in which he comments on "the secret of the manner in which the *sefirot* will function during the years of the *shemittah*," he cites the passage discussed above from the *Sefer ha-kanah* that describes the reign of each *sefirah* for five hundred years, but he leaves out the specific designation of the year 1490 as the time of redemption, and instead says that this passage merely means that the messiah will arrive at some point during the five hundred year reign of the *sefirah* of *Keter* during the sixth millennium. He points out that "we are now in the two hundred and sixty-ninth year of *Keter* of the sixth millennium (1509 CE), and during its reign the redeemer will arrive."[125] In an intriguing move to elide the inaccuracy of the specific messianic prediction in *Sefer ha-kanah*, while still retaining the kabbalistic framework advanced in that text for anticipating the messiah's arrival, Moses of Kiev suggests that the attribution of five hundred years for each *sefirah* is a true kabbalistic secret, and that the messiah will indeed arrive during the reign of *Keter*, just not necessarily in any specific year. He is nonetheless clearly aware that the passage he cited contained a prediction that did not come to pass. This may be the reason why he prefaced the citation with the comment that "this secret is precious and concealed, and few comprehend it."[126]

The messianic and apocalyptic discourses that proliferated after the expulsion were many, and a detailed analysis is beyond the scope of this chapter.[127] But one more fascinating example deserves mention. Writing in the wake of the expulsion, Abraham ben Eliezer ha-Levi was the first to relate the story of Rabbi Joseph Della Reina in Spain and his attempt the bring the messiah by using magical techniques to summon and bind Samael and his assistant, Ammon of No.[128] In the narrative account Ha-Levi provides, Della Reina's intention was to render Samael and his assistant, along with the Christian peoples under their dominion, powerless, thus enabling the final stages of messianic redemption to commence immediately. However, Samael tricked Della Reina into performing a forbidden act of offering incense on the altar of a church, which caused the exile to extend for another forty years. This meant that instead of arriving in 1490, the messiah would in fact appear in 1530—one of the dates that Ha-Levi himself argues for in many of his works.[129] When that year came and went and the messiah still did not appear, another series of recalculations of course began again. Yet the Jewish world carried on, and kabbalists did not refrain from anticipating the messiah's arrival and speculating about the date of his appearance. It is tempting at times to regard all such discourses as though their social power is purely conditional, and that if their predictions fail, they were of no use. But for readers of such texts before, and even in some cases even after the designated messianic date, they hold out the inspiring possibility that the Jewish tradition knows history's secrets. When the terrors of the present can be reimagined as the culmination of God's plan for the final stages of historical time, calculations of the messiah's arrival—however imperfect they may be—have accomplished their task.

Imagining Histories and Futures

Serving as both map and calendar, these texts advanced the notion that time and space are nothing like they appear. Their vast complexity can only be understood through the kabbalistic tradition, with the ironically comforting suggestion that exiles of the body and soul, as well as global war and violence against Jews, are all part of the final process that will initiate the messianic age. Then, the world will reverse itself, evil will cease, Jews will assume their proper place as the single ruling nation on earth, regain their luminous bodies, and settle their transmigrating souls, as time marches forth in the succession of ages and worlds. In this way, kabbalists contributed to the broader medieval Jewish project of countering what Chazan refers to as the Christian "assault on the Jewish future" that became prominent in anti-Jewish polemical discourse in the thirteenth and fourteenth centuries that sought to "pierce to the heart of Jewish capacity to struggle forward in the face of daunting circumstances."[130] For the kabbalists discussed above, the end of history was foreordained, and the inevitable inversion of Jewish fortune at the conclusion of historical time is encoded into the Godhead from which the world derives. Such a discourse offered medievals a privileged glimpse into the broader dimensions of a concealed divine plan in which Jews play a vital role in sustaining the multifaceted structure of being and time through the traumas that they suffer over the course of their exile. But that history does not continue indefinitely. The present world is of a finite duration, and the era of history is shorter still. Kabbalah offered medieval Jews a distinctive take on the venerable Jewish notion that history is moving inexorably toward the fulfillment of messianic promise. As Gershom Scholem has observed, by fusing the restorative and utopian tendencies, kabbalistic eschatologies depict "a past transformed and transfigured in a dream brightened by the rays of utopianism."[131]

By claiming such a bird's-eye view of the present eon of history, this discourse provided a tool for premodern Jews to understand their own present circumstance. By doing so, these texts sought to address cultural despair. How are Jews to understand their own history? And what are they to make of Jewish experiences of violence, displacement, and political disempowerment over time? Are these to be understood as signs of the impending end of Judaism, and validation of Christian or Muslim claims? The texts examined above asserted that Jews alone understand the real forces at work in history, and that those forces, both in terms of the extension of time and the dimensions of space, depart so sharply from the simple appearance of the world that only those who have received the divinely revealed secrets of the Kabbalah are able to understand the true nature of the world and workings of human history. In the kabbalistic imagination, it is non-Jews who lack sight and move through history blindfolded. By embracing such a claim, Jews could reimagine their own past and present. These texts offer important insight into how premodern Jews deployed discourses about the future to make sense of the present. Through an elaborate reframing of the structure of time and the theosophical secrets behind God's providence over historical events, kabbalists offered a way of perceiving a grand secret concealed within Jewish collective suffering on the stage of history. Descriptions of the redemption at history's end were an important part of how medieval kabbalists made sense of the purpose of Jewish suffering, and the important role that they assigned to Jews as the secret agents of history through the practice of Jewish law. By suffering through history as the subjects of powerful foreign nations over the course of their long exile, kabbalists suggested that Jews push history forward toward its transformative conclusion.

SIX

Shaping History

Kabbalistic Writing and Historical Agency

Kabbalists say much about the meaning of Jewish history, the destiny of the Jewish soul, and the orientation of the present to the approaching redemption.[1] Clearly, for them, the Jewish esoteric tradition provides tools for understanding the divine plan behind Jewish historical experience. But what do they think about the ability of kabbalistic discourses to *influence* Jewish history? And how might their claim help us to understand the strategies at play in the production of this literature? Discourse undoubtedly does do more than merely reflect the social environment. Under the right conditions, discourses shape the social environments that produce them. As Bruce Lincoln has observed, discourse is more than a mirror that reflects the social order—it is also an important mechanism for creating social change. While it is true that discourses only become meaningful within social contexts, it is also by means of discourse that social structures are challenged. As Lincoln puts it,

> All the tensions, contradictions, superficial stability, and potential fluidity of any given society *as a whole* are present within the full range of thought and discourse that circulates at any given moment. Change comes not when groups or individuals use "knowledge" to challenge ideological mystifications, but rather when they employ thought and discourse, including even such modes as myth and ritual, as effective instruments of struggle.[2]

The power of discourse lies not only in its intellectual content, but also in its capacity to structure social action and harness it for a particular purpose by being made manifest as a social phenomenon. It is not only kabbalistic thought, but the act of composing kabbalistic texts, that makes Kabbalah part of the social dynamic in Jewish societies. In that sense, Lincoln notes, "that which either holds society together or takes it apart is sentiment, and the chief instrument with which such sentiment may be aroused, manipulated, and rendered dormant is discourse."[3]

What "sentiment" did medieval kabbalists seek to activate through the act of writing books? Medieval kabbalistic texts reflect an aspiration to *shape* Jewish behavior and promote adherence to Judaism by describing the secret, history-shaping theurgic power encoded into Jewish religious practice. The fact that Judaism has persisted in the face of what could appear to be the historical failure of the covenantal promise is something of an enigma. Yet remarkably, despite the many challenges that Jews faced in the premodern world, many retained their identity. Kabbalistic texts from this period may help us to answer, for example, why there were any Jews left to be expelled from Spain in 1492. Jewish conversion to Christianity is not the only phenomenon worthy of inquiry. The fact that many Jews did *not* convert is in some ways even more surprising. What story did they tell themselves to make sense of Jewish identity and covenantal claims in light of Jewish historical experience?

Writing Kabbalah, Shaping History

Medieval kabbalists were remarkably uninterested in sharing personal biographical details or first-person attestations in their texts. They did not seem to find their own biographies to be the stuff of compelling writing. One can almost chart the growth of biographical material in kabbalistic literature against the onset of modernity and the rise of interest in the autonomous individual in the broader cultural milieu. For Jews living in earlier periods, what mattered most when they sat down to write was understanding Jewish collective identity. Despite this, premodern kabbalists did on occasion comment on their own method of writing and sharing kabbalistic ideas. This provides rare and precious visibility into the ways that kabbalists understood the purpose of their own work. In the examples to be considered here, we will see how kabbalists regarded the written dissemination of Kabbalah as a way for Jews to understand their history, and also a strategy for shaping it. Through the power of their words, and by disclosing kabbalistic secrets, they believed that they were providing an essential tool for Jewish survival in exile. The kabbalists considered below believed that their own texts were the key to sustaining Jewish identity in the face of a difficult history.

Many texts composed by kabbalists from the early fourteenth century through the generation of the Spanish expulsion were woven from quotations and adaptations taken from other texts. To greater or lesser degrees, the vast majority of these authors were eclectic compilers of earlier sources. Originality, in terms of creating entirely new ideas, was not the primary value that they perceived in writing books. Isaac of Acre[4] openly acknowledges his own tendency to repeat himself, as well as the words of others. In a passage in *Me'irat 'einayim*, he offered the following observation on the value of repetition and compilation in kabbalistic writing:

> And even though in this passage there are things that were made clear already in what I have written above, it is good in my view to write it out completely as it has been written, or as it has been heard. And if there be only a single novel idea articulated, or a single word alone, regarding that matter, it is of benefit to bring forth the entire passage in this way, which is the way of truth. For sometimes, a wise man who is proficient in wondrous secrets will allusively mention matters that appear to be simple and common discourse. One should not say that a wise man who finds a novel idea within a long passage, and who copies the entire passage for the sake of that [novel] matter, or even an entire book that is prolix in its language, has done so needlessly, since in many cases they repeat and repeat themselves. The response [to such an argument] is that if there is a good thing to be found in [a text], all who love and seek wisdom should not copy only the novel idea alone, but rather he should copy the entire book, since perhaps, for the person who studies it with perfect intention many times at length, concealed matters will be revealed to him that he will rejoice over all of his days.[5]

In this remarkably candid breach of the fourth wall, Isaac of Acre speaks directly to his readers about his own views on writing kabbalistic ideas and copying them from others. Repetition, he claims, is valuable. He suggests that reiterating ideas in their fullness, even if there is only "a single word" that is novel, is the best way to enable one's readers to understand the meaning and implications of the "new" idea. But beyond novelty, re-presenting one's own words or those of others from whom one copies is, Isaac claims, of benefit for those who are trying to learn. The reason, he argues, is that one may think that a particular idea is simple or straightforward, but one never knows which concepts are easily comprehended, and which are opaque to one's unknown, future readers. Mere allusion, he felt, is inadequate. He therefore asserts that if one finds a good or novel idea in a text, they should copy the entire context of that statement. One never knows if a future reader might need that additional material in order to understand the particular novel point. By giving the readers the necessary tools, Isaac believes that they may finally understand something that they had not previously known. They will then, he hopes, have concealed matters revealed to them, which they will "rejoice over" for the rest of their lives.

Is Isaac of Acre merely being hyperbolic? It would appear in this passage that he felt strongly enough about this to interrupt the flow of his discourse in order to give advice regarding the best way to share kabbalistic knowledge in written form. For him, saying more is better than saying less. His hope was that others will come upon the work and be enlightened. Based on statements found in other kabbalistic texts, it would seem that many shared the opinion that disseminating kabbalistic knowledge could bring life-long joy, to the point that it could help sustain Jewish identity as they endured the conditions of exile. Kabbalah, in their view, was a refuge. The authorship of the *Tiqqunei Zohar* described Zoharic literature in precisely these terms: "Permission is granted to the souls [of Israel] that are exiled from place to place, pursuing the Holy One, blessed be he and his *Shekhinah*, to nest in this composition, regarding which it is said, 'like a bird that wanders from its nest, so too a man wanders from his place' (Prov 27:8)."[6] Jews wandering in exile are like birds who have strayed from home,[7] and the Zohar is compared to a nest. As Biti Roi has shown, the image of the nest and the act of "nesting" in this passage invites the reader to regard the Zohar "as a space in which they can live and act."[8] The remedy for Jewish historical experience, in which they are driven from "place to place," is the Zohar itself. Those who pursue God and his *Shekhinah* have been given permission, according to this author, to literally nest in the text, finding a home in the words that kabbalists have written. Such a text, in their view, not only helps Jews understand the meaning of their history—it *shapes* Jewish history by enabling Jews to endure the realities of exile.

The authorship of the *Tiqqunei Zohar* offers a number of comments on the special nature of the Zohar and the divine approval of its composition and dissemination.[9] The images they deploy of the divine retinue that approves of the revelation of the book speak to the authorship's self-presentation as un-veilers of privileged knowledge. But to what end? The purpose of this special book is often described as both sustaining Jews in exile, as well as serving a role in bringing the Jewish experience of exile to an end.[10] Consider the fol-lowing comment: "Numerous people in the world below will be sustained by this composition[11] of yours when it is revealed below in the final generation at the end of days. Because of it, 'you shall declare freedom throughout the land' (Lev 25:10)."[12] Like the previous passage, this comment describes the function that the Zohar will play in supporting Jews during exile. At the same time, it says that the Zohar will be revealed during the final generation before redemp-tion, suggesting that Zoharic discourse serves an instrumental role in bring-ing history to a close. The declaration of freedom prophesied in Leviticus 25, which refers to the arrival of the Jubilee year, is interpreted here as a reference to messianic redemption. The author boldly states that "because of it," mean-ing, by means of the Zohar, redemption will arrive. In this passage, kabbalistic literature preserves Jewish life through a tumultuous history just as it helps to end history by ushering in the messianic age.

The *Ra'aya mehemna* section of the Zohar, which is, like the *Tiqqunei Zohar*, among the latter strata of this literature likely composed during the early fourteenth century, makes a very similar comment.

> The righteous will comprehend, from the aspect of *Binah*, which is the tree of life, regarding which it is said, "the righteous will shine with the splendor of the firmament" (Dan 12:3), with this composition of yours, which is *The Book of Splendor* (*sefer ha-zohar*), from the splendor of the supernal mother, Repentance. They will not require trials. Since Israel is destined to taste of the tree of life in the messianic future, which is this

Book of Splendor, they will depart from the exile in mercy by means of it, and in them the verse will be fulfilled, "the Lord alone guided them; no alien god with him" (Deut 32:12).[13]

In this passage, which uses language similar to the *Tiqqunei Zohar*, the knowledge contained in the Zohar is said to derive from the *sefirah* of *Binah*. The "taste" of the tree of life that is Israel's destiny in the messianic era is contained in the Zohar, which, for this author, means that by reading the Zohar in the present historical moment, Jews will be able to depart from exile "without trials." Escape from the pain of history can be acquired through a kabbalistic book. When Israel leaves the exile by means of the Zohar, they will fulfill the verse from Deuteronomy stating that God alone guides his people. That divine guidance, according to this author, is the Zohar. As this same author notes in a different anonymous text: "Redemption depends upon Kabbalah and masters of the Kabbalah, whose attribute is *Tifferet*. It releases the vow and oath[14] of the exile."[15]

Just as the composition of the Zohar was designed to aid Jews in exile and hasten redemption, the author of the *Tiqqunei Zohar* also claimed that those who reject Kabbalah lengthen the exile. For them, kabbalistic discourse and historical events are closely related. As this author puts it, "One who causes Kabbalah and wisdom to depart from the written and oral Torah, and who encourages [others] not to engage in them and says that there is nothing but the literal sense in the Torah and Talmud, truly it is as though he causes the divine flow to depart from that 'river' and 'garden.' Woe to him! Better for him never to have been created, and never to learn the written and oral Torah. He is regarded as though he caused the world to return to chaos, and caused poverty in the world and lengthening of the exile."[16] This author directs their fury at those who encourage the study of Scripture and rabbinic texts as though they have no kabbalistic meaning. The effect of this, they argue, is an interruption of the divine overflow from the "river," or *Yesod*, into the "garden," *Shekhinah*. This in turn causes a disordered historical reality of chaos, poverty, and extended exile.

The historical fate of the Jewish people is presented here as contingent upon the acceptance of Kabbalah. In another comment, the text describes students of Torah who neglect the study of Kabbalah, stating that they perform righteous acts only for themselves, which drives away "the spirit of the messiah." In reference to scholars such as these, the author declares: "Woe to those who cause [the messiah's spirit] to depart from the world, for they make the Torah desolate, and do not wish to study the wisdom of Kabbalah. . . . Woe to those who cause poverty, war, plunder, murder, and ruin in the world."[17] Just as the Zohar is instrumental in ushering in redemption, the rejection of the legitimacy of Kabbalah drives the messiah away, further delaying the long-awaited end of exile. And not only that—this text suggests that historical catastrophes will result in the interim. This author does not shy away from extreme language in suggesting that there are historical consequences to impeding the dissemination of kabbalistic texts.

Shem Tov ibn Shem Tov introduced his *Sefer ha-'emunot* with a history of Jewish knowledge, as well as an argument for the role of knowledge in shaping Jewish history. He begins by acknowledging that Jewish history is in an undeniably degraded state. In his view, "The truth, beyond doubt, is that the [the cause of the] great decline in fortune that has befallen us is this: just as it is the case that our people is intended to be superior to all other nations of the world as it pertains to the public manifestation of faith and wisdom and prophecy, so too, our great downfall has occurred as a result of their loss."[18] Loss of the unique Jewish wisdom correlates with historical exile. Moreover, in Ibn Shem Tov's view, the conditions of exile exacerbate the problem:

> Due to the length of the exile, the entryways of correct beliefs have been sealed in the parables and riddles of the prophets and the wise men in their books, and it is impossible to grasp the root of the beliefs from a single composition on all of the judgments of the Torah and the commandments. Regarding this, there have been significant disagreements in every generation, thus requiring many important men in Spain and other kingdoms, the notables of the exiled people, to investigate and inquire into the ways of the Greeks and the Muslims and the Christians, and other peoples who follow in their path of intellectual inquiry.[19]

The loss of the uniquely Jewish wisdom, now sealed behind incomprehensible hints in biblical and rabbinic literature, is an aspect of the tragedy of exile.[20]

This, according to Ibn Shem Tov, is what has led so many Jewish scholars to pursue philosophy—a field of learning that he regards as heretical.

A passionate desire to remedy this situation led Ibn Shem Tov to compose his book. He hoped that he would be able to share the true knowledge revealed by the prophets, which has been preserved exclusively by kabbalists. As he puts it, after studying the works of the Jewish philosophers, "a great fire burned within me, for a leprous affliction had broken out among the people of Israel. And I saw that in recent generations it is the experts in philosophical specula- tion who have become heretics and denied [their faith], and there is no doubt that, as we have been afflicted by tragedies and evil decrees, it is for this reason that our community has been lost, for the sophists and pretenders of wisdom have abandoned the tent [of faith] and burst its boundary, and the masses of the people have followed after them, until 'our bones have dried up and our hope has been lost.' "[21] The historical damage done to the Jewish people by the spread of philosophy is, according to Ibn Shem Tov, the destruction of their faith. It is philosophers, he claims, who have abandoned Judaism and con- verted to Christianity. And it is philosophy that has caused Jewish identity to become unsustainable in exile. At this point he then states plainly his reasons for writing his book: "For this reason it occurred to me over the course of days and years to compose and record in a book some of the matters retained in my possession from the paths of the Torah and the Kabbalah. . . . This is to say that even if the wellsprings of wisdom and goodness have been sealed before us, it is not impossible that 'one from a city or two from a family' (Jer 3:14) might still retain some trace of that which bears witness to the testimony of the Torah."[22] Composing a kabbalistic book, according to Ibn Shem Tov, was his way of preserving the knowledge that has declined as a result of exile.[23] This project of reclamation serves, in his view, to bolster waning Jewish identity. Given the growth of Jewish apostasy in the wake of the violence of 1391 when Ibn Shem Tov took up this project, the implications of his comments are clear—sharing Kabbalah is a way of preserving Judaism in the face of violent threats to its very existence.

A number of kabbalists describe their project of writing kabbalistic texts as one of reconstruction and recovery of a lost treasure. Michel de Certeau has observed that "only after a once-living unity has been decomposed into a thousand fragments—only after its death, in other words—can the scattered traces that attest to what it was be assembled as an object of discourse, a unity whose purpose is to create intelligibility."[24] Abraham Adrutiel, writing in the early sixteenth century in the wake of the Spanish expulsion, described his efforts in kabbalistic writing in a manner strikingly evocative of de Certeau's perceptive observation. In his *'Avnei zikkaron*,[25] Adrutiel noted that "in the present time, due to our many sins, the Torah has been forgotten in Israel due to the weight of exile, and the troubles that come one after the other."[26] That is not to say that there remains no valuable Jewish knowledge, including kabbalistic knowledge. Instead, the problem, as Adrutiel described it, was that kabbalistic knowledge had become fragmented. In speaking of the many valuable kabbalistic texts he had encountered, he noted, "when I, the young one, fox among lions, beheld their delightful words scattered one here and one there, it occurred to me to accrue benefit for myself, as well as for all those who are beginners in the study of Torah and this wisdom, to bring them together as one summation."[27] He also invoked the language of the introduction to the anonymous *Sefer ha-Shem*, written more than two hundred years earlier in Spain,[28] that the words of the kabbalists are scattered in "concealed scrolls," with each author describing kabbalistic ideas in their own manner through allusive language "in a terse way, in order to conceal the matter." The result could give, he feared, the mistaken impression that Kabbalah is incoherent, and one might therefore "entertain in his heart that division reigns among the wise ones."[29] His concern was that the teachings of the kabbalists would be "mocked, and people [would] cleave to foreign wisdoms." The situation, in his view, has gotten so dire that "the Torah was almost forgotten among Israel in all of the kingdoms of Sepharad, heaven forbid, were it not for the great tamarisks, the students of Rabbi Isaac Canpanton, who spread Torah in Israel; they and their students and their students' students; and were it not for the fact that the Lord of Hosts has permitted us the remnant of survivors who remain today in the kingdom of Fez."[30] Like Ibn Shem Tov, Adrutiel presented his project as one of preservation and reclamation, in order to spread the true message of Kabbalah and to counter the deleterious effects of "foreign wisdom" on the people of Israel as they endure their exile. In de Certeau's parlance, Adrutiel conceived of himself as one who gathers "scattered traces" in order to "create intelligibility."

The difficulties of coping with the problem of recovering kabbalistic knowledge had become, in Adrutiel's view, even more difficult since the death of Shimon bar Yohai, the great master of the Zohar. As he puts it,

> From the day that the eternal light was taken from us, he who is the great tree, Rabbi Shimon bar Yohai, may the memory of the righteous and pious be for a blessing, the grindstones were scattered and the manna departed. However, there remains for us a single flask, which is his holy and renowned book. By means of it, the millstones were rectified, and the waters were as they were at first. Those who came after tasted of them. Also, the holy book, whose light shines to all of the wise ones, *Sefer ha-bahir*, and Pirkei Heikhalot Rabbati, and Zutarti, and Ma'aseh Merkavah, and Seder Eliyahu Rabbah, and Seder Eliyahu Zuta, and the famous *Sefer yetzirah* of our father Abraham, peace be upon him, and *Sefer peli'ah* which is *Sefer ma'ayan hokhmah* of Moses, and *Sefer bitahon* of Rabbi Judah Batera, and *Sefer ha-kanah ben ha-Kanah*. All of these have come into our possession from the earlier wise men, excluding that which has been concealed from us in the myriads and thousands.[31]

Despite his protestations that the knowledge of Kabbalah had been lost, Adrutiel lists, in addition to the Zohar, quite a few books that have been preserved that were available to him. This is not a full accounting of the sources to which he had access, since there are other kabbalistic texts that he cites in his work that he did not mention here. But it demonstrates the nature of his project: he wanted to make Kabbalah both available and coherent for his readers, in order to help them survive in exile. To do this, he felt that he could contribute by bringing together a selection of sources in a way that would enable his readers to understand their own condition better. To that end, he says that he composed his work so that "it would be a reminder for myself, and for this reason I called it *'Avnei zikkaron* (Stones of memory), for they are words gathered together from the words of the wise, called 'stones,' since the word stones (*'avanim*) is from the word 'builders' (*bonim*), for they are the 'stones' and 'structure' (*binyan*), and 'sons' (*banim*), and 'builders' (*bonim*), who receive from the learned of the Lord."[32] Adrutiel's choice of title for his book suggests that it was simultaneously an act of memory and an act of creative construction. By recollecting Kabbalah, he hoped to recover and re/present the lost patrimony of the Jewish people. Exile has decreased this knowledge, but by composing kabbalistic books, Adrutiel and other kabbalists believed that they could give Jews access to memory of the secrets that they needed to survive history.[33]

The authorship of the *Sefer ha-meshiv*, which was likely composed in Spain several decades before the expulsion, was much less sanguine regarding the value of the surviving kabbalistic texts. The author argued that in many cases, the secrets contained in earlier kabbalistic writing are so deeply concealed that they can only be understood through new divine revelations, which are recorded in the first-person voice of God throughout *Sefer ha-meshiv*. At one point, for example, the divine persona in the text mentions that the true kabbalistic meaning of Abraham's encounter with the angels in Genesis 18 was not explicitly explained in Nahmanides's commentary on the Torah, despite the fact that "he inquired of me regarding this secret when he composed his book." God, according to this text, "responded to him with a hint and did not explain" because "the time had not arrived until now to reveal it."[34]

The voice of God in *Sefer ha-meshiv* praises the Zohar as a great text filled with important secrets, but often laments that with the death of Rabbi Shimon bar Yohai, "his book and his wisdom died along with him."[35] In many cases, the divine voice asserts that the explanations that it offers regarding the true meaning of passages in the Zohar are only permissible to share openly because the end of days is imminent.[36] In an introduction to the commentary on the parashah of *Lekh lekhah*, the text states: "I revealed [these secrets] to my son Shimon [bar Yohai], for they are the words of the living God, and I concealed them until the arrival of the time [of redemption]."[37] At one point, the divine voice provides a candid description of their objective:

> The secrets of my Torah and its hidden mysteries are without end. Behold, I reveal to you in this book most of those that have remained hidden until now. After my prophet Moses died, they remained concealed and hidden in the secret of the storehouses of wisdom. The secret of these storehouses are the secrets of my Torah and its hidden mysteries. Regarding these secrets the prophet alluded when he said, "With joy shall you draw waters

from the wellsprings of redemption" (Isa 12:3), hinting that at the time of redemption, all these secrets and hidden mysteries will be revealed to you through the power of my precious names. . . . These secrets . . . are the wellsprings of redemption, for it has not been permitted for them to be revealed until the "wellsprings of redemption" arrive. This is the secret of this verse that we are telling you, that these secrets will serve as a sign and allusion for you of the arrival of my messiah, may he be revealed speedily in your days. Permission has not been granted to reveal them until now.[38]

In this passage, a kabbalistic text purporting to be the first-person word of God describes itself as the revelation of divine secrets that have been hidden for the vast majority of Jewish history.[39] The reason God gives for finally uncovering these hidden mysteries of the Torah is that due to their connection to the "wellsprings of redemption," the time has finally arrived to make them known in the world. The implication is that this text serves as an instrument for disseminating the secrets that are part of the final stages of the redemptive process. Uncovering these unique mysteries is the immediate precursor to the messiah's arrival.[40] The author suggests that the open disclosure of hidden kabbalistic secrets began in the year 1403.[41] In order to usher in the final stages of history, an act of collective memory must take place in which the lost secrets of the kabbalistic tradition are finally recovered. The text speaking in the voice of God states, for example, "'In the future the Torah will be forgotten by Israel' (Sifrei Devarim 48:9) This refers to the present evil generation. And I have awakened your hearts despite yourselves in order to open this entryway, and it has been opened and inscribed and engraved in a book, by my power with my hands and my word and my command."[42] In this striking image, the act of recovery of the lost kabbalistic secrets of the Jewish people takes place through a book dictated by God himself revealing the concealed secrets of the Zohar.[43] As the author states elsewhere regarding why the Zohar was composed in Aramaic, or *lashon bavli*, instead of Hebrew, which is more accessible, "such it had to be until the arrival of the present time. The season has arrived to reveal them [the secrets of the Zohar] in accessible language (*lashon rahav*) so that you will be able to understand by making it clear in the language of this book."[44] For this author, the onset of the messianic era involves the composition of a kabbalistic book by God himself to explain another kabbalistic book from an earlier era. The end of exile is also the end of secrecy. As the text states elsewhere, "These secrets reside in the mystery of the concealed palaces, which have now been opened without any key so that all who wish may enter."[45]

The redemptive function of memory is not the only model for thinking about the role of kabbalistic books in ushering in the messianic age. As Moshe Idel has pointed out, the texts associated with the *Sefer ha-meshiv* and *Kaf ha-qetoret* add a new element of antagonism toward the study of philosophy.[46] The author of *Kaf ha-qetoret*, writing in the late fifteenth or early sixteenth centuries, described the "supernal yeshiva of Samael" (*metivta de-sama'el*), in which the "foreign wisdoms of philosophy" are taught. They claim that many books have descended into the world from this evil house of learning, which in turn, in his view, has harmed many Jews. In this author's telling,

> Due to their books written by them, they have lengthened the exile of Israel, because they have given power and dominion to Samael the wicked and his confidant, which are two foreign gods who deceive nations. They possess the "abomination" and the "bow" from the right hand of Samael the wicked. The "abomination" is the power of Esau, and in the left hand, the "bow," which is the power of Ishmael. . . . They anger the divine retinue, making it known that Israel will not be redeemed until they have forgotten these foreign wisdoms. At the time when the messianic king desires to be revealed, they will be sustained by the light from the books of the great light, Rabbi Shimon ben Yohai and his aid. One who studies these books draws the power of the *Shekhinah* down into the world.[47]

Redemption requires a double move of forgetting and remembering. The "foreign wisdoms" from the yeshiva of Samael manifest in the world in the form of philosophical books are like weapons, according to this author, in the hands of the Christian and Muslim nations. In order to move history toward its proper resolution, Israel must forget these books. At the same time, they must preserve and study kabbalistic books, since it is the Zohar, the works of Shimon bar Yohai, that will sustain them in the messianic period. The suggestion is that studying philosophical books mires the Jewish people in exile, while the study of kabbalistic works, by contrast, is a foretaste of the messianic days in which all Jews will be sustained by such wisdom. Writing and reading books of Kabbalah, and avoiding works of foreign philosophy, is how, according to the *Kaf ha-qetoret*, Jews will resolve their historical condition.

In one comment, the author is very direct in saying that his own book can be instrumental for Jews seeking to overcome the conditions of exile. In a discussion of the mystery of reincarnation, he breaks in with a direct address to the reader, warning them of the dire historical consequences of not believing in this particular kabbalistic doctrine.

> If you do not believe me and do not heed my book, "they shall say, the Lord did not appear unto you" (Exod 4:1), that you should know his secrets. "What is this in your hand? And he said, a rod. Cast it upon the ground. And he cast it upon the ground and it became a serpent" (Exod 4:2–3). This is the serpent from which the foreign nations were established. One who mocks and scorns these words, "it became a serpent." Due to the lack of faith in the reincarnations of the people of Israel, as the majority do not believe in these discussions of *gilgul*, this is the reason that the rod becomes a serpent that strikes Israel in the world. "Take hold of its tail" (Exod 4:4), which is the dominion of the serpent, "and it became a rod in his hand" (ibid.). This is the secret of the *Pan of Incense* (*Kaf ha-qetoret*).[48]

Disbelief in the kabbalistic secret of reincarnation is presented here as a cause for the continuation of the exilic condition of the Jewish people and the delay of their messianic redemption.[49] Disregard of this kabbalistic matter, and in particular, rejection of the author's own particular formulation of it in his book, turns the rod of Moses into a dangerous serpent. Given the associations throughout the book between the serpent, Samael, and Esau, the suggestion is that the rejection of kabbalistic wisdom empowers Christian nations to oppress Jews. Disarming the serpent entails taking hold of its tail, which means grasping the secret of the *Kaf ha-qetoret*—the very title of the book. In this bold formulation of the historical theurgic function of his own task of writing, the author claims that by embracing the authenticity of the secrets he shares with his readers, Christian power will be transformed from the deadly serpent to the rod in Moses's hand. By this account, writing and sharing kabbalistic books is how Jews will exert power and proactively resolve their historical predicament. As the author formulates it in a comment on Psalm 78:6, "'That a future generation might know; children yet to be born,' in the exiles, who go from defeat to defeat, and the Torah will be forgotten among Israel, and their yeshivot of Torah study will be destroyed. 'They shall rise up and tell their children.' By means of the composition of books."[50] Exile is characterized by the loss of Torah study and collective forgetfulness, while redemption, according to the author of Kaf ha-qetoret, is brought about by writing books.

Felling Cedars, Weaving Silk

Meir ibn Gabbai was born in Spain and exiled in 1492 at the age of thirteen.[51] He became an important kabbalist in the Ottoman eastern Mediterranean whose work enjoyed wide circulation. His three major books: Tola'at Ya'akov, written in 1507, 'Avodat ha-kodesh in 1531, and Derekh 'emunah in 1539, cite extensively from an eclectic array of earlier sources, and it is clear that he had access to a wide-ranging library of kabbalistic literature.[52] In the introduction to Tola'at Ya'akov he described his motivations for writing the book. He claimed that he wrote it largely for his own personal use to support his reflections on the meaning of prayer and the liturgy, and demurs from any claim to authority as an original kabbalist. In his description of himself, he says "I am merely one who transcribes from book to book, and scroll to scroll, 'for there is not a word upon my tongue' (Ps 139:4), 'for I am brutish, less than a man' (Prov 30:2), how can I attain the knowledge of the holy ones?"[53] And yet for all his humility, he also argues that the precious value of his book will be appreciated by those who are worthy to comprehend his far-reaching objective. Though Ibn Gabbai often depicted himself as merely a disseminator rather than an innovator of Kabbalah, he attributed significant value to the task of assembling and sharing kabbalistic ideas. Spreading knowledge of Kabbalah served an urgent social need, in his view, enabling Jews to understand the secret of their own power, their place in the world, and the meaning of their collective historical experience. In Ibn Gabbai's estimation, his books were necessary for supporting Jewish life in exile by demonstrating that the difficulties that Jews endured over the course of their history have not been in vain. He argued that only through the study of Kabbalah, and in particular, his formulation of it, can one properly understand that Jewish suffering and displacement serve a purpose.

An examination of the discursive strategies at play in his corpus reveals the social work that Kabbalah performed, or was perceived to perform, in the decades following the Spanish expulsion. Ibn Gabbai selectively organized a diverse array of kabbalistic texts and ideas in order to assign meaning to Jewish life under the conditions of exile, arguing that Jews possess a unique form of power and agency in the course of human events. His work is resistance literature par excellence.[54] He claimed that Jews wield power through words—the speech acts of prayer, the study of Torah, and the embodiment of the divine command through the observance of Jewish law. Ibn Gabbai explained in the introduction to his earliest kabbalistic book, *Tola'at Ya'akov* (The worm of Jacob), a work on the meaning of prayer, that he gave it that title because

> just as a worm's power is exclusively by means of its mouth, so too, the people of Israel's power is exclusively by means of their mouths. In the [midrash] Yelamdeinu[55] on the portion of *Yehi be-shalah* [it says,] "Why are the people of Israel compared to the worm? Just as the worm strikes down the cedar tree merely by means of its mouth, which is tender, and yet it strikes down that which is powerful, similarly, the people of Israel have only prayer, and the gentile nations are compared to cedar trees, as it is written, 'Assyria was a cedar in Lebanon' (Ezek 31:3)."[56]

Like the humble worm (or termite) that topples the mighty cedar tree with its tiny and delicate mouth, Ibn Gabbai argued that the people of Israel, despite their lack of physical and political power, can reign victorious over the rest of the nations of the world through their mouths, that is, their words. As he puts it, "They defeat their enemies through the power of their mouths, and for this reason they are compared to the worm."[57] Jewish discursive practices are an instrument of power for Ibn Gabbai, though a power of a particular sort— one that is less obviously strong in the conventional sense, but capable, after a long and concealed process, of ultimately producing victory. Jewish historical power in relation to other nations is, on this reading, akin to the worm's slow erosion of the tree from within.

Drawing upon a different midrashic image,[58] Ibn Gabbai compared the people of Israel and their words to another kind of worm—the silkworm. While both the worm that attacks the cedar and the worm that produces silk are referred to with the same Hebrew term, *tola'at*, it is a combination of these two senses that gives meaning to the title of Ibn Gabbai's earliest book. He notes that "in Bereishit Rabbah they say, 'Another matter: just as this worm brings forth silk from its mouth from which are made garments of glory, garments of royalty, similarly, the people of Israel pray with their mouths, glorifying the Holy One, blessed be he, granting him sovereignty over them.'"[59] In this image, the silkworm uses its mouth constructively rather than destructively, as it spins the fibers that compose the garments that adorn kings. The people of Israel, in Ibn Gabbai's comparison, adorn the divine through their utterances of prayer, accepting God as their king, and thus serving their role as subjects of the Israelite divine kingdom that will, one day, reign victorious.

In Ibn Gabbai's depiction, the people of Israel are actively engaged in an enterprise that will culminate in the victory of God's people over their enemies and the return of divine rule, even though this process remains invisible to those who are not privy to the secret workings of Jewish power. In an inversion of the apparent state of the Jewish people in exile, Ibn Gabbai suggests that the politically weak and fragile Jewish body politic wields a form of divine power on earth by means of their words. The image of the worm slowly gnawing at the wood of the cedar tree, combined with that of the silkworm spinning out the fibers that make up the strong and beautiful fabric of royal garments, provides insight into how Jews who were receptive to Ibn Gabbai's works may have made sense of their own historical predicament. Ibn Gabbai's articulation of the concealed means by which Jews secretly move forward on a path to historical victory has much to tell us regarding the role that ideas stemming from earlier medieval Spanish Kabbalah have played in the construction of Jewish identities in various times and places. For Ibn Gabbai, Jewish practices associated with words constitute the matrix of a meaningful and empowered Jewish place in the world. The only way, in his view, for Jews to properly access their full theurgic power is by studying Kabbalah. This, he claims, is why he wrote his books.

The historical stakes of disseminating kabbalistic knowledge, in Ibn Gabbai's view, could not be higher. Performing the law and engaging in prayer with the proper kabbalistic intentionality is the key to Jewish survival in the postrabbinic exile. The problem is a lack of direct divine revelation. Unlike the uniquely audacious author of the *Sefer ha-meshiv* literature who depicted God revealing kabbalistic secrets explicitly in the first person, Ibn Gabbai regarded the lack of firsthand communication with the divine as a challenge for Jews in exile. Kabbalistic texts, however, offer a solution to this problem. As Ibn Gabbai somewhat dolefully states the matter:

> Because the Holy Spirit has departed from the people of Israel, and the wise men of the Mishnah and the Talmud, may peace be upon them, have departed to their house of eternal rest, all that remains in our possession is the received tradition (*kabbalah*) of the unification of the lights encompassed in the great [divine] name, which everyone must unite unto *'ein sof* by directing the intention of the heart, and through thought devoid and cleansed of all inappropriate distraction. This is the secret meaning of, "sustain me with raisin cakes" (Song 2:5). This refers to the community of Israel [the *Shekhinah*] in this present exile, since the Tabernacle of David has fallen, she requires support.... To whom does she say this? To her children in the current exile, for she is exiled with them.... The one who knows how to unite the great [divine] name, even though there is no blessing to be found in this afflicted exile, such an individual assists and supports the community of Israel in the exile.... The one who unites the Great Name with his Glory in the manner that has been explained in this book, must unite harsh Judgment with Mercy together, to combine them with one another and to assure that all is one unity, to sweeten and rectify them with one another, such that they become a single bond and a single unity. The individual who knows this and directs their intentions regarding it, he is the one who supports and assists the community of Israel in this present exile. In praise of this unification, and those who unify it, the Holy Lamp [R. Shimon bar Yohai], peace be upon him, has said in the *Sefer ha-tiqqunim*,[60] "The masters of unification are inscribed in the concealed Thought."[61]

The problem that Jews face in the exile, according to Ibn Gabbai, is the lack of direct prophecy through the "holy spirit," and the loss of the now departed rabbinic sages. What does remain in Jewish hands is the Kabbalah—the secret teachings regarding the theurgic function of Jewish practices that bring about the "unification of the lights" in the divine realm. The one who knows these kabbalistic secrets and how to properly use them is the one who sustains the "community of Israel," another name for the *Shekhinah*, the last of the ten *sefirot*, as she experiences exile along with the people of Israel. Knowledge of Kabbalah, according to Ibn Gabbai, enables effective theurgic action, which brings about the amelioration of the forces of Judgment (the *sefirah* of *Din*) with the forces of Mercy (the *sefirah* of *Hesed*).[62] Supporting the indwelling of the *Shekhinah* in the world is the unique privilege of Jews who have received the kabbalistic tradition. Despite the fact that, as Ibn Gabbai notes, "there is no blessing to be found in this afflicted exile," Kabbalah enables Jews to cope with the conditions of exile by theurgically enacting the mandates of Jewish law. Their reward is to be "inscribed" in the highest reaches of the realm of the *sefirot*, referred to here in a citation Ibn Gabbai brings from the *Tiqqunei Zohar* as the divine "concealed thought." Writing books about the kabbalistic understanding of Judaism is thus an uncovering of the way that Jewish life is world-sustaining theurgic action. As Ibn Gabbai observes elsewhere, "This is the virtue of engaging in the work of the Torah and performing the commandments; by means of this the worlds are balanced and united as one, for the indwelling of the *Shekhinah* among the lower entities is the cause of the unification of all of the worlds and their balancing together, which is the unification of the supernal and lower entities."[63]

Prayer is a category of theurgic action in which Ibn Gabbai was particularly interested.[64] Two of his three books, *Tola'at Ya'akov* and *'Avodat ha-kodesh*, dealt extensively with this issue, and it is clear that Ibn Gabbai wished to present a fully kabbalistic rendering of petitionary prayer to his readers. One of the concerns that he addressed is the perception that Jewish prayers go unanswered.[65] Traditional Jewish liturgy entails a significant number of requests for safety, health, prosperity, and collective redemption that could seem at odds with Jewish historical misfortune, and particularly with the trauma of expulsion from Spain. Ibn Gabbai addresses this concern with a citation from an anonymous passage that he identified only as a matter that he has found among the "wise men of truth," but which is in fact taken word for word from a text deriving from the school associated with the *Sefer ha-temunah* in fourteenth-century Byzantium.[66] The text as Ibn Gabbai cites it reads:

One must know that there are four gradations of prayer, corresponding to four groups of the people of Israel. The first and highest gradation is prayer that ascends to and attains the level of *Tifferet*, which was utilized by Moses our teacher, peace be upon him, and he was answered immediately without any hindrance. The second gradation attains the level of *'Atarah*, which was used by all other prophets. They were answered, but not as quickly. The third gradation approaches close to the firmament of *'Aravot*,[67] which was employed by the early righteous ones, and they were sometimes answered, and other times not. The fourth gradation, with strenuous effort, can only approach the firmament of the moon. This is utilized by all of the rest of the people of Israel, and one in a hundred or one in a thousand [of these prayers] are answered. These four different gradations [of prayer] can be found in four different historical epochs: the era of the patriarchs and Moses; the era of the rest of the prophets; the era of the wise men of the Talmud; and the current era, in which the people of Israel are in exile. Not even one in a thousand of them are answered, for if they were, they would be redeemed.[68]

Ibn Gabbai embraces a notion of the decline of the generations,[69] in which there is a progressive loss of proximity to God from the era of the prophets, through the sages of the rabbinic period, and into the current exile.[70] This corresponds to the four levels of petitionary prayer, the highest of which was only attained by Moses, whose requests were always fulfilled by God immediately. The passage Ibn Gabbai cites here attributes this to the fact that his prayers ascended to the level of *Tifferet*, the sixth *sefirah*, while the rest of the prophets only attained the level of *'Atarah*, a cognomen for the tenth *sefirah*, or the *Shekhinah*. All other prayers since the time of the prophets only reach gradations within the regions below that of the *sefirot*, which accounts for the fact that the sages of the Talmud were "sometimes answered," and in the current exile since then, "not even one in thousand" are answered, and even that happens only with "strenuous effort." Ibn Gabbai appropriates this text from the *Temunah* literature as support for a comprehensive kabbalistic discourse to account for the historical predicament of the Jewish people from biblical times up to his own moment. This text acknowledges that if it were the case that all prayers were answered by God, the Jewish people "would be redeemed" immediately, since request for the swift arrival of the messiah is part of the daily liturgy. Ibn Gabbai, however, resorts instead to a text that professes a dispensational historiosophy according to which access to God has diminished, and Jewish petitions during prayer are unheeded due to the effects of exile in both the human *and* divine realms, causing a disruption in the fabric of being.

All of this begs the question of the efficacy of Jewish prayer in general. If requests for the safety and collective redemption of the Jewish people are not answered in the current epoch—if, in fact, prayers of that sort are not even acknowledged by God at all except in very exceptional cases—what is the purpose of prayer? What, indeed, is the purpose of Jewish life in exile if their voices are silenced and their God is aloof? To account for this harsh but undeniable aspect of Jewish historical experience, Ibn Gabbai turns once again to the kabbalistic notion of theurgy for an answer. The primary objective of prayer, he argues, is not for mundane matters in this world, but rather, the Jew who prays should aspire to unite the *sefirot* in order to address a *divine* need, expressed in terms of uniting the divine name, and bringing blessing into the world, even if the effects of that blessing do not create immediate positive material outcomes for that individual.[71] Proper intentionality based on knowledge of Kabbalah renders prayer powerful, but not in the sense of earthly reward. Ibn Gabbai regarded the allure of such mundane benefits as a deceptive ruse that "draws individuals after its false treasury, distancing them from the true treasure, which is cleaving to the supernal, shining light."[72] When prayer is offered in the proper manner, thought cleaves to its source in the divine, and "everything becomes like a column, and that supernal light is drawn below through the power of thought that draws it below, and the *Shekhinah* is found below. Thus, the brilliant light is drawn and spreads forth in the place where the master of that thought dwells."[73] Those who know the true power of prayer, according to Ibn Gabbai, do not seek earthly reward. Their goal should be to bask in divine light. The righteous are those who seek "to demonstrate that his desire is for his Lord, to know his ways, to find favor in his sight. For that individual, this is the essence [of prayer]."[74]

When understood in this way, even the loss of the Temple is not an irrecoverable obstacle to obtaining the theurgic objective of worship. Ibn Gabbai accepted the rabbinic notion that prayer is superior to sacrifice,[75] and that it is the Jewish practice of prayer that enacts *tiqqun*, or rectification of the divine and human worlds, bringing about the eventual messianic redemption. Jews awaiting the messiah are thus empowered through their prayers and actions, in Ibn Gabbai's view, but not for the purpose of reward in the form of earthly dominion.

> Isaiah the prophet, of blessed memory, has said, "And he said to me, 'You are my servant Israel, in whom I glory.' And I have thought, 'In vain have I toiled, for naught, for mere breath, my strength have I sapped. Yet my cause is with the Lord, and my wages with my God'" (Isa 49:3–4). The verse, "You are my servant Israel," alludes to us the reason why we are commanded to pray. The true worshipers are called by the name "Israel," referred to with terms of dominion and greatness, since by means of prayer, authority is placed upon their shoulders, and they are elevated above all other creatures in order that the great name should be glorified by them for their sakes.[76]

The act of "true worship" entails the unification of the divine name,[77] which then accords them an elevated status over all other creatures, but not that of this-worldly political power. Rather, they are the agents of a much higher, divine power, by means of prayer conducted with the necessary kabbalistic intention. Reward for such actions is delayed and only revealed fully at the moment of death:

> When people pass from this temporary life to everlasting life, it is shown and made known to them that their efforts bore fruit, and that this was through the rectification of the divine glory that they performed in this life. . . . How do they grasp and know this? The Holy One, blessed be he, reveals their reward to them at the moment when they pass from this world, and from this they come to know that the rectification of the divine glory, in the manner that we have explained, created for them such glorification.[78]

The act of "rectification of the divine glory," or uniting the *sefirot* and returning the *Shekhinah*, the tenth and final *sefirah*, to her proper place in the divine economy, is rewarded fully after death, according to Ibn Gabbai. At the moment of death, the veil is pulled back revealing the direct connection between theurgic acts in this life and reward in the next. In this passage, Ibn Gabbai boldly suggested that the kabbalistic tradition not only conveys the secret to eternal reward, but also that it transmits a tradition that details how the heretofore concealed connection between Jewish service to God in this life and reward in the next will finally be revealed. Kabbalah, and by extension, Ibn Gabbai himself, as an author who shares such knowledge, is thus a vehicle for the public sharing of divine secrets of the highest importance for understanding the place and role of Jews in the world and the flow of human history.

These notions regarding the theurgic power of the practice of Jewish law and ritual are not insights unique to Ibn Gabbai. He drew upon a substantial and rich corpus of kabbalistic works, as we have seen in the chapters above. The kabbalistic library was quite vast by the first decades of the sixteenth century, and while some texts were short and fairly simple, others were long and complex. Sharing the teachings of the Kabbalah by compiling these difficult and dispersed texts into lucid and readable books, as Ibn Gabbai did, was, in his estimation, a task of great importance. By disseminating kabbalistic ideas through his books, Ibn Gabbai, far from being a mere humble scribe, assumed a role of cosmic significance—that of the purveyor of knowledge (*in the manner that we have explained*, as he so often put it) necessary for enabling the attainment of the true telos of Jewish action.

Accounting for Exile

The question of exile recurs throughout Ibn Gabbai's corpus in a variety of contexts. In fact, it is the framing device of the introduction and conclusion to *'Avodat ha-kodesh*. In the opening passages of that book, he describes the soul, emanated from God, as only fully at home in the divine realm. He poetically gestures to the joys of the soul before birth, "while she was there in the bundle of life, in the secret of unity, perceiving wonders, beholding awesome matters in the [supernal] mirrors, standing before the King, the Lord of Hosts."[79] But, it was God's will to create a physical universe, according to Ibn Gabbai, so that there would be a material realm in which divine intention could be brought into action. As Ibn Gabbai puts it, "This is the awesome significance of creating the physical world, to bring forth the supernal divine thought to the perfection of performance and action, corresponding to the ultimate intention of supernal thought."[80]

The physical world, however, is not the soul's proper home.[81] Life in this world is defined by exile. The task before each Jew is to fulfill their divinely ordained role in the material world in order to return to their place in the divine realm. In Ibn Gabbai's estimation, feeling at home in the world is unnatural. Rather, "one must regard themselves as 'a foreigner in a foreign land' (Exod 2:22), and bind one's loins with righteousness to return to the Lord who sent them forth, to perform his work and to engage in his worship, progressing continuously in the direction of his purpose which he has come to complete, and to return to his destined place."[82] Ibn Gabbai argues that there is an inherent longing in the soul to return to its source within God. The question is how to achieve that goal while confined to material existence. The answer for Jews is that "a key has been given to them called 'repentance,' by means of which the gates of the world of mercy are opened; a supernal redemption bringing the enslaved into freedom. For there is a power in the soul that, while it dwells in the world below, arouses the supernal entities."[83] The theurgic capacity of the divine Jewish soul, in his view, brings the "enslaved" soul into freedom.

Commenting, in the voice of the soul, on the nature and purpose of the creation of humanity, Ibn Gabbai writes,

> "I am a sojourner in the land" (Ps 119:19), I am from among those who dwell in the supernal realm, and I have not come here to settle, but instead, to sojourn and to perform the will of my creator, and my destiny is to return to my land and birthplace. If so, how then shall I attain this in a short time? For I know not my time of departure; the day is short and the work is great (Avot 2:15). Therefore, this is the kindness that you shall do for me;[84] do not withhold the means of fulfilling this purpose. This is why it says, "Do not withhold your commandment from me" (ibid.). I performed them when I was still among the supernal entities, and though I have come to a foreign land, I will not engage in its modes of conduct, to convert to [this] world, subsisting in an ephemeral world. Therefore, there can be no worship or fulfillment of one's purpose except in this land

in which I have come to be a sojourner, for it was for this purpose that the world was created—for it to be a place of worship.[85]

Jewish service to God by means of Jewish law is described here as the purpose of the physical world. Pious Jews must therefore regard themselves as displaced, not merely as a result of their historical exile, but also as a condition of the nature of reality itself.[86] The soul in this world is always in foreign territory, no matter their physical location or political condition. This, according to Ibn Gabbai, is the larger divine purpose in creating humanity. The world exists for Jews to serve God, even when they are in exile and subject to foreign nations. This is why all Jews, in Ibn Gabbai's view, should regard themselves in this reality as displaced strangers resisting a foreign culture, refusing to become habituated to the ways of this world. Instead, the Jew's task is to fulfill the mandates of Jewish law and engage in prayer, just as the soul did before birth, in its true home in the divine realm of the *sefirot*. In this way, Jews imitate the ways of the patriarchs, who all described themselves as "strangers" or "foreigners," a self-appellation that Ibn Gabbai interprets as alluding to the ontological condition of the Jewish soul in the material world.[87]

In order to unite the divine name and accomplish the purpose for which Jews were created, Ibn Gabbai asserts that "there is no path other than through the attainment of the wonders of the Torah, for the secrets of the Torah . . . are the true wisdom; they guide one to this rectification. By means of them, peace will dwell upon the supernal will, which is unification, as will be made clear in this book with the help of heaven."[88] By means of the "secrets of the Torah," or Kabbalah, Jews are able to bring about the "rectification" and "unification" of the divine, balancing the upper and lower worlds and thus accomplishing the purpose for which they were created. While Ibn Gabbai endorses a highly exile-centric view of Jewish history and the nature of reality, he wants his readers to regard themselves not as passive subjects to the flow of history, but as the active agents of its proper unfolding. Crucially important here is Ibn Gabbai's full embrace of the notion that knowledge of Kabbalah is central to this objective. He describes "this book," that is, Ibn Gabbai's own *'Avodat ha-kodesh*, as the guide that will reveal and explain the secrets of this Jewish theurgical power. The self-effacing transmitter of kabbalistic lore is far more than a silent link in a chain of transmission. Ibn Gabbai places himself and his work as a writer within a grand narrative in which the very act of transmitting kabbalistic knowledge through the composition of kabbalistic texts is essential for enabling Jews to navigate the exile in which they find themselves. Such work, according to Ibn Gabbai, is essential for empowering his coreligionists to practice Judaism in a manner that fulfills the ultimate purpose of creation itself. It also reveals to them their central role as the agents of all human history.

This point is emphasized near the end of the introduction to *'Avodat hakodesh* where he enumerates the various reasons why he decided to write the book. After describing the theurgic purpose of the mandates of the Torah, he asserts that "all of this is accomplished by means of engaging in the Torah and performing its commandments for their own sake, in the manner that will be explained in this book. This is the path of true life that the faithful servants live all the days that they are foreign residents (*gerim*) in the land, until they return to the 'land of life,' their birthplace."[89] The Jews— strangers exiled in the strange land that is the physical universe—need kabbalistic instruction of the sort contained in "this book" in order accomplish their purpose in the world. As he states the matter in the continuation of the discussion:

> Everyone is obligated to complete his true purpose, to accomplish the intention for which he was created, which is the endeavor to live the true life, which is the pursuit of this knowledge to which we have alluded, which leads one to recognize their creator, and to worship him perfectly out of love, to do "that which is good and just in the eyes of the Lord" (Deut 12:28), in keeping with his will, as will be explained in this book, with the help of heaven.[90]

The "true life" of the exiled Jewish soul in the material world, now further exiled over the course of Jewish history, can only be attained through kabbalistic knowledge. Providing that knowledge is Ibn Gabbai's purpose. Writing his book is, in his view, a powerful contribution to the task of helping Jews to endure, and ultimately overcome, their historical condition.

Ibn Gabbai repeatedly underscores the importance of composing kabbalistic texts. Without such guidance, he feels that Jews would be lost in a kind of double exile: their souls would lack the necessary knowledge in order to serve the role for which they were emanated into physical bodies in the world, and their bodies would lack the instruction needed in order to fulfill the commandments properly and work toward their own liberation from the domination by foreign nations.[91] For Ibn Gabbai, his books bring refuge to Jews weathering their multilayered exilic reality. As he notes near the end of the introduction,

> There is great benefit and concealed mystery in the writing of books investigating the true wisdom, since it is the primary cause of the knowledge of God. By means of them, the dove, mentioned in the Song of Songs,[92] finds a place of rest for her feet in her exile. . . . The third benefit [of writing this book] . . . is for the one who "whose heart so moves him" (Exod 25:2), to come forth from the gloom of time (*mehashkhei ha-zeman*), to ascend from the abyss of his vanities and desires, that he may come and contemplate what is included in this book, and thus he will know his creator and worship him with true and complete worship.[93]

Ibn Gabbai imagines his readers—his fellow Jews seeking to make meaning out of the complex historical dramas of Jewish life in exile—to be like the dove in the Song of Songs seeking its lover. But the image of the dove finding "a place of rest for her feet" evokes Genesis 8:9, when the dove that Noah sent out to search for dry land "found no resting place for its foot." In bold terms, Ibn Gabbai depicted his own composition that teaches the "true wisdom" as a refuge for Jews enduring exile, adrift upon the great flood of history. Such texts, in his view, enable Jews to overcome history's terrors, or the "gloom of time," as Ibn Gabbai puts it. Through a discourse of escape from history, Ibn Gabbai attempted to help Jews see past the temporary matters of this world and to focus their attention on higher matters. Abandoning his humble posture, Ibn Gabbai asserted without reservation that those who "contemplate what is included in this book" will be able to worship God in a "true" and "complete" manner, which as noted above, was the purpose for creating the material world. As sojourners in foreign territory, Ibn Gabbai believed that Jews require proper kabbalistic instruction. His own work as an author of such books, in his view, responded to that need.

The preservation of the kabbalistic tradition is, for Ibn Gabbai, a matter of collective Jewish survival. He regarded it as an act of divine providence that this secret wisdom was never lost from among the Jewish people. The collective Jewish memory of kabbalistic secrets has, in Ibn Gabbai's view, enabled Jews to endure the events of history. For this reason, he disputed, in the most adamant terms, Maimonides's claim, echoed by other medieval Jewish philosophers, that the "secrets of the Torah" were lost to Jews, but were preserved among Greek philosophers in a corrupted form, from whom Jews then recovered it.[94] He asserted emphatically that the "books of the true wisdom were not lost" or transferred into the "possession of another people," but that "they remain in our hands today from the time of the first Temple."[95] The authenticity of the Jewish chain of esoteric transmission is so important to Ibn Gabbai because it grounds his claim as a purveyor of revealed secrets. Like Shem Tov ibn Shem Tov, *Sefer ha-meshiv*, and Abraham Adrutiel cited above, Ibn Gabbai maintains that rational speculation cannot supply the kind of knowledge that Kabbalah contains. For all of them, the act of composing texts that contain this knowledge and that make it accessible to others is a way of empowering Jews to endure history and to serve their purpose in exile.

Ibn Gabbai does acknowledge that many Jews are not as well versed in kabbalistic matters as they should be, and that this is in part the reason why the exile has persisted for so long. As he notes at one point in a discussion of the reasons for the persistence of the subjugation of the people of Israel by foreign powers, "Sin causes the absence of this wisdom and knowledge, and it is now only to be found among 'the elevated ones, and they are few' (b. Sukkah 45b), in particular in the present exile in which the divine unity has been concealed, 'and there are none who know, and no one considers.'[96] This is the cause of the length of the exile, and the many misfortunes, without question."[97] The absence of kabbalistic wisdom prolongs exile, and conversely, Ibn Gabbai believed, the dissemination of that knowledge—the *remembering* of Kabbalah— both enables Jews to cope with the difficulties of exile and teaches them how to bring about messianic redemption.[98]

As noted above, Ibn Gabbai did not regard himself as an innovator of new kabbalistic ideas. He paid homage to the many important authorities and texts that preceded him. This is particularly the case with regard to the Zohar, which he accepted as the most authoritative kabbalistic book. In the introduction to *Tola'at Ya'akov* he assured his readers that he relies upon "the great tamarisk tree to which I have affixed myself, the famous book of the true wise men of Israel, the midrash of Rabbi Shimon bar Yohai, peace be upon him, that boldly reveals the secrets of the Torah in a manner that was not permitted to any other."[99] In several places throughout his works, Ibn Gabbai described the chain of transmission of kabbalistic knowledge.[100] In one particularly interesting passage, he described the Zohar and its unique role in sustaining the Jewish people in exile. He noted, "Rabbi Shimon bar Yohai received the tradition from Rabbi Akiva, and this was after the destruction of the Temple. This holy one, peace be upon him, is the author of the *Midrash ha-ne'elam* which is called *Sefer ha-Zohar*, which was written by him. And he, peace be upon him, promised in that sacred text that multitudes would be sustained by it in the final days."[101] He then cites an interesting passage from the *Tiqqunei Zohar* that speaks with great reverence regarding "Rabbi Shimon and his companions" who "produced this text." The continuation of the passage cited by Ibn Gabbai reads,

This composition is like Noah's ark, into which every species gathered [during the flood]. . . . Now that this text has been revealed in the world, multitudes gather unto it, concerning whom it was said, "both those who are standing here [with us today], and those who are not standing here [with us this day]" (Deut 29:14). By means of this composition, they are here with us this day.[102]

Noah's ark appears here as a metaphor for the Zohar itself as a means of survival during a time of calamity.[103] The appearance of the Zohar after a period of concealment is regarded as a lifeline given by God to the Jewish people. The citation of Deuteronomy 29:14 implies that the Zohar enables Jews in their current exile to be like those who heard the direct word of God at Sinai. The implication is that the Zohar sustains Jewish life in exile by overcoming the linearity of time, enabling the past and present to converge in the constant remanifestation of the revelatory moment described in Deuteronomy 29.[104] Reading the Zohar is, according to this passage, to be present with all other generations at Sinai. The Zoharic "ark" provides access to a realm behind the contingencies of history.

The words of the *Tiqqunei Zohar* are certainly bold, and in many respects, Ibn Gabbai's suggestion regarding the value of his own contributions to kabbalistic literature was no less ambitious. Commenting on this passage, he goes on to say that through this "wondrous and sacred text" of the Zohar, comfort is brought to those who suffer

> this bitter and lengthy exile, for there is no comfort for the soul like the study of the soul of the Torah, which is the true, received wisdom. By means of it, one comes to know God's will, may he be blessed, regarding his worship and commandments. This, too, was wonderous divine providence bound to the beginning, that this wisdom not be lost or forgotten among the people. To demonstrate the powerful extent of this providence, this holy composition [the Zohar] was revealed in the world after having been concealed and hidden. When it was revealed in the world, many were drawn to it and turned to its meaning, as he [Shimon bar Yohai] promised, peace be upon him, [when he said,] "when this composition is revealed, multitudes will be drawn to it." . . . With the revelation of this composition, the light began to shine. . . . Then, the dove found a resting place to land in her exile.[105]

In this discussion in a kabbalistic text *about* another kabbalistic text, Ibn Gabbai returns to the image of Noah's dove searching for dry land after the flood. Here it is the Zohar, in his view, that is the metaphorical landing site for the dove, which, like his own compositions, served as the firm grounding for Jews seeking refuge in exile. Ibn Gabbai also underscored the notion that preserving knowledge of Kabbalah—the "soul of the Torah" that brings comfort to the people of Israel during this "bitter and lengthy exile"—was a matter of divine providence, since Jewish life would be unsustainable without it. He even cleverly suggested that the reason why the Zohar was "concealed and hidden" for a period, since it was an undeniable fact that mention of it did not begin until the late thirteenth century,[106] was to demonstrate that the revelation of the Zohar at that time was an intervention by God into Jewish history. While some notions of the secrets of the Torah were already well known, the particular form that they took in the Zohar answered the needs of Jews at that historical moment. That particular composition enabled the "light to shine," and has continued, in Ibn Gabbai's opinion, to support Jews in exile, sustaining them like Noah's ark upon the floodwaters of history. For Ibn Gabbai, the preservation of kabbalistic knowledge and books is proof that "the Lord our God protected his righteous ones, and did not abandon us in our exile."[107]

In this sense, the Zohar is more than a consolation. The study of this text serves an eschatological function, since "in the last generation, it will be revealed to those in the world below, and studying it will cause us to return to our possession, which is the arrival of redemption."[108] Judah Hayyat made a similar argument a few decades earlier in his *Minhat Yehudah*, declaring, "Happy are we and how fortunate is our lot that we have the great merit of the Zohar, which those who came before us did not . . . for in their time it had not been revealed. Do not be surprised by this, for in truth it was not to be revealed until the final generation, which we are in now. . . . Through the virtue of those who read and study it, the messiah will arrive."[109] Hayyat even associated his own survival of the many dangers and traumas that he experienced during his exile from Spain with his pre-expulsion activities of collecting Zohar manuscripts.[110] Like Hayyat and other kabbalists mentioned above, Ibn Gabbai connected the revelation and study of the Zohar with the onset of messianic redemption. But Ibn Gabbai's project, despite allusions to bringing about redemption through the writing of kabbalistic books, is not primarily one of activist messianism. His main concern was the construction of a sustainable vision of Jewish life under the conditions of exile. By situating himself and his books within this narrative, Ibn Gabbai advanced a strong claim regarding the positive social function of kabbalistic discourses like his own in the overall scope of Jewish history.

Kabbalah and the Exile from Spain in Ibn Gabbai's Project

The final two chapters of *'Avodat ha-kodesh* focus on the meaning of the exile in Egypt as an extended metaphor for the meaning of Jewish history and life in exile. While space does not permit a full presentation of his arguments, it is important to note that in that discussion he is more explicit in describing the parallels between the exile into Egypt and subsequent redemption, and processes that occur within the realm of the *sefirot*. The earthly Egypt correlates to the third *sefirah*, *Binah*, from which the lower seven *sefirot* emerged. According to Ibn Gabbai, within *Binah*, before the emanation of the world, "the powers of light and darkness, good and evil, and all opposites, were intermixed there, like silver and dross intermixed together."[111] The emergence of the lower *sefirot* and the cosmos from the "supernal Egypt" of *Binah* caused the disentanglement of these opposites, such that "the sacred and pure souls were distinguished from the impure souls."[112] Without this "exodus from the supernal Egypt," Ibn Gabbai argues, "nothing would exist, and neither the supernal nor lower entities would have been created."[113] The events that happened to the people of Israel in the physical land of Egypt were designed by God, according to Ibn Gabbai, in keeping with the divine "supernal pattern," in order that, in the earthly Egypt, "one nation would become intermixed with the other, pure and impure, good and evil, light and dark, Israel and Egypt." At the moment of redemption, through signs and wonders, "redemption and liberation were brought to Israel, and they were separated from the foreign peoples, and he refined and purified and distilled them from the dross that was intermixed with them. . . . Exodus from Egypt above, and exodus from Egypt below; deliverance of souls above, and deliverance of bodies below."[114] Ibn Gabbai interpreted the biblical exile of the Israelites in Egypt as a divine method for disentangling the forces of good and evil, both spiritual and physical. The experience of exile in Egypt was necessary in order to collectively refine and purify the Jewish people, and separate them from the rest of the nations of the world. Jewish distinctiveness, according to Ibn Gabbai, required collective Israelite suffering and disempowerment. The pain of exile, according to Ibn Gabbai, was a necessary aspect of God's selection of the Jewish people to be his holy, chosen nation.

On such a reading, history, including its many traumas, contains a grand secret. For those who are read in, that secret reveals the hidden truth that all human events on the historical plane—despite the many appearances to the contrary—have been for the benefit of Jewish people, preparing them to carry out their concealed mission. In Ibn Gabbai's kabbalistic looking glass, Jewish historical misfortunes signify divine favor instead of abandonment. The pangs of exilic suffering are necessary for enabling Jewish souls to attain their true purpose, which is the creation of a future that fulfills the original intention of creation.

Ibn Gabbai's discussion of exile as a remedy for past transgressions brings his kabbalistic reading of Jewish history full circle. The exile of the soul into the physical world, and the exile of the Jewish people into foreign territory, reflect an intradivine process playing out simultaneously on the stage of history. His primary aim is to situate collective Jewish experiences of displacement and disempowerment within a broader narrative arc that grants meaning to Jewish life and actions in the present, as well as hope for a transformed future. The sin of Adam, the sin of the golden calf, and ongoing Jewish laxity in the performance of the law, in Ibn Gabbai's telling, created effects in the divine realm that account for Jewish disempowerment and dislocation. At the same time, he argued that the true divine plan for creation is for Jews to be the most dominant nation on earth. The rectification of the world entails both a rebalancing of the forces of sanctity and impurity in the divine realm, as well as an inversion of the power relations between nations in the realm of human affairs.

It is tempting to draw a direct causal relationship between Ibn Gabbai's use of the image of the hardships of exile as national-collective refinement and his own experience of the Spanish expulsion. Gershom Scholem advanced such an argument, only to uncover later that one of Ibn Gabbai's extended discussions of the need for the refinement of souls through reincarnation in order to bring an end to exile and usher in messianic redemption in *'Avodat ha-kodesh* 2:37 was taken almost word-for-word from a text of responsa on kabbalistic matters exchanged between Joseph Alcastiel and Judah Hayyat that was written *before* the expulsion from Spain.[115] And in fact, as seen above in chapter 4, this idea was discussed in detail by many earlier kabbalists.

Scholem's mistaken surmise regarding the direct causal relationship between Ibn Gabbai's formulation of this idea and the experiences of his generation of Spanish Jews with expulsion offers an important insight into the relationship between Kabbalah and history. Rarely are kabbalistic discourses *created* by historical events in the immediate context in which a given text is written. In the case of Ibn Gabbai, Moshe Idel is correct to point out that he never refers to the expulsion of the Jews from Spain anywhere in his literary corpus.[116] Any attempt to draw a direct line between that event and the development of new kabbalistic ideas or images in his work is tenuous at best.[117] Scholem's argument, which he formulates in several places,[118] that kabbalists writing before the expulsion were mainly interested in the primordial beginning of time rather than its end, and only after the expulsion from Spain did messianic redemption become a topic of sustained interest, is, as we have seen in the previous chapter, hard to maintain. However, it is also worth noting that Ibn Gabbai does not refer to *any* contemporary events in his books. The fact that he chose not to write in the genre of a historical chronicle does not mean that he was unaware of or disengaged from contemporary historical events, especially major events with which he had firsthand experience, such as the expulsion from Spain. Ibn Gabbai's work was deeply engaged with the question of historical meaning, and it is not a coincidence that the need to address the meaning of exile had particular urgency for him, such that kabbalistic readings of Jewish exile bookend his magnum opus.

Any given historical moment presents Jewish communities with challenges that elicit engagement with certain aspects of kabbalistic discourse. The choices that are made in order to do that work—especially by authors whose choices met with significant acceptance—provide us with important insight into the ways that Jews construct viable discursive frameworks for giving meaning to Jewish life. In this particular case, Ibn Gabbai mined a vast trove of kabbalistic texts from before the expulsion from Spain in order to assemble a lucid picture of the meaning of Jewish history. He claimed that an important secret revealed by the kabbalistic tradition is that enduring expulsions is all part of a divine plan in which the souls of Israel will be purified to serve as the heroic instruments of divine power, bringing redemption to humanity and the entire cosmic order. Ibn Gabbai's vision of Jewish exile does more than simply summarize the views of kabbalists who came before him. He reassembles earlier ideas in order to emphasize the purifying, productive value of the collective experiences of the Jewish people with exile over the span of Jewish history, up to and including his moment in history.

Such a project, written in the aftermath of the expulsion from Spain, provides vital insight into how Jews at that time understood the meaning of the events of their own generation. Kabbalah enabled Ibn Gabbai to situate that experience within a long history and complex theosophy according to which

Jewish suffering in human historical terms is part of a broader plan for recovering the original divine intent of creation itself. By persisting through the traumas of exile and continuing to observe the law, Ibn Gabbai assured his readers, Jews advance human history toward its proper conclusion by means of, paradoxically, a return to history's origin. What we observe in the compositions of kabbalists like Ibn Gabbai is not the work that historical events like the exile from Spain perform in creating new kabbalistic ideas. Instead, we see the work performed by kabbalists through the creative reassembly of existing kabbalistic images and motifs to make the collective Jewish experience of history in their own moment, which in this case was the generation of the Spanish expulsion, meaningful and viable.

Ibn Gabbai's work reflects a broader phenomenon found in many other kabbalistic texts that came before him. In the kabbalistic imagination, the conditions of Jewish life manifest a secret divine plan. Kabbalistic discourses helped to account for the problems of Jewish history by conjuring an alternate world in which Jewish historical experience of misfortune is understood to be meaningful and powerful. The practice of writing and sharing kabbalistic texts was in many cases explicitly described as a strategy for giving Jews hope and providing them with the necessary tools for enduring the terrors of history. The catastrophic events of the Jewish past were recast as necessary and heroic. Jews were depicted as the central players in an epic narrative that culminates in Jewish triumph. By writing kabbalistic books, these authors sought to counter non-Jewish depictions of Jews as the passive victims of history who have been abandoned by God. For the kabbalists, all Jews living during the period of exile are the main actors of history. By exerting theurgic power through the practice of Jewish law, and by persevering through the painful ordeals of Jewish experience over time, Jews push history forward, while the nations of the world unwittingly watch from the sidelines. Messianic redemption and national triumph need not arrive within the span of an individual Jew's lifetime for that life to be imbued with power and meaning. Simply knowing the kabbalistic secret of Jewish historical experience was a way of making Jewish life in exile bearable. By revealing this mystery to their fellow Jews, kabbalistic authors were, as they saw it, shaping Jewish history by revealing its mysteries.

By sharing this knowledge of the kabbalistic meaning of *galut*, they believed that they were empowering Jews to persevere. Premodern kabbalistic literature is thus a rich repository of valuable evidence for the study of Jewish historical memory, and the strategies Jews have deployed to reconcile the promises of the Jewish tradition with the realities of Jewish life.

Conclusion

What do the catastrophes of Jewish history mean? At the most basic level, this is the question that informs the kabbalistic discourses examined in this book. Behind the many devices they deployed to assert that such misfortunes *do* mean something, that God has already written the entire story of the universe, and that Jews are the central, heroic characters in that drama, anxiety looms. By advancing audacious claims regarding God's secret plans, and by asserting that only the people of Israel know the true story of why the world is the way it is, these texts demonstrate that the problem of history and its terrors could not be easily dismissed. Kabbalistic attributions of meaning to history's disastrous course sought to mask the ghoulish specter of a world ruled by powerful, chaotic forces. The elaborate stories the kabbalists constructed to explain history's horrors reveal the urgency they felt to add something new to the traditional accounting of why the chosen people suffer under the growing weight of their historical misfortunes.

Concealing the nihilistic face of the uncontrolled and arbitrary powers of history is an important function of any culture. The survival of Jewishness as a viable identity over the course of the late Middle Ages suggests that somehow, despite peculiar and often difficult circumstances, Jews were able to find meaning in the collective Jewish historical experience. This book has charted some of the strategies evident in kabbalistic texts that attempted to uncover a purportedly secret key for decoding the meaning of Jewish history. The picture that emerges from the passages examined above is one in which the Jewish people are actively engaged in shaping human history. Ironically, they served as

agents of the divine plan for history by suffering at the hands of more powerful nations. But unlike the rest of the nations of the world, the Jewish people,
according to the kabbalists, are the only nation to whom God has revealed the
secret of history. As the exclusive inheritors, in their estimation, of an authentic divine revelation of the hidden forces behind the veil of world events, they
are the only people who understand the forces at play in human affairs. In
the kabbalistic imagination, it is only *Synagoga* who truly sees. The rest of the
world moves blindly through time. Such an assertion inverts the broadly held
view of Jews in the premodern Christian West as a people trapped in the past
and unable to perceive the reason for their condition in the present. The kabbalists claimed that Jewish historical misfortune was in fact a kind of progress.
By viewing the events of history in this way, kabbalists crafted a discourse of
Jewish historical memory that transformed disaster into power.

The passages examined here do not provide us with sufficient evidence for
making well-grounded scholarly claims about the role that these ideas played
in living Jewish societies. We can only very cautiously say to what extent kabbalistic discourses shaped Jewish history. While the kabbalists clearly hoped
that their texts would help their fellow Jews feel more committed to Judaism and less susceptible to despair in the face of their difficult history, we
can only speculate regarding the degree to which they had that social effect.
But these texts do provide us with a rich reservoir of primary evidence for
studying the *discursive practices* that, when publicly manifested, were part of
the social reality in which medieval Jewish lives and identities took on new
registers of meaning and addressed pressing social concerns. The production
of Jewish memory is an aspect of Jewish history. As I hope has been demonstrated above, premodern kabbalists were deeply invested in this vital cultural
enterprise.

Kabbalistic claims regarding secret knowledge revealed by God that explains the true course of history were one way that premodern Jews sought to
construct social coherence. In the discourses of the kabbalists, Jews remain
God's treasured people, exerting theurgic power and moving history toward
its final destiny, not only despite, but because of their suffering at the hands
of other nations. In the texts considered in this book, Jews are viewed as the
true agents of all historical events, for better or for worse. And as discussed

in the final chapter, some medieval kabbalists explicitly asserted that their own act of writing kabbalistic texts was a crucial step in the Jewish movement through time.

In the academic study of premodern Jews and Christians in Europe and throughout the Mediterranean, scholarship has tended to neglect kabbalistic sources. It is my hope that this book has shown the many ways that these texts provide ample evidence for expanding our knowledge of how late medieval Jews made sense of their place in history as active participants in a broader conversation. Medieval Jews are too often treated as though they really were Augustine's mute waymarks along the historical pathways traveled by Christians. To be sure, Jews and their history were frequently discussed by Christians. But, as we have seen above, medieval Jews also had a voice, and they articulated a detailed conception of their own role in history and relationship to other nations. This book is one contribution to the project of more fully uncovering that voice.

Medieval kabbalists were not the first to notice the gap between the covenantal promise and Jewish historical experience. Biblical and rabbinic authors were also painfully aware of this problem and had their own ways of describing Jewish historical suffering as divine punishment. Like the kabbalists, they could not accept the notion that history was arbitrary. Events, in their view, happen for reasons known only to God. And in the messianic future, God's chosen will reap their reward. Kabbalists added an intricately detailed new layer of meaning to these older conversations. The claim to secret knowledge of the ten divine *sefirot* and their interactions, and the notion that Jewish practices theurgically impact the world above, just as the dynamics of the divine realm drive events in the human world, created new opportunities for elaborating upon the dynamics of history. By building upon the allure of a divinely revealed esoteric tradition about the secret inner workings of God, the kabbalists attributed new meaning to human events in the world below. The misfortunes afflicting the people of Israel were transformed into the material manifestation of imbalances in the divine forces. Kabbalists decoded biblical and postbiblical events to reveal what they regarded as the divine plan for history that God has secretly shared with the Jewish people. The heavenly archons of the nations who control and empower peoples on earth, the kabbalists claimed, were usurpers of divine power within the realm of the *sefirot*, enabling the oppression on earth of the one true people of God. But, they promised, adherence to Jewish law and persevering through exile is how Jews theurgically correct the course of history.

Cyclical lives and worlds were another kabbalistic strategy for understanding history. The reincarnation of the soul, just like the successive regeneration of the cosmos under the aegis of different *sefirot*, considerably expanded the temporal framing for how to think about historical events. No individual lifetime or world stands alone. Each is an iteration in a series. The current historical age of the world is, the kabbalists claimed, the hardest possible stage of an enormous cosmic timeline. And for Jewish souls who endure the present stage of exile and oppression, these texts assured them that their hardships were not only virtuous, but also productive. Redemption cannot come until all Jewish souls have been purified through suffering on the stage of history. By conceiving of Jewish historical experience in this way, the kabbalists depicted historical misfortune as more than punishment that Jews must patiently and passively endure to atone for past and present transgressions of Jewish law. In their view, Jews move history forward by suffering. Kabbalistic descriptions of reincarnation and cosmic cycles suggest that God has mapped out the broad course of history. In the current stage of the world, history is kept on course only through the actions of Jews who accept their fate while continuing to observe the Torah. The great kindness that God has extended to the people of Israel, they argued, was that he revealed the secret of history to them. The sting of exile was, the kabbalists felt, vastly reduced by knowing its hidden purpose.

The final goal of Jewish historical suffering in the kabbalists' view is the end of history. With the arrival of the apocalyptic upheaval at the end of exile, which they warned will be preceded by the traumatic birth pangs of the messiah, Jews will be rewarded and vindicated—not within history, but beyond it. Kabbalists, of course, did not invent the notion of the messiah. What they added to the conversation was a way of imagining the time of redemption as a correction of the imbalance within the Godhead that has empowered foreign nations over Israel during the long course of their exile. They also claimed a new body of secret knowledge for saying when the messiah will come, and how to read recent historical events as harbingers of impending redemption. Like the discussions of the supernal archons, the forces of the divine realm, reincarnation, or the doctrine of the *shemittot*, the topic of messianic redemption was a way of talking about the Jewish historical past and present, and not just a fantasy of the future.

Gershom Scholem famously argued that the messianic idea has been a double-edged sword in Jewish history. On the one hand, the idea gave hope to Jews who longed for the return of their lost kingdom, and in that sense, "there is something grand about living in hope." But on the other hand, "the Messianic idea has compelled a *life lived in deferment*, in which nothing can be done definitively . . . there is nothing concrete which can be accomplished by the unredeemed."[1] While the idea of the messiah may have given Jews encouragement, it also, in Scholem's view, led them to live life outside of human history in a limbo state of passive waiting. But is it fair to say that the kabbalists discussed in this book advanced a passive doctrine? Are Jews, in the kabbalists' view, merely waiting for history to end? In the texts examined in the chapters above, Jews were imagined to be ironically active in their passivity. By suffering defeat and subjugation to foreign nations, and by bearing the pain of ongoing violence, expulsion, and dispossession, kabbalists believed that Jews—and only Jews—were theurgically exerting force on the stage of history. Enduring disempowerment while remaining faithful to God's law was, for the kabbalists, the secret to Jewish power. At the same time, the apparent dominance of non-Jewish nations was in fact merely the effect of their passive role as pawns in a divine scheme. The vindication of the Jewish people before the nations of the world at the end of history will only make clear what the kabbalists believed was happening the entire time—that history is driven by and for the Jews through hidden channels known only to the masters of the Kabbalah.

The texts discussed throughout this book cast into sharp relief the many ways that kabbalists sought to render meaning out of Jewish historical experiences. Such acts of collective memory are more than a lament, or an aspiration for the world to be otherwise, though they are often expressed in those terms. The project that emerges from these texts is one that constructed a Judaism of the present that was viable and meaningful by orienting it to the imagined divine plan for time in its totality. Through their musings on the origin of history and the meaning of its terrors, iterations of the soul and the cosmos, and dreams of redemption, the kabbalists sought to create the conditions for a robust and vibrant embrace of Jewish life in the here and now. Uncovering the divine plan concealed behind the catastrophes of history was, in their view, an urgent task.

Notes

Introduction

1. As Garb has observed, the development of autobiographical egodocuments is a hallmark of early modern Kabbalah. See Garb, *A History of Modern Kabbalah*, 6–7.

2. Bodleian Opp. 228, 239a. See Felix, *Perakim be-haguto ha-kabbalit*, 29n21. Angelet also mentions the exile of the Jews of France in *Livnat ha-sappir*, BL Add. 2700, 413b. See Asulin, "R. Joseph Angelet and the Doctrine," 23n120. Elsewhere in that same work, he mentions that in the ninth month of the year 5785 (1324/1325 CE), he observed a destruction of a Jewish "sanctuary" and the plunder of their property. Isaac Baer suggests that this is likely a reference to inquisitorial violence in Saragossa, see *History of the Jews*, 13–14, citing the printed edition of *Livnat ha-sappir*, 65b–66a. Carlebach discusses a sixteenth-century Hebrew chronograph in which the exile of the Jews of France is mentioned as part of a long list of historical events that are intended to situate the reader in time. See "Seeking the Symmetry of Time," 145. The anonymous early sixteenth-century *Kaf ha-qetoret*, 665, also mentions the exiles of "France, Ashkenaz, and England."

3. See the illuminating discussion in Goldberg, *Clepsydra*, 204–8.

4. Chazan, *From Anti-Judaism to Anti-Semitism*, xiv.

5. See, for example, Hasan-Rokem and Dundes, *The Wandering Jew*; Pedaya, "The Wandering Messiah and the Wandering Jew."

6. On Augustine's views on Jews and Judaism, see, for example, Fredriksen, *Augustine and the Jews*; Jeremy Cohen, *Living Letters of the Law*. See also the helpful review of literature by Jeremy Cohen, "'Slay Them Not': Augustine and the Jews in Modern Scholarship."

7. *De Genesi contra Manichaeos* I.23, PL 34:190–193, cited from Cohen, *Living Letters of the Law*, 25.

8. See, for example, Fredriksen, *Augustine and the Jews*, 260–89. On the application of this image to Jews in medieval Christian discourse, see Resnik, *Marks of Distinction*.

9. *Contra Faustum* 12.12–13, pp. 341–42, cited from Jeremy Cohen, *Living Letters of the Law*, 28. See also, Fredriksen, *Augustine and the Jews*, 270–72.

10. Jeremy Cohen, *Living Letters of the Law*, 24–54; idem, "Alterity and Self-Legitimation," 34–40; Fredriksen, *Augustine and the Jews*, 290–352.

11. Augustine, *Contra Faustum* 12.23, p. 351, cited from Cohen, *Living Letters of the Law*, 29.

12. Augustine, *Contra Faustum* 12.23, p. 351, cited from Cohen, *Living Letters of the Law*, 29.

13. Augustine, *Sermo* 199.I.2, PL 38:1027, cited from Cohen, *Living Letters of the Law*, 36.

14. Krummel, *The Medieval Postcolonial Jew*, 8–9.

15. See ibid.

16. Raz-Krakotzkin, "Jewish Memory between Exile and History," 536.

17. On the strategies employed by medieval Jewish polemicists to account for the length of Jewish exile, see Berger, "The Problem of Exile," 189–204.

18. See Chazan, *Fashioning Jewish Identity*, chapter 8.

19. Chazan, "Representation of Events," 40.

20. Chazan, "Representation of Events," 42.

21. Arnaldo Momigliano, for example, maintained that Jews were not interested in the meaning of historical events. See Idel, "Arnaldo Momigliano and Gershom Scholem"; Raz-Krakotzkin, "History, Exile, and Counter-History," 124–25.

22. See Myers, "Of Marranos and Memory."

23. Yerushalmi, *Zakhor*, 31. See also the Yerushalmi's conversations with Sylvie Anne Goldberg reflecting on this subject collected in *Transmitting Jewish History*, and the studies collected in Carlebach, Efron, and Myers, *Jewish History and Jewish Memory*.

24. Yerushalmi, "Clio and the Jews," 613 (emphasis in the original).

25. For a useful overview of the debates surrounding medieval Jewish historiography, see Ben-Shalom, *Medieval Jews and the Christian Past*, 1–11; Haverkamp, "Historiography," 836–59; Miron, *The Angel of Jewish History*; Gribetz and Kaye, "The Temporal Turn," 347–51.

26. Funkenstein, *Perceptions of Jewish History*, 11. On this debate, see Myers and Funkenstein, "Remembering 'Zakhor.'" Yerushalmi later suggested that he "had no intention of saying or even insinuating that Jews had no historical consciousness in the Middle Ages," and that he simply wanted to make "a clear distinction between

historical consciousness and the way it is expressed." In other words, medieval Jews were perfectly aware of history, but they did not write as historians. Yerushalmi claims that he and Funkenstein were able to come to an understanding about this many years later. See *Transmitting Jewish History*, 2.

27. Funkenstein, *Perceptions of Jewish History*, 17. See also, Urbach, "Halakhah and History."

28. Funkenstein, *Perceptions of Jewish History*, 2.

29. Ibid., 11.

30. Bonfil, "Jewish Attitudes toward History," 10 (emphasis in the original).

31. Ibid., 28.

32. See the classic study by Yitzhak F. Baer, *Galut*. For a general study of this theme in kabbalistic texts, see Elior, "Exile and Redemption in Jewish Mystical Thought." On exile in thirteenth-century kabbalistic sources, see Brown, "On the Passionality of Exile."

33. See Raz-Krakotzkin, "Jewish Memory between Exile," 531; idem, "History, Exile, and Counter-History," 126–27.

34. Raz-Krakotzkin, "Jewish Memory between Exile," 534–35.

35. Funkenstein, *Perceptions of Jewish History*, 36. See discussion in Biale, *Jewish Culture between Canon*, 44–45. David Biale has written extensively on the theme of counterhistory, but in a sense different from Funkenstein, in that a counterhistory is a form of historical writing in which the historian reconsiders or "transvalues" historical facts and sources that had been marginalized by earlier historians. See ibid., 46, as well as *Kabbalah and Counter-History*, in which Biale describes Scholem as a counterhistorian who created a new place for neglected kabbalistic texts in Jewish history. On the inclusion of the genre of apocalypses such as *Sefer Zerubavel* and *Sefer toldot Yeshu* in Funkenstein's conception of counterhistory, see Biale, "Counter-History and Jewish Polemic."

36. Ben-Shalom, *Medieval Jews and the Christian Past*, 5.

37. See Haskell, *Mystical Resistance*.

38. Ibid., 5.

39. Scholem, *On the Possibility of Jewish Mysticism*, 78.

40. Ibid.

41. Scholem, *Major Trends*, 20. Or as he puts it elsewhere, kabbalists writing before the Spanish expulsion were, "on the whole more concerned with creation than with redemption," ibid., 245.

42. Scholem, *Sabbatai Sevi*, 20.

43. Arendt, "Jewish History, Revised," in *The Jew as Pariah*, 96.

44. Scholem, *Major Trends*, 30, cited in Arendt, *The Jew as Pariah*, 97.

45. Arendt, *The Jew as Pariah*, 99.

46. See Huss, *Mystifying Kabbalah*, 58–59.

47. The works of Yitzhak Baer are a notable exception. See his insightful comments in "The Function of Mysticism."

48. Yerushalmi offered the valuable insight that "if Jews in the Middle Ages wrote relatively little history, that does not point to a flaw or lacuna in their civilization, nor, as has sometimes been alleged, that they lived 'outside of history.'" *Transmitting Jewish History*, 130.

49. Here I follow Garb's periodization, with the early modern period of Kabbalah beginning in the mid-sixteenth century with the school of Isaac Luria. See Garb, *A History of Modern Kabbalah*, 1–2; 5–8.

50. While the main emphasis in this book is on texts composed between the early fourteenth century and the generation of the expulsion from Spain, earlier sources are also occasionally cited when helpful for understanding later texts.

51. Fishbane, *The Art of Mystical Narrative*, 24.

52. Smith, *Relating Religion*, 48n63.

53. See, for example, Chazan, "Jewish Suffering."

54. Ibid., 1.

55. See, for example, Baron, "Newer Emphases in Jewish History." On Baron's caution regarding the lachrymose approach to premodern Jewish history in relation to his own understanding of the unrealized benefits of emancipation for European Jews, see Engel, "Salo Baron's View."

56. Teller, "Revisiting Baron's 'Lachrymose Conception,'" 439. See also, Birnbaum, "From Europe to Pittsburgh."

Chapter 1: Terrors of History

1. Scholem, *The Messianic Idea*, 43. Scholem attributed this view largely to the Lurianic Kabbalah, though we will see that this idea was fully operative in earlier sources that predate the expulsion from Spain. See also, idem, *Major Trends*, 248–50.

2. Taubes, *Occidental Eschatology*, 3.

3. Ibid., 32.

4. Eliade, *The Myth of Eternal Return*, 104.

5. Ibid.

6. Ibid.

7. Ibid., 105.

8. See, for example, Idel, *Mircea Eliade*, 145–47; idem, "Some Concepts of Time," 153–60; 176–79.

9. See Rickets, "Mircea Eliade and the *Terror of History*"; Ruiz, *The Terror of History*, 4–9.

10. Eliade, *The Myth of Eternal Return*, 96.

11. Ibid., 98 (italics in the original).

12. See ibid., especially 37–48.

13. Ibid., 102–3.

14. Ibid., 37–38.

15. Ibid., 105–6.

16. Ibid., 107.

17. Ibid.

18. Ibid., 112.

19. On this kabbalist, see Fishbane, *As Light before Dawn*.

20. Isaac of Acre, *'Otzar hayyim*, 86–87 (MS Moscow Guensburg 1062, 85a–b). On this passage, see Idel, "Prometheus in Hebrew Garb," 119–22; Fishbane, *As Light before Dawn*, 67n37.

21. See, for example, b. Megillah 29a.

22. See Dan, "Kabbalistic and Gnostic Dualism"; Dan, "Treatise on the Left Emanation," in *The Early Kabbalah*, 165–82; Ben-Shachar, "The Author of '*Sefer ha-Qelippot.*'"

23. Benjamin, *Illuminations*, 201. See Ruiz, *The Terror of History*, 10–11.

24. See Scholem, *On Jews and Judaism*, 198–236.

25. Ibid., 234–35.

26. See the discussion in Cooper, "A Medieval Jewish Version of Original Sin," especially 446–48, and sources cited in n6, n8. Cooper argues that "during the rabbinic period, contrary to the mainstream opinion, some Jews had a notion of original sin that included the idea that the first sin was transmitted from Adam and Eve to their descendants," 447. On this topic see also, Wolfson, *Venturing Beyond*, 40–41, and n105; Gross, *Iberian Jewry*, 125–29. On original sin in the thought of Hasdai Crescas, see Lasker, "Original Sin and Its Atonement." For a still useful treatment of this topic in pre-Augustinian sources, see Tennant, *Sources of the Doctrine*.

27. See Rembaum, "Medieval Jewish Criticism," and Jeremy Cohen, "Original Sin as the Evil Inclination." On original sin in Jewish philosophical literature from the thirteenth to fourteenth centuries, see Shechterman, "The Doctrine of Original Sin."

28. On Adam's sin in earlier medieval kabbalistic sources, see Yisraeli, *Temple Portals*, 50–66; Ben-Shachar, *Israel and the Archons*, 46n23.

29. See Safran, "Rabbi Azriel and Rabbi Nahmandies," 75–82. See also, Shem Tov ibn Shem Tov, *Sefer ha-'emunot*, 136; 142–43.

30. See Yisraeli, "The 'Messianic Idea,'" 33.

31. See Halbertal, *Nahmanides*, 109–12 and citations on 319n15. Meir ibn Gabbai follows his opinion on this matter. See *'Avodat ha-kodesh*, 2:19. On Nahmanides's reading of biblical events in relation to human history, see Diamond, "Maimonides vs. Nahmanides on Historical Consciousness."

32. Halbertal, *Nahmanides*, 107–8.

33. Ibid., 110–12; Pedaya, *Ramban: Cyclical Time*, 290.

34. See below, chap. 5, 180–83.

35. See, for example, Joshua ibn Shuib, *Peirush sodot ha-Torah le-Ramban*, 36–37.

36. b. Hagigah 14b.

37. See *Me'irat 'einayim*, in *Supercommentaries and Summaries*, 33.

38. Ibid., 34.

39. Ibid.

40. Bayha ben Asher, *Bi'ur 'al ha-Torah*, 68.

41. See discussion in Bereishit Rabbah 12:6.

42. Ibn Shuib, *Derashot 'al ha-Torah*, 3b (Lev Sameah 9). On Ibn Shuib, see Horowitz, *The Jewish Sermon in 14th Century Spain*.

43. *Ma'arekhet ha-'elohut*, 116a.

44. Ibid., 101b.

45. Ibid., 106a. A similar point is made in *Sefer 'ezrat ha-Shem*, Oron, ed., 22: "Before Adam sinned, he was worthy to perceive the concealed light. But at present, the foreskin prevents this, the filth that the serpent cast into Eve."

46. Ibid., 104a.

47. *A Kabbalistic Commentary*, 250.

48. See, for example, Gikatilla, *Sha'arei 'orah*, Ben Shlomo, ed., 1:203–4, 210–18; 2:17–20. On this idea in Gikatilla's corpus, see Ben-Shachar, *Israel and the Archons*, especially 18–21 and references, nn15–26. Gikatilla, *Sha'arei 'orah*, "Introduction," 1:36–39; Goetschel, "Le Motif de sarim"; Gottlieb, *Studies in Kabbalah Literature*, 158–59; Idel, "World of Angels in Human Form," 38–49; Pedaya, *Name and Sanctuary*, 223–33; Wolfson, *Venturing Beyond*, 98–99. See also, *Ma'arekhet ha-'elohut*, 151a-152b; Oron, "The Sefer Ha-Peli'ah and the Sefer Ha-Kanah," 287–89.

49. See *Pirkei de-Rebbi Eliezer* 24:8, 10.

50. See Nahmanides on Lev 18:25. See also Bahya ben Asher, *Rabbeinu Bahya on the Torah*, 1:130.

51. Gikatilla, *Sha'arei 'orah*, 1:218.

52. Ibid.,, 1:204–5. See also, *Sha'arei tzedek*, 1a–b; Ben-Shachar, *Israel and the Archons*, 18–19.

53. Gikatilla, *Sha'arei 'orah*, 1:210. In his earlier composition, *Ginat 'egoz*, Gikatilla also argues that the people of Israel are "the center of the point that is the sacred inner

courtyard, while the rest of the nations circle the perimeter that surrounds the point, and they remain outside," 343. See discussion in Lachter, "Kabbalah, Philosophy, and the Jewish-Christian Debate," 29.

54. Gikatilla, *Sha'arei 'orah*, 1:211–12.

55. Gikatilla, *Sha'arei 'orah*, 1:215–16. On exile and redemption in Gikatilla, see Gottlieb, *Studies in Kabbalah Literature*, 287–88.

56. On the construction of Esau, Edom, and Rome in some early medieval Jewish sources, see Gerson Cohen, *Studies in the Variety*, 243–69.

57. Gikatilla, *Sha'arei 'orah* 1:205.

58. Moscow Ginzberg 557, 38a, cited from Ben-Shachar, *Israel and the Archons*, 133. On this text, which is incorporated into Moses of Kiev's *Shoshan sodot*, see ibid., 83–86.

59. Rome Cazantenza 3158, 152a–152b, in Ben-Shachar, *Israel and the Archons*, 141. Idel attributes this composition to Gikatilla, *World of Angels*, 39–40. However, Ben-Shachar has argued that this attribution is not entirely certain, and that this text may be a reworking of Gikatilla by a later author, *Israel and the Archons*, 119.

60. On this text see Goldreich's comments in Isaac of Acre, *Sefer me'irat 'einayim*, Goldreich, ed., 76–89.

61. Bodleian Opp. Q. 43 (Neubauer 1645), 82a.

62. Ibid., 84b. Compare to Isaac of Acre's comment that "when the generation is blameworthy, the external gradations ascend, and the overflow is directed to that tenth [gradation] that is called 'harlot' (*zonah*), 'maidservant,' 'foreign woman.' 'Alas, she has become a harlot, that faithful city' (Isa 1:21), 'a maidservant who supplants her mistress' (Prov 30:23)," "*Hassagot* on Yehuda ibn Malka's Commentary," 149.

63. *Kaf ha-qetoret*, 334.

64. On this kabbalist, see Idel, *Kabbalah in Italy*, 106–16; idem, *Rabbi Menachem Recanati*.

65. Recanati, *Peirush 'al ha-Torah*, Exod 43.

66. Recanati, *Commentary on Prayer*, Carozzal, ed., 137.

67. *Ma'arekhet ha-'elohut*, 199b.

68. Ibid., 194b.

69. *Tiqqunei Zohar*, 76b.

70. *Hebrew Writings of the Author*, Gottlieb, ed., 62.

71. *Masekhet 'atzilut*, 26a.

72. On this text, see Scholem, *Kabbalah*, 67; *Sabbatai Sevi*, 20–21, who describes this composition as a counterpolemic against critics of the Kabbalah. In my estimation, this text could more accurately be categorized as a systematic introduction to kabbalistic lore.

73. Cambridge Add. 673, 25a–25b; *Sefer 'ohel mo'ed* (Jerusalem 2002), 51–52. See also, ibid., 136. On the archons receiving their sustenance from the tenth *sefirah*, see

ibid., 78. On the archons and their corresponding nations receiving sustenance from the "external chariot," see ibid., 138.

74. For more on this text, see below, 83–7.

75. Parma 2573, 191b.

76. Shemot Rabbah 21:5.

77. *Sefer Ziyyoni*, 93–94. See also, for example, *Kaf ha-qetoret*, 239: "When wars occur in the world, arrayment against arrayment, nations of the world against Israel, such is it among the supernal entities."

78. Gikatilla, *Sha'arei 'orah*, 1:151–52. See also the comments in *Sefer ha-temunah*, 70b, on the "disarray" of the archons.

79. Mark Jurgensmeyer has developed the idea of cosmic war as a way of understanding discourses of religious violence. See *Terror in the Mind of God*, 127–40.

80. Isaac of Acre, *Me'irat 'einayim*, 45. See also, ibid., 137–38.

81. A similar view regarding the derivative nature of the power of foreign peoples and their archons is found in the anonymous text from the circle of the *Sefer ha-temunah*, suggesting that it is because of the divine origin of their power "that they are called 'Gods' (*'elohim*)." See Ben-Shachar and Weiss, "The Order of Emanation," 303.

82. See, for example, Norman Cohen, "Shekhinta ba-Galuta."

83. b. Megillah 29a.

84. On this text, see Porat, *Sefer berit ha-menuhah*, 7–133.

85. Ibid., 314–15.

86. While Gershom Scholem, following other early scholars of Kabbalah, surmised that the *Sefer ha-temunah* was composed in mid-thirteenth-century Spain, Moshe Idel has argued that the text was composed in Byzantium in the fourteenth century. See Idel, "The Kabbalah in Byzantium," 679–88. This text seems to have circulated in multiple versions simultaneously, along with a commentary by a kabbalist also likely from the mid-fourteenth century that is included in many of the manuscripts, as well as the printed editions. See also the recent study by Roee Goldschmidt, "From Byzantium to Eastern Europe." Goldschmidt demonstrates the presence of the *Temunah* literature in Spain already before the end of the fourteenth century, and suggests the possibility that the lengthy anonymous commentary may in fact have been written in Spain. See ibid., especially 300–306. Numerous other texts emanated from this circle, including commentaries on the alphabet, three commentaries on the "divine name of seventy-two" (subsequently published in *Sefer razi'el*, 1701); a commentary on the Song of Songs mistakenly attributed to Joseph Gikatilla in Paris 790; a commentary on the Passover Haggadah mistakenly attributed Moses de Leon, "Peirush ha-Haggadah le-R. Moshe bar R. Shem Tov," and with an updated study and edition by Feuerstein, "Commentary on the Passover Haggadah"; another commentary on

the Passover Haggadah preserved in Parma 3511 and several other manuscripts; a text titled *Sod 'ilan ha-'atzilut* published by Gershom Scholem, another version of which is known as *Sod ha-Shem*, published at the end of the Constantinople edition of *Zohar Hadash*; and a shorter text, *Seder ha-'atzilut*, preserved in Vatican 194 and recently published by Na'ama Ben-Shachar and Tzahi Weiss.

87. *Sefer ha-temunah*, 3b.

88. *Ma'arekhet ha-'elohut*, 105b.

89. Joshua ibn Shuib, *Derashot 'al ha-Torah* (Lev Sameah 70).

90. Recanati, *Peirush ha-Recanati*, Deut, 54.

91. Recanati *Peirush ha-Recanati*, Deut, 27. A similar notion regarding the concubine and her children can be found in Joseph of Hamadan's commentary on the commandments. See discussion in Idel, *Ben*, 426–28. See also, Idel, *Kabbalah and Eros*, 109–17. On the theme of the divine concubine in Recanati and his indebtedness to Hamadan, see Idel, *Kabbalah and Eros*, 122–25.

92. Oxford Bodleian, Mich. 341, 4a.

93. This image, and the idea of the redemptive value of sacred blood-shedding, was an issue in Jewish-Christian polemics. See Biale, *Blood and Belief*, 61–65, 81–122. On the development of blood theology in medieval Christianity, see, for example, Rogers, *Blood Theology*; Bynum, *Wonderful Blood*.

94. See Janowsi and Stuhlmacher, *The Suffering Servant*. On the idea in the Zohar of the suffering messiah who bears the "maladies destined for Israel" in order to "alleviate Israel's sufferings and make them bearable," see Greenstone, *The Messiah Idea*, 179.

95. Zohar 3:218a.

96. MS Jerusalem NLI 144, 1a–1b.

97. *'Otzar hayyim*, 10.

98. Ibid., 55.

99. Based on the *'amri 'inashi* or "folk saying," mentioned in b. Hagigah 9b, "Poverty is good for the Jewish people, like a red bridle on a white horse." Joshua ibn Shuib, *Derashot 'al ha-Torah*, 4b (Lev Sameah 16), mentioned in Horowitz, *The Jewish Sermon*, 176. See also the early sixteenth-century *Kaf ha-qetoret*, 446.

100. *Peirush 'al sefer yetzirah*, 103.

101. Taubes, *From Cult to Culture*, 9. Compare with Cohen's insightful remark that "Jewish messianism was held in check by making inhibitions against messianic action part of the religious messianic affirmation," *Jewish History and Jewish Destiny*, 206.

102. See Scholem, *The Messianic Idea*, 35. On this theme in Scholem, see Biale, *Gershom Scholem*, 178, and below in the conclusion.

Chapter 2: Meaning in Exile

1. Ruiz, *The Terror of History*, 16.

2. Ibid., 17–18.

3. See Oron, "The Sefer Ha-Peli'ah and the Sefer Ha-Kanah" (especially 1–30 on the location and date of composition of these texts). See also, Idel, "The Kabbalah in Byzantium," 693–95, 700, 707; Bowman, "Who Wrote 'Sefer ha-Kaneh,'" 150–52; Netanyahu, "Establishing the Dates"; Baer, *A History of the Jews*, 369–73. See also, Fishman, "A Kabbalistic Perspective." On Jewish life and intellectual history in Byzantium, see Bowman, *The Jews of Byzantium*.

4. *Sefer ha-kanah*, 52.

5. Ibid., 53, On this passage, see Oron, "The Sefer Ha-Peli'ah and the Sefer Ha-Kanah," 311.

6. Based on Gen 25:5–6.

7. *Sefer ha-kanah*, 53–54. Similar discussion on the ascent of the cry can be found in *Sefer ha-peli'ah*, 46–47.

8. *Sefer ha-kanah*, 54.

9. Ibid.

10. Ibid., 54–55.

11. Ibid., 55.

12. *Sefer ha-peli'ah*, 42. See also, ibid., 52, and discussion in Hallamish, "The Kabbalists' Attitude," 308; Oron, "Exile and Redemption," 89–90.

13. Kabbalists are at times quite critical of their contemporaries. For a study of the phenomenon in the *Peli'ah* and *Kanah* texts, see Oron, "Bikoret ha-hevrah." On social critique in the latter strata of the Zohar, see Baer, "Ha-reka' ha-histori."

14. *Sefer ha-peli'ah*, 170.

15. *Sefer ha-kanah*, 92.

16. Ibid., 137.

17. *Sefer ha-peli'ah*, 43.

18. *Sefer ha-kanah*, 97–98.

19. Recanati, *Peirush ha-Recanati*, Num, 104.

20. b. Hagigah 13a.

21. *Sefer ha-peli'ah*, 48.

22. Ibid.

23. Ibid.

24. Ibid., 49.

25. See Wolfson, *Venturing Beyond*, 104n359; Idel in "World of Angels in Human Form," 39–40, as well as Gikatilla, Vatican ebr. 456, 16b.

26. *Sefer ha-peli'ah*, 49.

27. Wolfson notes that Bahya ben Asher observes in his commentary on Deut 30:7 that Jewish life is worse under Ishmael (Islam) than Edom (Christianity), *Venturing Beyond*, 157. See also, Septimus, "Better under Edom."

28. *Sefer ha-peli'ah*, 49.

29. Ibid., 254.

30. Ibid., 49.

31. Ibid., 254.

32. See, for example, b. Berakhot 5b.

33. *Sefer ha-peli'ah*, 85. See also, *'Ohel mo'ed*, Cambridge Add. 673, 48b.

34. *Sefer ha-peli'ah*, 367. See also the comment by Shem Tov ibn Shem Tov, "Ten pure gradations emerged, and ten other gradations emerged, like shells, to refine and purify beings," *Commentary on the Sefirot*, 72. The realm of impurity serves to purify Jewish souls.

35. *Sefer ha-peli'ah*, 199.

36. On the spelling of this name as "Canpanton," see Wolfson, "Judah ben Solomon Canpanton's," 7n2.

37. Canpanton, *Leqah tov*, Wolfson, ed., 64.

38. Ibid.

39. Citing Tanhuma, *Lekh lekha* 9. See discussion in Wolfson, "Judah ben Solomon Canpanton's," 63n384.

40. m. Tamid 7:4.

41. b. Berakhot 17a.

42. On the importance of this event as a rapture in the history of Spanish Jewry, see Ray, *Jewish Life in Medieval Spain*, 195–224. On Jewish intellectual creativity in Spain between 1391 and 1492, see Lawee, "Sephardic Intellectuals."

43. Based on Deut 31:17.

44. Shem Tov ibn Shem Tov, *Commentary on the Ten Sefirot*, Ariel, ed., 74–75.

45. See Huss, "*Sefer Pokeah 'Ivrim*: New Information"; idem, "On the Status of Kabbalah in Spain."

46. Parma 2572, 135b. For a similar argument, see, for example, Meir ibn Gabbai, *'Avodat ha-kodesh*, 1:54.

47. Job 33:30.

48. Parma 2572, 182b–183a.

49. See the discussion in Lawee, "Changing Jewish Attitudes," 2.

50. Parma 2572, 191b. See also, Huss, "On the Status of Kabbalah," 22.

51. Ps 44:23.

52. Ps 44:18.

53. Based on Judah ha-Levi, *Piyyut* for Purim, Parma 2572, 192a–192b. See also, Huss, "On the Status of Kabbalah," 22.

54. On this text, see Idel, "Neglected Writings." For a review of scholarship on the question of the attribution of this text to Joseph Titazak, see Ben-Zvi, *Pan of Incense,* 13–14, and the author's argument that the text was, in fact, written in Spain just before the expulsion, 15–26. Gross argues that this text was likely written shortly after the exile from Spain, but before the events in Portugal in 1497. See Gross, "Geirush Sefarad," 80–82, 90–91.

55. *Kaf ha-qetoret,* 314.

56. Ibid., 455.

57. Ibid., 415.

58. Ibid., 187.

59. Ibid., 242.

60. The manuscript has an erasure at this point, as Ben-Zvi notes, 244n31.

61. *Kaf ha-qetoret,* 243.

62. Ibid., 246.

63. Ibid., 432. See also, Idel, "The Attitude toward Christianity," 89n73.

64. Ibid., 429.

65. The following discussion of Ibn Gabbai has been adapted from my "Silkworms of Exile." For more on this kabbalist, see below, chapter 6, and Goetchel, *Meir ibn Gabbay.*

66. *'Avodat ha-kodesh,* 3:9, 266.

67. Ibid., 1:20, 54.

68. Ibid., 3:4, 242. On Israel and the archons, see also, ibid., 3:13, 291.

69. See Goetschel, *Meir ibn Gabbay,* 430–35.

70. See *Tola'at Ya'akov,* 4.

71. Ibid., 62. Shem Tov ibn Shem Tov makes a similar statement in his commentary on the Haggadah. See *'Otzar ha-rishonim 'al haggadah shel pesah,* 36.

72. b. Shabbat 146a.

73. See Goetschel, *Meir ibn Gabbay,* 452.

74. *'Avodat ha-kodesh,* 2:21, 153.

75. See Goetschel, *Meir ibn Gabbay,* 304–25; Idel, *New Perspectives,* 54–55, Scholem, *Kabbalah,* 175. For an overview of mystical union in Judaism, see Afterman, *And They Shall Be One Flesh.*

76. See Wolfson, *Venturing Beyond,* 109.

77. *'Avodat ha-kodesh,* 3:1, 234.

Chapter 3: The Shape of Time

1. An earlier version of the ideas presented here can be found in, Lachter, "Lives and Afterlives."

2. On this doctrine in medieval Kabbalah, see Scholem, *The Kabbalah of Sefer ha-Temunah*, 5–84; idem, *Kabbalah*, 120–22; idem, *Origins of the Kabbalah*, 461–75; Krinis, "Cyclical Time in the Isma'ili Circle," 20–108; Weinstock, *Studies in Jewish Philosophy and Mysticism*, 153–229; Asulin, "R. Joseph Angelet and the Doctrine of Seven Cosmic Cycles," 1–25; Goldschmidt, "Two Historical Conceptions in Kabbalah," 73–86; Idel, "Sabbath: On Concepts of Time," 167–70; idem, "'Higher than Time,'" 179–85; idem, "The Jubilee in Jewish Mysticism"; Pedaya, "The Divinity as Place," 91–94; Sed, "Le Sefer ha-temunah," 67–84; Schnytzer, "On the Secret of the Sabbatical."

3. Exod 23:10–11; Lev 25:1–7; Deut 15:2.

4. Lev 25:8–13. On the medieval kabbalistic interpretations of the Jubilee and *Binah*, see Idel, "The Jubilee in Jewish Mysticism."

5. See above, chap. 1, n8.

6. Goldberg, *Clepsydra*, 25.

7. See, for example, the studies collected in Wolfson, *Suffering Time*. See also, Wolfson, *Language, Eros, Being*, xi–xxxi; idem, *Heidegger and Kabbalah*, 29–60; idem, *Alef, Mem, Tau*.

8. Wolfson, *Suffering Time*, 151.

9. Ibid., 255.

10. Ibid., 596 (emphasis in the original).

11. Eliade, *The Myth of Eternal Return*, 118.

12. For a critique of Eliade's thinking in this regard, see Idel, *Mircea Eliade*, 145–47; idem, "Some Concepts of Time," 153–60; 176–79.

13. Eliade, *The Myth of Eternal Return*, 132.

14. Ibid.

15. Ibid., 133.

16. Ibid., 142.

17. Carlebach, "Seeking the Symmetry of Time," 144.

18. Scholem, *Origins of the Kabbalah*, 471.

19. Ibid., 474.

20. Pedaya suggests that this doctrine can be detected in the works of kabbalists from the first half of the thirteenth century, *Nahmanides: Cyclical Time*, 32.

21. See Sack, *The Kabbalah of Rabbi Moshe Cordovero*, 267–90; eadem, "'Al parashat yahaso"; Scholem, *The Kabbalah of Sefer ha-Temunah*, 84; idem, *Kabbalah*,

122. Goldschmidt, "Two Historical Conceptions," 80–84. Goldschmidt also points out that a number of post-Lurianic eastern European kabbalists embraced the doctrine of the *shemittot* and the *Sefer ha-temunah*, despite Cordovero's and Luria's strong reservations regarding the implications of this idea for theodicy and free will.

22. See Pedaya, *Nahmanides: Cyclical Time*, especially 209–73; Halbertal, *Nahmanides: Law and Mysticism*, 201–8.

23. See Gottlieb, *The Kabbalah in the Writings of R. Bahya*, 233–37; idem, *Studies in Kabbalah Literature*, 332–39; Idel, "The Jubilee in Jewish Mysticism," 220–23. On texts stemming from this group, see Abrams, "Orality in the School of Nahmanides," 90–93, Yisraeli, "*Keter Shem Tov* of Rabbi Shem Tov."

24. See Oron, "The Sefer Ha-Peli'ah and the Sefer Ha-Kanah," 294–300.

25. Jonathan Schnytzer has recently published an anonymous seventeenth-century text that summarizes the views of a number of fourteenth through seventeenth-century kabbalists. See idem, "On the Secrets of the Sabbatical," 227–40. Roee Goldschmidt has also demonstrated that the formulations of this doctrine as they are found in the *Sefer ha-temunah* texts were embraced by Ashkenazi kabbalists in eastern Europe in the seventeenth and eighteenth centuries. See "From Byzantium to Eastern Europe," 312–16.

26. David ben Judah he-Hasid, *Mara'ot ha-tzova'ot*, Matt, ed., 102. Also cited and translated in ibid., 32. See also, *Ma'arekhet ha-'elohut*, 179b–180a, 187a–190b; Weinstock, *Studies in Jewish Philosophy*, 162–64. Adrutiel cites this passage in *'Avnei zikkaron*, 251–52. On the indebtedness of this kabbalists to Joseph ben Shalom Ashkenazi on this doctrine, see Idel, "Some Concepts of Time," 168; idem, "An Additional Commentary to the Alphabet," 242–45.

27. On the diversity of views in some of the earlier sources regarding the difference between the Sabbatical and Jubilee years, see Krinis, "Cyclical Time in the Isma'ili Circle," 49–50.

28. *Ma'arekhet ha-'elohut*, 189b. See Pedaya, *Nahmanides: Cyclical Time*, 255. The passage from *Ma'arekhet ha-'elohut* expressing this view is appropriated in the pseudepigraphic sixteenth-century text *Ginat beitan*, Oxford Bodleian Opp. 419, 73a. See discussion in Gottlieb, *Studies in Kabbalah Literature*, 496–500.

29. See *Livnat ha-sappir* (Jerusalem, 1913), 1a–b, and the discussion in Asulin, "R. Joseph Angelet and the Doctrine," 6–9; Sachs-Shmueli, Felix, and Kara-Ivanov Kaniel, "Rabbi Joseph Angelet's Twenty-Four Secrets," 254–55. See also Angelet's comments in his "Twenty-Four *Sodot*," Columbia X 893 G 363, 91b. Despite this important difference, Angelet is as unequivocal as other kabbalists regarding the problematic nature of the present world, which he attributes to Adam's sin with the tree of

knowledge, which has brought death into the world, and placed it under the dominion of the sphere of the moon, which is "sometimes perfected, sometimes flawed," leading to the ups and downs of human history.

30. *Shoshan sodot*, 410. See also ibid., 247.

31. Adrutiel, *'Avnei zikkaron*, Turgeman, ed., 247.

32. Scholem, "The Book *Avnei Zikaron*," 269; *'Avnei zikkaron*, Turgeman, ed., 251. See discussion in Idel, "Intro to Alashkar, *Tzafnat Fa'aneah*," 34.

33. See, for example, *'Or ha-ganuz* on Bahir, (*'Amudei ha-kabbalah*), 28; Ziyyoni, *Sefer Ziyyoni*, 182–83.

34. Shem Tov ibn Gaon, *Keter Shem Tov* (*'Amudei ha-kabbalah*), 27. On this history of this work and the complex manuscript witnesses, see Yisraeli, "*Keter Shem Tov* of rabbi Shem Tov."

35. Ibid., 57.

36. Sachs-Shmueli, Felix, and Kara-Ivanov Kaniel, "Rabbi Joseph Angelet's Twenty-Four Secrets," 309.

37. Based on rabbinic exegesis. See, for example, Genesis Rabbah 2:22, "Rabbi Joshua ben Karha said, two entered the bed and seven left it; Cain and his twin sister, Abel and his two twin sisters." On this theme in rabbinic texts, see Teugels, "The Twin Sisters of Cain and Abel," 47–56.

38. b. Bava Batra 75a.

39. *Ma'arekhet ha-'elohut*, 177b. Adrutiel uses similar language regarding sevens in *'Avnei zikkaron*, Turgeman, ed., 248.

40. *Ma'arekhet ha-'elohut*, 187a.

41. Ibid., 187b.

42. On the doctrine of the *shemittot* in Bahya and other authors in the early fourteenth century, see Gottlieb, *Kabbalah in the Writings of R. Bahya*, 229–37.

43. Bahya ben Asher, *Commentary on the Torah*, 3:57.

44. Ibid., 3:58–59. Gottlieb notes that it is unclear what exactly the difference is here for Bahya between the "desolation" of *shemittah* and "chaos and void" of Jubilee, *Kabbalah in the Writings of R. Bahya*, 235–37. Bahya also discusses this topic in his *Commentary on the Torah*, 564–67. See also Gottlieb's discussion of the distinction between the end of each *shemittah* as a time when the world is "desolate" of all forms of life, and the Jubilee when the world is annihilated and then renewed, in Jabob ben Sheshet's writings, *Studies in Kabbalah Literature*, 24–25. Recanati also embraced the view that the world is renewed after the Jubilee. See Asulin, "R. Joseph Angelet and the Doctrine," 15.

45. *Sefer ha-peli'ah*, 147–48.

46. Ibid., 5.

47. Meir Aldabi, *Shevilei 'emunah*, 487.

48. *Sefer ha-kanah*, 170. Joseph Angelet is similarly cryptic in his remark that "the seven Sabbatical cycles function in accordance with the seven *sefirot*. At the conclusion of the activity, they return to Repentance to receive recompense, for from there they emanate, according to the secret of, 'To you, Lord, are greatness and might' (1 Chron 29:11). 'To you (*lekha*),' the sum [of the numerical value of its letters] according to *gematria* is fifty. They are the fifty gates of Understanding, and it is a concealed secret," *Twenty-Four Sodot*, 309.

49. The anonymous *Sefer 'ohel mo'ed*, likely from the fifteenth century, adopts this view as well, Cambridge Add. 673, 45b; *Sefer 'ohel mo'ed* (Jerusalem 2002), 117.

50. Bahya ben Asher, *Commentary on the Torah*, 2:564.

51. See Scholem, *The Kabbalah of Sefer ha-Temunah*, 52; idem, *Origins of the Kabbalah*, 468–69; idem, *Kabbalah*, 121; Idel, "On Concepts of Time," 168.

52. *Ma'arekhet ha-'elohut*, 198b–190a. See Gottlieb, *Studies in Kabbalah Literature*, 338.

53. Adrutiel, *'Avnei zikkaron*, Turgeman, ed., 249.

54. Anonymous marginal gloss on Joseph ben Shalom Ashkenazi's *Peirush 'al Sefer Yetzirah*, 3b. This comment is found in other sources, including BL Add. 26929, 177b and JTS 2203, 173b. See Idel, "Kabbalistic Material from the School," 202. See also, Isaac of Acre, "Commentary on Sefer Yetzirah," Scholem, ed., 392; *Sod ha-Shem*, in *Zohar Hadash* (Constantinople, 1739), 170b.

55. *Sod 'ilan ha-'atzilut*, Scholem, ed., 72.

56. See Scholem, *The Kabbalah of Sefer ha-Temunah*, 62–64, 68,

57. *Sefer ha-temunah*, 29a. See also, Scholem, *The Kabbalah of Sefer ha-Temunah*, 60–61; Goldschmidt, "Two Historical Conceptions," 77–78. From the grouping of texts associated with this literature, see also the anonymous *Seder ha-'atzilut*, Vatican 194, 100b, Ben-Shachar and Weiss, ed., 296, and "Peirush ha-Haggadah le-R. Moshe," 131, as well as the two other versions preserved in Vat. 233 and Vienna 148, published in Feuerstein, "Commentary on the Passover Haggada," 234–35.

58. See Idel, "The Meaning of Ta'amei Ha-'Ofot Ha-Teme'im,'" 18.

59. *Sefer ha-temunah*, 29a.

60. See Scholem, *The Kabbalah of Sefer ha-Temunah*, 53, 57; idem, "The Study of the Theory of Transmigration," 307–9.

61. Menahem Recanati also notes in his commentary on the Torah that reincarnation is an element of the current *shemittah*. See *Peirush ha-Recanati*, 1:295.

62. *Sefer ha-temunah*, 2b.

63. Goldschmidt, "Two Kabbalistic Historical Approaches," 184–92.

64. On esotericism and ineffability in the *Sefer ha-temunah* and related texts, see Wolfson, "Murmuring Secrets," 77–84.

65. *Sefer ha-temunah*, 39b.

66. The author of the introduction to the *Sefer ha-kanah* argues that the subjugation of the Jewish people by Christian and Muslim nations is a consequence of divine punishment. They identify the specific *sarim* of those peoples with Jesus and Muhammad. See the discussion in Oron, "The Sefer Ha-Peli'ah and the Sefer Ha-Kanah," 311.

67. *Sefer ha-temunah*, 58a.

68. Ibid., 63b.

69. Ibid.

70. *Sefer ha-peli'ah*, 359.

71. *Sefer ha-kanah*, 101.

72. Ibid., 30.

73. *Sefer ha-peli'ah*, 5.

74. Rubenstein, *Worlds without End*, 18.

75. Ibid., 235.

76. b. Avodah Zarah 3b.

77. Bodleian Opp. Q. 43 (Neubauer 1645), 91b.

78. Based on Ezek 1:10.

79. Ashkenazi, *A Kabbalistic Commentary*, 122.

80. Ibid., 128.

81. Isaac of Acre, *'Otzar hayyim*, 129.

82. See, for example, *Sefer ha-temunah*, 2a.

83. *Sefer ha-temunah*, commentary, 37b.

84. Ibid., 37b.

85. *Sefer ha-temunah*, commentary, 2a.

86. Ibid., 42b.

87. Ibid. This passage is cited in *Sefer ha-kanah*, 37, though there the author attributed these characteristics to the world of *Tifferet*.

88. *Sefer ha-temunah*, 43a–b. This passage is cited without attribution in the *Hakdamah to Sefer ha-kanah*, 42.

89. *Sefer ha-temunah*, 65b–66a.

90. Ibid.

91. Ibid., 66a.

92. Ibid.

93. Ibid.

94. Ibid., 56a. See a similar comment in *Sefer ha-kanah*, 17.

95. *Sefer ha-temunah*, 42b.

96. *Sefer ha-temunah*, commentary, 3b. See also ibid., 29b–30a, and discussion in Scholem, "Kabbalah shel Sefer ha-Temunah," 81; idem, *Kabbalah*, 121.

97. *Sefer ha-kanah*, 164.

98. Ibid., 139.

99. *Kaf ha-qetoret*, 183, states that the souls of Abraham, Isaac, and Jacob came from the previous *shemittah*.

100. *Sefer ha-kanah*, 17.

101. Ibid., 43.

102. *Sefer ha-peli'ah*, 404.

103. *Sefer ha-kanah*, 199.

104. Ibid., 200.

105. Ibid., 233. Moses of Kiev adopts this view in *Shoshan sodot*, 206.

106. Ibid., 237.

107. *Sefer ha-peli'ah*, 216.

108. See Idel, "The Jubilee in Jewish Mysticism," 222.

109. Asulin has shown that this was Angelet's view, "R. Joseph Angelet and the Doctrine," 6–7.

110. Recanati, *Peirush ha-Recanati*, Lev, 136. See also, Hayyat, *Minhat Yehudah*, 319.

111. *Migdol yeshu'ot*, 54a.

112. *Sefer ha-peli'ah*, 395.

113. Recanati, *Commentary on the Torah*, Lev, 122–23.

114. *Keter Shem Tov* ('*Amudei ha-kabbalah*), 57. *Sefer ha-kanah*, 68, similarly states that "the power of the gentile nations diminishes from one *shemittah* to the next."

115. *Ma'arekhet ha-'elohut*, 190a. This passage is reiterated in Adrutiel, '*Avnei zikkaron*, Turgeman, ed., 250.

Chapter 4: Living across Time

1. An earlier version of the ideas presented here can be found in Lachter, "Lives and Afterlives."

2. For an overview, see Scholem, *On the Mystical Shape*, 197–250; idem, *Kabbalah*, 344–50. On reincarnation in early modern Italian kabbalistic sources, see Ogren, *Renaissance and Rebirth*.

3. As Idel has noted, reincarnation "strengthens the theory of corporate personality, diachronically and synchronically, giving a sense of tight national cohesion," "The Secret of Impregnation," 378.

4. Scholem, *Major Trends*, 250. Or as Scholem notes elsewhere, for kabbalists, the "'Galut of souls' is transmigration," *The Messianic Idea*, 47.

5. For a discussion of reincarnation in early kabbalistic sources before Nahmanides, see Judith Weiss, "'Dehiyya,' 'halifah,' ve-'ibbur,'" 65–89. On Nahmanides's withholding of traditions related to reincarnation in his *Torat ha-'adam*, see Dauber, *Secrecy and Esoteric Writing*, 28–29. On the hints regarding reincarnation in Nahmanides's commentary on Job and the explications in his student Bahya ben Asher, see Kalman, *The Book of Job*, 100, 372–75.

6. Ibn Shuib, *Peirush sodot ha-Torah le-Ramban*, 105. See also, ibid., 209, 321.

7. On this text, see Scholem, "The Magid of R. Yosef"; Idel, "Inquiries into the Doctrine"; idem, "The Attitude to Christianity"; Ben-Zvi, *Pan of Incense*, 5–15.

8. *Sefer ha-meshiv*, 3. It is interesting to note that the same text also laments elsewhere that "many until now have denied the secrets of reincarnation." See ibid., 13.

9. Ziyyoni, *Seder Ziyyoni*, 58–59. See also, ibid., 116. Compare with the discussion of the range of perplexing questions regarding reincarnation discussed by Ibn Zimra in *Metzudat David*, as discussed by Hellner-Eshed, "Torat ha-gilgul be-sifrei ha-kabbalah," 29–47.

10. *Kaf ha-qetoret* discusses this, 186–87, 293. The *Sabba de-mishpatim* stratum of the Zohar discusses seven reincarnations of the soul. See Giller, "Love and Upheaval," 36.

11. On reincarnation in this thinker, see Ogren, *Renaissance and Rebirth*, 139–62.

12. Hayyat, *Minhat Yehudah*, 252.

13. See Joshua bar Samuel Nahmias, *Migdol yeshu'ot*, Cohen, ed., 55b. He notes that reincarnation is only for sinners who are more than half demerits, "for this matter applies only to the sinning soul that deserves to be cut off and lost."

14. Based on Job 33:29, "God does all these things, two and three times to a man."

15. *Ma'arekhet ha-'elohut*, 149b.

16. On the divinity of the soul in Nahmanides and his interpreters, see Idel, "Nishmat 'eloha."

17. Isaac of Acre, passage from Oxford 1638, fol. 48b–49a, published in Idel, *Rabbi Menahem Recanati*, 193.

18. Ibn Shuib, *Peirush sodot ha-Torah le-Ramban*, 327. See also, Ziyyoni, *Sefer Ziyyoni*, 167.

19. *Sefer ha-meshiv*, 68.

20. Cambridge Add. 673, 36a; *Sefer 'ohel mo'ed* (Jerusalem 2002), 87.

21. Ibid., 36b; (Jerusalem 2002), 88. On the wandering and suffering of the defiled soul after death, longing for redemption through *gilgul*, see ibid., 139. The *Sefer*

ha-meshiv offers a similar view, and asserts that those souls that do not perfect themselves after three lifetimes are forced to reincarnate as a dog, then undergo a painful death and endure the "crucible of fire that refines silver more than twenty times." After that, the soul reincarnates for a fourth time in order to "behold its goodness," and then it finally "cleaves to the place from whence it was hewn" in the divine. See *Sefer ha-meshiv*, 5.

22. b. Berakhot 7a.

23. *Sefer ha-temunah*, 37a–b.

24. Ibid., 43b.

25. Oron, "Sefer 'ezrat ha-Shem," 12.

26. A classic formulation of this idea in the late thirteenth century can be found in Joseph Gikatilla's *Sha'arei 'orah*, Ben-Shlomo, ed., 1:49–50.

27. *Tiqqunei Zohar*, 132a.

28. b. Hagigah 3a.

29. *Tiqqunei Zohar*, 96a.

30. According to the anonymous, fourteenth-century text *Sha'ar ha-shamayim*, 84, "One should not expound [upon the matter of reincarnation], for the one who expounds and says, 'Why was Abel punished?' and matters of this sort wastes time, and they are not possible. However, in the books of the kabbalists one can find many doubts." The second to last word in this citation is amended here according to the manuscript variant noted in n3.

31. *Sefer ha-kanah*, 78.

32. See *Shoshan sodot*, 283–84.

33. *Minhat Yehudah*, 252.

34. *Sefer ha-meshiv*, 4.

35. See *Sefer ha-peli'ah*, 331.

36. *'Or ha-ganuz* (*'Amudei ha-kabbalah*), 84. On the authorship of this text, see Galili, "On the Question of the Authorship."

37. *Migdol yeshu'ot*, Cohen, ed., 29a.

38. Moshe Idel cites an interesting passage from Paris 859, 42a, which asserts that certain souls are reincarnated into the world for the "needs of the world," including "Moses and Jeremiah and other righteous men." "Prometheus in Hebrew Garb," 121n9.

39. Le Goff, *In Search of Sacred Time*, 39.

40. Idel, "The Secret of Impregnation," 355–56, argues that the earliest citation of this idea is found in Shem Tov ibn Gaon's *Keter Shem Tov*, and was then adopted by other kabbalists, including Isaac of Acre and a number of anonymous texts.

41. *Tiqqunei Zohar*, 112a.

42. *Minhat Yehudah*, 200.

43. See, for example, Shem Tov ibn Gaon, *Keter Shem Tov*, 14, who claims to have discussed this secret with his teacher, Solomon ben Abraham ibn Adret. See also, Ibn Shuib, *Peirush sodot ha-Torah le-Ramban*, 132–33; *Sefer ha-peli'ah*, 374; Shem Tov ibn Shem Tov, *Sefer ha-'emunot ('Amudei ha-kabbalah)*, 156, 6:4, who describes this idea as a "hidden secret in the Zohar," where he also claims that this same soul is that of the messiah. See also, Isaac of Acre, *'Otzar hayyim*, 146; Meir Aldabi, *Shevilei 'emunah*, 462. The author of *Kaf ha-qetoret* relates a tradition according to which the reincarnations of Judah's sons Er and Onan were also part of the souls that must reincarnate in the generation of the messiah. See *Kaf ha-qetoret*, 219.

44. *Sefer ha-meshiv*, 3.

45. *Sefer ha-bahir*, §121.

46. Alluding to Isa 37:36; 2 Kings 19:35.

47. Based on Job 9:21.

48. Isaac of Acre, *Sefer me'irat 'einayim*, Goldreich, ed., 29–30.

49. See also Ziyyoni, *Sefer Ziyyoni*, 77.

50. See Idel, "Peirushim le-sod ha-'ibbur"; idem, "The Secret of Impregnation," 349–354, where he argues that this kabbalistic idea did not refer to the reincarnation of the soul from one body to another until Nahmanides.

51. This idea can be found in earlier sources. See, for example, *Sha'ar ha-shamayim*, Busi, ed., 81–82. This notion became common in later sources. See, for example, Moses of Kiev, *Shoshan sodot*, 196; *'Inyan ha-gilgul*, Oxford Hunt. 352, 30b. Scholem, *On the Mystical Shape*, 214, suggested that this interpretation of the letters of Adam's name may reflect a Christian influence, from Rom 5:17, in which Paul draws a correspondence between the biblical Adam and Jesus.

52. *Sefer ha-peli'ah*, 28. According to *Kaf ha-qetoret*, 373, Uriah was the reincarnation of Er, and Bat Sheva that of Tamar.

53. *Kaf ha-qetoret*, 346. This author also asserts that reincarnation is a way for the people of Israel to escape the grip of "the wicked Samael, who oppresses them," ibid., 409.

54. Ibid., 305. See also, Idel, "The Attitude toward Christianity," 82; Gross, "Satan and Christianity," 94; idem, *Iberian Jewry*, 133; Vajda, "Passages anti-chretiens," 48.

55. On the origins of this character in *Sefer Zerubavel* and its role in medieval Jewish eschatology, see Berger, "Three Typological Themes," 155–62. On the influence of this book on the incarnations of Jesus as depicted in *Galya raza*, see Gross, "Satan and Christianity," 95.

56. See Schnytzer, "Metempsychosis, Metensomatosis, and Metamorphosis."

57. Joseph ben Shalom Ashkenazi, *A Kabbalistic Commentary*, 151.

58. b. Yevamot 63b.

59. Joseph ben Shalom Ashkenazi, *A Kabbalistic Commentary*, 151–52.

60. On this concept in Ashkenazi's corpus, see Schnytzer, "Metempsychosis, Metensomatosis, and Metamorphosis," especially 231–32.

61. On Ashkenazi's understanding of reincarnation, see Judith Weiss, "'Dehiyya,' 'halifah,' ve-'ibbur,'" 89–97.

62. *Rabbenu Bahya on the Torah*, 3:480. On this passage, see the discussion in Idel, "Peirushim le-sod ha-'ibbur," 11–12.

63. Based on Ezek 33:11.

64. *Sefer ha-temunah*, 16a.

65. Yom Kippur Mahzor, Ashkenaz, Neila.

66. *Sefer ha-temunah*, 16a.

67. See Reigler, "Book Producing in the Galilee," 35; Zunz, *Zur Geschichte und Literature*, 522.

68. Oxford Bodleian Hunt. 352, 30b.

69. On this topic in Isaac of Acre's *Sefer me'irat 'einayim* and Joseph Alashkar's *Tzafnat fa'aneah*, see Idel, "Introduction to *Sefer Tzafnat Fa'aneah*," 26–27, and other sources cited in n40; idem, "The Secret of Impregnation," 363.

70. Ibid.

71. See Sachs-Shmueli, "The Rationale of the Negative Commandments," 191–98. On the influence of the late thirteenth-century Joseph of Hamadan on the *Temunah* texts with regard to this issue, see ibid., 192. On the relation of this idea to the Christian notion of purgatory, see ibid., 193–96.

72. b. Yevamot 62a, 63b; b. Avodah Zarah 5a; b. Nidah 13b.

73. See Verman, "Reincarnation and Theodicy," 414–15.

74. See Scholem, *On the Mystical Shape*, 205; Oron, "The Doctrine of the Soul and Reincarnation," 287–89.

75. *Peirush ha-Ramban*, 2:479. On kabbalistic interpretations of this secret, see Pedaya, *Nahmanides: Cyclical Time*, 444–52.

76. On this text and its relationship to Isaac of Acre, see Goldreich, *Sefer Me'irat 'Einayim by Rabbi Isaac of Acre*, 76–89.

77. Bodleian Opp. Q. 43 (Neubauer 1945), 96a. Isaac of Acre also cites this passage from *Kabbalat Saporta*. See *Sefer Me'irat 'Einayim by Rabbi Isaac of Acre*, Goldreich, ed., 239. See also the interpretation of Nahmanides's allusion in the anonymous supercommentary on Nahmanides, mistakenly attributed to Meir ibn Sahula, *Bi'ur le-peirush ha-Ramban* (Warsaw, 1875), 34a.

78. b. Yevamot 63b.

79. "Rabbi Joseph Angelet's Twenty-Four Secrets," Sachs-Shmueli, Felix, and Kaniel, eds., 306–7. See also his comment in the same composition: "Understand the secret of the souls, that they all return and complete those in the *guf*, for they no longer require refinement there, since they are refined and purified. Then, new souls are created from Repentance (i.e., the *sefirah* of *Binah*)," ibid., 311.

80. See Werblowsky, *Joseph Karo*, 237; Krinis, "Cyclical Time," 74; Oron, "The Sefer Ha-Peli'ah and the Sefer Ha-Kanah," 207.

81. *Sefer 'otzar hayyim*, 165.

82. *Sefer ha-kanah*, 114b. See discussion of this passage in Oron, "The Sefer Ha-Peli'ah and the Sefer Ha-Kanah," 304.

83. The author treats the separation caused between *Tifferet* and *Malkhut* as a kind of supernal manifestation of death.

84. *Sefer ha-peli'ah*, 241–42. Regarding the state of the soul in the present *shemittah*, the same author argues that "there is a war between the good and evil inclinations, and the soul is drawn after the flesh only in the current *shemittah*. . . . In this *shemittah* 'new souls' are prevented from entering the world . . . because the soul is drawn after the body to become a corporeal soul, pursuing bodily desires, and not spiritual ones," ibid., 410.

85. *Kaf ha-qetoret*, 172.

86. Ibid., 375.

87. *Sefer ha-temunah*, 56b–57a. See discussion in Pedaya, "Shabbat, Shabbetai, and the Diminution of the Moon," 189–90.

88. See also *Kaf ha-qetoret*, 382.

89. *Sod 'ilan ha-'atzilut*, Scholem, ed., 90.

90. *Sefer ha-temunah*, 56b. See Idel, "The Meaning of Ta'amei Ha-'Ofot Ha-Teme'im,'" 19; Elior, "The Doctrine of Transmigration in *Galya Raza*," 269n82.

91. *Sefer ha-temunah*, 57a.

92. On reincarnation in this author, see Shekalim, *Torat ha-nefesh ve-ha-gilgul*, 247–345.

93. *Sefer ha-'emunot*, 157–58. See also the discussion in Goetschel, "Providence et destinées de l'ame," LXX–LXXI.

94. See Idel, "R. Yehudah Haleiwah," 130.

95. MS Trinity College, Dublin, 26, 130a.

96. See Sachs-Shmueli, "The Rationale of the Negative Commandments," 187–208, 215–16; Scholem, *On the Mystical Shape*, 225–28; idem, *Kabbalah*, 346–47; Idel, "The Meaning of Ta'amei Ha-'Ofot Ha-Teme'im,'" 11–27; Hallamish, *An Introduction*

to Kabbalah, 300–302; Goldschmidt, "Two Historical Conceptions," 79; Elior, "The Doctrine of Transmigration," 259, 269n79. See also, Recanati, *Peirush ha-Recanati,* 2:34, 2:47–48, 2:104. On his qualified doubts regarding this matter, see ibid., 2:108–9. The legitimacy of this idea was the subject of an extended debate between Barukh Abraham da Spoleto and Abraham Yagel in Italy in the late sixteenth century. See Ruderman, "On Divine Justice, Metempsychosis."

97. Sachs-Shmueli, "The Rationale of the Negative Commandments," 188, 211–12. See also, Koren, "Kabbalistic Physiology," 334–36.

98. *Minhat Yehudah,* 253.

99. Recanati, *Peirush ha-Recanati,* 169–70.

100. On this expression in Recanati's works, see Idel, *Kabbalah in Italy,* 111.

101. See Hellner-Eshed, "Torat ha-gilgul be-sifrei ha-kabbalah," 38–43.

102. *Sefer ha-temunah,* 66b. See the discussion in Judith Weiss, "'Dehiyya,' 'halifah,' ve-'ibbur,'" 98–99, where she cites a version of this text found in Oxford Bodleian 309, 112a–113a. See also, Scholem, *The Kabbalah of Sefer ha-Temunah,* 57–58; Hellner-Eshed, "Torat ha-gilgul be-sifrei ha-kabbalah," 25; Pedaya, "Shabbat, Shabbetai, and the Diminution," 188–89. Idel notes that this passage, and the approach to reincarnation into animals more generally in the *Sefer ha-temunah,* also reflects the influence of Joseph ben Shalom Ashkenazi and David ben Judah he-Hasid. See, "The Meaning of Ta'amei Ha-'Ofot Ha-Teme'im,'" 18–20.

103. Here the text reflects a view first articulated in the works of Joseph ben Shalom Ashkenazi. See the study by Schnytzer, "Metempsychosis, Metensomatosis, and Metamorphosis," 221–44. *Kaf ha-qetoret,* 293, suggests that reincarnation into animals happens once a Jewish soul uses up all four of its human reincarnations. On reincarnation into animals more generally, see ibid., 297–99; 333; 413.

104. *Sefer ha-kanah,* 230. See also, *Sefer ha-kanah, Hakdamah,* 42, and Oron, "The Sefer Ha-Peli'ah and the Sefer Ha-Kanah," 303–4. On the influence of Joseph ben Shalom Ashkenazi and David ben Judah he-Hasid on the *Sefer ha-temunah* in relation to this idea, and this passage in particular, see Idel, "The Meaning of Ta'amei Ha-'Ofot Ha-Teme'im,'" 18–20.

105. *Sefer ha-temunah,* 39a.

106. See *Sefer ha-peli'ah,* 376–77.

107. *Sod 'ilan ha-'atzilut,* Scholem, ed., 90. Joseph Alcastiel makes a similar comment in a responsum written to Judah Hayyat before the expulsion from Spain, noting that the intermixing of pure and impure in the current state of the world is resolved through the purifying process of *gilgul.* See the text edited by Scholem in "Knowledge of Kabbalah," 182.

108. In addition to the writings of Joseph of Hamadan, this idea is found in other texts. See, for example, the *Sabba de-mishpatim* stratum of the Zohar, 2:96, and discussion in Giller, "Love and Upheaval," 38; Recanati, *Peirush ha-tefillot*, 52; Giller, *Reading the Zohar*, 44–48. See also, Hallamish, *An Introduction to Kabbalah*, 304–5. On this idea in Alcastiel and Ibn Gabbai, see Scholem, "The Kabbalistic Responsa of R. Joseph Alcastiel," 194–95.

109. Isaac of Acre, *Sefer me'irat 'einayim*, Goldreich, ed., 31.

110. Isaac of Acre, *'Otzar hayyim*, 38; "My teacher, the righteous one, may his memory be for a blessing, informed me that gentiles also undergo reincarnation, and he brought me proofs from the example of Judah, who fulfilled the commandment of levirate marriage before the Torah was given."

111. Isaac of Acre, *'Otzar hayyim*, 80. See also the discussion in Ziyyoni, *Sefer Ziyyoni*, 61, 149.

112. *Sefer ha-temunah*, 39b. Compare with *Kaf ha-qetoret*'s suggestion that Ruth's reincarnation was part of a broader divine stratagem to destroy gentile nations through the reincarnation of gentile women among Jews, 254.

113. According to *Sefer 'ohel mo'ed* (Jerusalem 2002), 85, Ruth 4:17 relates the people declaring "A son is born to Naomi!" upon the birth of Ruth's son Obed because he was, in fact, the reincarnation of Naomi's late eldest son Mahlon.

114. *Sefer ha-temunah*, 39b. Concerning gentiles who have a share in the world to come, the same text states, "Who are they? They are those gentiles for whom the souls of the righteous have reincarnated into their matter." On the question of gentiles and the afterlife in rabbinic literature, see Dov Weiss, "Jews, Gentiles, and Gehinnom."

115. *Sefer ha-'emunot*, 154. See Also, Goetschel, "Providence et destinées de l'ame," LXVI.

116. Isaac of Acre also mentions Ovadia among other famous converts whose souls, he claimed, were originally Israelite in origin. See *Sefer 'otzar hayyim*, Gross, ed., 80.

117. *'Avodat ha-kodesh*, 47. Ibn Gabbai cites another formulation of this purported passage from *Sefer ha-temunah* in ibid., 188.

118. *'Avodat ha-kodesh*, 480.

119. Isaac of Acre, *Me'irat 'einayim*, Goldreich ed., 34. See also the discussion in Ziyyoni, *Sefer Ziyyoni*, 201.

120. See, for example, Bereishit Rabbah 1:29; Bamidbar Rabbah 18:4; Tanhuma, *Korah*, 3:1; b. Sanhedrin 109b.

121. *Sefer ha-temunah*, 41a.

122. *Sefer ha-meshiv*, 11.

123. m. Toharot 3:12.

124. Prov 8:21.

125. Adrutiel, *'Avnei zikkaron*, Turgeman, ed., 252.

Chapter 5: History's Ends

1. See Howard, *Digital Jesus*, 114–17.

2. For a very instructive overview of rabbinic ideas regarding the notion of the world to come, see Hayes, "Heaven on Earth"; Dov Weiss, "*Olam Ha-ba* in Rabbinic Literature"; idem, "Gehinnom's Punishments."

3. Gerson Cohen, "Messianism in Jewish History," 211.

4. Scholem, *The Messianic Idea*, 37. See also, idem, *On the Possibility*, 31.

5. Wolfson, "Unveiling the Veil," 18.

6. Joseph ben Shalom Ashkenazi, *Commentary on Psalms*, Hallamish, ed., 64, argued that since redemption will entail the removal of the evil inclination, the practice of commandments will be in accord with the "dictates of natural law." On this see also Ziyyoni, *Sefer Ziyyoni*, 247. See also, *Berit menuhah*, 151–52, and discussion by Porat, 109–15, and 151n76. According to *Berit menuhah*, 52, in the seventh millennium, "Wisdom (*Hokhmah*) will overpower *Gevurah*, and human beings (*benei 'adam*) will lose their desire (*ta'avatam*)."

7. Yisraeli, "The 'Messianic Idea,'" 26–29, notes that Nahmanides offers several different portraits of what the messianic era will be like, one of which was "historical/realistic," and another that was more utopian.

8. Nahmanides, *Peirush ha-Torah*, 2:490. On this point, see Halbertal, *Nahmanides: Law and Mysticism*, 109–12, 120, 167; Pedaya, *Nahmanides: Cyclical Time*, 287–88. On Nahmanides's eschatology, see Yisraeli, *R. Moshe ben Nahman*, 301–17; Yisraeli, "The 'Messianic Idea,'" 29–35.

9. *Sefer ha-peli'ah*, 226, for example, states that "for the entirety of the seventh millennium, there is no *satan* or evil inclination."

10. *Sefer 'ohel mo'ed*, Cambridge Add. 673, 30a; *Sefer 'ohel mo'ed* (Jerusalem 2002), 67. See also, ibid., 91.

11. *Ma'arekhet ha-'elohut*, 105b.

12. See Pedaya, *Nahmanides: Cyclical Time*, 290, where she points out that this refers to historical time, while *zeman ha-sheleimut*, the time of perfection, refers to the messianic future time. The latter phrase may have some connection to Gal 4:4.

13. *Peirush ha-Recanati*, Exod, 128.

14. See Rom 5:12–21; 1 Cor 15:21–22; Col 3:9–10, and sources cited in Wolfson, "Re/Membering the Covenant," 238n54.

15. Wolfson, "Re/Membering the Covenant," 219. See also discussion in ibid., 220–21.

16. *Hebrew Writings of the Author*, Gottlieb, ed., 32.

17. *Tiqqunei Zohar*, 60b.

18. *Sefer ha-temunah*, 36a. *Kaf ha-qetoret*, 237, describes the progressive manifestations of the powers of *Binah*, *Hokhmah*, and *Keter* during redemption.

19. *Peirush ha-Recanati*, Lev, 142–43. This passage is discussed by Asulin, "R. Joseph Angelet and the Doctrine," 24. See also the appropriation of this comment in Hayyat, *Minhat Yehudah*, 319. See discussion in Pedaya, *Nahmanides: Cyclical Time*, 42n102. The anonymous sixteenth-century text *Ginat beitan* also adopted Hayyat's formulation of this passage. See Oxford Bodleian, Opp. 419, 73a, and discussion in Gottlieb, *Studies in Kabbalah Literature*, 498–99.

20. Isaac of Acre, *'Otzar hayyim*, 87–88.

21. See Krinis, "Cyclical Time in the Isma'ili Circle," 60–61, 67n162; Scholem, *Kabbalah*, 335.

22. See Scholem, *The Kabbalah of Sefer ha-Temunah*, 72.

23. *Sefer ha-temunah*, 58b. See Scholem, *The Kabbalah of Sefer ha-Temunah*, 69–73; idem, *Kabbalah*, 121.

24. *Sha'arei 'orah*, Ben Shlomo, ed., 1:215.

25. See *The Feast of Abraham*, 23–37. For a different view, see the more recent study by Daniel, "Abbott Joachim of Fiore." On the relationship between Fiore's view of history and that of thirteenth-century kabbalistic sources, see Pedaya, "The Sixth Millennium," 64–67.

26. On Jews in Joachim of Fiore's thought and that of the "Joachimites" who followed in his footsteps, see Jeremy Cohen, *The Salvation of Israel*, 113–24.

27. For some examples of the effacement of non-Jewish souls at the end of time, see Krinis, "Cyclical Time in the Isma'ili Circle," 76n195.

28. *Ma'arekhet ha-'elohut*, 151a.

29. *Migdol yeshu'ot*, Cohen, ed., 35a.

30. *Peirush ha-Recanati*, Exod, 70.

31. *Tiqqunei Zohar*, 24a.

32. Isaac of Acre, *Me'irat 'einayim*, Goldreich, ed., 100. See a similar formulation in Shem Tov ibn Gaon, *Keter Shem Tov*, 33.

33. In *'Utzar hayyim*, 32, Isaac of Acre suggests that both Christian and Muslim nations will be destroyed in the messianic future: "In the future he will judge the nations of the world and their archons. 'He lowers one,' they are the twelve princes of the children of Ishmael, and the twelve powers of the children of Edom. The singular lord will lower [them], and return them to the place of their emanation, which is their annulment. 'Elevates another,' they are the Israelites who live and cleave to eternal life. . . . It is written 'And [elevates] another' (*ve-zeh*), and not 'another' (*zeh*), since

the secret (numerical value) of *ve-zeh* is equal to 'life' (*ḥai* = 18), which is 'eternal life,' eighteen thousand worlds." Shem Tov ibn Shem Tov, by contrast, argues in *Sefer ha-'emunot* (*'Amudei ha-kabbalah*), 110 (1:5:4), that the descendants of Ishmael, or Muslim peoples, are "closer" to Israel, and will therefore repent and be preserved in the messianic age.

34. On the notion that Christianity, through its archon Samael, will be transformed through a forced acceptance of the covenant of circumcision at the end days in *Sefer ha-meshiv*, see Idel, "Attitude toward Christianity," 85–89. With regard to "Ishmael" or Islam, the author stated that their supernal archon will be banished during the time of redemption, "and he will wish to draw divine sustenance (*hashpa'ah*) from above, and he will be unable," *Sefer ha-meshiv*, 149, as well as 96. For an image of the destruction of the archons and their corresponding nations at the time of redemption see ibid., 122.

35. Moses ben Jacob of Kiev, *Shoshan sodot*, 64.

36. Ibid., 70.

37. *Sefer ha-temunah*, 14a.

38. The Babylonian Talmud describes a general deterioration of the world and of Jewish life in the period immediately before the arrival of the messiah in b. Sotah 49b (as well as b. Sanhedrin 98b), which is discussed in the *Ra'aya mehemna* section of the Zohar, 67b–68a.

39. Based on Lam 4:22.

40. *Berit menuḥah*, 220.

41. Ibid., 221. For a collection of rabbinic passages that describe the dark events that precede the arrival of the messiah, see Patai, *The Messiah Texts*, 97–100. See also, Scholem, *The Messianic Idea*, 10–13.

42. For some examples of this in earlier thirteenth-century sources, see Idel, "Mongol Invasions and Astrology."

43. *Berit menuḥah*, 222. See also, Silver, *A History of Messianic Speculation*, 109.

44. Scholem, *The Messianic Idea*, 7.

45. *Sefer ha-temunah*, 57b.

46. For a similar argument, see *Kaf ha-qetoret*, 283, and the comment from *Sefer ha-meshiv* adduced in Scholem, "The Magid of Rabbi Joseph," 104.

47. *Sefer ha-meshiv*, 27.

48. Ibid., 28.

49. Ibid., 147.

50. *Peirush ha-Recanati*, Lev, 144–145. See also, *Kaf ha-qetoret*, 310.

51. Joseph ben Shalom Ashkenazi, *A Kabbalistic Commentary*, 271–72.

52. *Tiqqunei Zohar*, 76b.

53. *Sefer ha-temunah*, 24a.

54. b. Yevamot 62a, 63b; b. Avodah Zarah 5a; b. Nidah 13b. For discussion of the *guf* of souls, see *'Or ha-ganuz* on *Bahir* (*'Amudei ha-kabbalah*), 20, 28, 65, 78.

55. *Peirush ha-Recanati al ha-Torah*, Lev, 142–43.

56. b. Yevamot 62a.

57. *Sefer ha-temunah*, 37a.

58. Based on Job 3:17. *Ma'arekhet ha-'elohut*, 183b.

59. *Sod 'ilan ha-'atzilut*, Ben-Shachar and Weiss, eds., 299.

60. On the sixth millennium as the time for preparation for the arrival of redemption in the main body of the Zohar, see Fishbane, *The Art of Mystical Narrative*, 191–96; Pedaya, "The Sixth Millennium."

61. *Sefer ha-temunah*, 44b.

62. See discussion above, 98–9.

63. Wolfson, *Suffering Time*, 596 (emphasis in the original).

64. See Idel, "The Jubilee in Jewish Mysticism," 215–16; 229–30.

65. *'Or ha-ganuz* on *Bahir* (*'Amudei ha-kabbalah*), 14.

66. *Rabbenu Bahya on the Torah*, 3:58–59. Gottlieb notes that it is unclear what exactly the difference is here for Bahya between the "desolation" of *shemittah* and "chaos and void" of Jubilee, *Kabbalah of R. Bahya*, 235–37. Bahya also discusses this topic in his *Commentary on the Torah*, 564–67.

67. In an interesting variation on the meaning of this idea, Moses of Kiev argues that the thousand years of desolation at the end of the *shemittah* means that the world will be "desolate" of the authority of gentile nations during the messianic millennium that will complete the present cycle. See *Shoshan sodot*, 318.

68. *Rabbenu Bahya on the Torah*, 3:59.

69. *Peirush ha-Recanati*, Lev, 144.

70. *Peirush ha-Recanati*, Lev, 140. See also, Recanati, *Ta'amei ha-mitzvot*, 76b–77a.

71. *Ma'arekhet ha-'elohut*, 188a.

72. Evoking Zech 9:9.

73. *Tanhuma*, *Ki tetze* 11.

74. b. Sanhedrin 97a.

75. *Ma'arekhet ha-'elohut*, 153a.

76. Based on Lev 25:48.

77. *Sefer ha-temunah*, 44b.

78. Adrutiel, *'Avnei zikkaron*, Turgeman, ed., 257.

79. See above, 98–9, 207–08.

80. *Migdol yeshu'ot*, Cohen, ed., 12a.

81. *Sod 'ilan ha-'atzilut*, Scholem, ed., 102.

82. See Krinis, "Cyclical Time," 61, 67.

83. *Sefer ha-temunah*, 58b. See Idel, "Multiple Forms of Redemption," 47–51; Scholem, *The Kabbalah of Sefer ha-Temunah*, 69; Pedaya, "Shabbat, Shabbetai, and the Diminution," 190–91. A version of this idea also appears in the anonymous commentary on the Haggadah mistakenly attributed to Moses de Leon, "Peirush ha-Haggadah le-R. Moshe bar R. Shem Tov de Leon," 130–31, and the version preserved in Vatican 194, printed in Feuerstein, "Commentary on the Passover," 233. See also, Pedaya, *Nahmanides: Cyclical Time*, 444–45.

84. *Sefer ha-temunah*, 45a.

85. Ibid.

86. Ibid., 59a.

87. For a still useful survey, see Silver, *A History of Messianic Speculation*, 82–108. See also, Gerson Cohen, *Studies in the Variety*, 271–97.

88. b. Sanhedrin 97b.

89. See Idel, "Jewish Apocalypticism," 359–60.

90. See Asulin, "R. Joseph Angelet and the Doctrine," 9, 22–23, Baer, *History of the Jews*, 20–21.

91. See Liebes, *The Messiah of the Zohar*, 9, interpreting the relevant passage in Zohar 2:9a–10b.

92. Zohar 1:139b. See Scholem, *Sabbatai Sevi*, 88, and the dated but still interesting discussion in Greenstone, *The Messiah Idea*, 173–78.

93. On the messianic doctrines associated with this text, see Idel, *Messianic Mystics*, 126–32.

94. See *Sefer ha-meshiv*, 81. Another passage, ibid., 158, suggests 1462 or 1464 as possible dates for the onset of the beginning of the messianic process, and ibid., 99, gives 1470 as the year. The text also suggests 1504 as the date for the resurrection of the patriarchs and matriarchs, and 1654 as the date for the resurrection of the dead from outside of the land of Israel, ibid., 159. In another passage, ibid., 95, the Gregorian year 1600 is predicted to be the year of resurrection.

95. *Sefer ha-meshiv*, 106.

96. See *Kaf ha-qetoret*, 231, and discussion in Ben-Zvi's introduction, 85–95. In the grouping of texts associated with *Sefer ha-meshiv*, many different possibilities are suggested as the date for the messiah's arrival, with most in the latter part of the fifteenth century or first half of the sixteenth century. See Scholem, "The Magid of R. Joseph," 78–79.

97. See Baer, "Ha-tenu'ah ha-meshihit be-Sefarad," 71–77; Idel, "Neglected Writings," 86; Robinson, "Two Letters." For an interesting comparison to other Jewish and Christian predictions from the same period in Spain, see Gutwirth, "Jewish and Christian Messianism."

98. See the introduction to his *Yeshu'ot meshiho*, and discussion in Lawee, *Isaac Abarbanel's Stance*, 144–45, 162; Sharot, "Jewish Millennial-Messianic Movements," 67; Benmelech, "Early Modern Messianism," 78–81; Lelli, "The Role of Early Renaissance," 192.

99. See Lawee, *Isaac Abarbanel's Stance*, 162. The *Sefer ha-meshiv*, 107, offers a somewhat earlier prediction of the messiah also based on the sack of Constantinople in 1451.

100. Tishby, "Geniza Fragments," 381.

101. Oxford Bodleian 5178, 63b. This text is adduced in Idel, *Mircea Eliade*, 146–47; idem, "Jewish Apocalypticism," 361.

102. Funkenstein, "A Schedule for the End of the World," 47.

103. Ibid., 49.

104. Ibid., 52.

105. See discussion in Halbertal, *Nahmanides: Law and History*, 234–38; Chazan, "Undermining the Jewish Sense of Future," 185; idem, *Barcelona and Beyond*, 172–94; Idel, "Jewish Apocalypticism," 361; Yisraeli, "The 'Messianic Idea,'" 26. On Nahmanides's dating and its influence on the Christian thinker Arnold of Villanova and its relationship to some early fourteenth-century millenarian thought influenced by Joachim of Fiore, see Kriegel, "The Reckonings of Nahmanides."

106. *Sefer ha-ge'ulah*, *Kitvei Ramban*, Chavel, ed., 1:290. See Halbertal, *Nahmanides: Law and History*, 235.

107. On the splitting of the messianic process into these two figures, the first of whom represents the apocalyptic events of the end, and the second the dawning of a utopian age, see Scholem, *The Messianic Idea*, 18.

108. See, for example, Joseph ben Shalom Ashkenazi, *A Kabbalistic Commentary*, 246, and discussion by Hallamish, ibid., 246–47n13.

109. *Sefer ha-peli'ah*, 35. On this passage see Oron, "The Sefer Ha-Peli'ah and the Sefer Ha-Kanah," 316.

110. *Sefer ha-temunah*, 57b.

111. This latter date, as noted above, was embraced by Abarbanel. It was also suggested by Abraham ben Eliezer ha-Levi in the early sixteenth century. See Scholem, *The Messianic Idea*, 42. Ruderman notes that 1530–31 was a year that both Jews and Christians regarded as messianically meaningful due to its astrological significance, see "Hope against Hope," 303.

112. *Sefer ha-meshiv*, 36. Interestingly, this prediction is based on a gematria calculation of the name of King Tid'al of Goiim in Gen 14:1, whose Hebrew name equals 504, which the author takes as an allusion to the Gregorian calendar year 1504. Abraham Zacuto also designated 1504 as a year of messianic import. See Tishby, "Acute Apocalyptic Messianism," 268.

113. *Sefer ha-meshiv*, 37.

114. Ibid., 40.

115. On this passage see Oron, "The Sefer Ha-Peli'ah and the Sefer Ha-Kanah," 315–16. On this passage in relation to a similar discussion in Moses of Kiev's *Shoshan sodot*, see Schneider, "The 'Judaizers' of Muscovite Russia," 230–33.

116. *Hakdamat ha-kanah* (*Torat ha-kanah* edition), 56.

117. See Oron, "The Sefer Ha-Peli'ah and the Sefer Ha-Kanah," 19; eadem, "Exile and Redemption," 92–93. On a version of this passage appearing in Yohanan Alemanno's work, see Lelli, "The Role of Early Renaissance," 196. Abraham Azulai (d. 1643) cited a text in the introduction to his commentary on the Zohar, *'Or ha-hamah*, that the prohibition against the public study of Kabbalah was dissolved in 1490. See Scholem, *Sabbatai Sevi*, 21; *Kabbalah*, 68–69. This may be an example of a transformation of a failed prediction for the date of the messiah's arrival offered by an earlier kabbalist into an accurate anticipation of something else by a later kabbalist.

118. *Kaf ha-qetoret* similarly argued that the revelation of kabbalistic secrets will characterize the messianic age, while the concealment of secrets is inherent to premessianic reality. See, for example, *Kaf ha-qetoret*, 154, 255.

119. The numerical value of the Hebrew letters of the word *ran* equals 250, which could be taken here as an allusion to the Hebrew date 5250, or 1490 CE.

120. *Hakdamat ha-kanah*, 56. For another translation, see Taube, *The Cultural Legacy*, 113–14.

121. *Sefer ha-peli'ah*, 31. See discussion in Idel, *Saturn's Jews*, 113, 117n52.

122. *Hakdamat ha-kanah* (*Torat ha-kanah* edition), 56-57.

123. See Krauss, "Le roi de France Charles," 95–96; Ruderman, "Hope against Hope," 305; Sharot, "Jewish Millennial-Messianic Movements," 72; Scholem, *Sabbatai Sevi*, 18n13.

124. See Tishby, "Acute Apocalyptic Messianism."

125. Moses of Kiev, *Shoshan sodot*, 317. On this passage see Zinberg, *A History of Jewish Literature*, 17; Taube, *The Cultural Legacy*, 68–69.

126. Ibid.

127. It is important to note that not all kabbalists who experienced the expulsion from Spain were focused on messianic speculation. Abraham Saba, for example, was

reluctant to offer such predictions. See the discussion in Gross, "R. Abraham Saba's Abbreviated," 390; idem, *Iberian Jewry*, 161–63.

128. See Scholem, "On the Legend of R. Joseph Della Reina"; idem, "The Magid of Rabbi Joseph," 108–10; Idel, "Inquiries into the Doctrine," 244–50; idem, *The Messianic Idea*, 15; idem, *Messianic Mystics*, 130–31, 133; Dan, "The Story of R. Joseph Della Reyna"; Benayahu, "Ma'aseh nora." On this story in Ha-Levi's work, See Robinson, "Abraham ben Eliezer ha-Levi," 137–38. On the connection between this story and *Sefer ha-meshiv*, see Idel, "Inquiries into the Doctrine," 209–12; 228–32; idem, "Attitude toward Christianity," 83–85. On the relationship between this story and the *Kaf ha-qetoret*, see Ben-Zvi, "Introduction to *Pan of Incense*," 96–108.

129. On the messianic speculation of this kabbalist, see Robinson, "Two Letters," 404, where he notes that Ha-Levi anticipates two "pre-messianic divine visitations" in 1520 and 1524, the messiah in 1530, and the rebuilding of the Temple in 1536/7. On Ha-Levi's messianism, see Robinson, "Abraham ben Eliezer ha-Levi," 87–160. Robinson notes on p. 93 that in his commentary on Daniel, Ha-Levi offers three possible dates for the messiah: 1530, 1540, and 1575. Moti Benmelech suggests that David Reuveni's messianic mission was deeply influenced by Ha-Levi's messianic Kabbalah, but with a novel agenda to create a form of "historical messianism" to "affect and design the historical events, and not merely passively watch and interpret them," "History, Politics, and Messianism," 47–48.

130. Chazan, "Undermining the Jewish Sense of Future," 180–81.

131. Scholem, *The Messianic Idea*, 4. See also, idem, *On the Possibility*, 107–8.

Chapter 6: Shaping History

1. An earlier version of the discussion of these ideas in the works of Ibn Gabbai can be found in Lachter, "Silkworms of Exile."

2. Lincoln, *Discourse and the Construction*, 5.

3. Ibid., 9.

4. On the creative reception of tradition in this kabbalist's works, see Fishbane, *As Light before Dawn*, 49–76.

5. Isaac of Acre, *Me'irat 'einayim*, 164.

6. *Tiqqunei Zohar*, 1b.

7. On this image in the *Tiqqunei Zohar*, see Roi, *Love of the* Shekhinah, 168–91; 232–36.

8. Ibid., 228.

9. See, for example, *Tiqqunei Zohar*, 17a.

10. This extends the position taken in the *Idra Rabba* section of the Zohar that the merit of the generation of Rabbi Shimon bar Yohai "upholds the world until the messiah shall arrive." See Liebes, *Studies in the Zohar*, 8. On the necessity of keeping kabbalistic secrets concealed until the time of redemption in the main stratum of the Zohar, see Fishbane, *The Art of Mystical Narrative*, 203–4.

11. Roi points out that the term *hibur* or "composition" carries a double meaning of both text and union of the divine attributes, which also characterizes the state of redemption. See *Love of the* Shekhinah, 230.

12. *Tiqqunei Zohar*, 23b–24a.

13. Zohar 3:124b. See Elior, "Breaking the Boundaries," 101–2, 194–95; Roi, *Love of the* Shekhinah, 232.

14. Based on Num 30:14.

15. *Hebrew Writings of the Author*, Gottlieb, ed., 110.

16. *Tiqqunei Zohar*, 23b–24a. See Elior, "Breaking the Boundaries of Time and Space," 194.

17. *Tiqqunei Zohar*, 73b.

18. *Sefer ha-'emunot*, 3. Ibn Shem Tov similarly notes in his *Commentary on the Sefirot*, 59, "From the day that our forefathers cut [the shoots] and nullified these wisdoms [of Kabbalah], they were separated, and this is the reason for the withdrawal of the divine glory, and [why] power was granted to the opposer to oppose by means of his people Amalek and Edom."

19. *Sefer ha-'emunot*, 3.

20. As Ibn Shem Tov notes in his *Commentary on the Sefirot*, 6, "Due to the secrecy of Kabbalah and its names and the loss of the wisdom of our wise men, our rabbis of blessed memory have said, 'Why do Israel pray and they are not answered? Because they do not know to whom they are praying.' That is to say, [they do not know] the proper divine attribute or aspect."

21. Ezek 37:11. *Sefer ha-'emunot*, 5.

22. *Sefer ha-'emunot*, 5.

23. As Pely has argued, the authorship of the *Peli'ah* and *Kanah* texts regard the preservation of Kabbalah as a way of retrieving even the halakhic traditions of the oral Torah that have been lost over subsequent generations. See "The Book of 'Kanah.'"

24. De Certeau, "History and Mysticism," 441.

25. See the discussion in Ben-Shachar, "The Author of '*Sefer ha-Qelippot*,'" 160.

26. Adrutiel, *'Avnei zikkaron*, Turgeman, ed., 80.

27. See also Adrutiel, *'Avnei zikkaron*, Turgeman, ed., 82. See also his comments in ibid., 409.

28. See *Sefer ha-Shem*, Oron, ed., 53.

29. Adrutiel, *'Avnei zikkaron*, Turgeman, ed., 80.

30. Ibid. Scholem, "Once More," 458, noted that Adrutiel claimed in his *Hashlamah le-sefer ha-kabbalah* that his father was a student of the disciples of Canpanton.

31. Adrutiel, *'Avnei zikkaron*, Turgeman, ed., 81; Scholem, "Once More," 459.

32. Ibid., 82, echoing the language of b. Berakhot 64a.

33. Moshe Idel observes that books such as Adrutiel's *'Avnei zikkaron* and Alashkar's *Tzafnat fa'aneah* constitute "wide-ranging anthologies comprised of diverse kabbalistic material from Spain, some of which is unknown to us from other sources," "R. Yehudah Haleiwah ve-hiburo," 121. On the similarities between Alashkar's disavowal of his own originality and Adrutiel's, both of whom were from the generation of the expulsion from Spain, see Idel, "Introduction to *Sefer Tzafnat Fa'aneah*," 18.

34. *Sefer ha-meshiv*, 73.

35. See ibid., 56. See also, ibid., 54, and discussion in Scholem, "The Magid of R. Joseph," 78.

36. For example, *Sefer ha-meshiv*, 61, states, "I have revealed this mystery to my son Shimon, and he alluded to it in his book and knew the secret and concealed it . . . for people were not worthy of this secret until the arrival of the time of the birth pangs of the messiah." See also discussion in Idel, *Enchanted Chains*, 114–21.

37. *Sefer ha-meshiv*, 24.

38. Cited from Scholem, "The Maggid of Rabbi Joseph," 100. See also *Sefer ha-meshiv*, 9–10.

39. Moshe Idel has noted that a parallel version of this passage can be found at the beginning of *Kaf ha-qetoret*, MS Paris 845, 5b, see "Inquiries into the Doctrine," 196–98. See also, *Pan of Incense*, Ben-Zvi, ed., 154. In the version preserved in *Kaf ha-qetoret*, the passage is stripped of its first-person divine voice, and related as merely an interpretation of the verse from Isaiah 12:3. The *Kaf ha-qetoret* passage does not include the direct reference to the composition of the book itself as a way of sharing hidden secrets for redemptive purposes.

40. See also the passage transcribed by Scholem, *Kitvei yad be-kabbalah*, 87–88. This same author asserts elsewhere that there were ten books of Solomon that were concealed in order to hide them from the gentile nations during Israel's exile. They will be revealed in the final stages before the messiah's arrival. See Scholem, "The Magid of Rabbi Joseph," 110.

41. *Sefer ha-meshiv*, 109.

42. Ibid., 145.

43. See also the text transcribed by Scholem, ibid., 102–3. There it is the Zohar's secrets that will finally be revealed in the fullness at the end of days. On the image of the recovery of the memory of the secrets contained in the Zohar in relation to messianic redemption, in *Kaf ha-qetoret*, see Idel, "Neglected Writings," 82.

44. *Sefer ha-meshiv*, 44. See also, ibid., 61. On Aramaic as a language associated with secrecy in the Zoharic literature, as well as a number of later kabbalistic compositions, see Mopsik, "Late Judeo Aramaic."

45. *Sefer ha-meshiv*, 154. See also, ibid., 160.

46. See Idel, "Inquiries into the Doctrine," 232–39.

47. *Kaf ha-qetoret*, 331–32. See also the discussion of part of this passage in Idel, "Neglected Writings," 79–80; idem, "Particularism and Universalism," 333.

48. *Kaf ha-qetoret*, 437.

49. See Ben-Zvi, introduction to *Pan of Incense*, 66.

50. *Kaf ha-qetoret*, 466.

51. On this kabbalist see Lachter, "Silkworms of Exile"; Goetschel, *Meir ibn Gabbay*.

52. On Ibn Gabbai's sources in Spanish, Byzantine, and Ashkenazi esoteric literature, see Garb, *Manifestations of Power*, 232. For a listing of specific sources cited in Ibn Gabbai's corpus, see Goetschel, *Meir ibn Gabbay*, 34–36.

53. *Tolaʿat Yaʿakov*, 8. On this passage see Garb, *Manifestations of Power*, 233.

54. On this phenomenon in Zoharic Kabbalah, see Haskell, *Mystical Resistance*.

55. Tanhuma, *Be-shelah* 9:2. A similar formulation can be found in Mekhilta de-Rabbi Yishmaʾel 14:10.

56. *Tolaʿat Yaʿakov*, 8. See also, Bahya ben Asher on Exod 14:10.

57. Ibid.

58. Ibn Gabbai seems to be drawing upon a passage from Midrash Rabbah that is not extant in any of the standard editions. See the discussion in Ginsburg, *Sod ha-shabbat*, 77n.17.

59. *Tolaʿat Yaʿakov*, 8.

60. Based on *Tiqqunei Zohar*, 123b.

61. *ʿAvodat ha-kodesh*, 4:15, 521. See Goetschel, *Meir ibn Gabbay*, 455.

62. See also Ibn Gabbai's discussion in *Derekh ʾemunah*, 83–84.

63. *ʿAvodat ha-kodesh*, *Hakdamah*, 9.

64. See, for example, Goetschel, *Meir ibn Gabbay*, 273–344; Gottlieb, *Studies in Kabbalah Literature*, 38–55; Faierstein, "God's Need," 55–56.

65. See *Tolaʿat Yaʿakov*, 6.

66. This text has been preserved in two versions: "Sod 'ilan ha-'atzilut," Scholem, ed., 83, and *Sod ha-Shem*, 171a.

67. See b. Hagigah 12b.

68. *'Avodat ha-kodesh*, 2:12, 114.

69. See the discussion in Kellner, *Maimonides*, 7–26.

70. Jacobus de Voragine, an important Dominican in northern Italy in the late thirteenth century and author of *The Golden Legend*, interestingly, also divided history into four distinct periods: Adam to Moses was the time of "deviation," Moses to the nativity of Christ was the time of "renewal," from Easter to Pentecost was the time of "reconciliation," and the era of "pilgrimage" is the current historical era. See Le Goff, *In Search of Sacred Time*, 18–19.

71. See Garb, *Manifestations of Power*, 237; Hallamish, *Introduction to Kabbalah*, 239.

72. *'Avodat ha-kodesh*, *Hakdamah*, 5. See also the discussion in Gottlieb, *Studies in Kabbalah Literature*, 31, 55.

73. *Tola'at Ya'akov*, 35. On this passage, see Garb, *Manifestations of Power*, 238.

74. Ibid.

75. See b. Berakhot 32b.

76. *'Avodat ha-kodesh*, 2:7, 100.

77. See Garb, *Manifestations of Power*, 242.

78. *'Avodat ha-kodesh*, 2:7, 101.

79. *'Avodat ha-kodesh*, *Hakdamah*, 1.

80. Ibid., 3.

81. See Goetschel, *Meir ibn Gabbay*, 223–26.

82. *'Avodat ha-kodesh*, *Hakdamah*, 1.

83. Ibid., 2.

84. Based on Gen 20:13.

85. *'Avodat ha-kodesh*, *Hakdamah*, 2.

86. See Goetschel, *Meir ibn Gabbay*, 223–26.

87. As Ibn Gabbai notes, *'Avodat ha-kodesh*, *Hakdamah*, 4, "Further proof of this can be seen from the holy forefathers who were foreigners in the land. Of Abraham it was said, 'I am a foreign resident [*ger ve-toshav*] among you' (Gen 23:4). Of Isaac it is said 'reside [*gur*] in this land' (Gen 36:3). Of Jacob it was said, 'the length of my sojourn (*megurai*)' (Gen 47:9). Yet, by means of their actions, they completed the divine intention, and they merited the treasury and the success that derives from it."

88. *'Avodat ha-kodesh*, *Hakdamah*, 3.

89. Ibid., 11.

90. Ibid., 11.

91. On the double exile of bodies and souls in Ibn Gabbai, see Idel, "Multiple Forms," 56–57.

92. Song 2:14; 5:2; 6;9.

93. *'Avodat ha-kodesh, Hakdamah*, 14.

94. Maimonides makes a claim of this sort in his *Guide for the Perplexed*, 1:71. For a discussion of Maimonides and other philosophers on this matter, see Roth, "Theft of Philosophy." On Ibn Gabbai's rejection of this claim, see Diamond, *Maimonides and the Shaping*, 145, 150.

95. *'Avodat ha-kodesh*, 3:18, 326.

96. Based on Isa 57:1; Jer 12:11.

97. *'Avodat ha-kodesh*, 3:70, 471–72. See Goetschel, *Meir ibn Gabbay*, 453.

98. On Ibn Gabbai's views of redemption, see Idel, "Multiple Forms of Redemption," 51–57.

99. *Tola'at Ya'akov*, 8. See Huss, *The Zohar*, 121.

100. On this issue, see Yisraeli, "Jewish Medieval Traditions"; Goetschel, *Meir ibn Gabbay*, 86–87.

101. *'Avodat ha-kodesh*, 3:18, 327. See also the discussion in ibid., 3:23, discussed by Scholem, *The Messianic Idea*, 298–300.

102. *Tiqqunei Zohar*, 94a.

103. See Goetschel, *Meir ibn Gabbay*, 86.

104. See the discussion of Wolfson's notion of the linear circularity of time in kabbalistic temporality above, p. 98–9, 207–08.

105. *'Avodat ha-kodesh*, 3:18, 328. Idel notes that this view, based upon the *Tiqqunei Zohar*'s own self-perception, is discussed by earlier kabbalists, including Judah Hayyat in *Minhat Yehudah*, and the anonymous *Sefer ha-meshiv* literature. See Idel, "Neglected Writings," 80–82; idem, *Messianic Mystics*, 138.

106. The author of *Sefer pokeah 'ivrim* MS Parma 1397, 169a, mentions that even great sages who know the Talmud need Kabbalah, noting that there was a sage who didn't know the mysteries of the *'arayot*, Balak, and other things, because he was born in a generation before the Zohar became publicly known.

107. *'Avodat ha-kodesh*, 3:18, 329. See also ibid., 4:1, 473.

108. Ibid., 3:18, 328.

109. Hayyat, *Minhat Yehudah*, 2a–2b. See Elior, "Messianic Expectations and Spiritualization," 37.

110. Ibid.

111. *'Avodat ha-kodesh*, 4:35, 601. See also ibid., *Hakdamah* 3, and discussion in Gottlieb, *Studies in Kabbalah Literature*, 16; Wolfson, "Min u-minut," 245.

112. Ibid.

113. Ibid.

114. Ibid. See Goetschel, *Meir ibn Gabbay*, 434.

115. See Scholem, "The Kabbalistic Responsa," 172–73, referring to his argument in "Ra'ayon ha-ge'ulah be-kabbalah," published in *Explications and Implications*, 213–14. See also the discussion in Goetschel, *Meir ibn Gabbay*, 458–59.

116. See Idel, *Primeval Evil*, 224; see also his critique of Scholem's assumptions in *Major Trends*, 244–50, regarding the influence of the Spanish expulsion on the development of Lurianic Kabbalah, *New Perspectives*, 264–67. See also his comments in, "Religion, Thought, and Attitudes," 124–25, 136–39, and "Spanish Kabbalah after the Expulsion," 170–72.

117. See the discussion in Idel, "Encounters between Spanish and Italian Kabbalists," especially 189–92.

118. See, for example, Scholem, *The Messianic Idea*, 38–41; *On the Possibility*, 109; *Major Trends*, 244–49.

Conclusion

1. Scholem, *The Messianic Idea*, 35. Italics in the original. See the discussion by Morgan and Weitzman in *Rethinking the Messianic Idea*, 1–12.

Bibliography

Primary Sources

Adrutiel, Abraham ben Solomon. *Sefer 'avnei zikkaron*. Edited by Yehuda Ohad Turgeman. Jerusalem: Makhon Hakhmei Yerushalayim ve-ha-Maʿarav, 2020.

Aldabi, Meir. *Shevilei 'emunah*. Edited by Joseph Cohen. Jerusalem: M. Abramowitz, 2017.

Angelet, Joseph. *Kupat ha-ruchlin*. MS Oxford Bodleian, Opp. 228.

Angelet, Joseph. *Livnat ha-sappir*. Jerusalem, 1913.

Angelet, Joseph. *Peirush 'al sha'arei 'orah*. MS Jerusalem, NLI 144.

Angelet, Joseph. *Twenty-Four Secrets*. In Leore Sachs-Shmueli, Iris Felix, and Ruth Kara-Ivanov Kaniel, "Rabbi Joseph Angelet's Twenty-Four Secrets (Introduction, Study, Edition)." *Kabbalah: Journal for the Study of Jewish Mystical Texts* 50 (2021): 293–320.

Ashkenazi, Joseph ben Shalom. *Commentary on Psalms*. In Hallamish, "Remnants of the Commentary of Rabbi Yoseph Ashkenazi to Psalms." *Daat* 10 (1983): 57–70 (Hebrew).

Ashkenazi, Joseph ben Shalom. *A Kabbalistic Commentary of Rabbi Yoseph ben Shalom Ashkenazi on Genesis Rabbah*. Edited by Moshe Hallamish. Jerusalem: Magnes, 1984 (Hebrew).

Ashkenazi, Joseph ben Shalom. *Peirush 'al sefer yetzirah*. In *Sefer yetzirah ha-meyuhas le-Avraham Avinu*. Jerusalem: Lewin-Epstein, 1965.

Bahya ben Asher. *Rabbenu Bahya on the Torah*. Edited by Rabbi C. B. Chavel. 3 vols. Jerusalem: Mosad HaRav Kook, 1966–68.

Bi'ur le-feirush ha-Ramban. Warsaw, 1875.

Canpanton, Judah ben Solomon. *Leqah tov*. Edited by Elliot Wolfson. *Kabbalah* 43 (2019): 31–85.

"Commentary on the Passover Haggadah from the Circle of *Sefer ha-Temunah*—Study and Edition." Edited by Hillel Feuerstein. *Kabbalah* 54 (2022): 115–254.

Gikatilla, Joseph. *Ginat 'egoz*. Jerusalem: Yeshivat ha-Hayyim ve-ha-Shalom, 1989.

Gikatilla, Joseph. *Sha'arei 'orah*. Edited by Joseph ben-Shlomo. 2 vols. Jerusalem: Mosad Bialik, 1996.

Gikatilla, Joseph. *Sod ha-nahash u-mishpato*. Edited by Raphael Cohen. Jerusalem: 1998.

Ginat beitan. MS Oxford Bodleian, Opp. 419.

Hakdamah le-Sefer ha-kanah. In *Torat ha-kanah*. Jerusalem: Makhon Nezer Shraga, 2011.

Haleiwah, Judah. *Tzafnat fa'aneah*. MS Trinity College Dublin, 26.

Hayyat, Judah. *Minhat Yehudah*. In *Sefer 'amudei ha-kabbalah*. Jerusalem: Makhon Nezer Shraga, 2005.

Hebrew Writings of the Author of Tiqqunei Zohar *and* Ra'aya Mehemna. Edited and Annotated by Efraim Gottlieb. Jerusalem: Academy of Sciences and Humanities, 2003.

Ibn Gabbai, Meir. *'Avodat ha-kodesh*. Jerusalem: Yarid ha-Sefarim, 2004.

Ibn Gabbai, Meir. *Derekh 'emunah*. Jerusalem: Makhon Pithei Magidim, 1997.

Ibn Gabbai, Meir. *Tola'at Ya'akov*. Jerusalem: Makor Hayyim, 1967.

Ibn Shuib, Joshua. *Derashot 'al ha-Torah*, facsimile of the Cracow 1573 edition, with an introduction by Shraga Abramson. Jerusalem: Makor, 1969. (Modern edition, *Derashot 'al ha-Torah u-mo'adei ha-shanah*. Edited by Zev Metzger. Jerusalem: Lev Sameah, 1992).

'Inyan ha-gilgul. MS Oxford Bodleian Hunt. 352, 30b–34a.

Isaac of Acre. *Sefer Me'irat 'Einayim by Rabbi Isaac of Acre: A Critical Edition*. Edited by Amos Goldreich. PhD diss., Hebrew University, 1981.

Isaac of Acre. "*Hassagot* on Yehuda ibn Malka's Commentary on *Pirkei de-Rebbi Eliezer*." Edited by Paul Fenton. *Sefunot* 6 (1993): 115–65.

Isaac of Acre. *'Otzar hayyim*. Tel Aviv: Amnon Gross, 2020.

Kabbalat Saporta. MS Bodleian Opp. Q. 43 (Neubauer 1645), 80b–98b.

Kaf ha-qetoret (Pan of Incense: Kabbalistic Commentary on the Book of Psalms). Edited by Aryeh Ne'eman Ben-Zvi. Tel Aviv: Idra, 2018.

Ma'arekhet ha-'elohut. Mantua, 1558.

Ma'arekhet ha-'elohut. In *Sefer 'amudei ha-kabbalah*. Jerusalem: Makhon Nezer Shraga, 2005.

Masekhet 'atzilut. Kaunas: M. Guttman, 1931.

Moses ben Nahman (Nahmanides). *Peirush ha-Ramban 'al ha-Torah.* Edited by Hayim Chavel. 2 vols. Jerusalem: Mosad HaRav Kook, 1994.

Moses of Kiev. *Shoshan sodot.* Petah Tikvah: Or ha-Ganuz, 1995.

Nahmias, Joshua bar Samuel. *Migdol yeshu'ot.* Edited by Raphael Cohen. Jerusalem, 1998.

'Or ha-ganuz on *Sefer ha-bahir.* In *Sefer 'amudei ha-kabbalah.* Jerusalem: Makhon Nezer Shraga, 2005.

'Otzar ha-rishonim 'al haggadah shel pesah. Edited by Dovid Holzer. Miami Beach, 2006.

"Peirush ha-haggadah le-R. Moshe bar R. Shem Tov me-'Ir Leon." In *Haggadah Shelemah: The Complete Passover Haggadah,* 103–32. Jerusalem: Torah Shelemah Institute, 1967.

Peirush ha-Torah 'al derekh ha-peshat ve-ha-kabbalah. MS Oxford Bodleian, Mich. 341, 1a–68b.

Recanati, Menahem. *Peirush he-Recanati 'al ha-Torah.* Edited by Amnon Gross. Tel Aviv, 2003.

Recanati, Menahem. *Peirush ha-tefillot le-R. Menahem Recanati.* In *Menahem Recanati: Commentary on Daily Prayers.* Edited by Giacomo Corazzol. Torino: Nino Aragno Editore, 2008.

Seder ha-'atzilut. Edited by Na'ama Ben-Shachar and Tzahi Weiss. "The Order of Emanation regarding 'The Unity of Our God and Our Torah for Our People'—A Commentary on the Ten Sefirot from the 'Circle of the *Sefer ha-Temunah.'*" *Kabbalah* 41 (2018): 290–304.

Seder ha-'atzilut. Vatican MS Ebr. 194, 99b–103a.

Sefer brit ha-menuhah (Book of Covenant of Serenity): Critical Edition and Prefaces. Edited by Oded Porat. Jerusalem: Magnes, 2016.

Sefer 'ezrat ha-Shem. Edited by Michal Oron. *Jerusalem Studies in Jewish Thought* 12 (1991): 177–99.

Sefer ha-kanah. In *Torat ha-kanah.* Jerusalem: Makhon Nezer Shraga, 2011.

Sefer ha-meshiv. Edited by Aryeh Ne'eman Ben Zvi. Gush Etzion, 2015.

Sefer ha-peli'ah. In *Torat ha-kanah.* Jerusalem: Makhon Nezer Shraga, 2011.

Sefer ha-Shem Attributed to R. Moses de Leon. Edited by Michal Oron. Los Angeles: Cherub Press, 2010.

Sefer ha-temunah. Lemberg, 1892.

Sefer ha-zohar. Jerusalem: Mosad HaRav Kook, 1999.

Sefer 'ohel mo'ed. MS Cambridge Add. 673, 13a–55a. (Printed edition: *Sefer 'ohel mo'ed.* Edited by Elimelech Parush. Jerusalem, 2002)

Sefer pokeah 'ivrim. MS Parma, 2572 (Catalogue De-Rossi, 1397).

Sefer yetzirah. Jerusalem: Lewin-Epstein, 1965.

Sha'ar ha-shamayim. In *The Gate of Heaven: Flavius Mithridates' Latin Translation, The Hebrew Text, and an English Version*. Edited by Susanne Jurgan and Saverio Campanini. Torino: Nino Aragno Editore, 2012.

Shem Tov ibn Gaon. *Keter Shem Tov*. In *'Amudei ha-kabbalah*. Jerusalem: Makhon Nezer Shraga, 2001.

Shem Tov ibn Shem Tov. *Commentary on the Sefirot*. In *Shem Tov ibn Shem Tov's Kabbalistic Critique of Philosophy in the* Commentary on the Sefirot: *Study and Text*, edited by David S. Ariel, 1–129 (Hebrew section). PhD diss., Brandeis University, 1982 (Hebrew).

Shem Tov ibn Shem Tov. *Sefer ha-'emunot*. Ferrara, 1556.

Sod 'ilan ha-'atzilut. Edited by Gershom Scholem. *Qovetz 'al yad*, n.s. 5 (1951): 67–102.

Sod ha-Shem. In *Zohar Hadash*, 168a–178b. Constantinople, 1739.

Supercommentaries and Summaries by Students of the Rashba on the Kabbalah of the Ramban. Edited by A. Eizenbach, D. Kamenetsky, Y. Becker, and J. Sternbuch. Jerusalem: Mosad HaRav Kook, 2020.

Tiqqunei Zohar. Jerusalem: Mosad HaRav Kook, 2013.

Ziyyoni, Menahem ben Meir. *Sefer Ziyyoni*. Tel Aviv: A. Gross, 2005.

Secondary Sources

Abrams, Daniel. "Orality in the School of Nahmanides: Preserving and Interpreting Esoteric Traditions and Texts." *Jewish Studies Quarterly* 3, no. 1 (1996): 85–102.

Afterman, Adam. *And They Shall Be One Flesh: On the Language of Mystical Union in Judaism*. Leiden: Brill, 2016.

Arendt, Hannah. *The Jew as Pariah: Jewish Identity and Politics in the Modern Age*. New York: Random House, 1978.

Asulin, Shifra. "R. Joseph Angelet and the Doctrine of Seven Cosmic Cycles: Between the Zohar and Nahmanides's Kabbalah." *AJS Review* 43, no. 2 (2019): 1–25 (Hebrew).

Baer, Yitzhak. "The Function of Mysticism in Jewish History." *Zion* (1942): 55–64 (Hebrew).

Baer, Yitzhak F. *Galut*. New York: Schocken, 1947.

Baer, Yitzhak. "Ha-reka' ha-histori shel ha-*Ra'aya mehemna*." *Zion* 5 (1940): 1–44.

Baer, Yitzhak. "Ha-tenu'ah ha-meshihit be-Sefarad be-tekufat ha-gerush." *Zion* 5 (1933): 61–77.

Baer, Yitzhak F. *A History of the Jews in Christian Spain*. 2 vols. Philadelphia: Jewish Publication Society, 1966.

Bar-Asher, Avishai. *Journeys of the Soul: Concepts and Imageries of Paradise in Medieval Kabbalah*. Jerusalem: Magnes, 2019.

Baron, Salo. "Newer Emphases in Jewish History." *Jewish Social Studies* 25, no. 4 (1963): 245–58.

Benayahu, Meir. "On the History of the Jews in Tiria." *Zion* 12 (1948): 37–48 (Hebrew).

Benayahu, Meir. "Ma'aseh Norah of Rabbi Joseph Della Reina." *'Areshet* 5 (1972): 170–88 (Hebrew).

Benjamin, Walter. *Illuminations*. Translated by Harry Zohn. New York: Houghton Mifflin Harcourt, 2019.

Benmelech, Moti. "History, Politics, and Messianism: David ha-Reuveni's Origin and Mission." *AJS Review* 35, no. 1 (2011): 35–60.

Benmelech, Moti. "Medieval Messianism between Ashkenaz and Sepharad." In *Sephardim and Ashkenazim: Jewish-Jewish Encounters in History and Literature*, edited by Sina Rauschenbach, 73–88. Berlin: De Gruyter, 2020.

Ben-Shachar, Na'ama. "The Author of '*Sefer ha-Qelippot*' (The Book of Shells)." *Kabbalah* 50 (2021): 153–64.

Ben-Shachar, Na'ama. *Israel and the Archons of the Nations: War, Purity and Impurity*. In collaboration with Tzahi Weiss. Los Angeles: Cherub Press, 2021.

Ben-Shachar, Na'ama, and Tzahi Weiss. "The Order of Emanation Regarding 'The Unity of Our God and Our Torah for Our People'—A Commentary on the Ten Sefirot from the 'Circle of the *Sefer ha-Temunah*.'" *Kabbalah* 41 (2018): 279–304.

Ben-Shalom, Ram. *Medieval Jews and the Christian Past*. Oxford: Littman Library of Jewish Civilization, 2017.

Ben-Zvi, Aryeh Ne'eman. Introduction to *Pan of Incense: Kabbalistic Commentary on the Book of Psalms*, by Joseph Titazak, edited by Aryeh Ne'eman Ben-Zvi, 13–136. Tel Aviv: Idra, 2018.

Berger, David. "The Problem of Exile in Medieval Jewish-Christian Polemic." In *In the Dwelling of a Sage Lie Precious Treasures: Essays in Jewish Studies in Honor of Shnayer Z. Leiman*, edited by Y. Berger and C. Milikowsky, 189–204. New York: KTAV, 2020.

Berger, David. "Three Typological Themes in Early Jewish Messianism: Messiah Son of Joseph, Rabbinic Calculations, and the Figure of Armilus." *AJS Review* 10, no. 2 (1985): 141–64.

Biale, David. *Blood and Belief: The Circulation of a Symbol between Jews and Christians*. Berkeley: University of California Press, 2007.

Biale, David. "Counter-History and Jewish Polemics against Christianity: The 'Sefer Toldot Yeshu' and the 'Sefer Zerubavel.'" *Jewish Social Studies* 6, no. 1 (1999): 130–45.

Biale, David. *Gershom Scholem: Kabbalah and Counter-History*. 2nd ed. Cambridge, MA: Harvard University Press, 1982.

Biale, David. *Gershom Scholem: Master of the Kabbalah*. New Haven, CT: Yale University Press, 2018.

Biale, David. *Jewish Culture between Canon and Heresy*. Stanford, CA: Stanford University Press, 2023.

Birnbaum, Pierre. "From Europe to Pittsburgh: Salo W. Baron and Yosef H. Yerushalmi between the Lachrymose Theory and the End of the Vertical Alliance." In *Salo Baron: The Past and Future of Jewish Studies in America*, edited by Rebecca Kobrin, 174–91. New York: Columbia University Press, 2022.

Bonfil, Robert. "Jewish Attitudes toward History and Historical Writing in Pre-Modern Times." *Jewish History* 11, no. 1 (1997): 7–40.

Bowman, Steven. *The Jews of Byzantium (1204–1453)*. Tuscaloosa: University of Alabama Press, 1985.

Bowman, Steven. "Who Wrote the Sefer ha-Kaneh and Sefer ha-Peli'ah?" *Tarbiz* 45, no. 2 (1985): 50–52 (Hebrew).

Brown, Jeremy Philip. "On the Passionality of Exile in Medieval Kabbalah." In *Land of Stark Choices: Faith-Based Responses to Homelessness in the United States*, edited by Manuel Mejido Costoya, 250–74. New York: Fordham University Press, 2021.

Bynum, Caroline Walker. *Wonderful Blood: Theology and Practice in Late Medieval Northern Germany and Beyond*. Philadelphia: University of Pennsylvania Press, 2007.

Carlebach, Elisheva, J. M. Efron, and D. N. Myers, eds., *Jewish History and Jewish Memory: Essays in Honor of Yosef Hayim Yerushalmi*. Hanover, NH: Brandeis University Press, 1998.

Chazan, Robert. *From Anti-Judaism to Anti-Semitism: Ancient and Medieval Constructions of Jewish History*. New York: Cambridge University Press, 2016.

Chazan, Robert. "Jewish Suffering: The Interplay of Medieval Christian and Jewish Perspectives." In *Lectures on Medieval Judaism at Trinity University: Occasional Papers II*, 1–33. Kalamazoo: Western Michigan University, 1998.

Chazan, Robert. "Representation of Events in the Middle Ages." *History and Theory* 27, no. 4 (1988): 40–55.

Chazan, Robert. "Undermining the Jewish Sense of Future: Alfonso of Valladolid and the New Christian Missionizing." In *Christians, Muslims, and Jews in Medieval and Early Modern Spain*, edited by Mark D. Meyerson and Edward D. English, 179–94. Notre Dame, IN: University of Notre Dame Press, 2000.

Cohen, Gerson. *Jewish History and Jewish Destiny*. New York: Jewish Theological Seminar of America, 1997.

Cohen, Gerson. *Studies in the Variety of Rabbinic Cultures*. Philadelphia: Jewish Publication Society, 1991.

Cohen, Jeremy. "Alterity and Self-Legitimation: The Jew as Other in Classical and Medieval Christianity." In *The Jew as Legitimation: Jewish-Gentile Relations beyond Antisemitism and Philosemitism*, edited by David J. Wertheim, 33–45. Cham: Springer International, 2017.

Cohen, Jeremy. *Living Letters of the Law: Ideas of the Jew in Medieval Christianity*. Berkeley: University of California Press, 1999.

Cohen, Jeremy. "Original Sin as the Evil Inclination: A Polemicist's Appreciation of Human Nature." *The Harvard Theological Review* 73, nos. 3–4 (1980): 495–520.

Cohen, Jeremy. *The Salvation of Israel: Jews in Christian Eschatology from Paul to the Puritans*. Ithaca, NY: Cornell University Press, 2022.

Cohen, Jeremy. "'Slay Them Not': Augustine and the Jews in Modern Scholarship." *Medieval Encounters* 4 (1998): 78–92.

Cohen, Norman. "Shekhinta ba-Galuta: A Midrashic Response to Destruction and Persecution." *Journal for the Study of Judaism in the Persian, Hellenistic, and Roman Period* 13, no. 1/2 (1982): 147–59.

Cooper, Alan. "A Medieval Jewish Version of Original Sin: Ephraim of Luntshits on Leviticus 12." *Harvard Theological Review* 97, no. 4 (2004): 445–59.

Dan, Joseph. "Kabbalistic and Gnostic Dualism." *Binah* 3 (1994): 19–33.

Dan, Joseph. "The Story of R. Joseph Della Reyna." *Sefunot* 6 (1962): 313–26 (Hebrew).

Dan, Joseph, ed. *The Early Kabbalah*, translated by Ronald C. Kiener. New York: Paulist Press, 1986.

Davis, Joseph. *Yom Tov Lipman Heller: Portrait of a Seventeenth-Century Rabbi*. Oxford: Littman Library of Jewish Civilization, 2004.

De Certeau, Michel. "History and Mysticism." Translated by Arthur Goldhammer. In *Histories: French Constructions of the Past*, edited by Jacques Revel and Lynn Hunt, 437–47. New York: The New Press, 1995.

De Lang, Nicholas. "Hebrew Scholarship in Byzantium." In *Hebrew Scholarship and the Medieval World*, edited by Nicholas de Lang, 23–37. Cambridge: Cambridge University Press, 2001.

Diamond, James A. *Maimonides and the Shaping of the Jewish Canon*. Cambridge: Cambridge University Press, 2014.

Diamond, James A. "Maimonides vs. Nahmanides on Historical Consciousness and the Shaping of Jewish Identity." In *History, Memory, and Jewish Identity*, edited by Ira Robinson, Naftali S. Cohen, and Lorenzo Ditommaso, 92–115. Boston: Academic Studies Press, 2016.

Elior, Rachel. "Breaking the Boundaries of Time and Space in Kabbalistic Apocalypticism." In *Apocalyptic Time*, edited by Albert Baumgarten, 187–97. Leiden: Brill, 2000.

Elior, Rachel. "The Doctrine of Transmigration in *Galya Raza*." In *Essential Papers on Kabbalah*, edited by Lawrence Fine, 243–69. New York: New York University Press, 1995.

Elior, Rachel. "Exile and Redemption in Jewish Mystical Thought." *Studies in Spirituality* 14 (2004): 1–15.

Elior, Rachel. "Messianic Expectations and Spiritualization of Religious Life in the Sixteenth Century." *Revue des études juives* 145, nos. 1–2 (1986): 35–49.

Engel, David. "Salo Baron's View of the Middle Ages in Jewish History: Early Sources." In *Studies in Medieval Jewish Intellectual and Social History: Festschrift in Honor of Robert Chazan*, edited by David Engel et al., 299–315. Leiden: Brill, 2012.

Faierstein, Morris. "God's Need for the Commandments in Medieval Kabbalah." *Conservative Judaism* 36 (1982): 45–59.

Felix, Iris. "Perakim be-haguto ha-kabbalit shel ha-Rav Yosef Angelet." MA thesis, Hebrew University, 1991.

Feuerstein, Hillel. "Commentary on the Passover Haggadah from the Circle of *Sefer ha-Temuna*—Study and Edition." *Kabbalah* 54 (2022): 115–254 (Hebrew).

Fine, Lawrence. "Dimensions of Kabbalah from the Spanish Expulsion to the Dawn of Hasidism." In *The Cambridge History of Judaism*. Vol. 7, *The Early Modern World, 1500–1815*, edited by Jonathan Karp and Adam Sutcliffe, 437–74. Cambridge: Cambridge University Press, 2018.

Fishbane, Eitan. *The Art of Mystical Narrative: A Poetics of the Zohar*. New York: Oxford University Press, 2018.

Fishbane, Eitan. *As Light before Dawn: The Inner World of a Medieval Kabbalist*. Stanford, CA: Stanford University Press, 2009.

Fishman, Talya. "A Kabbalistic Perspective on Gender-Specific Commandments: On the Interplay of Symbols and Society." *AJS Review* 17, no. 2 (1992): 199–245.

Fredriksen, Paula. *Augustine and the Jews: A Christian Defense of Jews and Judaism.* New Haven, CT: Yale University Press, 2010.

Funkenstein, Amos. *Perceptions of Jewish History.* Berkeley: University of California Press, 1993.

Funkenstein, Amos. "A Schedule for the End of the World: The Origins and Persistence of the Apocalyptic Mentality." In *Visions of Apocalypse: End or Rebirth?,* edited by S. Friedländer, G. Holton, L. Marc, and E. Skolnikoff, 44–60. London: Holmes & Meier, 1985.

Galili, Ze'ev. "On the Question of the Authorship of the Commentary '*Or ha-Ganuz*' Attributed to Rabbi Meir Ben Solomon Abi Sahula." *Jerusalem Studies in Jewish Thought* (1985): 83–96 (Hebrew).

Gampel, Benjamin, ed. *Crisis and Creativity in the Sephardic World, 1391–1648.* New York: Columbia University Press, 1997.

Garb, Jonathan. *A History of Modern Kabbalah: From the Early Modern Period to the Present Day.* Cambridge: Cambridge University Press, 2020.

Garb, Jonathan. *Manifestations of Power in Jewish Mysticism from Rabbinic Literature to Safedian Kabbalah.* Jerusalem: Magnes, 2004.

Giller, Pinchas. "Love and Upheaval in the Zohar's *Sabba de-Mishpatim*." *The Journal of Jewish Thought and Philosophy* 7 (1997): 31–60.

Giller, Pinchas. *Reading the Zohar: The Sacred Text of the Kabbalah.* New York: Oxford University Press, 2001.

Ginsburg, Elliot K. *Sod ha-Shabbat: The Mystery of the Sabbath.* Albany: State University of New York Press, 1989.

Goetschel, Roland. "Le Motif de *sarim* dans les écrits de Joseph Giqatilla." In *Michael: On the History of the Jews in the Diaspora,* edited by S. Simonsohn, 9–31. Tel Aviv: Diaspora Research Institute, 1989.

Goetschel, Roland. *Meir Ibn Gabbay: Le Discours de la kabbale espagnole.* Leuven: Peters, 1981.

Goetschel, Roland. "Providence et destinées de l'ame dans le *Sefer ha-Emunot* de Shem Tob ibn Shem Tob (1380–1441)." In *Misgav Yerushalayim: Studies in Jewish Literature,* LIII–LXXI. Jerusalem: Institute for Research on Sephardi and Oriental Jewish Heritage, 1987.

Goldberg, Sylvie Anne. *Clepsydra: Essay on the Plurality of Time in Judaism.* Stanford, CA: Stanford University Press, 2016.

Goldberg, Sylvie Anne, and Yosef Hayim Yerushalmi. *Transmitting Jewish History: Yosef Hayim Yerushalmi in Conversation with Sylvie Anne Goldberg*. Waltham, MA: Brandeis University Press, 2021.

Goldreich, Amos. "Sefer Me'irat 'Einayim by Rabbi Isaac of Acre: A Critical Edition." PhD diss., Hebrew University, 1981 (Hebrew).

Goldschmidt, Roee. "From Byzantium to Eastern Europe: The Textual Versions of *Sefer ha-Temunah* and Their Circulation in Manuscript and in Print." *Kabbalah* 46 (2020): 287–316 (Hebrew).

Goldschmidt, Roee. "Two Historical Conceptions in Kabbalah: Between Safed and Byzantine Kabbalah." *Judaica Petropolitana* 11 (2019): 73–86 (Hebrew).

Goldschmidt, Roee. "Two Kabbalistic Historical Approaches: Between Safed and Byzantium." *Journal of Jewish Thought and Philosophy* 29 (2011): 177–204.

Gottlieb, Ephraim. *The Kabbalah in the Writings of R. Bahya ben Asher ibn Halawa*. Jerusalem: Kiryat Sefer, 1970 (Hebrew).

Gottlieb, Ephraim. *Studies in Kabbalah Literature*, edited by Joseph Hacker. Tel Aviv: Tel Aviv University Press, 1976 (Hebrew).

Greenspoon, Leonard J., ed. *Olam ha-zeh v'olam ha-ba: This World and the World to Come in Jewish Belief and Practice*. West Lafayette, IN: Purdue University Press, 2017.

Greenstone, Julius H. *The Messiah Idea in Jewish History*. Philadelphia: The Jewish Publication Society, 1906.

Gribetz, Sarit Kattan, and Lynn Kaye, eds. "The Temporal Turn in Ancient Judaism and Jewish Studies." In *Currents in Biblical Research* 17, no. 3 (2019): 332–95.

Gross, Abraham. "Geirush Sefarad ve-yetziratam ha-sifrutit shel ha-megurashim." *Pe'amim: Studies in Oriental Jewry* (Spring 1998): 75–93.

Gross, Abraham. *Iberian Jewry from Twilight to Dawn: The World of Rabbi Abraham Saba*. Leiden: Brill, 1995.

Gross, Abraham. "R. Abraham Saba's Abbreviated Messianic Commentary on Haggai and Zecharia." In *Studies in Medieval Jewish History and Literature*, edited by Isadore Twersky, 2:398–401. Cambridge, MA: Harvard University Press, 1984.

Gross, Abraham. "Satan and Christianity: The Demonization of Christianity in the Writings of Abraham Saba." *Zion* (1993): 91–105 (Hebrew).

Gutwirth, Eleazar. "Jewish and Christian Messianism in XVth Century Spain." In *The Expulsion of the Jews and the Emigration to the Southern Low Countries*, edited by Luc Dequeker and Werner Verbeke, 1–22. Leuven: Leuven University Press, 1998.

Hacker, Joseph. "Patterns in the Intellectual Activity of Ottoman Jewry in the 16th and 17th Centuries," *Tarbiz* 53 (1984): 569–603 (Hebrew).

Hacker, Joseph. "The Rise of Ottoman Jewry." In *The Cambridge History of Judaism*. Vol. 7, *The Early Modern World, 1500–1815*, edited by Jonathan Karp and Adam Sutcliffe,77–112. Cambridge: Cambridge University Press, 2018.

Halbertal, Moshe. *Nahmanides: Law and Mysticism*. New Haven, CT: Yale University Press, 2020.

Hallamish, Moshe. *An Introduction to Kabbalah*, translated by R. Bar-Ilan and O. Wiskind-Elper. Albany: State University of New York Press, 1999.

Hallamish, Moshe. "The Kabbalists' Attitude to the Nations of the World." *Jerusalem Studies in Jewish Thought* 14 (1988): 289–311 (Hebrew).

Hasan-Rokem, Galit, and Dundes, Alan, eds. *The Wandering Jew: Essays in the Interpretation of a Christian Legend*. Bloomington: Indiana University Press, 1986.

Haskell, Ellen. *Mystical Resistance: Uncovering the Zohar's Conversations with Christianity*. Oxford: Oxford University Press, 2016.

Haverkamp, Eva. "Historiography." In *The Cambridge History of Judaism*. Vol. 4, *The Middle Ages: The Christian World*, edited by Robert Chazan, 836–903. Cambridge: Cambridge University Press, 2018.

Hayes, Christine. "Heaven on Earth: The World to Come and Its Dislocations." In Greenspoon, *Olam ha-zeh v'olam ha-ba*, 69–90.

Heidi, Laura. "Connected Traditions and Scattered Secrets: Eclecticism and Esotericism in the Works of the 14th Century Ashkenazi Kabbalist Menahem Ziyyoni of Cologne." *Nordisk Judaistic* 20, nos. 1–2 (1999): 19–44.

Hellner-Eshed, Melila. "Torat ha-gilgul be-sifrei ha-kabbalah shel R. David ibn Zimra." *Pe'amim* 43 (1990): 16–50.

Horowitz, Carmi. *The Jewish Sermon in 14th Century Spain: The Derashot of R. Joshua ibn Shuib*. Cambridge, MA: Harvard University Press, 1989.

Howard, Robert Glenn. *Digital Jesus: The Making of a New Christian Fundamentalist Community on the Internet*. New York: New York University Press, 2011.

Huss, Boaz. *Mystifying Kabbalah: Academic Scholarship, National Theology, and New Age Spirituality*, translated by Elana Lutsky. New York: Oxford University Press, 2020.

Huss, Boaz. "On the Status of Kabbalah in Spain after the Decrees of 1391: The Book Pokeah 'Ivrim." *Pe'amim* 56 (1993): 20–32 (Hebrew).

Huss, Boaz. "*Sefer Pokeah 'Ivrim*: New Information on the History of Kabbalistic Literature." *Tarbiz* 61 (1992): 489–504 (Hebrew).

Huss, Boaz. *The Zohar: Reception and Impact*, translated by Yudith Nave. Oxford: Littman Library of Jewish Civilization, 2016.

Idel, Moshe. "An Additional Commentary to the Alphabet by R. David ben Yehudah he-Hasid and *Sefer ha-Temunah.*" *'Alei sefer* 26/27 (2017): 237–45 (Hebrew).

Idel, Moshe. "Arnaldo Momigliano and Gershom Scholem on Jewish History and Tradition." In *Momigliano and Antiquarianism: Foundations of the Modern Cultural Sciences*, edited by Peter N. Miller, 312–33. Toronto: University of Toronto Press, 2007.

Idel, Moshe. "The Attitude to Christianity in *Sefer ha-Meshiv.*" *Immanuel* 12 (1981): 77–95.

Idel, Moshe. *Ben: Sonship and Jewish Mysticism*. New York: Continuum, 2007.

Idel, Moshe. *Enchanted Chains: Techniques and Rituals in Jewish Mysticism*. Los Angeles: Cherub Press, 2005.

Idel, Moshe. "Encounters between Spanish and Italian Kabbalists in the Generation of the Expulsion." In *Crisis and Creativity in the Sephardic World: 1391–1648*, edited by Benjamin Gampel, 189–222. New York: Columbia University Press, 1997.

Idel, Moshe. "'Higher than Time': Observations on Some Concepts of Time in Kabbalah and Hasidism." In *Time and Eternity in Jewish Mysticism*, edited by Brian Ogren, 179–210. Leiden: Brill, 2015.

Idel, Moshe. "Inquiries into the Doctrine of Sefer ha-Meshiv." *Sefunot* 17 (1983): 185–266 (Hebrew).

Idel, Moshe. Introduction to *Sefer Tzafnat Fa'aneah: R. Yosef ben Moshe Alashqar*. Jerusalem: Misgav Yerushalayim, 1991 (Hebrew).

Idel, Moshe. "Jewish Apocalypticism, 670–1670." In *The Continuum History of Apocalypticism*, edited by Bernard McGinn, John J. Collins, and Stephen J. Stein, 354–79. New York: Continuum, 2003.

Idel, Moshe. "The Jubilee in Jewish Mysticism." In *Fins de Siècle—End of Ages*, edited by Y. Kaplan, 209–32. Jerusalem: Shazar, 2005 (Hebrew).

Idel, Moshe. *Kabbalah and Eros*. New Haven, CT: Yale University Press, 2005.

Idel, Moshe. "The Kabbalah in Byzantium: Preliminary Remarks." In *The Jews in Byzantium: Dialectics of Minority and Majority Cultures*, edited by R. Bonfil, O. Irshai, G. Stroumsa, and R. Talgam, 661–710. Leiden: Brill, 2012.

Idel, Moshe. *Kabbalah: New Perspectives*. New Haven, CT: Yale University Press, 1988.

Idel, Moshe. "The Meaning of 'Ta'amei Ha-'Ofot Ha-Teme'im' of Rabbi David ben Yehuda He-Hasid." In *'Alei Shefer: Studies in the Literature of Jewish Thought Presented to Rabbi Dr. Alexandre Safran*, edited by Moshe Hallamish, 11–27. Ramat Gan: Bar-Ilan University Press, 1990 (Hebrew).

Idel, Moshe. *Mircea Eliade: From Magic to Myth*. New York: Peter Lang, 2014.

Idel, Moshe. "Mongol Invasions and Astrology: Two Sources of Apocalyptic Elements in 13th Century Kabbalah." *Hispania Judaica Bulletin*, Vol. 10, no. 1 (2014): 145-168.
Idel, Moshe. "Multiple Forms of Redemption in Kabbalah and Hasidism." *Jewish Quarterly Review* 101, no. 1 (2011): 27–70.
Idel, Moshe. "Neglected Writings from the Author of *Sefer Kaf ha-Qetoret*." *Pe'amim* 53 (1993): 75–89 (Hebrew).
Idel, Moshe. "Nishmat 'eloha: 'Elohiyut ha-neshamah 'etzel ha-Ramban ve-ha-'eskolah shelo." In *Midrash ha-hayyim*, edited by S. Arzy, B. Fachler, and B. Kahana, 338–80. Tel Aviv: Yedi'ot Aharonot, 2000 (Hebrew).
Idel, Moshe. "On Mobility, Individuals, and Groups: Prolegomenon for a Sociological Approach to Sixteenth-Century Kabbalah." *Kabbalah* 3 (1998): 145–73.
Idel, Moshe. "Particularism and Universalism in Kabbalah, 1480–1650." In *Essential Papers on Jewish Culture in Renaissance and Baroque Italy*, edited by David B. Ruderman, 324–44. New York: New York University Press, 1992.
Idel, Moshe. "Peirushim le-sod Ha-'ibbur be-kabbalot Catalonia be-me'ah ha-13 u-mashma'utam le-havanatah shel ha-kabbalah be-reishitah u-le-hitpathutah." *Da'at* 72 (2012): 5–49; *Da'at* 73 (2012): 5–44.
Idel, Moshe. *Primeval Evil in Kabbalah: Totality, Perfection, Perfectibility.* New York: KTAV, 2020.
Idel, Moshe. "Prometheus in Hebrew Garb." *'Eshkolot* 5–6 (1980): 119–27 (Hebrew).
Idel, Moshe. *Rabbi Menahem Recanati ha-Mekubal.* Jerusalem: Schocken, 1998.
Idel, Moshe. "R. Yehudah Haleiwah ve-hiburo Sefer Tzafnat Fa'aneah." *Shalem* 3 (2009): 119–48.
Idel, Moshe. "Religion, Thought, and Attitudes: The Impact of the Expulsion on the Jews." In *Spain and the Jews: The Sephardic Experience 1492 and after*, edited by Elie Kedourie, 123–39. London: Thames and Hudson, 1992.
Idel, Moshe. "The Secret of Impregnation as Metempsychosis in Kabbalah." In *Verwandlungen: Archäologie der literarischen Kommunikation IX*. Munich: Wilhelm Fink, 2006.
Idel, Moshe. "Some Concepts of Time and History in Kabbalah." In Carlbach, Efron, and Myers, *Jewish History and Jewish Memory*, 153–88.
Idel, Moshe. "Spanish Kabbalah after the Expulsion." In *Moreshet Sepharad: The Sephardi Legacy*, edited by Haim Beinart, 123–39. Jerusalem: Magnes, 1992.
Idel, Moshe. "World of Angels in Human Form." In *Studies in Jewish Mysticism, Philosophy, and Ethical Literature Presented to Isaiah Tishby on His Seventy-Fifth Birthday*, edited by Joseph Dan and Joseph Hacker, 1–66. Jerusalem, Magnes, 1986 (Hebrew).

Jacobson, Yoram. "The Problem of Evil and Its Sanctification in Kabbalistic Thought." In *The Problem of Evil and Its Symbols in Jewish and Christian Tradition*, edited by H. G. Reventlow and Y. Hoffman, 97–121. London: T & T Clark, 2004.

Janowsi, B., and P. Stuhlmacher, eds. *The Suffering Servant: Isaiah 53 in Jewish and Christian Sources*, translated by Daniel P. Bailey. Grand Rapids, MI: Eerdmans, 2004.

Jurgensmeyer, Mark. *Terror in the Mind of God: The Global Rise of Religious Violence.* Berkeley: University of California Press, 2017.

Kalman, Jason. *The Book of Job in Jewish Life and Thought.* Cincinnati, OH: Hebrew Union College Press, 2021.

Kellner, Menachem. *Maimonides on the "Decline of the Generations" and the Nature of Rabbinic Authority.* Albany: State University of New York Press, 1996.

Koren, Sharon. "Kabbalistic Physiology: Isaac the Blind, Nahmanides, and Moses de Leon on Menstruation." *AJS Review* 28, no. 2 (2004): 317–39.

Krauss, Samuel. "Le Roi de France Charles VIII et les espérances messianiques." *Revue des études juives* 51 (1906): 87–96.

Kriegel, Maurice. "The Reckonings of Nahmanides and Arnold of Villanova: On Early Contacts between Christian Millenarianism and Jewish Messianism." *Jewish History* 26 (2012): 17–40.

Krinis, Ehud. "Cyclical Time in the Isma'ili Circle of the Ihwan al-Safa (Tenth Century) and in Early Jewish Kabbalistic Circles (Thirteenth and Fourteenth Centuries)." *Studia Islamica* III (2016): 20–108.

Krummel, Miriamne Ara. *The Medieval Postcolonial Jew, In and Out of Time.* Ann Arbor: University of Michigan Press, 2022.

Lachter, Hartley. "Kabbalah, Philosophy, and the Jewish-Christian Debate: Reconsidering the Early Works of Joseph Gikatilla." *Journal for Jewish Thought and Philosophy* 16, no. 1 (2008): 1–58.

Lachter, Hartley. "Lives and Afterlives: Reincarnation and the Medieval Jewish Present." In *The Life of the Soul: Jewish Perspectives on Reincarnation from the Middle Ages to the Modern Period*, edited by Andrea Gondos and Leore Sachs-Shmueli. Albany: State University of New York Press (forthcoming).

Lachter, Hartley. "Silkworms of Exile: Jewish History and Collective Memory in the Kabbalistic Works of Meir ibn Gabbai." *Shofar* 40, no. 3 (2022): 1–37.

Lasker, Daniel. "Original Sin and Its Atonement according to Hasdai Crescas." *Da'at* 20 (1988): 127–35 (Hebrew).

Lawee, Eric. "Changing Jewish Attitudes towards Christian Spain: The Case of Spain in the Late Middle Ages." *York University Centre for Jewish Studies Annual* 3 (2001): 2–15.

Lawee, Eric. *Isaac Abarbanel's Stance toward Tradition: Defence, Dissent, and Dialogue.* Albany: State University of New York Press, 2001.

Lawee, Eric. "Sephardic Intellectuals: Challenges and Creativity (1391–1492)." In *The Jew in Medieval Iberia: 1100–1500*, edited by Jonathan Ray, 352–94. Boston: Academic Studies Press, 2012.

Le Goff, Jacques. *In Search of Sacred Time: Jacobus de Voragine and* The Golden Legend. Princeton, NJ: Princeton University Press, 2014.

Lelli, Fabrizio. "The Role of Early Renaissance Geographical Discoveries in Yohanan Alemanno's Messianic Thought." In *Hebraic Aspects of the Renaissance*, edited by Ilana Zinguer, Abraham Melamed, and Zur Shalev, 192–210. Leiden: Brill, 2011.

Liebes, Yehuda. *Sections of the Zohar Lexicon.* Jerusalem: Hebrew University, 1977 (Hebrew).

Liebes, Yehuda. *Studies in the Zohar*, translated by A. Schwartz, S. Nakache, and P. Peli. Albany: State University of New York Press, 1993.

Lincoln, Bruce. *Discourse and the Construction of Society.* 2nd ed. Oxford: Oxford University Press, 2014.

Lincoln, Bruce. *Gods and Demons, Priests and Scholars: Critical Explorations in the History of Religions.* Chicago: University of Chicago Press, 2012.

Matt, Daniel. "The Mystic and the Mizwot." In *Jewish Spirituality from the Bible through the Middle Ages*, edited by Arthur Green, 367–404. New York: Crossroad, 1986.

McMichael, Steven J., and Susan E. Myers, eds. *Friars and Jews in the Middle Ages and Renaissance.* Leiden: Brill, 2004.

Miron, Ronny. *The Angel of Jewish History: The Image of the Jewish Past in the 20ᵗʰ Century.* Boston: Academic Studies Press, 2014.

Mopsik, Charles. "Late Judeo-Aramaic: The Language of Theosophic Kabbalah." *Aramaic Studies* 4, no. 1 (2006): 21–33.

Mopsik, Charles. *Les Grands textes des cabala: Les rites qui font dieu.* Lagrasse: Verdier, 1993.

Morgan, Michael L., and Weitzman, Steven, eds. *Rethinking the Messianic Idea in Judaism.* Bloomington: Indiana University Press, 2015.

Myers, David. "Of Marranos and Memory: Yosef Hayim Yerushalmi and the Writing of Jewish History." In Carlebach, Efron, and Myers, *Jewish History and Jewish Memory*, 1–21.

Myers, David, and Amos Funkenstein. "Remembering 'Zakhor': A Super-Commentary [with Response]." *History and Memory* 4, no. 2 (1992): 129–48.

Netanyahu, Benzion. "Establishing the Dates of the Books 'Ha-Kane' and 'Ha-Peliah.'" In *Salo Wittmayer Baron Jubilee Volume*, edited by Saul Lieberman, 247–58. New York: Columbia University Press, 1974 (Hebrew).

Ogren, Brian. *Renaissance and Rebirth: Reincarnation in Early Modern Italian Kabbalah*. Leiden: Brill, 2009.

Oron, Michal. "Bikoret ha-hevrah be-sifrut ha-kabbalah." *Masekhet* 2 (2004): 133–46.

Oron, Michal. "The Doctrine of the Soul and Reincarnation in Thirteenth-Century Kabbalah." In *Studies in Jewish Thought*, edited by Sara O. Heller-Willensky and Moshe Idel, 277–89. Jerusalem, Magnes, 1989 (Hebrew).

Oron, Michal. "Exile and Redemption according to 'Ha-Peli'ah' and 'Ha-Kanah.'" *Da'at* 8 (1982): 87–93 (Hebrew).

Oron, Michal. "The Sefer Ha-Peli'ah and the Sefer Ha-Kanah: Their Kabbalistic Principles, Social and Religious Criticism, and Literary Composition." PhD diss., Hebrew University, 1980 (Hebrew).

Patai, Raphael. *The Messiah Texts: Jewish Legends of Three Thousand Years*. Detroit: Wayne State University Press, 1979.

Pedaya, Haviva. "The Divinity as Place, Time, and Holy Place in Jewish Mysticism." In *Sacred Space: Shrine, City, Land*, edited by B. Z. Kedar and R. J. Zwi-Werblowsky, 84–111. New York: New York University Press, 1988.

Pedaya, Haviva. *Nahmanides: Cyclical Time and Holy Text*. Tel Aviv: Am Oved, 2003 (Hebrew).

Pedaya, Haviva. *Name and Sanctuary in the Teaching of R. Isaac the Blind*. Jerusalem: Magnes, 2001 (Hebrew).

Pedaya, Haviva. "Shabbat, Shabbetai, and the Diminution of the Moon: The Holy Conjunction, Sign and Image." In *Eshel Be'er Sheva*, 4:143–91. Be'er Sheva: Ben-Gurion University Press, 1996 (Hebrew).

Pedaya, Haviva. "The Sixth Millennium: Millenarism and Messianism in the Zohar." *Da'at* 72 (2012–2013): 51–98 (Hebrew).

Pedaya, Haviva. "The Wandering Messiah and the Wandering Jew: Judaism and Christianity as a Two-Headed Structure and the Myth of His Feet and Shoes." In *Religion und Politik: Das Messianische in Theologien, Religionswissenschaften und Philosophien des zwansigsten Jahrhunderts*, edited by Gesine Palmer and Thomas Brose, 73–103. Tübingen: Mohr Siebeck, 2013.

Pely, Hagai. "The Book of 'Kanah' and the Book of 'Peli'ah': Literal and Esoteric Meaning of the Halakha." *Tarbiz* 77 (2008): 271–93 (Hebrew).

Porat, Oded. *Sefer Berit ha-Menuhah (Book of Covenant of Serenity): Critical Edition and Prefaces.* Jerusalem: Magnes, 2016 (Hebrew).

Ray, Jonathan. *After Expulsion: 1492 and the Making of Sephardic Jewry.* New York: New York University Press, 2013.

Raz-Krakotzkin, Amnon. "History, Exile, and Counter-History: *Jewish Perspectives.*" In *A Companion to Global Historical Thought*, edited by Prasenjit Duara, Viren Murthy, and Andrew Sartori, 122–35. Oxford: Wiley Blackwell, 2014.

Raz-Krakotzkin, Amnon. "Jewish Memory between Exile and History." *The Jewish Quarterly Review* 97, no. 4 (Fall 2007): 530–43.

Rembaum, Joel E. "Medieval Jewish Criticism of the Doctrine of Original Sin." *AJS Review* 7/8 (1982/1983): 353–82.

Resnik, Irven. *Marks of Distinction: Christian Perceptions of Jews in the High Middle Ages.* Washington, DC: The Catholic University Press of America, 2012.

Ricketts, Mac Linscott. "Mircea Eliade and the *Terror of History.*" In *Mircea Eliade: Between the History of Religions and the Fall into History*, edited by Mihaela Gligor, 35–65. Cluj: Presa Universitara Clujeana, 2014.

Robinson, Ira. "Abraham ben Eliezer ha-Levi: Kabbalist and Messianic Visionary of the Early 16th Century." PhD diss., Harvard University, 1980.

Robinson, Ira. "Two Letters of Abraham ben Eliezer Halevi." In *Studies in Medieval Jewish History and Literature*. Vol. 2, edited by Isaiah Twersky, 403–22. Cambridge, MA: Harvard University Press, 1984.

Roi, Biti. *Love of the* Shekhinah: *Mysticism and Poetics in* Tiqqunei Zohar. Ramat Gan: Bar-Ilan University Press, 2017 (Hebrew).

Roth, Norman. *Conversos, Inquisition, and the Expulsion of the Jews from Spain.* Madison: University of Wisconsin Press, 1995.

Roth, Norman. "The 'Theft of Philosophy' by the Greeks from the Jews." *Folia* 31 (1978): 53–67.

Rubenstein, Mary Jane. *Worlds without End.* New York: Columbia University Press, 2014.

Ruderman, David B. "Hope against Hope: Jewish and Christian Messianic Expectations in the Late Middle Ages." In *Essential Papers on Jewish Culture in Renaissance and Baroque Italy*, edited by David B. Ruderman, 299–323. New York: New York University Press, 1992.

Ruderman, David B. "On Divine Justice, Metempsychosis, and Purgatory: Rumina-
tions of a Sixteenth-Century Italian Jew." *Jewish History* 1, no. 1 (1986): 9–30.

Ruiz, Teofilo F. *The Terror of History: On Uncertainties of Life in Western Civilization.*
Princeton, NJ: Princeton University Press, 2011.

Sachs-Shmueli, Leore. "The Rationale of the Negative Commandments by
Rabbi Joseph Hamadan: A Critical Edition and Study of Taboo in the Time
of the Composition of the Zohar." Vol. 1. PhD diss., Bar-Ilan University, 2018
(Hebrew).

Sachs-Shmueli, Leore, Iris Felix, and Ruth Kara-Ivanov Kaniel. "Rabbi Joseph Angelet's Twenty-Four Secrets (Introduction, Study, Edition)." *Kabbalah: Journal for
the Study of Jewish Mystical Texts* 50 (2021): 193–290 (Hebrew).

Sack, Bracha. "'Al parashat yahaso shel Rabbi Moshe Cordovero le-*Sefer ha-Temunah*."
In *Massu'ot: Studies in Kabbalistic Literature and Jewish Philosophy in Memory of
Prof. Ephraim Gottlieb*, edited by Michal Oron and Amos Goldreich, 186–98. Jeru-
salem: Mosad Bialik, 1994 (Hebrew).

Sack, Bracha. *The Kabbalah of Rabbi Moshe Cordovero.* Beer Sheva: Ben-Gurion University, 1995 (Hebrew).

Schneider, Michael. "The 'Judaizers' of Muscovite Russia and Kabbalistic Eschatology." In *Jews and Slavs.* Vol. 24, *The Kanaanites—Jews in the Medieval Slavic
World*, edited by Wolf Moskovich, Mikhail Chlenov, and Abram Torpusman,
222–58. Jerusalem: Gesharim, 2014.

Schnytzer, Jonathan. "Metempsychosis, Metensomatosis, and Metamorphosis: On
Rabbi Joseph ben Shalom Ashkenazi's Systematic Theory of Reincarnation."
Kabbalah 45 (2019): 221–44 (Hebrew).

Schnytzer, Jonathan. "On the Secret of the Sabbatical and Jubilee Years." *Kabbalah* 52
(2022): 197–240 (Hebrew).

Scholem, Gershom. "Again on the Book Avnei Zikkaron." *Kirjath sefer* 7, no. 3 (1930):
457–65 (Hebrew).

Scholem, Gershom. "The Book 'Abne Zikkaron.'" *Kirjath sefer* 6, no. 2 (1929): 259–76
(Hebrew).

Scholem, Gershom. *Explications and Implications.* Tel Aviv: Am Oved, 1976 (Hebrew).

Scholem, Gershom. *Kabbalah.* New York: Meridian, 1978.

Scholem, Gershom. *Ha-kabbalah shel Sefer ha-temunah ve shel-Avraham Abulafia*,
edited by Joseph Ben-Shlomo. Jerusalem: Akademon, 1965.

Scholem, Gershom. "The Kabbalistic Responsa of R. Joseph Alcastiel to R. Judah
Hayyat." *Tarbiz* 24 (1955): 167–206 (Hebrew).

Scholem, Gershom. *Kitvei yad be-kabbalah, Catalogus Codicum Hebraicorum.* Jerusalem: Hebrew University, 1930.

Scholem, Gershom. "Knowledge of Kabbalah in Pre-Expulsion Spain." *Tarbiz* 24, no. 2 (1955): 167–206 (Hebrew).

Scholem, Gershom. "The Magid of R. Yosef Taitazak and the Revelations Attributed to Him." *Sefunot* 11 (1971–1977): 69–112 (Hebrew).

Scholem, Gershom. *Major Trends in Jewish Mysticism.* New York: Schocken, 1954.

Scholem, Gershom. *The Messianic Idea in Judaism and Other Essays on Jewish Spirituality.* New York: Schocken, 1971.

Scholem, Gershom. *On Jews and Judaism in Crisis: Selected Essays*, edited by Werner J. Dannhauser. New York: Schocken, 1976.

Scholem, Gershom. "On the Legend of R. Joseph Della Reina." In *Studies in Jewish Religious and Intellectual History: Presented to Alexander Altmann on the Occasion of his Seventieth Birthday*, edited by Raphael Loewe and Siegfried Stein, 124–230. Tuscaloosa: University of Alabama Press, 1979 (Hebrew).

Scholem, Gershom. *On the Mystical Shape of the Godhead.* New York: Schocken, 1991.

Scholem, Gershom. *On the Possibility of Jewish Mysticism in Our Time and Other Essays.* Philadelphia: Jewish Publication Society, 1997.

Scholem, Gershom. *Origins of the Kabbalah*, edited by R. J. Zwi Werblowsky, translated by Allan Arkush. Princeton, NJ: Princeton University Press, 1987.

Scholem, Gershom. *Sabbatai Sevi: The Mystical Messiah*, translated by R. J. Zwi Werblowsky. Princeton, NJ: Princeton University Press, 1973.

Scholem, Gershom, ed. "Sod 'ilan ha-'atzilut le-R. Yitzhak: Kuntrus mi-mesoret ha-kabbalah shel *Sefer ha-Temunah.*" *Qovetz 'al yad*, n.s. 5 (1951): 67–102 (Hebrew).

Scholem, Gershom. "The Study of the Theory of Transmigration during the XIII Century." *Tarbiz* (1945): 135–50 (Hebrew).

Sed, Nicholas. "Le Sefer ha-Temunah et la doctrine des cycles cosmiques." *Revue des études juives* 126, no. 4 (1967): 399–415.

Septimus, Bernard. "'Better under Edom Than under Ishmael': The History of a Saying." *Zion* 47 (1982): 103–11.

Sharot, Stephen. "Jewish Millennial-Messianic Movements: A Comparison of Medieval Communities." In *Comparing Jewish Societies*, edited by Todd M. Endelman, 61–87. Ann Arbor: The University of Michigan Press, 1997.

Shechterman, Deborah. "The Doctrine of Original Sin in Jewish Philosophy of the Thirteenth and Fourteenth Centuries." *Da'at* 20 (1988): 65–90 (Hebrew).

Shekalim, Rami. *Torat ha-nefesh ve-ha-gilgul be-reishit ha-kabbalah.* Tel Aviv: 1998.

Silver, Abba Hillel. *A History of Messianic Speculation in Israel*. New York: Macmillan, 1927.

Stuckrad, Kocku von. "Discursive Study of Religion: From States of Mind to Communication and Action." *Method and Theory in the Study of Religion* 15 (2003): 255–71.

Taube, Moshe. *The Cultural Legacy of the Pre-Ashkenazic Jews in Eastern Europe*. Oakland: University of California Press, 2023.

Taubes, Jacob. *From Cult to Culture: Fragments toward a Critique of Historical Reason*, edited by Elisheva Fonrobert and Amir Engel. Stanford, CA: Stanford University Press, 2010.

Taubes, Jacob. *Occidental Eschatology*, translated with a preface by David Ratmoko. Stanford, CA: Stanford University Press, 2009.

Teller, Adam. "Revisiting Baron's 'Lachrymose Conception': The Meanings of Violence in Jewish History." *AJS Review* 38, no. 2 (2014): 431–39.

Tennant, Frederick R. *The Sources of the Doctrine of the Fall and Original Sin*. Cambridge: Cambridge University Press, 1903.

Teugels, Lieve M. "The Twin Sisters of Cain and Abel: A Survey of the Rabbinic Sources." In *Eve's Children: The Biblical Stories Retold and Interpreted in Jewish and Christian Traditions*, edited by Gerard P. Luttikhuizen, 47–56. Leiden: Brill, 2003.

Tishby, Isaiah. "Acute Apocalyptic Messianism." In *Essential Papers on Messianic Movements and Personalities in Jewish History*, edited by Marc Saperstein, 259–86. New York: New York University Press, 1992.

Tishby, Isaiah. "Geniza Fragments of a Messianic-Mystical Text on the Expulsion from Spain and Portugal." *Zion* (1983): 347–85 (Hebrew).

Urbach, Ephraim E. *The Sages: Their Concepts and Beliefs*, translated by Israel Abrahams. Cambridge, MA: Harvard University Press, 1975.

Vajda, George. "Passages anti-chretiens dans *Kaf ha-Qetoret*." *Revue de l'histoire des religions* 197, no. 1 (1980): 45–58.

Verman, Mark. "Reincarnation and Theodicy: Traversing Philosophy, Psychology, and Mysticism." In *Be'erot Yitzhak: Studies in Memory of Isadore Twersky*, edited by Jay M. Harris, 399–426. Cambridge, MA: Harvard University Press, 2005.

Weinstock, Israel. *Studies in Jewish Philosophy and Mysticism*. Jerusalem: Mosad HaRav Kook, 1969 (Hebrew).

Weiss, Dov. "Gehinnom's Punishments in Classical Rabbinic Literature." In *Jewish Culture and Creativity: Essays in Honor of Professor Michael Fishbane on the Occasion of His Eightieth Birthday*, edited by Eitan P. Fishbane and Elisha Russ-Fishbane, 77–90. Boston: Academic Studies Press, 2023.

Weiss, Dov. "Jews, Gentiles, and Gehinnom in Rabbinic Literature." In *Studies in Rabbinic Narratives*. Vol. 1, edited by Jeffrey Rubenstein, 337–75. Providence: Brown Judaic Studies, 2021.

Weiss, Dov. "*Olam Ha-ba* in Rabbinic Literature: A Functional Reading." In Greenspoon, *Olam ha-zeh v'olam ha-ba*, 91–103.

Weiss, Judith. "'Dehiyya,' 'halifah,' ve-'ibbur': Tefisot sefiratiyot be-davar gilgul neshamot bein gufim be-sifrut ha-kabbalah ha-mukdemet ve-ha-da'eihen." *Mada'ei ha-yahadut* 57, no. 1 (2022): 65–103.

Werblowsky, R. J. Zwi. *Joseph Karo: Lawyer and Mystic*. Philadelphia: Jewish Publication Society, 1977.

Wolfson, Elliot. *Alef, Mem, Tau: Kabbalistic Musings on Time, Truth, and Death*. Berkeley: University of California Press, 2006.

Wolfson, Elliot. *Heidegger and Kabbalah: Hidden Gnosis and the Path of Poesis*. Bloomington: Indiana University Press, 2019.

Wolfson, Elliot. "Judah ben Solomon Canpanton's *Leqah Tov*: Annotated Edition and Introduction." *Kabbalah* 43 (2019): 7–85.

Wolfson, Elliot. *Language, Eros, Being: Kabbalistic Hermeneutics and Poetic Imagination*. New York: Fordham University Press, 2005.

Wolfson, Elliot. "Min u-minut be-heker ha-kabbalah." *Kabbalah* 6 (2001): 231–62.

Wolfson, Elliot. "Murmuring Secrets: Eroticism and Esotericism in Medieval Kabbalah." In *Hidden Intercourse: Eros and Sexuality in the History of Western Esotericism*, edited by J. Kripal and W. Hanegraff, 65–109. Leiden: Brill, 2008.

Wolfson, Elliot. "Mystical Rationalization of the Commandments in *Sefer ha-Rimmon*." *Hebrew Union College Annual* 59 (1988): 217–51.

Wolfson, Elliot. "Mystical-Theurgical Dimensions of Prayer in *Sefer ha-Rimmon*." In *Approaches to Judaism in Medieval Times*. Vol. 3, edited by David. R. Blumenthal, 41–79. Atlanta: Scholars Press, 1984.

Wolfson, Elliot. "Re/Membering the Covenant: Memory, Forgetfulness, and the Construction of History in the Zohar." In Carlbach, Efron, and Myers, *Jewish History and Jewish Memory*, 153–88.

Wolfson, Elliot. "Retroactive Not Yet: Linear Circularity and Kabbalistic Temporality." In *Time and Eternity in Jewish Mysticism: That Which Is Before and That Which Is After*, edited by Brian Ogren, 15–52. Leiden: Brill, 2015.

Wolfson, Elliot. *Suffering Time: Philosophical, Kabbalistic, and Hasidic Reflections on Temporality*. Leiden: Brill, 2021.

Wolfson, Elliot. "Unveiling the Veil: Apocalyptic, Secrecy, and the Jewish Mystical Imaginaire." *AJS Perspectives* (Fall 2012): 18–20.

Wolfson, Elliot. *Venturing Beyond: Law and Morality in Kabbalistic Mysticism*. Oxford: Oxford University Press, 2006.

Yerushalmi, Yosef Hayim. "Clio and the Jews: Reflections on Jewish Historiography in the Sixteenth Century." *Proceedings of the American Academy for Jewish Research* 46/47 (1979–1980): 607–38.

Yerushalmi, Yosef Hayim. *Zakhor: Jewish History and Jewish Memory*. Seattle: University of Washington Press, 1996.

Yisraeli, Oded. *The Interpretation of Secrets and the Secret of Interpretation: Midrashic and Hermeneutic Strategies in* Sabba de-Mishpatim *of the Zohar*. Los Angeles: Cherub Press, 2005 (Hebrew).

Yisraeli, Oded. "Jewish Medieval Traditions Concerning the Origins of the Kabbalah." *Jewish Quarterly Review* 106, no. 1 (Winter 2016): 21–41.

Yisraeli, Oded. "*Keter Shem Tov* of Rabbi Shem Tov de Leon: A Chapter in the History of Nahmanides' Kabbalah in the 13th-14th Centuries." *Tarbiz* 89, no. 3 (2023): 455–80 (Hebrew).

Yisraeli, Oded. "The 'Messianic Idea' in Nahmanides' Writings." *Jewish Studies Quarterly* 1 (2022): 23–45.

Yisraeli, Oded. *R. Moshe ben Nahman: Biographiyah 'intelektu'alit*. Jerusalem: Magnes, Hebrew University, 2020.

Yisraeli, Oded. *Temple Portals: Studies in Aggadah and Midrash in the Zohar*, translated by Liat Karen. Berlin/Boston: De Gruyter and Magnes, 2018.

Zinberg, Israel. *A History of Jewish Literature: The German-Polish Cultural Center*. Vol. 6. Translated by Bernard Martin. Cincinnati/New York: Hebrew Union College Press and Ktav, 1972.

Index

Note: page numbers followed by "n" indicated endnotes.